The EU and the Rule of Law in International Economic Relations

The LAwTTIP Project

Developments related to the negotiation, conclusion and implementation of the new generation of EU free trade agreements (FTAs) represent one of the major challenges concerning the consolidation of the external dimension of the European Union. On the one hand, they impact on the allocation of competences between the Union and its Member States, contributing to reshaping the scope of the external action of the Union. On the other, they raise questions in terms of protection of EU fundamental values and rights. More generally, as clearly demonstrated by developments related to the dispute settlement mechanisms enshrined in those agreements, they require a re-assessment of the autonomy of the EU legal order vis-à-vis international law. These volumes constitute one of the most comprehensive legal analyses of EU FTAs. The volumes' findings are mostly based on the activities of a consortium of three well established research centres – the International Centre on European Law of the University of Bologna (CIRDE), the Centre of European Law of the King's College London (CEL) and the Institut de l'Ouest Droit et Europe of the University of Rennes 1 (IODE), carried out under the auspices of the European Commission Jean Monnet Network 'LAwTTIP – Legal Ambiguities withstanding TTIP'.

Editorial Board

Andrea Biondi, Professor of EU Law, King's College London
Isabelle Bosse-Platière, Professor of Public Law, Université de Rennes 1
Federico Casolari, Associate Professor of EU Law, University of Bologna
Cécile Rapoport, Professor of Public Law, Université de Rennes 1
Lucia Serena Rossi, Professor of EU Law, University of Bologna and Judge at European Union Court of Justice

The EU and the Rule of Law in International Economic Relations

An Agenda for an Enhanced Dialogue

Edited by

Andrea Biondi

Professor of EU Law and Director, Centre of European Law, King's College London and Academic Associate, 39 Essex Chambers, UK

Giorgia Sangiuolo

Legal Adviser, Department for International Trade, Government Legal Department and Fellow of the Centre of European Law, King's College London, UK

 Edward Elgar
PUBLISHING

Cheltenham, UK • Northampton, MA, USA

With the support of the Jean Monnet Action (Erasmus+ Programme), Project No 575478-EPP-1-2016-1-IT-EPPJMO-NETWORK.

This publication reflects the views only of the authors, and the European Commission cannot be held responsible for any use which may be made of the information contained herein.

Co-funded by the
Erasmus+ Programme
of the European Union

Published by
Edward Elgar Publishing Limited
The Lypiatts
15 Lansdown Road
Cheltenham
Glos GL50 2JA
UK

Edward Elgar Publishing, Inc.
William Pratt House
9 Dewey Court
Northampton
Massachusetts 01060
USA

A catalogue record for this book
is available from the British Library

Library of Congress Control Number: 2021945175

This book is available electronically in the **Elgar**online
Law subject collection
http://dx.doi.org/10.4337/9781839103353

MIX
Paper from
responsible sources
FSC   FSC® C013056
www.fsc.org

ISBN 978 1 83910 334 6 (cased)
ISBN 978 1 83910 335 3 (eBook)

Printed and bound in Great Britain by TJ Books Limited, Padstow, Cornwall

Contents

Contributors

Andrea Biondi, Professor of EU Law and Director, Centre of European Law, King's College London and Academic Associate, 39 Essex Chambers

Sonja Boelaert, Legal Adviser at the Council of the European Union and agent for the Council in Opinion 1/17 (CETA)

Frank J. Büchel, College Member of the EFTA Surveillance Authority, and an alumnus of King's College London. Solicitor admitted in England and Wales

Quentin Declève, Associate at Van Bael & Bellis, member of the Brussels Bar

Rosana Garciandia, Research Fellow, British Institute of International and Comparative Law (BIICL), Visiting Lecturer in Public International Law, King's College London

Steffen Hindelang, Professor of International Investment and Trade Law at Uppsala University, Professor (wsr) of European and International Law at the University of Southern Denmark, and adjunct faculty at the Humboldt-Universität zu Berlin and Technische Universität Berlin

Sir Francis G. Jacobs, KCMG QC, President of the Centre of European Law, King's College London, former British Advocate General at the European Court of Justice

Urszula Jaremba, Assistant Professor in EU law, University of Utrecht, School of Law

Adam Łazowski, Professor of EU Law, Westminster Law School, University of Westminster, London and Visiting Professor at College of Europe, Natolin

Elisa Longoni, PhD Bocconi University and Policy Senior Associate at the Financial Conduct Authority (FCA)

Federico Ortino, Professor of International Economic Law, King's College London

Giancarlo Piscitelli, Research assistant and LRM student, University of Utrecht, School of Law

Fausto Pocar, Professor emeritus, University of Milan; former President, ICTY and appeals Judge ICTY and ICTR

Giorgia Sangiuolo, Legal Adviser, Department for International Trade, Government Legal Department and Fellow of the Centre of European Law, King's College London

Hugo H. Siblesz, Secretary-General, Permanent Court of Arbitration

Raymundo Tullio Treves, JD State University of Milan; LLM New York University School of Law

Susanna Villani, PhD Post-Doc Research Fellow in EU Law at the Department of Political and Social Sciences, University of Bologna

Philippa Webb, Professor of Public International Law, King's College London

Simon Weber, Research Assistant to Prof J. Martin Hunter, Visiting Lecturer, King's College London

Carsten Zatschler, Director of Legal and Executive Affairs of the EFTA Surveillance Authority, and a Fellow of the Centre of European Law of King's College London. Barrister admitted in England & Wales and Ireland

Ewa Żelazna, Lecturer, University of Leicester

Foreword

1. THE RULE OF LAW AND THE INTERNATIONAL RULE OF LAW

Under Article 2 of the Treaty on European Union, one of the values on which the Union is founded is the rule of law. Indeed, the European Union can be regarded as totally dependent on the rule of law, notably in its relations with its Member States, where it lacks other relevant instruments of cohesion. As has been demonstrated over many years, the Court of Justice of the European Union has a central role in this respect, ensuring the implementation of the rule of law in the interpretation and application of the Treaties.

The European Union has also developed an important role, beyond the Member States, in the international legal order. It has developed over the years a wide treaty-making power; it has concluded many treaties – some together with its Member States, some exclusively; it is a member, in its own right, of many international organisations; and it is a major subject of international law.

The rule of law also occupies a fundamental role in the international relations of the EU. And by Article 3(5) of the Treaty, the Union is required to contribute to the strict observance and the development of international law, including respect for the principles of the United Nations Charter. As it might be expressed, the Union is required to uphold the international rule of law.

This book has as its focus important recent developments in the relations of the European Union with international law.

Here it is appropriate to focus on the most recent developments, as highlighted in this book. The main focus is on recent cases of the CJEU; two issues in particular stand out and raise several fundamental questions, all of considerable importance for the relationship of the European Union with the rule of law.

2. ACCESSION BY THE EUROPEAN UNION TO THE EUROPEAN CONVENTION ON HUMAN RIGHTS

As long ago as 1979 the European Commission proposed that the European Community should accede to the European Convention on Human Rights. The issue was referred by Belgium to the Court of Justice, which held that such accession would require an explicit Treaty amendment. Such an amendment was made by the Treaty on European Union as amended by the Lisbon Treaty, which not merely empowered, but obliged, the European Union to accede to the Convention. In due course an agreement on accession was successfully negotiated. The Court had been involved in the negotiations and had secured important safeguards for the legal order of the Union. However, the Court, going much further than the Opinion of Advocate General Kokott, raised what seemed novel and, in its view, fundamental objections. It objected to what it saw as the Strasbourg Court having the last word on the interpretation of EU law, without the Court of Justice having its say. The Court's objection is based on the notion of the 'autonomy' of EU law. While I take no position here on that objection, it might be noted that such situations are not unusual in international dispute settlement systems: international courts may decide questions which have not been raised before national courts. Moreover the ECHR itself imposes a requirement, before a case can be considered by the European Court of Human Rights, of the exhaustion of domestic remedies.

But the objection of the Court of Justice raises a further question: it might be said that an international court or tribunal, and the European Court of Human Rights here, does not in any circumstances make a definitive and authentic interpretation of municipal law – including European Union law. Rather, the international courts interpret the treaties which they are required to apply. In the judgments of international courts, statements of municipal law (including EU law) are to be regarded in the same way as findings of fact. Those interpretations in no way bind other courts in future cases. Thus the Strasbourg Court interprets the Convention, and rules on how the Convention so interpreted applies in all the circumstances of the case. In relation to the European Union, the Strasbourg Court would thus interpret the Convention and decide whether, on the basis of all the facts, including the way in which any provisions of national or EU law were applied by the national or EU authorities, there has been a breach of the Convention as so interpreted. On that view, a decision of an international court or tribunal containing a finding on EU law does not in any event affect the 'autonomy' of the EU legal order.

3. INTERNATIONAL DISPUTE SETTLEMENT: *ACHMEA* AND *CETA*

Going even further, and much discussed in this book, is the *Achmea* judgment. The main issue was, in essence, whether a system of international arbitration mechanism for the settlement of Investor-State disputes, under which questions of EU law could not be referred to the Court of Justice, was compatible with EU law. The Court's ruling, going against the opinion of Advocate

General Melchior Wathelet, also raises some new questions. In particular the Court's reliance, in support of its conclusion, on Articles 267 and 344 TFEU, is novel and has proved controversial.

Moreover, in contrast to earlier opinions of the Court, for example on the draft EEA Agreement, on the proposed European Patent Court, and on EU accession to the ECHR, all of which examined proposed *future* agreements, the ruling in *Achmea* concerned past proceedings and could be read as over-turning a well-established and widely used mechanism for the settlement of international disputes which had been established for apparently good reasons and had been functioning for many years. The Court did not rule on the con-sequences of its judgment for past or for ongoing procedures. But once the judgment was given, the referring court quashed the arbitral award at issue in the main proceedings.

Moreover, a declaration subsequently adopted by certain Member States at the instigation of the European Commission stated that the Court's ruling had immediate effect so as to invalidate ongoing procedures and even past awards. While such declarations have no effect as a matter of law, they may have some impact in practice. Here the question has been raised whether such retroactive consequences are consistent with fundamental rights, or indeed – of particular importance for the subject of this book – with the international rule of law.

These issues remain live. The more recent CETA Opinion of the Court of Justice – here in line with the opinion of Advocate General Bot – appears to retreat partially from the earlier case-law. In particular, it accepts that a dispute settlement mechanism can be compatible with EU law even without any involvement of the Court of Justice; and it recognises that questions of EU law can be decided by an international tribunal as a matter of fact.

It has even been suggested that the CETA Opinion might be a basis for the Court of Justice to re-consider the issue of EU accession to the ECHR. At all events it seems likely that this very important area of law on the relationship between EU law and international dispute settlement mechanisms will con-tinue to evolve: it is to be hoped in the right direction. As will be apparent, it raises central questions on the observance by the European Union of the international rule of law.

Sir Francis G. Jacobs

PART I

Rule of law: Between autonomy and judicial dialogue

1. The EU: Unifying or fragmenting force in international law?

Philippa Webb[1]

1. INTRODUCTION

In this chapter, I focus on the interaction between the Court of Justice of the European Union ('CJEU') and the International Court of Justice ('ICJ'), which is the principal judicial organ of the United Nations and a symbol of general international law. I consider whether the European Union is a unifying or fragmenting source in international law by focusing on the case law of its judicial branch.

Fragmentation is not merely a matter of having different interpretations.[2] 'Genuine fragmentation' occurs where judicial decisions give rise to conflicting developments in the law that are either unconscious due to lack of awareness of other courts' decisions or are a conscious departure from existing case law. Cases of genuine fragmentation are rare in standing courts with public decisions. Greater risk of fragmentation occurs in ad hoc arbitral tribunals, which may not have public decisions. 'Apparent fragmentation' arises where judicial decisions have variations due to contextual factors and therefore appear to be conflicting, although through clarification and interpretation the underlying legal reasoning can be resolved and rendered compatible. It occurs most commonly where judges are interpreting different legal instruments on the same legal issue.

In international law, the aim is not to have uniformity, but rather to achieve unification or integration so that similar factual scenarios and legal issues are treated in a consistent manner and any disparity in treatment is explained and justified. The desired outcome is harmony and compatibility, with allowances

---

[1]   I am grateful to Giulia Bernabei for excellent research assistance and to Niccolò Ridi for helpful conversations on citation analysis.
[2]   Philippa Webb, *International Judicial Integration and Fragmentation* (OUP 2013), Chapter 1.

for minor variations and the tailoring of solutions to disputes that come before the courts.

The assessment of unification or fragmentation in this chapter is not a rigorous empirical exercise. I have not analysed the 11,000 or so CJEU Judgments. Instead, I have looked at a sample of cases where the CJEU directly cites the case law of the ICJ and a very small sample of one case in which the ICJ cited the CJEU. Citations are an imperfect metric.[3] We do not know the number of times the CJEU *could* have cited the ICJ but chose not to (and for what reason). It is not always clear whether ICJ case law was pleaded by one or more of the parties or by the winning party. It is beyond our knowledge as to whether the ICJ approach was deliberated upon by the judges or simply ignored as irrelevant or exotic. Instead, in this chapter, I am interested in the overall posture and attitude of the courts to each other.

Some recent writing on the CJEU's dialogue with the ICJ characterised it as follows:

> the CJEU has proven, so far at least, a *shy disciple, rather than an enquiring peer* ... showing a high degree of deference to the case law of the ICJ.[4]

I do not perceive the CJEU to be a 'shy disciple'. I instead see a robust and independent Court that wishes to avoid fragmentation with international law, but also has little incentive to actively promote integration through dialogue.

In this chapter, I first examine the CJEU's posture towards the ICJ and then contrast it with the only case in which the ICJ has cited the case law of the CJEU. I then identify three explanatory factors for the CJEU's approach and conclude with some thoughts on how a self-referential approach to autonomy is compatible with greater judicial dialogue.

---

[3]　Niccolò Ridi, 'Mirages of an Intellectual Dreamland? Ratio, Obiter and the Textualisation of International Precedent' (2019) 10(3) *Journal of International Dispute Settlement* 361.

[4]　Eva Kassoti, 'Fragmentation and Inter-Judicial Dialogue: The CJEU and the ICJ at the interface' (2015) 8 *European Journal of Legal Studies* 21, 46 (emphasis added). See also Eva Kassoti and Lisa Louwerse, 'Like Ships in the Night? The CJEU and the ICJ at the Interface', Geneva Jean Monnet Working Paper 06/2016, 21 https://www.ceje.ch/files/3314/6122/9300/Geneva_JMWP_06-Kassoti-Louwerse.pdf, accessed 18 May 2019:

> However, the previous exposition showed that the Court has shied away from delving too deeply into international law. It is noteworthy that, in none of the cases discussed above, did the Court take a proactive stance by exploring the relevant questions beyond the ICJ's dicta: it merely, unquestioningly deferred to the latter's authority. In this sense, the CJEU has proven, so far at least, a shy disciple, rather than an enquiring peer – a fact that somewhat diminishes the quality of judicial dialogue between the two courts.

2.   THE CJEU's POSTURE TOWARDS THE ICJ

Although the primary task of the CJEU is 'to examine the legality of EU measures and ensure the uniform interpretation and application of EU law',[5] there is a legal basis for a unified approach to *international* law. Article 3(5) of the Treaty of the European Union provides that in 'its relations with the wider world', the EU contributes to the 'eradication of poverty and the protection of human rights, in particular the rights of the child, as well as to *the strict observance and the development of international law, including respect for the principles of the United Nations Charter*'.[6] And Article 21 on principles inspiring the EU's external action refers to 'respect for the principles of the United Nations Charter of 1945 and international law'.

At the same time, international law, including the case law of other courts, is not expressly part of the applicable law of the CJEU, unlike the reference to other 'judicial decisions' in Article 38 of ICJ Statute.[7] Neither the Statute of the CJEU nor its Rules of Procedure refer to what law can be applied by the Court.

Over 30 CJEU Judgments between 1955 and January 2019 have directly cited the ICJ.[8] Citations have also appeared in opinions of the Advocate-General.

---

[5]   Court of Justice of the European Union, 'The Court of Justice in the legal order of the European Union', https://curia.europa.eu/jcms/jcms/Jo2_7024/en/#competences, accessed 18 May 2019.

[6]   Emphasis added.

[7]   The main treaties stipulate the jurisdiction of the CJEU (Consolidated Versions of the Treaty on European Union (TEU) and the Treaty on the Functioning of the European Union (TFEU) 2016/C 202/01, Part Six, Title I, Chapter 1, Section 5; Consolidated Version of the Treaty Establishing the European Atomic Energy Community, Title III, Chapter 2, Section 4) but do not mention the 'applicable law' as such.

[8]   Case C-266/16 *Western Sahara Campaign UK v Commissioners for Her Majesty's Revenue and Customs and Secretary of State for Environment, Food and Rural Affairs* [2018] ECLI:EU:C:2018:118, paras 38, 41; Case C-104/16 P *Front Polisario* (n 7), paras 28, 29, 88, 91, 104–105; Case T-512/12 *Front Polisario* (n 8), paras 7, 8, 9, 206, 208; Joined Cases C-464/13 and C-465/13 *Europäische Schule München v Silvana Oberto and Barbara O'Leary* [2015] ECLI:EU:C:2015:163, para 61; Case C-179/13 *Raad van bestuur van de Sociale verzekeringsbank v LF Evans* [2015] ECLI:EU:C:2015:12, para 36; Joined Cases T-208/11 and T-508/11, *Liberation Tigers of Tamil Eelam (LTTE) v Council of the European Union* [2014] ECLI:EU:T:2014:885, para 69; Case T-468/08 *Tisza Erőmű kft, formerly AES-Tisza Erőmű kft v European Commission* [2014] ECLI:EU:T:2014:235, para 321; Case C-466/11 *Gennaro Currà and Others v Bundesrepublik Deutschland* [2012] ECLI:EU: C:2012:465, paras 6, 7, 20; Case C-347/10 *A. Salemink v Raad van bestuur van het Uitvoeringsinstituut werknemersverzekeringen* [2012] ECLI:EU:C:2012:17, para 32; Case C-366/10 *Air Transport Association of America and Others v Secretary of State for Energy and Climate Change* [2011] ECR I-13755, para 104; Joined Cases C-402/05

The most recurrent legal issue that the CJEU has referred to is the ICJ's interpretation of the principle of good faith.[9] The next most recurrent clusters

---

P and C-415/05 P, *Yassin Abdullah Kadi and Al Barakaat International Foundation v Council of the European Union and Commission of the European Communities* [2008] ECR I-06351, para 88; Case T-231/04 *Hellenic Republic v Commission of the European Communities* [2007] ECR II-00063, paras 2, 85; Case C-459/03 *Commission of the European Communities v Ireland* [2006] ECR I-04635, para 15; Case T-306/01 *Ahmed Ali Yusuf and Al Barakaat International Foundation v Council of the European Union and Commission of the European Communities* [2005] ECR II-03533 paras 233, 234, 282; Case T-315/01 *Yassin Abdullah Kadi v Council of the European Union and Commission of the European Communities* [2005] ECR II-03649, paras 183, 184, 231; Case T-353/00 *Jean-Marie Le Pen v European Parliament* [2003] ECR II-01729, para 61; Case C-37/00 *Herbert Weber v Universal Ogden Services Ltd* [2002] ECR I-02013, para 34; Case T-196/99 *Area Cova, SA and Others v Council of the European Union and Commission of the European Communities* [2001] ECR II-03597, para 7; Case C-162/96 *A Racke GmbH & Co v Hauptzollamt Mainz* [1998] ECR I-03655, paras 24, 50; Case T-115/94 *Opel Austria GmbH v Council of the European Union* [1997] ECR II-02739, para 90; Case T-572/93 *Odigitria AAE v Council of the European Union and Commission of the European Communities* [1995] ECR II-02025, para 4; Case C-432/92 *The Queen v Minister of Agriculture, Fisheries and Food, ex parte S. P. Anastasiou (Pissouri) Ltd and others* [1994] ECR I-03087, paras 35, 49; Case C-286/90 *Anklagemyndigheden v Peter Michael Poulsen and Diva Navigation Corp* [1992] ECR I-06019, para 10; Joined Cases C-138/81 and 139/81 *Directeur des Affaires Maritimes du Littoral du Sud-Ouest and Procureur de la République v Javier Marticorena-Otazo and Manuel Prego Parada* [1982] ECR 03819, pp. 3831, 3832; Case C-181/80, *Procureur général près la Cour d'Appel de Pau and others v José Arbelaiz-Emazabel* [1981] ECR 02961, p 2974; Ruling 1/78 *Ruling delivered pursuant to the third paragraph of Article 103 of the EAEC Treaty - Draft Convention of the International Atomic Energy Agency on the Physical Protection of Nuclear Materials, Facilities and Transports* [1978] ECR 02151, pp. 2154, 2155 and para 10, p. 2169; Case C-3/76 *Cornelis Kramer and others* [1976] ECR 01279, p. 1290; Case C-37/74 *Chantal Van den Broeck v Commission of the European Communities* [1975] ECR 00235, para 2 (a), p. 240; Case C-48/69 *Imperial Chemical Industries Ltd v Commission of the European Communities* [1972] ECR 00619, para 1 (A) (a) p. 624, para 1 (B) (b) (aa) p. 628, 629, para (D) (c) (aa) p. 633; Case C-52/69 *J. R. Geigy AG v Commission of the European Communities* [1972] ECR 00787, para 1 (A) (b) page 794, para 1 (B) (a) p. 796, 797, para 1 (C) p. 798, para 1 (D) (a) p. 800, para 2 p. 803; C-5/55-ITRP *Associazione Industrie Siderurgiche Italiane (ASSIDER) v High Authority of the European Coal and Steel Community* [1955] ECR 00263, para 3, p. 142.

[9]   *Tisza Erőmű kft, formerly AES-Tisza Erőmű kft v European Commission*, ibid, para 321; *Hellenic Republic v Commission of the European Communities*, ibid, para 85; *Opel Austria GmbH v Council of the European Union*, ibid, para 90. See also Case C-104/16 P *Front Polisario*, ibid, para 3.

are law of the sea;[10] the relationship between the UN Charter and treaties;[11] the customary status of treaties; and issues of territory, sovereignty and recognition.[12]

A typical citation appears in *Hellenic Republic v Commission of the European Communities*. This case concerned an agreement between the Commission and several Member States, including Greece, on the sharing of costs relating to the housing of representations in the Commission's offices in Abuja, Nigeria. Having decided that Greece had not paid its share of the costs according to the agreement, the Commission proceeded to recovery by offsetting the relevant sums. Greece brought an action for annulment against the act of offsetting and argued, *inter alia*, that it was not bound by the agreement in question since it had not ratified it. The Court ruled that, as well as the act of ratification, Greece's conduct and more particularly the expectations that its conduct led others to entertain were also relevant in assessing the case:[13]

> In that regard, the Court would point out that the principle of good faith is a rule of customary international law, the existence of which has been recognised by the Permanent Court of International Justice [...] (*German interests in Polish Upper Silesia*), and subsequently by the International Court of Justice and which, consequently, is binding in this case on the Community and on the other participating partners.
>
> That principle has been codified by Article 18 of the Vienna Convention of 23 May 1969 on the Law of Treaties, [...]
>
> It should also be noted that the principle of good faith is the corollary in public international law of the principle of protection of legitimate expectations which, according to the case-law, forms part of the Community legal order (Case T-115/94 *Opel Austria v Council* [1997] ECR II-39, para 93).

Three features of this citation may be highlighted. First, the ICJ is cited by the CJEU for a rule of CIL without the CJEU conducting its own examination of state practice and *opinio juris*. It cites the ICJ as an indicator of the state

---

[10] *Anklagemyndigheden v Peter Michael Poulsen and Diva Navigation Corp* (n 7), para 10; *Herbert Weber v Universal Ogden Services Ltd* (n 7), para 34, cited by Judge Allan Rosas, 'The European Court of Justice and Public International Law, Meeting of the Council of Europe Committee of Legal Advisers on Public International Law (CAHDI)' (23 March 2018), 9 https://rm.coe.int/statement-delivered-by-judge-allan-rosas-at-the-55th-cahdi-meeting-55t/16807b3b04, accessed 19 May 2019.

[11] *A Racke GmbH & Co v Hauptzollamt Mainz* (n 8), paras 24, 50, cited by Judge Allan Rosas, ibid.

[12] Case C-104/16 P *Front Polisario* (n 7), paras 28, 88, 91, cited by Judge Allan Rosas, ibid.

[13] *Hellenic Republic v Commission of the European Communities* (n 8), paras 85–87.

of public international law.[14] Second, a link is made to an international treaty – the Vienna Convention on the Law of Treaties. Third, and importantly, the CJEU draws a link back to its own case law and the Community legal order.

Another illustration of citation techniques is found in the *Wightman* case[15] on whether Article 50 could be unilaterally revoked. In that case, the CJEU had the opportunity to deliver a judgment resting on international law principles, but it instead asserted its central role in the European legal order.[16] It stated:[17]

> [...] it must be borne in mind that the founding Treaties, which constitute the basic constitutional charter of the European Union [...] established, unlike ordinary international treaties, *a new legal order, possessing its own institutions,* for the benefit of which the Member States thereof have limited their sovereign rights, in ever wider fields, and the subjects of which comprise not only those States but also their nationals (Opinion 2/13 (Accession of the European Union to the ECHR) of 18 December 2014, EU:C:2014:2454, para 157 and the case-law cited).
>
> According to settled case-law of the Court, that autonomy of EU law with respect both to the law of the Member States and to international law *is justified by the essential characteristics of the European Union and its law, relating in particular to the constitutional structure of the European Union and the very nature of that law.* EU law is characterised by the fact that it stems from an independent source of law, namely the Treaties, by its primacy over the laws of the Member States, and by the direct effect of a whole series of provisions which are applicable to their nationals and to the Member States themselves. Those characteristics have given rise to a structured network of principles, rules and mutually interdependent legal relations binding the European Union and its Member States reciprocally as well as binding its Member States to each other (judgment of 6 March 2018, Achmea, C-284/16, EU:C:2018:158, para 33 and the case-law cited).

This reasoning represents what Takis labels 'autonomy' as a 'self-referential blueprint'.

Interestingly, the Advocate-General's opinion had based its reasoning on the substance of the Vienna Convention on the Law of Treaties and cited the

---

[14] Judge Allan Rosas (n 10), 9.

[15] Case C-621/18 *Andy Wightman and Others v Secretary of State for Exiting the European Union* [2018] ECLI:EU:C:2018:999.

[16] Oliver Garner, 'Case C-621/18, Wightman v Secretary of State for Exiting the European Union: The European Court of Justice confirms that Article 50 notification can be unilaterally revoked' (*European Law Blog*, 11 December 2018) https://europeanlawblog.eu/2018/12/11/case-c-621-18-wightman-v-secretary-of-state-for-exiting-the-european-union-the-european-court-of-justice-confirms-that-article-50-notification-can-be-unilaterally-revoked/, accessed 18 May 2019.

[17] *Andy Wightman and Others v Secretary of State for Exiting the European Union* (n 15), paras 44–45 (emphasis added).

ICJ.[18] By contrast, the judgment's starting point is the specific constitutional features of the EU, with its reasoning firmly grounded within EU law. The provisions of the Vienna Convention are only cited in corroboration of the main argument, and even then they are explicitly hooked to the source of EU law through their utilisation in the preparatory work of the Treaties.[19]

3.   THE ICJ's POSTURE TOWARDS THE CJEU

Strikingly, only one ICJ Judgment has cited the CJEU since 1946.[20] The ICJ has traditionally been reluctant to cite the case law of other courts, as it considers its role as the principal judicial organ of the UN as setting itself apart. However in the last two decades it has started to cite decisions of international and regional courts and arbitral tribunals.[21]

The only ICJ case in which the Court has referred to a case of the CJEU was the *Application of the Interim Accord of 13 September 1995*.[22] The ICJ held that Greece's objections to the Former Yugoslav Republic of Macedonia's ('FYROM') application for membership of the North Atlantic Treaty Organization ('NATO') breached Greece's obligations under international law. Specifically, Greece violated Article 11(1) of the Interim Accord with the FYROM of 13 September 1995, which was intended to improve the strained relations between the two states and establish a roadmap for the resolution of the underlying dispute over the official name of the FYROM. The ICJ's judgment did not determine the controversial naming issue that has long divided Greece and the FYROM.[23]

In its Judgment, the ICJ cited Case 10/61 *Commission v Italy* and Case C-249/06 *Commission v Sweden*:[24]

> Turning to the Respondent's interpretation of Article 22 [of the Interim Accord], the Court notes the breadth of the Respondent's original contention that its 'rights' under a prior agreement (in addition to its 'duties') take precedence over its obliga-

---

[18]   Opinion of -G Campos Sánchez-Bordona (4 December 2018) (1), points 63–85.
[19]   Garner, (n 16).
[20]   Citations have also appeared in dissenting and separate judicial opinions.
[21]   See e.g., Vladyslav Lanovoy, 'The Authority of Inter-state Arbitral Awards in the Case Law of the International Court of Justice' (2019) 32(3) *Leiden Journal of International Law* 561.
[22]   *The former Yugoslav Republic of Macedonia v Greece,* Judgment of 5 December 2011, [2011] ICJ Rep 644, para 109.
[23]   Following a compromise under which Greece lifted its objections to Macedonia joining NATO and the EU, and ratification by the parliaments of both states, the Republic of North Macedonia become the official name in February 2019.
[24]   Case 10/61 *Commission v Italy* [1962] ECR 1, 10 and Case C-249/06 *Commission v Sweden* [2009] ECR I-1348, para 34, cited in *The former Yugoslav Republic of Macedonia v Greece* (n 21), para 109 (emphasis added).

tion not to object to admission by the Applicant to an organization within the terms of Article 11, paragraph 1. That interpretation of Article 22, if accepted, would vitiate that obligation, because the Respondent normally can be expected to have a 'right' under prior agreements with third States to express a view on membership decisions. The Court, considering that the parties did not intend Article 22 to render meaningless the first clause of Article 11, paragraph 1, is therefore unable to accept the broad interpretation originally advanced by the Respondent [Greece]. In this regard, *the Court notes that the Court of Justice of the European Communities [...] has interpreted a provision of the Treaty establishing the European Economic Community which states that 'rights and obligations' under prior agreements 'shall not be affected by' the provisions of the treaty. The European Court has concluded that this language refers to the 'rights' of third countries and the 'obligations' of treaty parties, respectively* (see Case 10/61 *Commission v Italy* [1962] ECR, p. 10; see also Case C-249/06 *Commission v Sweden* [2009] ECR I-1348, para. 34).

The citation is matter of fact, technical and descriptive. There is no comment from the ICJ on the weight to be accorded to the CJEU case law.

4.   WHAT EXPLAINS THE POSTURE OF THE CJEU?

Three factors help explain the posture of the CJEU to international law as represented by its citation of ICJ case law: its institutional features, its sense of identity, and the distinction between jurisdiction and applicable law.

4.1   Institutional Features

Several institutional features of the CJEU militate against an extensive and proactive dialogue with international law.

First, the CJEU does not have a provision such as Article 38(1)(d) of the ICJ Statute providing that judicial decisions are a secondary source of law. It is entirely possible for them not to even consider a relevant judicial decision. Second, the CJEU will not necessarily hold an oral hearing or obtain an official opinion from the Advocate General, which limits the opportunities for an exploration of international law issues.[25] Third, the CJEU does not publish separate opinions, which makes it difficult to assess whether in practice international law issues were discussed. Fourth, there is a large volume of cases which limits the amount of time and energy that can be allocated to the consideration

---

[25]   Arts 20, 53 and 59 of the Statute of the CJEU; Art 76 of the Rules of Procedure of the Court of Justice of 25 September 2012 (OJ L 265, 29.9.2012), as amended on 18 June 2013 (OJ L 173, 26.6.2013, 65) and on 19 July 2016 (OJ L 217, 12.8.2016, 69); Art 252 TEU and TFEU (ex Art 222 TEC).

of international law and efforts to integrate it into the jurisprudence.[26] Finally, the Court's location in Luxembourg rather than the 'international legal capital' of The Hague restricts opportunities for judicial exchanges in person.

In 2006, the then President of the ICJ, Judge Rosalyn Higgins, referred to the burgeoning of international courts and tribunals over the preceding decades. She noted that '[w]e are forging cordial relationships with each other. The Court has set up an informal system of exchange whereby judges at the ICTY and ICC receive summaries and/or relevant excerpts of our cases that address legal questions of particular interest, and vice versa'.[27] President Higgins observed:

> The authoritative nature of ICJ judgments is widely acknowledged. It has been gratifying for the International Court to see that these newer courts and tribunals have regularly referred, often in a manner essential to their legal reasoning, to judgments of the ICJ with respect to questions of international law and procedure. Just in the past five years, the judgments and advisory opinions of the ICJ have been expressly cited with approval by the International Tribunal for the Law of the Sea, the European Court of Human Rights, the European Court of Justice, the United Nations Commission on Human Rights, the Inter-American Commission on Human Rights, the International Centre for Settlement of Investment Disputes, the International Criminal Tribunal for the former Yugoslavia, and arbitral bodies including the Eritrea-Ethiopia Claims Commission. The International Court, for its part, has been following the work of these other international bodies closely.

In 2007, she explained to the legal advisers of UN Member States:[28]

> I remain convinced that so-called 'fragmentation of international law' is best avoided by regular dialogue between courts and exchanges of information. A detailed pro-gramme of co-operation between the ICJ and other international judicial bodies is now in place. We have an especially advanced programme of co-operation with the International Criminal Tribunal for the former Yugoslavia (ICTY).

---

[26] 37,127 judgments and orders have been delivered between 1952 and January 2019, of which roughly 21,703 by the Court of Justice, 13,875 by the General Court (since 1989) and 1,549 by the Civil Service Tribunal (2005–2016): CJEU website, https://curia.europa.eu/jcms/jcms/P_80908/en/, accessed 18 May 2019.

[27] HE Judge Rosalyn Higgins, President of The International Court Of Justice, 'Speech to The General Assembly of The United Nations' (26 October 2006), 7 https://www.icj-cij.org/files/press-releases/9/13149.pdf, accessed 18 May 2019.

[28] HE Judge Rosalyn Higgins, President of The International Court of Justice, 'Speech At The Meeting Of Legal Advisers Of The Ministries Of Foreign Affairs' (29 October 2007), 3–5 https://www.icj-cij.org/files/press-releases/7/14097.pdf, accessed 18 May 2019.

The CJEU was not part of the programme of cooperation among the courts, most of which were based in The Hague, with the exception of ITLOS and the European Court of Human Rights.

4.2   Sense of Identity

The second factor is that the CJEU has tended not to see itself as an *international* court, but rather as a constitutional or supreme court in a supranational system. As mentioned above, the CJEU is not part of the inter-court dialogue set up by the ICJ. However, the CJEU does regularly meet with national supreme and constitutional courts. The CJEU prefers to act as a 'protectionist domestic court' rather than committing itself to international dialogue with international law courts.[29]

President Lenaerts has described the CJEU as 'the guarantor of the rule of law within the EU, whose role is, in effect, to act as both the Constitutional and Supreme Court of the European Union'.[30] He has also defined 'autonomy' as the 'European Union legal system functioning as a self-referential, complete legal system'.[31]

The Court of Appeal of England and Wales had cause to consider the role of the CJEU in a case on state immunity:

> We accept that the CJEU's primary role is to decide matters of EU law. However, its role with regard to international law is just like that of a domestic court. It may be necessary for the CJEU – or a domestic court – *to decide directly or indirectly a question of international law in order to decide disputes properly brought before it* (see, for example, Case C-466/11 Curra v. Bundesrepublic Deutschland, 12 July 2012 (Third Chamber) at [18].[32]

---

[29]   Szilard Gaspar-Szilagyi, 'The CJEU: An Overzealous Architect of the Relationship between the European Union Legal Order and the International Order' [2016] *Revista de Drept Constitutional* 44, 63.

[30]   Koen Lenaerts, 'The ECHR and the CJEU: Creating Synergies in the Field of Fundamental Rights Protection' (Solemn hearing for the opening of the Judicial Year, 26 January 2018) https://www.echr.coe.int/Documents/Speech_20180126_Lenaerts_JY_ENG.pdf, accessed 18 May 2019.

[31]   Koen Lenaerts, 'Keynote Speech' (III LAwTTIP Conference: EU Law, Trade Agreements, and Dispute Resolution Mechanisms: Contemporary Challenges, King's College London, 21–22 March 2019) https://www.youtube.com/watch?v=qBOeopzvPBY, accessed 18 May 2019.

[32]   *Benkharbouche & Anor v Embassy of the Republic of Sudan* (Rev 1) [2015] EWCA Civ 33, [2016] QB 347, para 52.

In deciding such a question of international law, the CJEU has the power to do more than make a passing citation to the ICJ – it could engage in dialogue, but its identity is closer to that of a domestic court rather than an international one.

4.3   Jurisdiction v Applicable Law

The third factor for the CJEU's posture towards international law is the relationship of the concepts of jurisdiction and applicable law.

The logical sequence of decision-making is:

(1)   Jurisdiction;
(2)   Applicable law;
(3)   Interpretation;
(4)   Application.

But these categories are not neat: 'application' often inevitably involves some measure of 'interpretation';[33] and provisions on applicable law and jurisdiction can easily be conflated. These concepts need to be kept distinct if the Court is not to exceed, or be thought to exceed, the jurisdiction conferred upon it by the parties to the dispute before it.

The CJEU, highly aware of its jurisdictional reach, keeps a tight rein on its applicable law. The *Mox Plant* dispute was illustrative of this. In this dispute, three linked sets of litigation arose out of the UK's decision to authorise the construction and operation of a plant to make mixed oxide fuel ('MOX'): first, proceedings instituted by Ireland against the UK under OSPAR Convention;[34] second, proceedings instituted by Ireland against the UK under the 1982 United Nations Convention on the Law of the Sea;[35] and third, proceedings instituted by the European Commission against Ireland before the European Court of Justice complaining that it had breached Article 292 Treaty estab-

---

[33] 'Art. 19. Interpretation of Treaties. Draft convention on the law of treaties' (1935) 29 AJIL Supp2 937, 938. There is, however, a recognised distinction between the two processes. Interpretation is the process of determining the meaning of a text; application is the process of determining the consequences which, according to the text, should follow in a given situation.'

[34] *Mox Plant Case (Ireland v United Kingdom)*, PCA, Order No 3 (24th June 2003) 126 ILR 310, (2003) 42 ILM 1187, ICGJ 366 (PCA 2003); and *Dispute Concerning Access to Information Under Article 9 of the OSPAR Convention (Ireland v United Kingdom)*, PCA, Final Award, (2nd July 2003) XXIII RIAA 59, (2003) 42 ILM 1118, ICGJ 377 (PCA 2003).

[35] *Mox Plant Case (Ireland v United Kingdom)*, ITLOS Case No 10, ICGJ 343 (ITLOS 2001), Order, Request for Provisional Measures (3rd December 2001); and *Mox Plant Case (Ireland v United Kingdom)*, PCA, Annex VII Tribunal, Order No 6 (6th June 2008).

lishing the European Community,[36] which required EC Member States not to submit disputes concerning EC law to a body other than the European Court of Justice.[37]

The European Court of Justice found that it had *exclusive jurisdiction* over the interpretation or application of mixed agreements like the UN Convention.[38] It was a robust assertion of jurisdiction matched by the application of European law to an international dispute, as seen in *Wightman*.

A more unifying approach would have been to safeguard the integrity of exclusive jurisdiction while taking a broad approach to applicable law, including using international law as an aid in the interpretation of European law.

5.   CONCLUSIONS

In the relationship of the EU and its judicial branch to general international law, we do not see *genuine* fragmentation, but we also do not observe genuine *engagement*. This lack of engagement by the CJEU with the case law of the ICJ is not a product of shyness, but rather of a strong sense of self-confidence and a concept of autonomy that equates to it being self-referential.

The EU and the CJEU do not, however, exist in a vacuum. Although the CJEU is the guardian of the European legal order, it also has a role in the international legal order and being self-referential should not require self-containment. As Bruno Simma, a former ICJ Judge, has observed: 'The EU's claim to autonomy is not problematic to the unity of the system since it conforms to a fundamental rule thereof, namely the *lex specialis* rule.'[39] A claim to autonomy is not incompatible with a horizontal, decentralised international legal system or with a constructive dialogue among courts.

---

[36]   Case C-459/03 *Commission of the European Communities v Ireland* [2006] ECR I-04635.

[37]   Robin R Churchill, 'Mox Plant Arbitration and Cases', *The Max Planck Encyclopedia of Public International Law* (June 2018) http://opil.ouplaw.com/home/EPIL, accessed 19 May 2019.

[38]   Ireland was therefore in breach of Art 292 EC Treaty by instituting proceedings against the UK before the Annex VII Tribunal (*Commission v Ireland* (n 36), paras 80–139).

[39]   Bruno Simma and Dirk Pulkowski, 'Of Planets and The Universe: Self-Contained Regimes in International Law' (2006) 17 *European Journal of International Law* 483, 500.

2.   Three years after *Achmea*: What is said, what is unsaid, and what could follow

Andrea Biondi and Giorgia Sangiuolo[1]

1.   INTRODUCTION

On 6 March 2018, the Court of Justice of the European Union delivered its decision in the case of *Achmea*.[2] The Grand Chamber of the CJEU found that Articles 267 and 344 TFEU preclude the Investor-State Dispute Settlement (ISDS) arbitration clause in Article 8 of the Dutch-Slovak Bilateral Investment Treaty (BIT). The case has rightly been regarded as of 'constitutional' prominence in that the Court was called on to add an important tile to the mosaic of the concept of 'autonomy' of the EU, by analysing for the first time the compatibility with the Union's legal order of the ISDS arbitration provision of a BIT in force between Member States (intra-EU). Yet, despite the significance of the case, the final judgment of the Court in *Achmea* is quite a 'skinny' one – and its many 'unsaids' leave much scope for further clarifications on its meaning and effects. With the 'Agreement for the Termination of intra-EU BITs' (Termination Agreement) signed in May 2020[3] almost all Member States have *de facto* interpreted the Court decision as determining the incompatibility of intra-EU BITs and intra-EU ISDS arbitration with EU law. The interpretation of *Achmea* set out in the Termination Agreement – the culmination of over ten years of efforts by the European Commission – is certainly rooted in important considerations of unity and full effectiveness of EU law. Yet, it arguably goes under many aspects well beyond the decision of the Court

---

[1]   The views and opinions expressed in the text are those of the authors and do not necessarily reflect the official policy or position of the UK's Government.

[2]   Case C-284/16, *Slovak Republic v Achmea BV* [2018] ECLI:EU:C:2018:158.

[3]   Agreement for the termination of Bilateral Investment Treaties between the Member States of the European Union (SN/4656/2019/INIT), OJ L 169/2020 ('Termination Agreement'). Austria, Ireland, Finland, Sweden, and the UK have not signed the Termination Agreement.

in ways that potentially raise questions of protection of intra-EU investors and compatibility with certain aspects of the rule of law. First, the wording of *Achmea* does not clearly encompass *all* intra-EU ISDS arbitration clauses, as the Termination Agreement suggests. The point is relevant and will require clarification, as this interpretation may have the undesirable effect of depriving investors of an effective route to safeguard their international protection (ISDS arbitration) even when that route does not interfere with the 'autonomy' of the EU. The interpretation of the Court's decision in *Achmea* endorsed by the Termination Agreement may further have questionable retroactive effects on arbitration proceedings that are pending at the date of its entry into force, leaving investors in the unenviable position of having to restart years of litigation to protect their rights or effectively being retroactively deprived of a forum for their protection. While the Termination Agreement seems to try to mitigate these issues through a transitional regime that 'phases-out' these intra-EU BITs, it is argued that that regime in itself may not be sufficient, and a combined effort of national courts, Member States, the Commission, and of the Court itself, through its interpretative role, will be necessary to overcome these issues. With this in mind, it is thus important to take a step back and reassess the significance of the *Achmea* decision.

2.   *ACHMEA*: WHAT THE DECISION SAYS

The main elements of the *Achmea* litigation are very well known but it may be useful to rapidly recap its essential tenets and certain details that will be useful for the rest of our analysis. The case arose in the context of the 1992 Dutch-Slovak BIT ('the BIT'). In particular, the ISDS arbitration clause included in Article 8 of the BIT, now terminated by the Termination Agreement, allowed investors of one of the contracting parties to bring claims directly against the other contracting party before an international tribunal for the alleged breach of the standards set out therein. The BIT was one among numerous investment protection agreements signed between western European countries that, at the time of conclusion, were members of the EU and eastern European countries that acceded to the block between 2004–2007. In 2008, a Dutch investor operating in the sickness insurance market (Achmea, formerly Eureko) brought arbitral proceedings against the Slovak Republic under that clause. Achmea argued before the investment tribunal constituted under the BIT that the reversal of the liberalisation of the sickness insurance market by the Slovak Republic had infringed its rights under the BIT to fair and equal treatment and free transfer of payments. The proceeding was governed by the 1976 UNCITRAL arbitration rules, and the seat of the arbitration was

Frankfurt am Main. Article 8(6) of the BIT, on the applicable law, provided that investor-state disputes shall be decided:

> on the basis of the law, taking into account in particular though not exclusively: the law in force of the Contracting Party concerned; the provisions of this Agreement, and other relevant agreements between the Contracting Parties; the provisions of special agreements relating to the investment; and the general principles of international law.

The tribunal eventually found in favour of the Dutch investor and ordered the Slovak Republic to pay EUR 22.1 million in damages.

The Slovak Republic brought an action before the German courts to have the final award set aside. Particularly, the Slovak Republic contended that the entire arbitration agreement in the Dutch-Slovak BIT was null and void and contrary to public policy inter alia for violation of EU law, in the form of Articles 18 (prohibition of discrimination on the grounds of nationality), 267 (preliminary reference), and 344 (exclusivity of the Court's jurisdiction) TFEU. Although unconvinced by the Slovak Republic's arguments,[4] the German Federal Court of Justice (*Bundesgerichtshof*) decided nonetheless to seek guidance from the CJEU due to the novelty of the issues raised. Specifically, the questions asked by the German court were phrased as follows:

(1)   Does Article 344 TFEU preclude the application of a provision in a bilateral investment protection agreement between Member States of the European Union (a so-called intra-EU BIT) under which an investor of a Contracting State, in the event of a dispute concerning investments in the other Contracting State, may bring proceedings against the latter State before an arbitral tribunal where the investment protection agreement was concluded before one of the Contracting States acceded to the European Union but the arbitral proceedings are not to be brought until after that date?

If Question 1 is to be answered in the negative:

(2)   Does Article 267 TFEU preclude the application of such a provision? If Questions 1 and 2 are to be answered in the negative: Does the first paragraph of Article 18 TFEU preclude the application of such a provision under the circumstances described in Question 1?

In reply to those questions, the CJEU eventually ruled that Articles 267 and 344 TFEU 'must be interpreted as precluding a provision in an international

---

[4]   *Achmea* (n 2), paras 14–22.

agreement concluded between Member States, such as Article 8' of the Dutch-Slovak BIT.[5] The Court deemed it unnecessary to decide on the issue of non-discrimination under Article 18 TFEU.

The reasoning of the CJEU is articulated in three main parts, in which the Court analyses in turn:

(i)   whether the arbitral tribunal constituted on the basis of the BIT may be called upon to decide on the interpretation or application of EU law;

(ii)   if that's the case, whether the arbitral tribunal is a court or tribunal of a Member State under Article 267 TFEU able to make a reference to the CJEU;

and

(iii)   should that conclusion be negative, is the arbitral award liable to be reviewed by the national courts of Member States.

Analysing these points in turn, in the *first part* of its decision, the Court concluded that the disputes which the arbitral tribunal mentioned in Article 8 of the Dutch-Slovak BIT is called to resolve are liable to relate to the interpretation or application of EU law.[6] The Court observed that, considering that EU law is, by definition, a constituent part of the domestic legal order of the Member States, the broad wording of the applicable law clause in Article 8(6) of the relevant BIT – which allowed it to decide based on the 'law in force of the Contracting Party concerned' – meant that the tribunal 'may be called on to interpret or indeed to apply EU law, particularly the provisions concerning the fundamental freedoms, including freedom of establishment and free movement of capital'.[7]

In the *second part* of its decision, the Court stated that an arbitral tribunal 'such as that referred to in Article 8 of the BIT cannot be regarded as a court or tribunal of a Member State within the meaning of Article 267 TFEU' and is thus 'not entitled to make a reference to the Court for a preliminary ruling'.[8] Importantly, the Court decided that the 'exceptional nature' of investment tribunals does not allow them to be considered part of the judicial system of either Member State involved (the Netherlands or the Slovak Republic).[9]

In the *third part* of its decision, the Court concluded that an arbitral award delivered by an arbitral tribunal, 'such as' the tribunal referred to in Article 8

---

[5]   Ibid., para 60.
[6]   Ibid., paras 39–42.
[7]   Ibid., para 42.
[8]   Ibid., paras 43–49.
[9]   Ibid., para 45.

of the BIT is not subject to review by a court of a Member State.[10] The reasoning of the Court on this point revolves around the flexibility intrinsic to the functioning of investment tribunals. The Court found that the discretion left to investment tribunals to determine their own rules of procedure – in particular, the seat and applicable law – coupled with the limited grounds for review under the national law eventually selected – mostly public policy – entailed the possibility that these awards might escape judicial review by the national courts of the Member States. The Court acknowledged that, as previously affirmed in its judgment *Eco Swiss*,[11] a limited review of arbitral award is, in principle, essential for arbitration to function efficiently. However, it then moved on to find that ISDS tribunals constitute an exception to that rule. The Court then distinguished commercial arbitration, at issue in *Eco Swiss*, from the case of investment arbitration at issue in *Achmea*, reasoning that while the former 'originates in the freely expressed wishes of the parties', the latter derives:

> from a treaty by which Member States agree to remove from the jurisdiction of their own courts, and hence from the system of judicial remedies which the second subparagraph of Article 19(1) TEU requires them to establish in the fields covered by EU law disputes which may concern the application or interpretation of EU law.[12]

For these reasons, the Court then concluded that the fact that mechanisms 'such as' the one under Article 8 of the BIT call into question the effectiveness of EU law, affect the preliminary ruling procedure provided for in Article 267 TFEU and are incompatible with the principle of sincere cooperation and the autonomy of EU law.

3.   *ACHMEA*: WHAT THE DECISION DOES NOT SAY AND HOW IT HAS BEEN INTERPRETED

The Court's decision in *Achmea* is more criticisable for what it does not say than for what it does. First, the brevity of the decision, only 31 paragraphs long, is particularly noticeable when compared to the 240 paragraphs of the Opinion rendered by Advocate General Wathelet. That brevity stands in stark contrast with the 'constitutional' importance of this case, in which the Court for the first time intervenes in the longstanding heated debate on the interface between the EU constitutional order and international investment arbitration.

---

[10]   Ibid., paras 50–59.
[11]   Case C-126/97, *Eco Swiss China Time Ltd v Benetton International NV* [1999] ECLI:EU:C:1999:269.
[12]   *Achmea* (n 2), para 55.

Second, it is also noteworthy that the Court spends most part of the decision re-stating certain constitutional principles of EU law established in its own previous case law – particularly the autonomous nature of the EU, the definition of court or tribunal of a Member State, and the importance of the preliminary reference procedure to ensure the effective functioning of the EU legal system and the unity of EU law.[13] The Court instead avoids responding directly to the first, general question posed by the referring court – of whether Article 344 TFEU precludes the application of a BIT arbitration clause in intra-EU BITs concluded before one of the Contracting States acceded to the EU, after accession has taken place – which it instead rephrases to fit a narrower response. It also carefully declines to decide the third preliminary question on the compatibility of the intra-EU ISDS arbitration clause in question with the principle of non-discrimination in Article 18 TFEU. The CJEU further seems reluctant to engage with the substance of the facts of the case or the broader picture of international law, the absence of any references to the Vienna Convention on the Law of the Treaties (VCLT) or to general rules of treaty interpretation or application is noteworthy. As a result, the judgement seems more of a restatement of some general features of EU law, rather than the critical and specific guidance that one would expect in a decision where the Court 'breaks new ground'.[14] Closer to a 'guidance' decision is, in the specific field of ISDS mechanisms, *Opinion 1/17* on the compatibility with EU law of the ISDS mechanism in the Comprehensive Economic Trade Agreement (CETA) between Canada and the EU. In that opinion, the Court elaborates on the importance of 'reciprocity' in the international relations of the EU and spends some time looking at the specific interactions between the wording of certain clauses of the CETA and EU treaty provisions, particularly from a standpoint of the 'autonomy' of the block.

One may only speculate why the CJEU adopted such a restrained approach in such an important constitutional decision – a disagreement among judges in the deliberation, deference to the executive in such a politically controversial matter, or other. Yet, the 'unspoken' in *Achmea* has sparked an intense debate – and, to some extent, confusion on the scope and effects of the 'preclusion' found by the Court, as well as its effects on pending arbitration proceedings among national and international courts, and Member States.[15] *Achmea* has

---

[13] Ibid., paras 31–37.

[14] Takis Tridimas, 'Constitutional Review of Member State Action: The Virtues and Vices of an Incomplete Jurisdiction' (2011) 9(3–4) *International Journal of Constitutional Law* 737.

[15] A good overview of the opposing arguments on the interpretation of *Achmea* is found in Ivana Damjanovic and Nicola de Sadeleer, 'I Would Rather Be a Respondent State before a Domestic Court in the EU than Before an International Investment

been mainly interpreted as establishing the incompatibility with EU law of all intra-EU ISDS arbitration clauses. That is the legal position that the Commission has held for a long time: already in 2006, the Commission's Economic and Financial Committee had argued that intra EU-BITs conflicted with EU law in that they created a risk of fragmentation for the internal market. The Committee further argued that intra-EU BITs had been 'superseded' upon accession and recommended a review of the need for these agreements by the following year.[16] As only two Member States – Ireland and Italy – terminated all their intra-EU BITs,[17] the Commission started infringement proceedings against five other Member States in 2015,[18] ultimately with little overall success, considering that the quasi-totality of the intra-EU BITs remained in

---

Tribunal' (2019) 4(1) European Papers, Special Section – The Achmea Case between International Law and European Union Law, Ségolène Barbou des Places, Emanuele Cimiotta, Juan Santos Vara (eds). Dimopulous and Hindelang argue that *Achmea* finds a full incompatibility between investment agreements and EU law, which requires that Member States must either terminate or amend BITs: Angelos Domopolous '*Achmea*: The principle of Autonomy and its implications for intra and extra- EU BITs' (*EJIL: Talk!* 27 March 2018); Steffen Hindelang 'The Limited and Immediate Effects of CJEU's *Achmea* Judgment' (*Verfassungblog*, 9 March 2019). On the other hand, other authors (Quentin Declève 'Does Achmea invalidates all intra-EU BITs? Not Necessarily!' (*International Litigation Blog*, 24 July 2018)) and many arbitral tribunals have instead argued that *Achmea* can only produce effects when EU law comes into play in the case at issue (e.g., *Addiko Bank v Croatia*, ICSID Case No. ARB/17/37, Decision on Croatia's Jurisdictional Objection Related to the Alleged Incompatibility of the BIT with the EU Acquis (12 June 2020); *Eskosol v Italy*, ICSID Case No. ARB/15/50, Decision on Termination Request and Intra-EU Objection (7 May 2019); *AMF Aircraftleasing v Czech Republic*, PCA Case No. 2017-15, Final Award (11 May 2020)). Some have argued that the wording of *Achmea* may extend to extra-EU BITs (Quentin Declève 'Achmea: Consequences on Applicable Law and ISDS Clauses in Extra-EU BITs and Future EU Trade and Investment Agreements' (2019) 4(1) European Papers, Special Section – The Achmea Case between International Law and European Union Law, Ségolène Barbou des Places, Emanuele Cimiotta, Juan Santos Vara (eds)) and to the Energy Charter Treaty (notably, that's also the interpretation of Advocate General Saugmandsgaard Øe in his Opinion dated 29 October 2020 in Joined Cases C-798/18 and C-799/18 *Federazione nazionale delle imprese elettrotecniche ed elettroniche (Anie) and Others*, [2020] ECLI:EU:C:2020:876, see fn 55) while others disagree (Anna Bilanova and Jaroslav Kudrna 'Achmea: The End of Investment Arbitration As We Know It?' (2018) 3(1) *European Investment Law and Arbitration Review*. See also the different positions on the application of *Achmea* to the Energy Charter Treaty adopted by the Member States in the three 2019 Declarations (n 23)).

[16]   Economic and Financial Committee, Annual EFC Report to the Commission and the Council on the Movement of Capital and the Freedom of Payments ECFIN/ CEFCPE (2006)REP/56882, 7.

[17]   Respectively, in 2012 and 2013.

[18]   Sweden, Austria, the Netherlands, Romania, and Slovak Republic.

force. In 2006 the Commission also started participating as *amicus curiae* in support of Member States in numerous ISDS arbitration proceedings based on intra-EU BITs, arguing that intra-EU BITs and their arbitration clauses had to be considered incompatible with EU law and terminated under Articles 59(1) (termination of the operation of a treaty implied by conclusion of a later treaty) or Article 30 (*lex posterior*) of the VCLT at the act of accession of the last Member State to the EU, thus depriving of jurisdiction all arbitral tribunals constituted after that date. Yet, that approach of the Commission had for over ten years before *Achmea* been unsuccessful, with most Member States remaining recalcitrant to take a position on the status of their intra-EU BITs and arbitral tribunals regularly rejecting what has become known as the 'intra-EU' objection.[19]

Against this background, it is interesting to see how *Achmea* was then immediately heralded by the Commission as a longed-for endorsement by Court of its longstanding legal position: the Commission, in a quickly issued Communication,[20] opined that *Achmea* implies that:

> all investor-State arbitration clauses in intra-EU BITs are inapplicable and that any arbitration tribunal established on the basis of such clauses lacks jurisdiction due to the absence of a valid arbitration agreement. As a consequence, national courts are under the obligation to annul any arbitral award rendered on that basis and to refuse to enforce it. Member States that are parties to pending cases, in whatever capacity, must also draw all necessary consequences from the Achmea judgment.[21]

The Communication evidenced how intra-EU BITs may overlap with single market rules and prevent the full application of EU law, for instance when they constitute the basis for the award of unlawful State aid in violation of the level playing field in the single market. The Communication also highlighted how the fact that these intra-EU BITs can confer rights only in respect of investors from one of the two Member States concerned may conflict with the principle of non-discrimination among EU investors within the single market and that intra-EU BITs may be regarded as taking away from the national judiciary litigation concerning national measures and involving EU law. On this basis, the

---

[19]   To date, no arbitral tribunal has accepted 'intra-EU objections' moved by either the Commission or a respondent Member State.

[20]   'The Court of Justice confirmed that investor-State arbitration clauses in intra-EU BITs are unlawful.': Commission, 'Communication from the Commission to the European Parliament and the Council: Protection of intra-EU investment' (17 June 2018) COM(2018) 547 final ('2018 Communication').

[21]   2018 Communication, ibid.

Commission thus called all on EU Member States to terminate their intra-EU BITs based on the 'legal consequences' of the Court's decision.[22]

This time, the Member States followed suit. In three political declarations dated 15 and 16 January 2019 on the 'Legal Consequences of the *Achmea* Judgement' (2019 Declarations), all Member States of the EU declared their intention to 'terminate all bilateral investment treaties concluded between them by means of a plurilateral treaty or, where that is mutually recognised as more expedient, bilaterally'.[23] While the legal effects of the 2019 Declarations are unclear, the coronation of the Commission's longstanding efforts to overcome ISDS arbitration among Member States is the conclusion by the majority of the Member States of the Termination Agreement, which formally terminates all the 134 intra-EU BITs set out in its Annex, including their sunset clauses.[24] The Termination Agreement further 'confirms' that intra-EU arbitration clauses are 'inapplicable' and, therefore, they 'cannot serve as legal basis for Arbitration Proceedings' as of the date on which the last of the parties to a Bilateral Investment Treaty became a Member State of the European Union.[25] National courts of the Member States, bound to a duty of loyalty to the EU, seem to date to be attempting to conform to this interpretation.[26]

The Termination Agreement is indeed a success for the Commission as it effectively signals a new era for investment protection within the EU, where intra-EU ISDS arbitration is most certainly going to be phased-out. That success is even more noteworthy because the interpretation of *Achmea*

---

[22]   See title of the 2019 Declarations (n 23) and Art 4(a) of the Termination Agreement (n 3).

[23]   Declaration of the Representatives of the Governments of the Member States, of 15 January 2019 on the Legal Consequences of the Judgment of the Court of Justice in Achmea and on Investment Protection in the European Union https://ec.europa .eu/info/sites/info/files/business_economy_euro/banking_and_finance/documents/ 190117-bilateral-investment-treaties_en.pdf, accessed 1 June 2020; Declaration of the Representatives of the Governments of the Member States, of 15 January 2019 on the Legal Consequences of the Judgment of the Court of Justice in Achmea and on Investment Protection in the European Union, issued by the Governments of Finland, Luxembourg, Malta, Slovenia and Sweden https://www.regeringen.se/48ee19/ contentassets/d759689c0c804a9ea7af6b2de7320128/achmea-declaration.pdf, accessed 1 June 2020; Declaration of the Representative of the Government of Hungary, of 16 January 2019 on the Legal Consequences of the Judgment of the Court of Justice in Achmea and on Investment Protection in the European Union https://www.kormany .hu/download/5/1b/81000/Hungarys%20Declaration%20on%20Achmea.pdf, accessed 1 June 2020 ('2019 Declarations').

[24]   Art 1 of the Termination Agreement (n 3).

[25]   Ibid., Art 4.

[26]   Although a number of preliminary references on the interpretation of *Achmea* have been reported.

pushed by the Commission and accepted by the majority of the Member States in the Termination Agreement, is not self-evident, but rather seems to go beyond what the Court actually held. Specifically, the interpretation adopted by the Commission and taken by the Termination Agreement seems to add supplementary meaning to the Court's decision in two main ways. First, by expanding the scope of *Achmea* to all intra-EU arbitration clauses. Second, by assuming that in *Achmea* the Court confirmed the Commission's thesis that intra-EU ISDS arbitration clauses became inapplicable as of the date when both parties to the BIT acceded to the EU, thus invalidating the jurisdiction of arbitral tribunals in pending ISDS proceedings.

It certainly is in the power of the Member States, as a matter of international law, to agree on this interpretation, whose effects ultimately also potentially benefit the EU project in so far as they ensure the unity of the law and pre-empt undue interferences of international law with Union law. However, it is argued that the expansive interpretation of *Achmea* embraced in the Termination Agreement raises issues in terms of reducing the protection of investors and curtailing the role of international tribunals of upholding the rule of law beyond what is necessary from a standpoint of Union law. The next two sections will look in turn at each of the two interpretative points discussed, how they sit with what the Court actually said in *Achmea*, and what issues they raise in practice.

3.1   Does (and Should) *Achmea* Really Target All Intra-EU Arbitration Clauses?

By terminating all the BITs in force among Member States together with the sunset clauses of those BITs that are no longer in force, but continue to produce effects, the Termination Agreement embraces the Commission's position that in *Achmea* the Court of Justice confirmed that *all* investor-State arbitration clauses in intra-EU BITs are incompatible with EU law.[27] Yet, that conclusion is not clear-cut from the wording of the Court's decision, which can be read (as indeed it has been read by arbitral tribunals) as grounded in considerations of applicable law, i.e., whether the arbitral tribunal in each case is actually able to interpret or apply EU law. That reading is also in line with the consideration that the protection offered by investment agreements and ISDS tribunals arguably does not fully overlap with that offered by EU law and EU courts and there will be instances where investors' rights are not protected, or are not effectively protected, under EU law. Therefore, the broad interpretation of *Achmea* endorsed in the Termination Agreement may have the undesirable effect of depriving investors of an effective additional tool of

---

[27]   2018 Communication (n 20).

protection of their rights under international law, ISDS tribunals, even in the absence of actual incompatibilities with EU law. Finally, from a more principled standpoint, even in the areas where the protection offered by EU law and investment agreements do actually overlap, it is widely acknowledged that EU law may still not offer in practice the same level of substantive and procedural protection provided in investment agreements. One may thus wonder whether, based on the need to ensure effective protection of individuals' rights, it would have been possible and advisable to maintain in some form a double-tracked system of protection until the process of reform and improvement of this area of law is completed.

3.1.1   The Court's decision is based on the applicable law clause of the Dutch-Slovak BIT

The wording of the CJEU's decision in *Achmea* seems centred around the question of applicable law, as set out in Article 8(6) of the Dutch-Slovak BIT and arguably does not extend to other ISDS arbitration clauses in other intra-EU BITs that do not require investment tribunals to interpret or apply EU law. The focus of the Court on the applicable law clause first emerges from the fact that the CJEU does not directly answer the widely-phrased first question posed by the *Bundesgerichtshof* (i.e., whether Art 344 TFEU precludes intra-EU ISDS arbitration) and concludes that its decision is addressed to intra-EU arbitration clauses 'such as' the one included in the Dutch- Slovak BIT. The reasoning of the Court further appears based on the specific wording of Article 8 of the BIT at issue, which, in the Court's view, created the 'risk' that the arbitral tribunal may be called on to interpret or apply EU law. That in itself suggests the necessity of a link between the law applicable to the arbitration proceeding and EU law, which would exclude that arbitration tribunals called to solve a dispute on the grounds of international law and/or of the law of a third country may be captured by the CJEU decision in *Achmea*. And indeed, the arbitral tribunal in *Achmea* was interpreting EU law to solve the dispute before it.

Admittedly, making recourse to the concept of 'autonomy' of EU law, the CJEU has in the past adopted quite a broad interpretation of what creates a risk that an international court or tribunal may 'interpret or apply' EU law for the purposes of Article 344 TFEU. In some cases, the Court has gone as far as finding that the mere, distant, possibility of that happening would have sufficed to triggering the incompatibility of their jurisdiction with Articles 267 and 344 TFEU. That was for instance the case of *Mox Plant*[28] and a number of opinions of the Court under Article 218(11) TFEU, from *Inland Waterways* to

---

[28]   Case C-459/03, *Commission of the European Communities v Ireland* [2006] ECLI:EU:C:2006:345.

Opinion 2/13 on the accession of the EU to the ECHR.[29] However, not only is that line of case law far from uncontroversial,[30] but, most recently, the Court also appears to have reconsidered this approach, notably in relation to specifically investor-State disputes: *Opinion 1/17*, on the compatibility with EU law of the ISDS mechanism included in the CETA, suggests that international dispute settlement mechanisms may not require an interpretation or application of the *acquis Communautaire*.[31] It may be remembered that, on that occasion, the Court found that the CETA tribunal could legitimately take into account EU law as a 'matter of fact',[32] and so accepted its potential jurisdiction by *renvoi*.

One may argue that the different conclusion reached by the CJEU in CETA is motivated by the 'extra-EU' nature of that agreement, signed between the EU and a third country rather than among Member States of the EU. And indeed, the President of the CJEU at the III LAwTTIP conference expressed the view that *Achmea* is fundamentally aimed at tackling an issue of 'mutual trust' among Member States. Essentially, President Lenaerts explained, the Court considered that such principle excludes that Member States may sign an international treaty to disempower their judiciaries, particularly of Eastern European countries, because they are not trusted with protecting the interest of investors, particularly of western European countries.[33]

---

[29]   Respectively, Opinion 1/76, Draft Agreement establishing a European laying-up fund for inland waterway vessels [1977] ECLI:EU:C:1977:63; Opinion 2/13, Accession of the European Union to the European Convention for the Protection of Human Rights and Fundamental Freedoms [2014] ECLI:EU:C:2014:2454.

[30]   The breadth of the Court's interpretation of autonomy vis-à-vis international law had been criticised in certain quarters already before *Achmea*: see among others Jed Odermatt, 'When a Fence Becomes a Cage: The Principle of Autonomy in EU External Relations Law' European University Institute (EUI) Working Papers, Max Weber Programme 2016/2017, https://cadmus.eui.eu/bitstream/handle/1814/41046/MWP_2016_07.pdf?sequence=1, accessed 1 June 2020; Piet Eeckhout, 'Opinion 2/13 On EU Accession to the ECHR and Judicial Dialogue: Autonomy or Autarky?' (2013) 38(1) *Fordham International Law Journal*; Jan W Rossem, 'The Autonomy of EU Law: More is Less?' in R A Wessel and O Blockmans, *Between Autonomy and Dependence - The EU Legal Order under the Influence of International Organisations* (Asser Press 2013).

[31]   Opinion 1/17, Comprehensive Economic and Trade Agreement between Canada, of the one part, and the European Union and its Member States, of the other part [2019] ECLI:EU:C:2019:341, para 130. See also Steffen Hindelang, Chapter 7 in this volume.

[32]   Ibid., paras 130–131.

[33]   Koen Lenaerts, 'Keynote Speech' (III LAwTTIP Conference: EU Law, Trade Agreements, and Dispute Resolution Mechanisms: Contemporary Challenges, King's College London, 21–22 March 2019), minutes 52:00 ss https://www.youtube.com/watch?v=qBOeopzvPBY, accessed 1 June 2020.

Yet, one may also argue that this interpretation is not part of the text of the decision in *Achmea*, which instead remains far from clear on this point. It would also make sense that the more relaxed approach adopted by the Court in CETA to the interaction between international dispute settlement mechanisms and EU law arises from the nature of ISDS disputes as falling outside the strictly inter-State, and thus outside of the scope of Article 344 TFEU. In fact, *Opinion 1/09* on the establishment of a Patent Court found that Article 344 TFEU 'merely prohibits Member States from submitting a dispute concerning the interpretation or application of the Treaties to any method of settlement other than those provided for in the Treaties' and does not prohibit disputes involving private persons.[34] If that holds true, then there is no reason why one should interpret the 'risk' of interference of ISDS tribunals with EU law found by the Court in *Achmea* as applicable to the entirety of intra-EU ISDS clauses.

3.1.2   The scope of protection of investors' rights offered by investment agreement and ISDS tribunals arguably does not fully overlap with the scope of protection offered by EU law and EU courts

A narrow interpretation of the decision in *Achmea*, as applicable only to intra-EU ISDS arbitration clauses where tribunals are called on to interpret or apply EU law, is also in line with the competence-based nature of the EU, whose scope is arguably more limited compared to the subject matter of investment treaties. Investment treaties indeed (i) have a somewhat different scope compared to the EU Treaties; and (ii) are implemented through procedural mechanisms that are different from EU law.

It may be argued that, outside the areas of competence of the EU, ISDS tribunals in intra-EU BITs perform an important function of protection for investors and of the rule of law, offering an efficient tool for resolution of disputes that may arise with the Member States. Therefore there is no reason why, in principle, the two systems of protection, European and international, should not continue to work side-by-side where the jurisdiction of investment tribunals does not directly interfere with EU law.

Discussing these points in turn, first, EU law is based on the concept of attributed competence and can thus only afford protection to activities falling within the scope of the EU Treaties (exclusively) or, in the case of mixed competences, where and to the extent that the EU has exercised its powers in that area. EU competences, as set out in the EU Treaties, however, seem to fall short of overlapping with investment treaties and the Court's decision

---

[34]   Opinion 1/09, *Creation of a unified patent litigation system* [2011] ECLI:EU:C: 2011:123, paras 61–63.

in *Achmea* does not support any other conclusion. It is true that the CJEU has found that the Treaty provisions on free movement of capital offer 'equivalent' protection to Member States' extra-EU BIT provisions on free transfer of funds.[35] Yet, as noted by the tribunal in *Eastern Sugar*[36] and by the Advocate General in *Achmea*,[37] while EU law deals with intra-EU investments, the scope of the substantive protections offered to investors under the EU Treaties is not comparable to those found under BITs, either because their scope is narrower, or because EU law does not offer any equivalent protection. For instance, the principle of national treatment under EU law does not allow the nationals of one Member State to benefit in another Member State from treatment which the latter State grants to nationals of a third Member State on the basis of a bilateral agreement. As for the protection from expropriation, while Article 345 TFEU provides that 'the Treaties shall in no way prejudice the rules in Member States governing the system of property ownership' and the Charter of Fundamental Rights of the EU (CFREU) provides for the conditions for legitimate expropriation in Article 17, the regulation of the conditions for expropriation are mostly a matter for domestic law. EU law also does not offer express protection from indirect expropriation, as many BITs do. No equivalent of the clause of full protection and security, which covers protection against physical and legal infringements of the host State directed at foreign investors, seems to exist under EU law. The Fair and Equitable Treatment (FET) standard does not overlap with the fundamental freedoms under EU law and goes beyond the prohibition of discrimination under the Treaties.[38] The different scope of the protections for investors under EU law and intra-EU BITs seems to have also been acknowledged by the Commission in its Communication on the 'Protection of intra-EU investment,' where it declared that 'EU law does not solve all problems investors may face in their activities. However, *in the single market*, EU investors' rights are protected by EU law, which allows for the pursuit and development of economic activities in all Member States'.[39]

---

[35] Case C-205/06, *Commission of the European Communities v Republic of Austria* [2009] ECLI:EU:C:2009:118; Case C-118/07, *Commission of the European Communities v Republic of Finland* [2009] ECLI:EU:C:2009:715; Case C-249/06, *Commission of the European Communities v Kingdom of Sweden* [2009] ECLI:EU:C: 2009:119.

[36] *Eastern Sugar BV v Czech Republic*, SCC Case No. 088/2004, Partial Award (17 March 2017), para 180.

[37] *Achmea*, Opinion of AG Wathelet ECLI:EU:C:2017:699, paras 100–109.

[38] *AMF Aircraftleasing v Czech Republic*, PCA Case No. 2017-15, Final Award (11 May 2020), paras 359–360.

[39] 2018 Communication (n 20) (emphasis added).

Second, procedurally, domestic or EU courts do not necessarily offer a protection equivalent to international arbitration in terms of fairness and efficiency of the proceedings. On the one hand, ISDS arbitration allows investors to directly 'sue' States for their policies, in virtually whichever form they may be implemented, i.e., primary, secondary, etc. That is not always the case in proceedings before the national courts of the Member States or before the EU courts: while it is uncontested that EU law requires Member States to put in place an effective system of judicial remedies, that obligation only covers matters of EU law. Further, State laws can and do set various limitations on what can be reviewed judicially and on how investors may, in practice, claim State liability.[40] On the other hand, it is well known that the gap between the duty of Member States to set up an effective system of judicial protection and its implementation in practice still has not been fully bridged in all EU countries, potentially leaving investors exposed to a de facto lack of effective remedies. That is for instance confirmed by the annual Justice Scoreboard of the Commission, which evidences that across Member States of the EU there are likely to be potential large disparities in terms of real or perceived efficiency, quality, and independence of courts and tribunals. The Commission itself is well aware of this deficiency, having included among its objectives in this area the increase of the effectiveness of the enforcement system in the EU, including actions to support administrative capacity building or to strengthen justice systems, and to tackle breaches of EU law by national authorities.[41] It is precisely for this reason that arbitration clauses have in practice traditionally been regarded as the most essential provisions of BITs: the power to address an international arbitral tribunal independent of the host State is the best guarantee that the investment will be protected against potential undue infringements by that same host State.[42] The Termination Agreement itself seems to acknowledge the difference in the procedural and substantive standards of protection between BITs and EU law where it provides in the preamble that Member States and the European Commission 'will intensify discussions to ensure that effective protection of investments is provided to all investors within the EU'.[43]

---

[40]   On the point on State liability, ibid.
[41]   Ibid.
[42]   *Emilio Agustin Maffezini v Spain*, ICSID Case No. Arb/9717, Decision on Objections to Jurisdiction (25 January 2000), point 54; *Gas Natural Sdg, Sa. v Argentina*, ICSID Case No. Arb/03/10, Decision of the Tribunal on Preliminary Questions on Jurisdiction (17 June 2005), point 31; *Suez, Sociedad General De Aguas de Barcelona SA. and Interagua Servicios Integrales de Agua SA. v Argentina*, ICSID Case No. Arb/03/17, Decision on Jurisdiction (16 May 2006), point 57.
[43]   Preamble of the Termination Agreement (n 3).

The above is also confirmed in the discussed 2018 Commission Communication[44] and the 'Action Plan on the Capital Markets Union', which puts the accent on the importance of reviewing the system of investment protection and facilitation within the EU through three pillars of substantive rules to ensure consistent protection, improvement of the enforcement of these rules, and facilitation of cross-border investments.[45] Yet, such an ambitious reform project, started in 2006 with the Commission's Economic and Financial Committee[46] is not likely to for many years. It remains unclear how it will develop and to what extent EU investors will be able to really obtain a level playing field of protections that resembles the one offered by ISDS tribunals.

3.2 *Achmea* and Pending Intra-EU ISDS Arbitration Proceedings

The Termination Agreement and the Commission interpret *Achmea* as supporting the illegality of intra-EU ISDS arbitration clauses 'as of the date on which the last of the parties to a Bilateral Investment Treaty became a Member State of the European Union'. Yet, that conclusion is not supported by the wording of the CJEU's decision: the judgment merely looks at the interpretation under EU law of the question referred by the German court on the specific point of the 'preclusion' under EU law of intra-EU ISDS clauses. The Court also remains very vague with regard to the overall effects of its pronouncement: notably, the original French version of the *Achmea* decision is much more nuanced, compared to the English version. The English version employs the verb 'to preclude' which might imply that the TFEU imposes some supervening illegality that renders investor-State arbitration per se invalid. In contrast, the French text uses the verb '*s'opposer*'. This may indicate more of a 'tension' between EU law and ISDS arbitration under intra-EU BITs rather than a clear-cut supervening illegality.[47] That suggests that national courts of Member States should be left some scope to module the potential impacts of the decision, taking into account the specific circumstances of the case before them.

---

[44] 2018 Communication (n 20).

[45] Commission, 'Communication from the Commission to the European Parliament, the Council, the European Economic and Social Committee and the Committee of the Regions: A Capital Markets Union for People and Businesses-New Action Plan' (24 September 2020) COM/2020/590 final.

[46] Economic and Financial Committee, 'Annual EFC Report to the Commission and the Council on the Movement of Capital and the Freedom of Payments' ECFIN/CEFCPE (2006) REP/56882, 7.

[47] 'Les articles 267 et 344 TFUE doivent être interprétés en ce sens qu'ils s'opposent à une disposition [aux termes de laquelle un investisseur peut] introduire une procédure [...] devant un tribunal arbitral.'

The Termination Agreement also 'confirms' that ISDS arbitration clauses in intra-EU BITs are 'inapplicable' and 'cannot serve as legal basis for Arbitration Proceedings' as of the moment when both contracting parties acceded to the EU.[48] This interpretation effectively deprives arbitration tribunals of jurisdiction as of that date. And after all, the referring *Bundesgerichtshof* in *Achmea* eventually set aside the investment award obtained by the Dutch investor against the Slovak Republic and many others have resisted the enforcement of intra-EU awards obtained by investors against Member States. The Termination Agreement further expands the scope of the arbitration proceedings affected by the *Achmea* decision to those arisen on the basis of sunset clauses of intra-EU BITs no longer in force. Although unclear in the face of the Termination Agreement, these effects on pending arbitration proceedings seem to be based on the longstanding argument of the Commission that intra-EU BITs would have been succeeded or terminated by the Treaties at the moment when they became agreements between Member States on the basis of Articles 59(1) or 30 of the VCLT. Yet, once again, the Court in *Achmea* makes no reference to Articles 59(1) or 30 of the VCLT in its decision. The argument of the Commission of the termination of intra-EU BITs from the moment of accession is indeed a highly controverted one, having been questioned by Member States and commentators alike, and consistently rejected by arbitral tribunals.[49] That could also explain why neither the 2018 Commission's Communication nor the Termination Agreement makes specific reference to it. If that is true, then ISDS clauses are valid until the moment when Member States officially terminated them (i.e., the date when the Termination Agreement entered into force) and the Termination Agreement may thus have questionable *retroactive* effects on pending proceedings arising from intra-EU BITs, both before national courts, which are asked to set aside arbitral awards, and before arbitral tribunals, which are asked to decline their jurisdiction regardless of whether their decision impacts on EU law.

Whilst some commentators have argued that the VCLT would allow contracting parties to afford retroactive effects to treaties,[50] and retroactivity is not

---

[48]   Art 4 of the Termination Agreement (n 3).

[49]   To the knowledge of the authors, none of the many international investment tribunals' awards or dissenting opinions that have dealt with the intra-EU jurisdictional objection based on Art 59 VCLT have accepted it. The intra-EU objection based on Art 30 VCLT was endorsed only in the dissent of Prof Kohen in *Theodoros Adamakopoulos and others v Republic of Cyprus*, ICSID Case No. ARB/15/49, Statement of Dissent of Professor Marcelo Kohen (3 February 2020).

[50]   Tanya Voon and Andrew D Mitchell, 'Denunciation, Termination and Survival: The Interplay of Treaty Law and International Investment Law' (2016) 31(2) *ICSID Review – Foreign Investment Law Journal*.

per se prohibited under international or EU law,[51] it remains doubtful whether the retroactive effects of the Termination Agreement are compatible with EU law for a number of reasons. First, retroactivity sits uncomfortably with Article 351(2) TFEU. Article 351(2) TFEU safeguards the pre-accession international obligations of the Member States, within the limit that they 'shall take all appropriate steps to eliminate the incompatibilities' deriving from rights and obligations going forward.[52] Admittedly, where it refers to 'Member States on the one hand, and one or more third countries on the other', that article has been in the past interpreted by the Court as referring to agreements between the Member States and third countries concluded before accession, and would thus exclude agreements between Member States.[53] However, that interpretation appears not entirely suited to ISDS arbitration provisions, due to their specific characteristics. To begin with, it may be argued that intra-EU BITs produce effects for parties *other* than the contracting Member States: on the one hand, while intra-EU BITs have been concluded between Member States, they have been interpreted as conferring rights beyond the States parties', also directly to individuals. ISDS arbitration clauses seem to confer certain rights to redress for the violations by the host State of basic standards of protection of their investments before an international, independent, forum directly to investors, disentangling them from the rights of their home State. For that reason, some commentators have argued that international investment arbitration constitutes a type of 'global administrative law', able to shield investors from States' interference.[54] On the other hand, procedural features of ISDS arbitration, such as the ability of an investor to succeed in a claim despite the their home State asserting that the tribunal lacks jurisdiction, the ability of investors to waive their rights to bring a claim, the fact that investors are not always required to exhaust domestic remedies before bringing a claim in the absence of a specific

---

[51] While the principle of non-retroactivity is considered an element of the rule of law, as part of legal certainty, the retroactive application of rules is in certain cases accepted. See Art 28 of the Vienna Convention on the Law of Treaties for international treaties; 'The Rule of Law Checklist' adopted by the Venice Commission at its 106th Plenary Session (Venice, 11–12 March 2016). For an overview of the principle of non-retroactivity in EU law, see Juha Raitio 'Legal Certainty, Non-Retroactivity and Periods of Limitation in EU Law' (2008) 2(1) *Legisprudence.*

[52] On this argument see also Michael De Boeck, 'Disagreement on intra-EU BITs continues: Infringement actions over intra-EU BITs' (*EU Law Blog*, 2020) https://europeanlawblog.eu/2020/06/15/disagreement-on-intra-eu-bits-continues-infringement-actions-over-intra-eu-bits/, accessed 23 December 2020.

[53] Among others, Case C-301/08, *Irène Bogiatzi, married name Ventouras v Deutscher Luftpool and Others* [2009] ECLI:EU:C:2009:649, para 19.

[54] Gus Van Harten and Martin Loughlin, 'Investment Treaty Arbitration as a Species of Global Administrative Law' (2006) 17(1) *European Journal of International Law.*

treaty provision, single out international investment arbitration as a unique legal regime in which investors are granted unseen rights that cannot logically unilaterally and retroactively be revoked by those same States that have conferred them, on pain of frustrating the rationale itself of the agreement. Therefore, there is an argument to say that ISDS arbitration clauses cannot be limited, as to their effects, to an agreement between Member States.

Second, intra-EU BITs are placed in a larger network of international obligations of the Member States with third countries, such as the ICSID Convention and the 1958 New York Convention. The ICSID Convention in particular sets up a specific regime of international law, in relation to which States cannot simply withdraw consent unilaterally once they have given that consent.[55] The Convention also sets out a specific procedure for its denunciation, which cannot be implicit.[56] So, unilateral changes by the parties to the Convention to their domestic law in a way that denies access to ICSID dispute settlement sit uncomfortably with their obligations under the Convention.[57] It is therefore at least debatable that matters of alleged succession or termination of intra-EU BITs may simply be considered as a matter internal to EU law.

For all these reasons, it would seem that the safeguards for the pre-accession obligations of Member States set out in Article 351(2) TFEU should also be considered applicable to ISDS provisions in intra-EU BITs. These include the fact that difficulties to square rights and obligations in previous international agreements with EU law should normally be addressed by formally denouncing those agreements (rather than assuming their implicit termination),[58] preserving legitimate expectations of those involved, and that there is an obligation on the national courts of the Member States to attempt to minimise possible incompatibilities between the EU Treaties and the international agreements of the Member States 'to the extent possible and in compliance with international law, in such a way that it is consistent with Community law', so arguably avoiding retroactive interpretations that impair investors' rights.[59]

Further, while it was said that retroactivity is not as such prohibited under international or EU law,[60] the temporal effects of the law must be set within the

---

[55]   Art 25 of the Convention on the Settlement of Investment Disputes Between States and Nationals of Other States (International Centre for Settlement of Investment Disputes (ICSID) 575 UNTS 159.

[56]   Ibid., Art 71.

[57]   *Micula v Romania (II)*, ICSID Case No. ARB/14/29, Award (5 March 2020), paras 268–278.

[58]   Case C-62/98, *Commission of the European Communities v Portuguese Republic* [2000] ECLI:EU:C:2000:358, para 58.

[59]   Case C-216/01, *Budějovický Budvar, národní podnik v Rudolf Ammersin GmbH* [2003] ECLI:EU:C:2003:618, paras 167–169.

[60]   See to this effect (n 51).

boundaries of the rule of law, including legal certainty, legitimate expectations, and access to justice. Article 351 TFEU can be considered an expression of this principle, in the sense that it safeguards the principles of legality and legal certainty by allowing Member States to fulfil the obligations under international law undertaken before accession. Along the same lines, Article 69(2)(b) of the VCLT, for example, provides that while treaty invalidity is grounds to render the provisions of such treaty without legal force, 'if acts have nevertheless been performed in reliance on such a treaty' and 'in good faith before the invalidity was invoked', those acts 'are not rendered unlawful by reason only of the invalidity of the treaty', unless expressly provided otherwise. Equally, it is an essential element of any democratic legal system that independent mechanisms for the resolution of disputes should be subject to a number of safeguards, including legal certainty, due process, and access to justice. The CJEU itself in *Opinion 1/17* specifically prohibited any retroactive effect of joint binding interpretations by the Joint Committee set up by Canada and the EU on pending proceedings, including investor-State proceedings. That is particularly true for proceedings involving a control over States' powers, such as ISDS tribunals, whose role is precisely that of keeping them in check vis-à-vis standards of protection of individuals willingly undertaken by State parties to the investment agreement. The case law of the Court in other areas also traditionally stresses the importance of the observance of the principles of legal certainty and the protection of legitimate expectations of individuals, requiring inter alia that EU law can be applied to situations existing before their entry into force only in so far as it follows clearly from their terms, and that the termination of individuals' rights should be coupled with a transitional period, especially where there may be negative consequences on individuals and undertakings.[61]

Those guarantees may not be safeguarded by, effectively, 'terminating' retroactively pending ISDS proceedings. It is noteworthy that treaties terminating ISDS arbitration protection in recent decades provide also specific 'phasing out' mechanisms for disputes arising from acts or omissions carried out before the termination. That is the case, for instance, of the new US-Mexico-Canada Agreement (USMCA) in relation to Canada, which, in Annex 14-C, provides that claims of US or Canadian investors with respect to investments established or acquired while NAFTA is still in effect, will be entitled to bring ISDS claims for three years following the termination of this latter agreement. Article 30.8 of the Comprehensive Economic and Trade Agreement (CETA) between the EU and Canada replaces the survival clause of terminated BITs

---

[61] Case C-347/06, *ASM Brescia SpA v Comune di Rodengo Saiano* [2008] ECLI: EU:C:2008:416, paras 69–71.

between Canada and the Member States with a three-year survival clause.[62] Considerations of rule of law require, in our view, that any decision on invalidity of dispute settlement procedures cannot have retroactive effects, but rather requires careful prospective implementation taking into account principles such as legal certainty, legitimate expectations, and due process for all those involved. For instance, an interpretation of *Achmea* as retroactively 'invalidating' arbitration clauses relied upon in good faith by investors in pending proceedings risks impairing their access to court by depriving them of a forum to resolve their disputes where – due to time-limits and other formal preclusions, such as nationality – they cannot start proceedings before national courts.

The Termination Agreement seems to take into account such a concern and attempts to mitigate the consequences of a retroactive interpretation of *Achmea* by providing a transitional regime for the 'phasing-out' of intra-EU ISDS proceedings. However, it is questionable whether that regime achieves its aim as, among other things, the transitional regime, agreed in May 2020, strikingly is construed around the date of the publication of *Achmea two years earlier*, in March 2018.[63] The rationale for this choice is probably that *Achmea* was regarded by the Member States as having provided some clarity on the law. Yet, the decision falls short of doing so. If anything, *Achmea* raises more questions on the interpretation of the law rather than clarifying it. As a consequence, that transitional regime in the Termination Agreement does not provide any phasing-out provision for 'new' arbitration proceedings – i.e., proceedings started after the CJEU rendered its decision in *Achmea*. Numerous intra-EU BIT proceedings that were initiated over two years before the entry into force of the Termination Agreement are simply considered null and void for its purpose and no arrangement is made for investors to rely on the transitional provisions set out therein for other pending arbitration proceedings.

---

[62]   Tanya Voon and Andrew D Mitchell, 'Denunciation, Termination and Survival: The Interplay of Treaty Law and International Investment Law' (n 50); Natalia Bernasconi-Osterwalder, Sarah Brewin et al 'Terminating a Bilateral Investment Treaty' IISD Best Practice Series (March 2020).

[63]   The Termination Agreement distinguishes among three categories of ISDS arbitration proceedings: (i) 'concluded' arbitration proceedings, where a final award had been rendered and executed before 6 March 2018 (date of publication of the *Achmea* decision) are left untouched; (ii) 'pending' arbitration proceedings, initiated before that date, are deemed 'invalid' and without a legal basis but certain transitional arrangements for their conclusions are put in place; while (iii) 'new' arbitration proceedings, started after that date, are deemed as based on an 'invalid' provision.

4.   CONCLUSIONS

Despite its constitutional importance, the decision of the CJEU in *Achmea* provides little help to define the status of intra-EU ISDS arbitration clauses in EU law. The decision has been interpreted by the Member States that signed the Termination Agreement as, among other things, determining the incompatibility with EU law of *all* ISDS arbitration provisions in intra-EU BITs, regardless of their interference with EU law, and 'confirming' the lack of jurisdiction of ISDS tribunals as of the date when both parties to the BIT acceded to the EU, potentially bearing retroactive effects on pending proceedings. That interpretation seems based on the longstanding views of the Commission on the matter, based on considerations of unity and effectiveness of EU law.

This contribution tried to argue that the interpretation adopted in the Termination Agreement is not fully supported by the Court's decision in *Achmea* and goes beyond it in many ways which may seem unnecessary and problematic from an EU law standpoint. That is, first, because the interpretation of the Court in the *Achmea* judgment can (and probably should) be regarded as specifically limited to the applicable law clause at issue in that case, which allowed the tribunal to interpret and apply EU law and does not impinge on the broader jurisdiction of the tribunals when that is not the case. Second, *Achmea* does not validate the Commission's claims on the *ex tunc* lack of jurisdiction of arbitration tribunals based on Articles 59(1) and 30 VCLT, and thus risks having retroactive effects on pending proceedings, questionable from a rule of law standpoint.

So, what now? Regardless of whether one agrees or not with it, the conclusion of the Termination Agreement seems to signal the end of intra-EU ISDS arbitration going forward. Intra-EU BITs have formally been terminated and there is no sign that the Commission or the Member States will have a change of heart on their compatibility with EU law.

It could be argued that, while not strictly necessary, the termination of intra-EU BITs may, in effect, remove any potential threat to the unity and effectiveness of EU law, by sparing all parties involved from having to assess their effects on a case-by-case basis. However, hopefully something remains to be done in relation to the most problematic effects of the Termination Agreement, its potentially retroactive effects on pending proceedings and its 'clumsy' transitional regime. It will be for national courts, Member States, and the Commission alike to use all the tools in their arsenal to ensure that pending arbitration proceedings at the date of the Termination Agreement are handled within the boundaries of the rule of law. National courts are already showing their willingness to do so by referring preliminary questions to the CJEU which may modify the mainstream interpretation of *Achmea* followed in the Termination Agreement to take account of rule of law considerations. For instance, the Svea Court of Appeal has recently considered that if Member States do not object to the jurisdiction of ISDS tribunals within the procedural time periods prescribed, they are considered to be contractually agreeing to arbitration with the investors. In so doing the Swedish court effectively tried to circumvent the considerations of mutual trust in *Achmea* by shifting the legal framework from an agreement between Member States, prohibited under Article 344 TFEU to an agreement between an individual and a Member State, which falls outside the scope of that provision. The question has now been referred to the CJEU.[64]

The Court of Justice itself will have an important role to play when deciding these questions. It cannot be excluded that, possibly as a reflection of its decisions in commercial arbitration cases,[65] the Court will eventually end up 'scaling back' its position on the interface of EU law and ISDS arbitration and so enable arbitral tribunals to play their part in upholding the rule of law internationally.

---

[64] Högsta Domstolen (Swedish Supreme Court), Decision of 12 December 2019 in Case T 1569-19 https://www.italaw.com/sites/default/files/case-documents/italaw11099.pdf (Swedish), accessed 1 June 2020.

[65] Eco Swiss (n 11); Case C-567/14, *Genentech Inc. v Hoechst GmbH and Sanofi-Aventis Deutschland GmbH* [2016] ECLI:EU:C:2016:526.

3. Opinion 1/17 of the Court of Justice on the legality, under EU law, of the investor-to-state dispute settlement mechanism included in the CETA agreement. A case of legal pragmatism or the dawn of a new era?

Sonja Boelaert[1]

1. INTRODUCTION

On 7 September 2017 Belgium requested the opinion of the Court of Justice of the European Union on whether the provisions on investor-to-state dispute settlement (ISDS) included in the draft Comprehensive Economic and Trade Agreement (CETA)[2] are compatible with EU law.

In its Opinion 1/17, issued on 30 April 2019,[3] the Court (in Full Court formation) gave its legal blessing to the ISDS mechanism set out in the CETA texts.[4] These provisions are set out in part F of Chapter 8 of the CETA

---

[1]   The author is writing in a strictly personal capacity. No opinion in this contribution may be attributed to the Council or to its Legal Service.

[2]   Comprehensive Economic and Trade Agreement (CETA) between Canada, of the one part, and the European Union and its Member States, of the other part [2017] OJ L 11/ 23.

[3]   Opinion 1/17 *EU-Canada CET Agreement* [2019] EU:C:2019:341.

[4]   In addition to the text of the CETA itself, a number of additional documents and declarations were agreed between parties. Art 1 of the Council (of the European Union) signature decision refers to the text of the Agreement itself, together with the 'Joint Interpretative Instrument' and the related Statements and Declarations: see Council Decision (EU) 2017/37 of 28 October 2016 on the signing on behalf of the European Union of the Comprehensive Economic and Trade Agreement (CETA) between Canada, of the one part, and the European Union and its Member States, of the other part [2017] OJ L 11/1. For the purposes of the ICS and Opinion 1/17, the 'Joint Interpretative Instrument' carries particular weight and importance: see Joint

('Resolution of investment disputes between investors and states'). It is referred to by parties to CETA as the 'Investment Court System' (ICS)[5] and needs to be read together with the 'Joint Interpretative Instrument'.[6] The ICS is intended as a two-tier bilateral standing permanent tribunal system, with appointed members, but that still retains some features of investment arbitration.[7] The parties have also agreed to set up an Appellate Tribunal,[8] which is loosely modelled on the WTO's Appellate Body, and expressed the intention that the future multilateral investment tribunal could replace the bilateral ICS.[9]

Under the CETA texts, 'foreign' investors[10] have two options in terms of dispute resolution. They may choose to bring a claim before the domestic courts of the Parties, but in that case they cannot rely on the provisions of the

---

Interpretative Instrument on the Comprehensive Economic and Trade Agreement (CETA) between Canada and the European Union and its Member States [2017] OJ L 11/3 ('Joint Interpretative Instrument'). There is also a list of 38 statements that have been entered into the Council minutes and in relation to which the EU has internally agreed that they 'form an integral part of the context in which the Council adopts the decision to authorise the signature of CETA on behalf of the Union'. For the purposes of Opinion 1/17 and the ISDS/ICS system, statements 23 (Slovenia), 36 (Council and Commission), 37 (Belgium) and 38 (Council Legal Service) carry particular interest: see Statements to be entered in the Council minutes [2017] OJ L 11/9.

[5]   See part 2 below for an explanation of this system.
[6]   See Joint Interpretative Instrument.
[7]   See Arts 8.27, 8.28, and 8.30 of Chapter 8, section F of the CETA and points 6 f), g), h) and f) of the Joint Interpretative Instrument.
[8]   See Art 8.28 of Chapter 8, section F of the CETA.
[9]   See Art 8.29 of Chapter 8, section F of the CETA, which reads as follows:
      The Parties shall pursue with other trading partners the establishment of a multilateral investment tribunal and appellate mechanism for the resolution of investment disputes. Upon establishment of such a multilateral mechanism, the CETA Joint Committee shall adopt a decision providing that investment disputes under this Section will be decided pursuant to the multilateral mechanism and make appropriate transitional arrangements.
[10]   That is to say, Canadian investors in the EU and EU investors in Canada: see Opinion 1/17 (n 3), paras 180–181.

CETA.[11] Or they can resort to the ICS, which allows them to invoke the investment protection provision of the CETA.[12]

In its request to the Court of Justice Belgium raised 'concerns' regarding three aspects of the ICS as proposed for the CETA. First, it expressed doubts as to the compatibility of the envisaged ICS with the autonomy of the EU legal order. Secondly, it had doubts regarding the compatibility of the envisaged ICS with the general principle of equal treatment and the requirement of effectiveness. Last, it expressed doubts as to the compatibility of the envisaged ICS with the right of access to an independent tribunal. The Court dismissed all the concerns expressed by Belgium.[13]

This chapter will concentrate of the first question posed by Belgium, relating to the question of the autonomy of the EU legal order.

The response to Belgium's first question is set out in section V. A, paragraphs 106 to 161 of its Opinion. The Court considers that the proposed investment dispute resolution mechanism, even though it allows Canadian investors to bypass EU courts (and vice versa*)*, does not *adversely* affect the autonomy of the EU legal order. The Court's reasoning regarding this first question closely followed the Opinion of the late AG Bot delivered on 29 January 2019.[14] and is entirely in line with the pleadings of the Council, the Commission, and most, but not all, Member States that participated in the proceedings.[15]

There were formidable legal obstacles that had to be overcome to achieve that outcome, most of which had been erected by the Court itself. For a proper understanding of the impact of Opinion 1/17 it is useful to recall why efforts to include ISDS in its EU-level trade agreements faced heavy criticism from civil

---

[11]   See Art 30.6 of Chapter 30 of the CETA, entitled 'Private Rights', which reads as follows:

>   1.   Nothing in this Agreement shall be construed as conferring rights or imposing obligations on persons other than those created between the Parties under public international law, nor as permitting this Agreement to be directly invoked in the domestic legal systems of the Parties.
>   2.   A Party shall not provide for a right of action under its domestic law against the other Party on the ground that a measure of the other Party is inconsistent with this Agreement.

[12]   See Art 8.28 of Chapter 8, section F of the CETA.

[13]   For a summary of the Court's answers to the three questions: see ECJ, 'Opinion 1/17'_Press release No 52/19 (Luxembourg, 30 April 2019) https://curia.europa.eu/jcms/upload/docs/application/pdf/2019-04/cp190052en.pdf, accessed 29 June 2021.

[14]   Opinion 1/17 *EU-Canada CET Agreement* [2019], Opinion of AG Bot EU:C: 2019:72.

[15]   The European Parliament did not participate. Apart from Belgium, the Member States that participated in the proceedings were the following: Denmark, Germany, Estonia, Greece, Spain, France, Lithuania, the Netherlands, Austria, Slovenia, Slovakia, Finland and Sweden.

society as well as serious legal obstacles coming from case law of the Court of Justice. All these interlacing developments will be addressed in Part 2 below. Part 3 of this chapter dives into the key points of the Opinion 1/17 viewed against the Court's previous case law. Part 4 presents some reflections on the place of the CETA in the EU legal order. Part 5 offers some final remarks and ends with a few words of caution against reading too much into the opinion.

2.   THE COMPLEX BACKGROUND TO THE BELGIAN REQUEST

2.1   ISDS Generally

There are thought to be about 3,000 bilateral investment treaties world-wide. Investor-to-State dispute settlement (ISDS) is included as a mechanism in about 93 per cent of these investment treaties. EU Member States are report-edly party to around 1,400 bilateral investment treaties (BITs) with third States, 125 of which with OECD countries. Many of these include ISDS provisions.[16]

In its traditional form, ISDS is a dispute-resolution mechanism set out in bilateral or multilateral investment treaties that allows a 'foreign' investor (natural or legal person) to directly bring a dispute against the state in which an investment was made, and have this resolved by an ad hoc arbitral tribunal, appointed in accordance with terms agreed by the disputing parties, independ-ent from the host state's court system. The treaty-based mechanism entails that the host state accepts, by way of a 'standing offer', to be brought before an arbitral tribunal by any foreign investor covered by the investment treaty and that these investors do not need to resort to seeking diplomatic protection from their home state. One of the principal features, and no doubt its *raison d'être*,[17] is that ISDS allows investors to side-step the judicial systems of host states. As AG Bot rightly pointed out, ISDS is used where there are '*perceived shortcomings in the judicial systems of certain host States, which have fostered distrust amongst investors in those systems*'.[18] This also explains why the

---

[16]   Sources reported, inter alia, by the European Commission http://ec.europa.eu/trade/policy/accessing-markets/dispute-settlement/investment-disputes/, accessed 28 June 2021.

[17]   Case C-284/16 *Slovak Republic v Achmea* EU:C:2018:158, para 45. As noted by the Court of Justice in the *Achmea* case:

> In the case in the main proceedings, the arbitral tribunal is not part of the judicial system of the Netherlands or Slovakia. Indeed, it is precisely the exceptional nature of the tribunal's jurisdiction compared with that of the courts of those two Member States that is one of the principal reasons for the existence of Article 8 of the BIT.

[18]   Opinion of AG Bot (n 14), paras 11–13.

principle of exhaustion of local remedies is not a principle of international investment law.[19]

It is no secret that ISDS remains a contentious form of dispute settlement. The literature on this subject is voluminous and many voices from civil society continue to be vocal in their opposition.[20] Among the criticisms levelled are the complaint that 'investment' is usually defined in a broad manner in the investment treaties, and places few limits on the standing of natural and legal persons who can claim protected investor status to bring claims against the defendant host state; that ISDS tends to generate large monetary awards, which sets it apart from other international dispute settlement mechanisms. In addition, like most international arbitrations, it is also a fairly costly process. There are also concerns that ISDS poses a threat to the host state's 'right to regulate' and more broadly, has a deterrent effect and leads to what is known as the 'regulatory chill'. Furthermore, opinion is divided as to whether ISDS provides an incentive or disincentive to improve domestic adjudication systems. In addition, it is not clear whether ISDS provisions directly contribute to increasing foreign direct investment. Other criticisms of ISDS relate to genuine or perceived conflicts of interest between the small number of specialists who can serve either as arbitrator or counsel in investment arbitration and accusations that the system leads to a professional bias towards investors' claims. Others point to discrimination: ISDS gives 'foreign' investors a direct right of action to enforce the 'investment protection' provisions against the host state in circumstances where 'local' companies may not have the same rights. Finally, it is claimed that there is genuinely no need to allow foreign investors to bypass domestic courts in well-developed legal systems.

To his credit, the late AG Bot acknowledged most of these criticisms in his Opinion on the CETA agreement.[21] His Opinion, which is entirely in line with arguments made by the Council, the Commission, the Council and most

---

[19]   Steffen Hindelang, *Part II: Study on Investor-State Dispute Settlement (ISDS) and Alternative Dispute Resolution in International Investment Law* (European Parliament, INTA Committee 2012), 1.3.2.21; Markus Krajewski, 'Modalities for investment protection and Investor-State Dispute Settlement (ISDS) in TTIP from a Trade Union Perspective' (2014), 18.

[20]   Laurens Ankersmit, 'The Compatibility of Investment Arbitration in EU Trade Agreements with the EU Judicial System' (2016) 13 *Journal for European Environmental and Planning Law* 46; Kyla Tienhaara, 'Regulatory Chill and the Threat of Arbitration: A View from Political Science' in Chester Brown and Kate Miles (eds), *Evolution in Investment Treaty Law and Arbitration* (CUP 2011); Johannes Schwarzer, 'Investor-State Dispute Settlement: An Anachronism Whose Time Has Gone' Policy Brief 2018/1 https://www.cepweb.org/wp-content/uploads/2018/09/CEP-Policy-Brief-ISDS-1.pdf, accessed 28 June 2021.

[21]   Opinion of AG Bot (n 14), para 15.

Member States that participating in the proceedings, provides an elaborate defence of the EU policy decision to include (as was eventually done in the case of the CETA) a modernised version of ISDS in its trade and investment agreements with third countries. AG Bot started by referring to the EU's substantial efforts to improve on the traditional ISDS mechanism. He opined that ultimately its inclusion in the CETA was the outcome of a democratic debate and furthermore is a matter at the political discretion of EU institutions. His preliminary conclusion was that the 'only issue' before him and the Court, is a narrow legal question: '[…] whether, by adopting the practice of investment arbitration whilst at the same time developing it with a view to moving towards a judicial model, the agreement envisaged is, from a purely legal perspective, compatible with primary EU law'.[22]

However, further on in his opinion AG Bot could not resist the temptation to answer one of the more pointed contemporary criticisms levelled against ISDS/ICS: why is there a need at all for such a mechanism among countries, which presumably have well-developed, well-functioning, independent and unbiased judicial systems? Why indeed should investors from Canada be allowed to by-pass EU domestic courts and vice versa?

In responding to these doubts, AG Bot embarked on vigorous defence of the EU's policy decision to include an ISDS mechanism in the CETA. He elaborated on the need for reciprocity in view of the legitimate fear that foreign investors may have of being placed at a disadvantage before the host state's courts;[23] pointed to the lack of mutual trust (as that principle is understood in the case law of the Court) governing the relations between the EU and its Member States on the one hand, and Canada, on the other;[24] explained the need for the EU to agree on a 'blind' model with Canada which does not require it to examine whether or not the latter offers judicial protection on a par with that provided in the EU; as well as the need for the EU to be able to replicate this model in trade and investment agreements with countries other than Canada.[25] In other words, AG Bot acknowledged that Canada's judicial system may not leave anything to be desired, but that the same may not necessarily be true for other states that the EU wishes to have investment treaty protection with. Hence the need for a 'one-size-fits-all' approach. Lastly, AG Bot concluded

---

[22]   Ibid., paras 15–33.
[23]   Ibid., paras 72–78.
[24]   Ibid., paras 79–86.
[25]   Ibid., paras 86–90.

that the policy decision to include ISDS/ICS in the CETA should not be taken as reflecting poorly on the EU's judicial system:

> [...] establishing a dispute settlement mechanism such as that under examination does not, in my view, mean calling into question the judicial system of the European Union and of its Member States or the ability of that system to deal effectively, independently and impartially with actions brought by foreign investors. By establishing such a mechanism in its bilateral relations in the field of investment, the European Union intends to satisfy a demand for neutrality and speciality in the resolution of disputes between investors and States, bearing in mind that it will also benefit European investors when they invest in a third State.[26]

In its Opinion of 30 April 2019, the Court itself did not endorse any of these remarks, no doubt because they exceed the bounds of the limits of the narrow legal question that AG Bot had said was before him and before the Court.[27]

2.2   ISDS and the EU Investment Policy

What has often been overlooked by those opposing ISDS as part to the EU's trade policy is that already in the 1990s, the EU had concluded an international agreement that includes ISDS. The agreement in question is the Energy Charter Treaty (ECT) to which the EU, EURATOM and initially all EU Member States were a party.[28] As both the Union and its Member States are Contracting Parties to the ECT, investors may bring claims against a Member State and/or the Union before an international investment tribunal (Art 26(1) ECT).[29] The ISDS currently included in the ECT is of the traditional kind. Until very recently, the only arbitrations that were brought under the ECT were against EU Member States. However, since the summer of 2019, this has changed. The EU is now party to two arbitrations brought against the EU under that treaty, including the high-profile case brought by the Nord Stream

---

[26]   Ibid., para 88.

[27]   Ibid., paras 72–90.

[28]   Council and Commission Decision of 23 September 1997 on the conclusion, by the European Communities, of the Energy Charter Treaty and the Energy Charter Protocol on energy efficiency and related environmental aspects [1998] OJ L 69/1.

[29]   Juliane Kokott and Christoph Sobottan, 'Investment Arbitration and EU Law' (2016) 18 *Cambridge Yearbook of European Legal Studies* 3. More generally on the EU and the ECT see Matthew Happold and Michael De Boeck, 'The European Union and the Energy Charter Treaty: What next after *Achmea*?' in Mads Andenas, Matthew Happold and Luca Pantaleo (eds), *The European Union as an Actor in International Economic Law* (TMC Asser Press 2019) (forthcoming).

2 consortium.[30] The Council of the EU has as recently as July 2019, adopted
a negotiation mandate for the 'modernisation' of the ECT.[31] The negotiating
directives issued to the Commission aim, inter alia, at bringing the ECT's
investment protection provisions in line with the EU's reformed approach,
including its goal to bring the ECT eventually under the umbrella of the
Multilateral Investment Court (MIC).[32]

Leaving the ECT aside, it is useful to recall the timeline of the inclusion
of ISDS/CETA in EU trade and investment agreements. The negotiation
mandates for the CETA, Singapore FTA and other similar agreements in the
area of the EU's Common Commercial Policy (or trade policy) predate the
Lisbon Treaty. With the entry into force of this treaty, significant amendments
were made to the EU's trade policy. Among these is the explicit reference in
Articles 206 and 207 TFEU that this policy area allows the EU include foreign
direct investment (FDI). Soon after the Lisbon Treaty entered into force the
European Commission proposed an ambitious EU investment policy, driven
by the Commission's understanding of the Lisbon Treaty. In that view international investment agreements – including investment protection – would
now fall entirely under the exclusive competence of the EU, which means
that ISDS involving EU Member States should be brought under the EU's
umbrella. Furthermore, the Commission took the view that the EU is the legal
successor to all investment agreements concluded by EU Member States with
third states and that eventually all such agreements should be replaced by
EU-level agreements.[33] At the same the Commission maintained that bilateral

---

[30]   See for information on some of these arbitrations brought under the ECT against
the EU: European Commission's DG Trade website http://ec.europa.eu/trade/policy/
accessing-markets/dispute-settlement/investment-disputes/, accessed 28 June 2021.

[31]   Council document 10745/19 of 15 July 2015 authorising the opening of negotiations on the modernisation of the Energy Charter Treaty, to the extent this falls
within the competence of the Union; See also Council document 10745/19 ADD1 of 10
July 2015 http://trade.ec.europa.eu/doclib/press/index.cfm?id=2049, accessed 28 June
2021.

[32]   Following the *Achmea* judgment and Opinion 1/17, sooner or later the Court
of Justice will be seised of questions regarding the compatibility with the EU legal
order of the old-style ISDS mechanism included in the ECT, including the question of
whether ISDS among EU Member States under the ECT remains, at least from the point
of view of the EU legal order, a legally viable path. It comes as no surprise that neither
AG Bot nor the Court itself refer to the ECT in their opinions.

[33]   This goal is also included in internal EU legislation in the so-called
'Grandfathering' regulation, that provides an interim authorisation and supervision
regime of investment agreements concluded by EU Member States with third countries:
Regulation (EU) No 1219/2012 of the European Parliament and of the Council of 12
December 2012 establishing transitional arrangements for bilateral investment agree-
ments between member states and third states, [2012] OJ L 351/40.

investment agreements concluded by EU Member States among themselves are incompatible with the EU treaties.

However, the Commission's views were not universally shared within the EU. The Council and Member States, whilst not opposed at all to an ambitious EU investment policy, maintained that 'investment' as such, insofar it goes beyond trade-related FDI, is a shared competence under the TFEU, and hence, that all EU agreements that include investment and investment protection going beyond FDI, will need to be concluded as 'mixed' agreements on the EU side. On the equally divisive question of the legality of intra-EU investment agreements and intra-EU ISDS, the Council took no position, as this was judged to be a matter for the Commission and the Member States.

Both controversies rankled EU inter-institutional debates on the EU's investment policy for years. It took about a decade for those questions to be brought before the Court of Justice.

2.3   Opinion 2/15 (Singapore FTA)

The question of whether EU Member States can keep intra-EU bilateral investment treaties in place was – arguably at least partially – resolved in the *Achmea* judgment of 6 March 2018. As is well-known, the Court largely sided with the views of the Commission, confirming the legal precariousness, under EU law, of keeping intra-EU investment treaties in place.[34] The equally important question of the scope of the EU's competences as regards 'investment' and 'investment protection' under the Lisbon Treaty, was resolved by the Court in its Opinion 2/15, issued in May 2017.[35] This Opinion, dealing with the proposed Singapore Free Trade Agreement, was issued following a request pursuant to Article 218(11) TFEU that the Commission had filed with the Court on 10 July 2015. Like the CETA, the proposed Singapore FTA covers a whole series of trade-related matters in addition to investment and investment protection.

In its Opinion 2/15 the Court came to a rather fascinating Solomon's judgement, holding that the Commission, the Council and the Member States had all been right, but only on certain points. In summary, the Court held that all the provisions of the envisaged agreement fell under the exclusive competence of the EU in trade matters pursuant to Articles 3(1)(e) and 207(1) TFEU, except for the ISDS mechanism itself and except for the subject matter of indirect investment.[36] With regard to the latter, the Court sided with the Council and

---

[34]   *Achmea* (n 17).
[35]   Opinion 2/15 *Free Trade Agreement between the European Union and the Republic of Singapore* [2017] EU:C:2017:376.
[36]   The Court thus confirmed that whilst the threshold for finding that the EU does possess exclusive competences covering the whole of international agreements has

most of the Member States, who had argued that indirect ('portfolio') investment falls under shared competence. The Court later clarified that the EU
could nonetheless decide to exercise this competence if a political decision
was taken in the Council to do so. In essence, the Court's opinion means that
the subject matter of indirect (or portfolio investment) falls under potential EU
competence, i.e., it is a case of facultative 'mixity'.[37]

Crucially however, as regard the ISDS mechanism itself, in Opinion 2/15
the Court rather emphatically indicated that it would reserve judgment on
whether the mechanism as such is compatible with the EU legal order.[38] It
only pronounced on whether this mechanism falls under the EU's exclusive
competence, as the Commission maintained, or under shared competence, as
the Council and most Member States argued. The Court agreed with the latter
view, but on grounds that no one had argued. The Court notes that a dispute
settlement mechanism such as the proposed ISDS deprives ordinary courts and
tribunals of Member States from their ordinary jurisdiction, no doubt implying
that inevitably, the Court itself is also deprived of its jurisdiction, and hence
requires the unanimous consent of all Member States. Hence, from the point of
EU internal law, ISDS is 'shared' competence, but of a singular kind: its inclusion in an EU-level agreement leads unavoidably to 'mixity' on the EU side,
requiring the consent of all EU Member States in addition to that of the EU
and the third state(s). The policy choice to be made, following Opinion 2/15, is
whether to include investment protection and investment dispute resolution in
one overarching EU-level trade and investment agreement, such as the CETA,
which will then require ratification by the EU and all its Member States in
addition to ratification by Canada; or whether to separate the 'trade' part from
the investment part, and conclude two separate standalone agreements, one
'EU-only' covering the trade part and the other, a mixed agreement dealing
with investment and investment protection.[39]

---

since the Lisbon Treaty become significantly lower, mixity remains a legally valid
hypothesis, including in the area of the EU's trade policy and investment policy; See
my forthcoming article: 'Mixity versus unity: a view from the other side of the Rue
de la Loi', in 'Studies in EU External Relations' Marc Maresceau (ed.), in course of
publication.

[37] See Opinion 2/15 (n 35), paras 241–244, as clarified by the Court in Case
C-600/14 *OTIF (Germany v Council)* EU:C:2017:935, para 68 and Joined Cases
C-626/15 and C-659/16 *AMP Antarctique (Commission v Council)* EU:C:2018:925,
paras 126–127.

[38] Opinion 2/15, ibid., paras 30, 290 and 300.

[39] See Council conclusions of May 2018 on the 'new architecture' of trade and
investment agreements http://data.consilium.europa.eu/doc/document/ST-8622-2018
-INIT/en/pdf, accessed 28 June 2021. A first example of this is the Singapore FTA
which has been separated from the investment protection agreement: see https://www

2.4 ISDS Reform, Opinions 1/09 (European Patent Court) and 2/13 (Accession to the ECHR)

The divergent opinions as regards the competences involved in trade and investment under the Lisbon Treaty notwithstanding, the Commission nonetheless convinced the Council to include ISDS in the negotiation mandate for ongoing or new Trade and Investment Agreements with a whole series of third countries, including Canada (CETA), the US (TTIP), Singapore, Vietnam, Thailand, Japan and others. In addition, in 2014 the Council and the EP adopted the Financial Responsibility Regulation (FRR).[40] The FRR establishes rules concerning the apportionment of financial responsibility between the EU and its Member States identifies in which cases the EU and/or the Member States can act as respondents in ISDS, settle disputes and be liable to pay damages to investors.

By that time however, the EU's forays into ISDS faced heavy headwinds. As is well-known, in 2013 the EU's TTIP negotiations came under heavy criticism from EU civil society, including because of the proposed inclusion of traditional ISDS. In an effort to allay the critics and to seek support for its incipient ideas on ISDS reform, the Commission launched an online public consultation on investment protection and ISDS in TTIP. The consultation used the ISDS provisions included initially in the CETA negotiations (which were similar to those included in the Singapore FTA[41] that were put before the Court in Opinion 1/15) as an example. The public consultation ran from 27 March 2014 to 13 July 2014 and brought 150,000 online contributions. In its report on the public consultation, published on 13 January 2015, the Commission identified four areas of work that it proposed to explore further: the protection of the right to regulate; the establishment and functioning of arbitral tribunals; the relationship between domestic judicial systems and ISDS; and the review

---

.consilium.europa.eu/en/press/press-releases/2018/10/15/eu-singapore-council-adopts -decisions-to-sign-trade-and-investment-agreements/, accessed 28 June 2021. The free trade part of the agreement covers only subject matters of exclusive EU competence and requires only the Council's approval and the European Parliament's consent. But the investment protection agreement, because it covers indirect investment and includes an ISDS mechanism, requires signature and ratification not only in by the EU but also by its 28 Member States.

[40] Regulation (EU) No 912/2014 of the European Parliament and of the Council of 23 July 2014 establishing a framework for managing financial responsibility linked to investor-to-state dispute settlement tribunals established by international agreements to which the European Union is party [2014] OJ L 257/121.

[41] In other words, the investment protection chapter initially proposed for the Singapore FTA that were put before the Court included an ISDS mechanism of the traditional, arbitral, judicial-system bypassing kind.

of ISDS decisions for legal correctness through an appellate mechanism. The Commission then set out its first ideas for a reform of ISDS in a 'Concept Paper' publicly released on 4 May 2015.[42] The key elements of this concept paper formed the basis of the investor-to-state dispute resolution included in part F of Chapter 8 of the CETA that would, eventually, about four years later, be blessed by the Court of Justice Opinion 1/17.

Interestingly though, the Commission's concept paper of May 2015 was silent about the implications of Opinion 2/13, which had been rendered by the Court (Full Court) in December 2014,[43] months after the closure of the ISDS/ TTIP public consultation, but well before the issuing of the concept paper. In that Opinion the Court struck down the draft accession agreement of the EU to the EHCR, judging that there were insufficient guarantees to preserve the autonomy of the EU legal order when EU acts are submitted to external judicial review by the Strasbourg-based European Court of Human Rights. The Commission's concept paper was also silent about how to avoid the complications of the Court's earlier Opinion 1/09 on the European Patent Court. In that Opinion, issued on 8 March 2011, the Court had rejected the idea of the EU signing up to an international agreement for the establishment of a specialised court which would have exclusive jurisdiction to decide on the interpretation and validity of EU patent law, even if it was envisaged that this specialised court could refer a preliminary reference to the Court of Justice.[44] In Opinion 1/09 the Court held that this set-up was incompatible with the EU legal system insofar as it would deprive the national courts of the Member States of their tasks as 'ordinary' courts in the EU legal system.[45]

Whilst the Commission was formally silent on what lessons, if any, should be drawn from these recent Court opinions when designing an EU-level modernised ISDS mechanism, plenty of suggestions were made in the literature. According to some, the pitfalls that the Court had found in its Opinions 1/09 and 2/13 could only be avoided by bringing EU-agreed ISDS mechanisms in from the cold and somehow within the fold of the EU legal system. Among the suggestions made were: including the requirement of exhaustion of domestic remedies (including before EU courts); ensuring that ISDS tribunals can refer

---

[42]   See Commission, 'Concept Paper: Investment in TTIP and beyond – the path for reform: Enhancing the right to regulate and moving from current ad hoc arbitration towards an Investment Court' (5 May 2015) https://trade.ec.europa.eu/doclib/docs/ 2015/may/tradoc_153408.PDF, accessed 28 June 2021.

[43]   Opinion 2/13 *Accession of the European Union to the European Convention for the Protection of Human Rights and Fundamental Freedoms* [2014] EU:C:2014:2454.

[44]   See Art 4 of the draft agreement referred to in Opinion 1/09 *Creation of a Unified Patent Litigation System* [2011] EU:C:2011:123, para 12.

[45]   Opinion 1/09, ibid., para 80.

questions to the Court of Justice under a preliminary ruling procedure; establishing a procedure of 'prior' involvement of the Court of Justice; and ensuring
that ISDS tribunals do not render awards that would affect the validity of EU
law.[46]

Yet, in designing the new-style ISDS provisions the Commission took a radically different path. Apart from engaging in a major rebranding exercise in
a bid to avoid the 'toxic' ISDS label, the Commission placed its faith firmly in
investment arbitration and public international case. It proposed that a Chinese
wall be erected between the provisions of the international agreement on
the one hand, and the remainder of EU law on the other.[47] Accordingly, the
investment tribunals would only be able to apply and interpret the provisions
of the agreement itself as well as public international law; would be explicitly
prohibited from interpreting EU law; would not have jurisdiction to review the
validity of EU law; would need to treat EU law as 'domestic law' and 'consider' EU law as a matter of fact only. Furthermore, the EU, as a contracting
party, would be able to provide the tribunals with prevailing interpretations on
its law, which would bind the tribunals. And, equally importantly, the explicit
provision now included in all EU trade and investment agreements on lack
of direct effect would mean that the provisions of the agreement itself cannot
be invoked before the domestic courts of the parties. In addition, unlike the
draft accession agreement for the ECHR, there would be no power for the
investment tribunals to deal with the division of competence between the EU
and its Member States, as this would be internally settled between the EU and
its Member States in accordance with the FRR regulation. And, unlike for the
ECHR, there would be no complex co-respondent mechanism either: it would
be either the EU or a Member State that would defend the claim before the
ISDS tribunals. Furthermore, unlike for the ECHR, there would be no 'prior
involvement procedure' allowing the Court of Justice to give its views EU
law. Finally, the Commission proposed that the prohibition of the investment
tribunals to interfere with a party's right to regulate be beefed up.

In essence, what the Commission proposed to do was to create as much
distance as legally and politically possible between the proposed revamped
ISDS on the one hand, and the draft agreements that the Court had struck
down in Opinions 1/09 and 2/13, on the other hand. The Commission secured
the support of the Council, most of the Member States and of the European

---

[46] See e.g., Angelos Dimopoulos, 'The Involvement of the EU in the investor-state
dispute settlement: a question of responsibilities' *51 CMLR* 1671, 1699; Hindelang (n
19), 113–14; Caroline Henckels, 'Protecting Regulatory Autonomy through Greater
Precision in Investment Treaties: The TPP, CETA, and TTIP' (2016) 19 *Journal of
International Economic* Law 27.

[47] The same would apply vice versa to law of the third state.

Parliament for this endeavour. It was able to agree a text with Canada along those lines, set out in part F of Chapter 8 of the CETA text.

In the summer of 2016, the Commission presented the CETA text for signature, provisional application and conclusion to the Council. Even though the Court had not yet rendered its opinion on the competences involved in the Singapore FTA yet, the Commission (correctly) anticipated that the Member States would not accept that a similar trade and investment agreement, *in casu*, the CETA, should fall entirely under the EU's exclusive competence. The Commission therefore presented the CETA as a mixed agreement, acknowledging, ostensibly for political reasons and possibly as an afterthought, that it required on the EU side the consent of each of the 28 Member States, next to the EU's own decision. It was then that the world was made aware of the constitutional set-up in Belgium, where competence in trade matters has been devolved to its constituent regions. Following the strenuous opposition to the ISDS/ICS system expressed by some of Belgium's regional parliaments, certain regional and community governments, and in particular by Wallonia, it was clear that the idea to have a quick entry into force of the first EU-level ISDS mechanism with a third state into effect, would have to be put on ice. A Joint Interpretative Instrument, meant to offer additional assurances as regards the fairness and the legality of the CETA's ICS was negotiated with Canada. It was agreed in the Council that the CETA text would be signed and provisionally applied only insofar as the EU has competence over the agreement.[48] The investment protection part would possibly need to be re-examined at a later stage, following the statement by Belgium that it would request the opinion of the Court of Justice on its legality. In October 2016, an internal agreement was reached in Belgium as to the questions that would be raised with the Court on the investment protection part of the CETA.[49] In the meantime, the provisional

---

[48]   See Council Decision (EU) 2017/37 of 28 October 2016 (n 3); Council Decision (EU) 2017/38 of 28 October 2016 on the provisional application of the Comprehensive Economic and Trade Agreement (CETA) between Canada, of the one part, and the European Union and its Member States, of the other part, [2017] OJ L 11/1080.

[49]   See Statement 37 by the Kingdom of Belgium on the conditions attached to full powers, on the part of the Federal State and the federated entities, for the signing of CETA, point B:

>   Belgium will ask the European Court of Justice for an opinion on the compatibility of the ICS with the European treaties, in particular in the light of Opinion A-2/15. Unless their respective parliaments decide otherwise, the Walloon Region, the French Community, the German-speaking Community, the French-speaking Community Commission and the Brussels-Capital Region do not intend to ratify CETA on the basis of the system for resolving disputes between investors and Parties set out in Chapter 8 of CETA, as it stands on the day on which CETA is signed. The Flemish Region, the Flemish Community

application of CETA has taken effect as from 1 September 2017, but insofar as investment is concerned only insofar as these refer to FDI, but does not include the ICS mechanism itself.[50]

3. INTERNATIONAL AGREEMENTS PROVING FOR EXTERNAL DISPUTE SETTLEMENT AND THE AUTONOMY OF THE EU's LEGAL ORDER: A TURNING POINT

3.1 Two Sides of the Same Coin: Internal and External Autonomy of the EU Legal Order

The EU's treaties contain several provisions that set out how the EU should position itself in the world. For starters, there is the unmistakable principled intention of the EU to contribute to the international legal order, set out in Article 3(5) TEU:

> [I]n its relations with the wider world [...] shall contribute to peace, security, the sustainable development of the Earth, solidarity and mutual respect among peoples, free and fair trade, eradication of poverty and the protection of human rights, in particular the rights of the child, as well as to the strict observance and the development of international law, including respect for the principles of the United Nations Charter.

More concretely, the second paragraph of Article 21(1) TEU states that the EU shall be a strong builder of partnerships and promoter of multilateralism: 'The Union shall seek to develop relations and build partnerships with third countries, and international, regional or global organisations [...]' and that it 'shall promote multilateral solutions to common problems, in particular in the framework of the United Nations'.

At the same time, early on in its case law the Court of Justice held that it regarded the EU (and its predecessors)[51] as a new legal order, which is distinct from international law in general reaching far into the domestic sphere of its Member States. As to how this new legal order should operate, the Court

---

and the Brussels-Capital Region welcome in particular the joint statement by the European Commission and the Council of the European Union on the Investment Court System (n 3).

[50]   See Notice concerning the provisional application of the Comprehensive Economic and Trade Agreement (CETA) between Canada, of the one part, and the European Union and its Member States, of the other part, [2017] OJ L 238/9.

[51]   The notion 'EU' is used here also to refer to its legal predecessors, i.e., the European Communities and the European Community.

developed the twin doctrines of 'direct effect' and 'supremacy' of EU law.[52] The focus of this seminal case law was initially mainly inward looking, insofar as it concentrated on the relationship between the Union law on the one hand, and the domestic law (including constitutional law) of the Union's Member States on the other. An allusion to these two facets of the principle of the autonomy of the EU legal system (internal and external) can be found in Opinion 1/17, paragraph 109:

> That autonomy, which exists with respect both to the law of the Member States and to international law, stems from the essential characteristics of the European Union and its law. EU law is characterised by the fact that it stems from an independent source of law, namely the Treaties, by its primacy over the laws of the Member States, and by the direct effect of a whole series of provisions that are applicable to their nationals and to the Member States themselves. Those characteristics have given rise to a structured network of principles, rules and mutually interdependent legal relations binding the European Union and its Member States reciprocally as well as binding its Member States to each other (see, inter alia, judgment of 10 December 2018, *Wightman and O*thers, C-621/18, EU:C:2018:999, para 45 and the case-law cited).

Nonetheless, over time, the judge-made principle of the special nature and the 'autonomy' of the EU legal order also set the tone for the relationship between the Union and the 'outside world' in the Court's case law.[53] One of the main canons is what appears to be the 'protective shield' function of the principle of the autonomy of the EU's legal order in the external sphere: the EU and/or its Member States should never be forced into a position whereby the outside world and potential international obligations could negatively affect the autonomy of the EU's legal order and the constitutional principles set out in Union law. The Court's Opinions 1/09 (European Patent Court), 2/13 (Accession to ECHR) and also the most recent Opinion 1/17 (CETA) as well as the Court's judgment in Case C-284/16, *Achmea*, contain vivid reminders of the clear lines drawn in the sand. Some of these principles that follow from this main doctrine are by now well-known. They have been repeated almost religiously in the jurisprudence rendered since the entry into force of the Lisbon Treaty. But as will be explained below, Opinion 1/17 opens up a fresh perspective on these matters.

---

[52]   Cases 26/62 *Van Gend & Loos* EU:C:1963:1 and C-6/64 *Flaminio v Costa Enel* EU:C:1964:66.

[53]   On the question of the distinction and the historical relationship between internal and external autonomy see the excellent blog post by Francisco de Abreu Duarte, 'Autonomy and Opinion 1/17 – a matter of coherence?' (*European Law Blog*, 31 May 2019) http://europeanlawblog.eu/2019/05/31/autonomy-and-opinion-1-17-a-matter-of -coherence/, accessed 28 June 2021.

3.2   The Judge-Made Essential Principles of the Autonomy of the EU Legal Order

The main principles that Court consistently cites relate to mutual trust, the powers of the EU's institutions and of the features of the EU's judicial system.

As regards the first of these principles, the Court has consistently held that an international agreement cannot affect the fundamental principle of 'mutual trust' between the EU Member States which is based on the premise that the common values on which the Union is founded, are shared and respected among these Member States. This principle occupies a prominent place in the Opinions 2/13 and the recent *Achmea* judgment.[54] Or in the words of the Court in Opinion 1/17, in paragraph 128:

> The Member States are, in any area that is subject to EU law, required to have due regard to the principle of mutual trust. That principle obliges each of those States to consider, other than in exceptional circumstances, that all the other Member States comply with EU law, including fundamental rights, such as the right to an effective remedy before an independent tribunal laid down in Article 47 of the Charter (see, inter alia, to that effect, *Opinion 2/13* (Accession of the Union to the ECHR) of 18 December 2014, EU:C:2014:2454, para 191, and judgment of 26 April 2018, *Donnellan*, C-34/17, EU:C:2018:282, paras 40 and 45).

Whereas the principle of mutual trust played a central role in the Court's judgment in *Achmea*, it was nigh irrelevant in the CETA Opinion.[55] No one disputes that this principle can only apply between Member States of the EU, or by extension to those forming part of Schengen or the EEA,[56] but cannot, under any circumstance, apply to Canada's relations with the EU and its Member States.

As regards the second principle, the Court has also consistently held that an international agreement can affect the powers of EU institutions but only if the 'indispensable conditions for safeguarding the essential character of those powers' is satisfied. This is possibly one of the most crucial mantras consist-

---

[54]   Opinion 2/13 (n 43), paras 168 and 173; *Achmea* (n 17), para 34.

[55]   Opinion 1/17 (n 3), Opinion of AG Bot (n 14), paras 81, 98, 105, 107.

[56]   See for cases on the principle of 'mutual trust' in relations involving EU and Schengen States: Joined Cases C-411/10 and C-493/10 *NS and Others* EU:C:2011:875, para 78; C-680/17 *Vethanayagam* EU:C:2019:627, paras 78–88.

ently cited by the Court, e.g., rather prominently in Opinion 2/13.[57] All this has been recalled in Opinion 1/17 (CETA), at paragraphs 106–107 as follows:

> It must be recalled, at the outset, that an international agreement providing for the creation of a court responsible for the interpretation of its provisions and whose decisions are binding on the European Union, is, in principle, compatible with EU law. Indeed, the competence of the European Union in the field of international relations and its capacity to conclude international agreements necessarily entail the power to submit to the decisions of a court that is created or designated by such agreements as regards the interpretation and application of their provisions (*Opinion 2/13* (Accession of the Union to the ECHR) of 18 December 2014, EU:C:2014: 2454, para 182; see also *Opinion 1/91* (EEA Agreement — I) of 14 December 1991, EU:C:1991:490, paras 40 and 70, and *Opinion 1/09* (Agreement on the creation of a unified patent litigation system) of 8 March 2011, EU:C:2011:123, para 74).

> 107: An international agreement entered into by the Union may, moreover, affect the powers of the EU institutions provided, however, that the indispensable conditions for safeguarding the essential character of those powers are satisfied and, consequently, there is no adverse effect on the autonomy of the EU legal order (see, inter alia, Opinion 1/00 (Agreement on the establishment of a European Common Aviation Area) of 18 April 2002, EU:C:2002:231, paras 20 and 21, and *Opinion 2/13* (Accession of the Union to the ECHR) of 18 December 2014, EU:C:2014: 2454, para 183).

However, it is not always clear or predictable what the Court regards as 'indispensable conditions'. What is clear though is that the Court is – or perhaps was – before Opinion 1/17 firm on the following point: an international agreement cannot affect the judicial system set out in the treaties, which is intended to ensure consistency in the interpretation of EU law. This judicial system comprises the ordinary courts and tribunals of Member States which need to ensure the full application of Union law and effective judicial protection. It also implies that the Court of Justice is solely competent to decide on the validity of EU acts and to give a definitive interpretation of EU law, and which ensures a judicial dialogue with the courts and tribunals of Member States through the 'keystone' preliminary reference procedure.[58] In paragraph 111 of Opinion 1/17 the Court recalls the features of the EU's judicial system as guarantor of the specific characteristics and the autonomy of the legal order as follows:

> In order to ensure that those specific characteristics and the autonomy of the legal order thus created are preserved, the Treaties have established a judicial system intended to ensure consistency and uniformity in the interpretation of EU law. In accordance with Article 19 TEU, it is for the national courts and tribunals and the

---

[57] Opinion 2/13 (n 43), para 183.
[58] Opinion 1/09 (n 44), para 68; Opinion 2/13, ibid., paras 174–176 and 246; *Achmea* (n 17), paras 35–36.

Court to ensure the full application of that law in all the Member States and to ensure effective judicial protection, the Court having exclusive jurisdiction to give the definitive interpretation of that law. To that end, that system includes, in particular, the preliminary ruling procedure provided for in Article 267 TFEU (*Opinion 2/13* (Accession of the Union to the ECHR) of 18 December 2014, EU:C:2014:2454, paras 174–176 and 246).

This brings us to a third important related principle that is dear to the Court: an international agreement cannot have the effect of binding the EU and its institutions, in the exercise of their internal powers, to a particular interpretation of the rules of EU law. It is worth citing in full what the Court stated on this question in Opinion 2/13 at paragraph 184:

> In particular, any action by the bodies given decision-making powers by the ECHR, as provided for in the agreement envisaged, must not have the effect of binding the EU and its institutions, in the exercise of their internal powers, to a particular interpretation of the rules of EU law (see *Opinions 1/91*, EU:C:1991:490, paras 30–35, and *1/00*, EU:C:2002:231, para 13).

3.3   The Turning Point in the CETA Opinion

Opinion 1/17 appears to diverge from previous case law on these two afore-mentioned issues, namely, the EU judicial system and the power to interpret EU law. As observed below, the Court has now accepted that a dispute settlement body outside the EU judicial system can (exclusively) interpret provisions of EU law, provided that a number of conditions are fulfilled.

This is arguably a crucial turning point in the Court's case law and a consequential step that the Court has taken in Opinion 1/17. But it comes at a price: it required that the Court downplay the consequences of Article 216(2) TFEU and of its previous case law on the implications of international agreements concluded by the EU. This approach is in marked contrast with the Court's line in Opinion 2/13, where the Court held that one of the major difficulties posed by the proposed EU accession to the ECHR is that the latter would become, pursuant to Article 216(2) TFEU and the Court's case law, an integral part of EU law.[59] The Court left no room for doubt in Opinion 2/13 that this would render the EU and its institutions, including the Court itself, subject to external judicial control. This, the Court held, could only be accepted if the indispensable conditions for safeguarding the essential character of *its* powers are satisfied and, consequently, there is no adverse effect on the autonomy of the EU legal order.[60]

---

[59]   Opinion 2/13, ibid., paras 179–181.
[60]   Ibid., paras 182–183.

It is interesting to see how this jurisprudence has been rephrased and down-played by the Court of Justice in Opinion 1/17. The starting point is – or should be – uncontroversial: based on Article 216(2) TFEU and the Court's consistent case law the CETA will become an integral part of the EU order, once it is concluded by Canada and the EU (and as it is a mixed agreement, also by all EU Member States). In the hierarchy of sources of EU law, the CETA will rank below primary law but above EU secondary law, including above EU legislation.[61] Legally speaking therefore, the CETA agreement will be (part of) EU law. Rather curiously, in his Opinion AG Bot seems to have overlooked this point almost entirely. Indeed, throughout most of his opinion he treats the CETA as distinct from EU law.[62]

But in a marked contrast to AG Bot's approach, the Court of Justice tackles the obstacle of the CETA forming part of EU law, head on. The Court starts by repeating its previous case law confirming that the CETA will of course, upon its conclusion, form an integral part of the EU's legal order. However, for the purposes of its analysis as to whether the CETA adversely affects the autonomy of the EU legal order, the Court makes a crucial distinction between the provisions of the agreement on the one hand and the rest of EU law.[63]

---

[61]   C- 308/06 *Intertanko* EU:C:2008:312, para 42; C-61/94 *Commission v Germany* EU:C:1996:313, para 52; and C-311/04 *Algemene Scheeps Agentuur Dordrecht* EU:C: 2006:23, para 25.

[62]   There is however a telling point in the opinion that shows that AG Bot did realise the oversight, albeit rather belatedly. In para 122 AG Bot states that the CETA tribunal will be 'confined to applying that agreement and other rules and principles of international law applicable between the Parties, and consequently it does not have jurisdiction to apply rules of EU law'. In view of Art 216(2) TFEU and the Court's case law, this is of course legally incorrect: the CETA will become integral part of EU law. In footnote 107 to this paragraph AG Bot then corrects himself:

> I am referring here to the rules of EU law other than those contained in the CETA since, as I have previously stated, from the date of its entry into force, that agreement will be integrated automatically into the EU legal order, of which it will form part in the same way as other sources of EU legislation.

Further on his opinion, AG Bot continues to struggle with the question of whether the CETA Tribunals will, in one way or another, somehow must take EU law in consideration: see for example, his Opinion at paras 124–126. At one point AG Bot even acknowledges that the investment protection provisions of the CETA agreement themselves demonstrate that there is a substantial overlap with EU internal law on these provisions: see Opinion of AG Bot (n 14), para 157.

[63]   Although the Court does not explain what this 'other' EU law could entail, logically, it must encompass the primary law treaties (TEU, TFEU, Euratom), the Charter of Fundamental Rights of the EU, other international agreements binding the EU, as well as other secondary EU acts including EU legislation.

Opinion 1/17 sets the tone for this apparent turn in paragraphs 115–118, which are worth citing in full:

> However, the fact that the envisaged ISDS mechanism stands outside the EU judicial system does not mean that that mechanism adversely affects the autonomy of the EU legal order.
>
> 116: Indeed, with respect to international agreements entered into by the Union, the jurisdiction of the courts and tribunals specified in Article 19 TEU to interpret and apply those agreements does not take precedence over either the jurisdiction of the courts and tribunals of the non-Member States with which those agreements were concluded or that of the international courts or tribunals that are established by such agreements.
>
> 117: Accordingly, while those agreements are an integral part of EU law and may therefore be the subject of references for a preliminary ruling (see, inter alia, judgments of 30 April 1974, *Haegeman*, 181/73, EU:C:1974:41, paras 5 and 6; of 25 February 2010, *Brita*, C-386/08, EU:C:2010:91, para 39; and of 22 November 2017, *Aebtri*, C-224/16, EU:C:2017:880, para 50), they concern no less those non-Member States and may therefore also be interpreted by the courts and tribunals of those States. It is, moreover, precisely because of the reciprocal nature of international agreements and the need to maintain the powers of the Union in international relations that it is open to the Union, as is clear from the case-law cited in para 106 of the present Opinion, to enter into an agreement that confers on an international court or tribunal the jurisdiction to interpret that agreement without that court or tribunal being subject to the interpretations of that agreement given by the courts or tribunal of the Parties.
>
> 118: It follows from the foregoing that EU law does not preclude Section F of Chapter Eight of the CETA either from providing for the creation of a Tribunal, an Appellate Tribunal and, subsequently, a multilateral investment Tribunal or from conferring on those Tribunals the jurisdiction to interpret and apply the provisions of the agreement having regard to the rules and principles of international law applicable between the Parties. On the other hand, since those Tribunals stand outside the EU judicial system, they cannot have the power to interpret or apply provisions of EU law other than those of the CETA or to make awards that might have the effect of preventing the EU institutions from operating in accordance with the EU constitutional framework.

It is based on this crucial distinction between EU law set out in the international agreement and the rest of EU law, that the Court then frames its further enquiry into whether the provisions of CETA adversely affect the autonomy of the EU legal order. As per paragraph 119 of its Opinion, the Court proposes to examine whether the CETA Tribunals (1) have any power to interpret or apply EU law 'other than the provisions of that agreement'; and (2) may issue awards which have the effect of preventing the EU institutions from operating in accordance with the EU constitutional framework.

3.4   A Chinese Wall Between the CETA and Other EU Law

In response to the first question set out in section V.A.2 of the Opinion, the Court starts by noting that the ICS tribunals will have to apply the CETA agreement and other rules of international law applicable between the parties, but will have no competence to review the legality of a measure under the domestic law of the parties.[64] This, in the Court's view, sets the CETA provisions apart from the (draft) agreements that the Court struck down in Opinion 1/09 and *Achmea.* In these cases, the Court notes, the possibility that the external tribunals could rule on directly applicable (internal) EU law was legally problematic.[65] Moreover, the Court points out that *Achmea* concerned an agreement between two Member States, whereas the EU is a party to the CETA.[66] The Court stresses, furthermore, that the principle of mutual trust, which was very much at play in *Achmea*, and Opinion 2/13, does not apply in the EU's relations with a third state.[67] As indicated before, none of this strikes as particularly controversial. However, what follows then is the key part of the reasoning. The Court accepts that pursuant to the text of the CETA,[68] in cases where ICS tribunals would need to take cognisance of 'domestic' law of the

---

[64]   Opinion 1/17 (n 3), para 121.
[65]   Ibid., paras 123–126.
[66]   Ibid., para 127.
[67]   Ibid., paras 128–129.
[68]   See, in particular, Art 8.28 of Chapter 8, section F, entitled 'Applicable law and interpretation', which reads as follows:

1.   When rendering its decision, the Tribunal established under this Section shall apply this Agreement as interpreted in accordance with the Vienna Convention on the Law of Treaties, and other rules and principles of international law applicable between the Parties.
2.   The Tribunal shall not have jurisdiction to determine the legality of a measure, alleged to constitute a breach of this Agreement, under the domestic law of a Party. For greater certainty, in determining the consistency of a measure with this Agreement, the Tribunal may consider, as appropriate, the domestic law of a Party as a matter of fact. In doing so, the Tribunal shall follow the prevailing interpretation given to the domestic law by the courts or authorities of that Party and any meaning given to domestic law by the Tribunal shall not be binding upon the courts or the authorities of that Party.
3.   Where serious concerns arise as regards matters of interpretation that may affect investment, the Committee on Services and Investment may, pursuant to Article 8.44.3(a), recommend to the CETA Joint Committee the adoption of interpretations of this Agreement. An interpretation adopted by the CETA Joint Committee shall be binding on the Tribunal established under this Section. The CETA Joint Committee may decide that an interpretation shall have binding effect from a specific date.

Parties, they would need to confine themselves to considering this as a matter of fact:

> 130: The finding made in paragraph 122 of the present Opinion is not invalidated by Article 8.31.2 of the CETA, which provides, that 'in determining the consistency of a measure with this Agreement, the Tribunal may consider, as appropriate, the domestic law of a Party as a matter of fact' and further states that, 'in doing so, the Tribunal shall follow the prevailing interpretation given to the domestic law by the courts or authorities of that Party', adding that 'any meaning given to domestic law by the Tribunal shall not be binding upon the courts or the authorities of that Party'.

> 131: Those provisions serve no other purpose than to reflect the fact that the CETA Tribunal, when it is called upon to examine the compliance with the CETA of the measure that is challenged by an investor and that has been adopted by the invest-ment host State or by the Union, will inevitably have to undertake, on the basis of the information and arguments presented to it by that investor and by that State or by the Union, an examination of the effect of that measure. That examination may, on occasion, require that the domestic law of the respondent Party be taken into account. However, as is stated unequivocally in Article 8.31.2 of the CETA, that examination cannot be classified as equivalent to an interpretation, by the CETA Tribunal, of that domestic law, but consists, on the contrary, of that domestic law being taken into account as a matter of fact, while that Tribunal is, in that regard, obliged to follow the prevailing interpretation given to that domestic law by the courts or authorities of that Party, and those courts and those authorities are not, it may be added, bound by the meaning given to their domestic law by that Tribunal.

Moreover, the Court accepts that as a result of the aforementioned FRR, the decision as to whether a case is to be brought against the Union or against a Member State remains subject to the exclusive jurisdiction scrutiny of the Court, unlike the draft agreement that was the subject of Opinion 2/13:

> 132: The fact that there is no jurisdiction to interpret the rules of EU law other than the provisions of the CETA is also reflected in Article 8.21 of that agreement, which confers not on the CETA Tribunal, but on the Union, the power to determine, when a Canadian investor seeks to challenge measures adopted by a Member State and/or by the Union, whether the dispute is, in the light of the rules on the division of powers between the Union and its Member States, to be brought against that Member State or against the Union. The exclusive jurisdiction of the Court to give rulings on the division of powers between the Union and its Member States is thereby pre-served, and Section F of Chapter Eight of the CETA must be distinguished in that regard from the draft agreement that was the subject of Opinion 2/13 (Accession of the Union to the ECHR) of 18 December 2014, (EU:C:2014:2454, paras 224–231).

Furthermore, whilst the Court acknowledged that the ICS tribunals may need to give meaning to domestic EU law, it found additional reassurance in the 'backstop' included in the CETA text for this purpose: any such exercise by

ICS tribunals does not amount to 'interpreting' EU law and any such meaning given by ICS tribunals would not bind the EU.[69]

This approach may not strike as particularly novel to those familiar with international investment and public international law litigation, but it is of course a *première* in the Court's case law. The Court was apparently genuinely persuaded by the path that the Commission proposed following the public consultation on ISDS/TTIP held in 2014: the autonomy of the EU legal system can be preserved through the erection of a Chinese wall between the provisions of the international agreement and the remainder of EU law.

What is more, the Court's new-found ease with the barrier that has been erected in the CETA text leads it even to relinquish the erstwhile sacrosanct demand for EU courts, including of course the Court itself, to have a say in the external dispute resolution process. It accepts that there is no need for a preliminary ruling procedure, nor for a 'prior involvement procedure', which it should be recalled, the Court itself had insisted on in relation to the EU accession project to the ECHR. Furthermore, the Court sees no need to insist on a procedure allowing for the re-examination by domestic courts, subject to the exceptions provided for in the CETA text, of awards rendered by an ICS tribunal.[70]

On the basis of this analysis the Court to concludes, in response to the first question that it proposed to answer, that Section F of Chapter Eight of the CETA does not confer on the envisaged tribunals any jurisdiction to interpret or apply EU law other than that relating to the provisions of that agreement.[71]

3.5   The Right to Regulate as a New Building Block of the Autonomy of the EU Legal Order?

In response to the second question, which deals with the Parties' right to regulate and the problem of the 'regulatory chill', the Court acknowledges that there may be a concern insofar as the ICS tribunals can be asked to review measures of general application. The Court also acknowledges that whilst the ICS tribunals cannot annul a measure or impose a penalty, the losing party, and hence possibly also the EU, will be asked the pay the award or damages, which the Court notes is a distinguishing feature of investment arbitration.[72] However, also on this issue the Court accepts that the CETA texts are expressly intended

---

[69]   Opinion 1/17 (n 3), paras 130–133.
[70]   Ibid., paras 134 and 135.
[71]   Ibid., para 136.
[72]   Ibid., paras 143–147.

to allay such concerns.[73] Whilst judging that these are in principle legally sufficient, the Court nonetheless seizes this opportunity to add a new element to the edifice of the protective shield of the autonomy of the EU's legal order. Earlier on in the Opinion, in paragraph 110, the Court recalled its own case law on what it regards as the 'constitutional framework' of the EU.[74] The Court then adds a new substantive element to what it regards as part of the essence of the EU's 'constitutional framework': in an elaborate treatise set out in paragraphs 137–161, and in particular paragraphs 148–160, the Court cautions that an international agreement, such as the CETA, cannot have the power of calling into question the level of protection of the public interest, as established by the Union's institutions following a democratic process, relating, inter alia, to the protection of public order or public safety, the protection of public morals, the protection of health and life of humans and animals, the preservation of food safety, protection of plants and the environment, welfare at work, product safety, consumer protection or, equally, fundamental rights.[75]

This new building block of the EU's judge-made constitutional framework is remarkable, not only because it is entirely new: it appears to elevate, in one fell swoop, EU measures that may have been adopted via EU secondary legislation to the rank of a constituent element of the 'autonomy of the EU legal order'. The foregoing is also noteworthy in view of the principle, recalled above, that EU secondary legislation ranks below norms set out in international agreements concluded by the EU.

In reply to the second question the Court holds that '*it must be concluded that Section F of Chapter Eight of the CETA does not adversely affect the autonomy of the EU legal order*'. In short, the Court accepts that the assurances set out in the CETA texts are sufficient insofar as they would not allow the CETA ICS tribunals to call into question the level of protection of public interest determined by the Union following a democratic process. That said, the Court does not elaborate on possible consequences if an ICS tribunal interfering with the EU's power to regulate.

---

[73]   See Art 8.9.1 of the CETA text, referred to in *Opinion 1/17*, para 154; Point 1(d) and point 2 of the Joint Interpretative Instrument, referred to in Opinion 1/17, para 155.

[74]   See *Opinion 1/17* (n 3), para 111, which summarises the Court's own case law on the EU's constitutional framework as encompassing the founding values of the EU, the values of respect for human dignity, freedom, democracy, equality, the rule of law, and respect for human rights, the general principles of EU law, the provisions of the Charter, and the provisions of the TEU and TFEU, which include, inter alia, rules on the conferral and division of powers, rules governing how the EU institutions and its judicial system are to operate, and fundamental rules in specific areas, structured in such a way as to contribute to the implementation of the process of integration described in the second paragraph of Art 1 TEU.

[75]   Ibid., paras 148–160.

4.   SOME REFLECTIONS ON THE CETA AS PART OF THE EU LEGAL ORDER

4.1   The CETA's Lack of Direct Effect in the Domestic Legal Order

As already alluded to earlier in this chapter, there are a few interesting points of difference between AG Bot's Opinion and the (Full) Court's opinion. One of these has been noted before. Whereas AG Bot belatedly acknowledged, and then only in a footnote, that it is legally problematic not to regard the CETA agreement, once it is concluded, at least formally, as part and parcel of EU law, the Court itself tackles this issue from the very start of its Opinion. A second point of difference is that AG Bot accepted that there may be a 'substantive overlap' between EU (domestic) law as regards the investment protection standards,[76] but the Court itself stays mute on this issue, apparently in keeping with the strict line that there is a Chinese wall between EU (domestic) law on the one hand, and the provisions of the agreement itself, on the other.

More significantly, on the question of the autonomy of the EU legal order AG Bot attached great importance[77] to Article 30.6.1 in the CETA, which excludes its direct effect.[78] But the Court itself only fleetingly refers to this aspect once, and not in the part dealing with the autonomy of the EU legal order.[79] It does seem as if the Court, unlike AG Bot, did not regard the absence of direct effect of the CETA particularly important for the preservation of the autonomy of the EU legal order. But the Court's approach, on reflection, is rather puzzling, because the lack of direct effect of the CETA has undeniably considerable consequences. Whereas it is formally correct to state, as the Court did in paragraph 117 of its Opinion, that the CETA will upon its conclusion form '*an integral part of EU law and may therefore be the subject of references for a preliminary ruling*', the lack of direct effect means that there are

---

[76]   Opinion of AG Bot (n 14), para 157.

[77]   Ibid., paras 63, 93, 94, and section 3. A 4 of his opinion, entitled 'A mechanism consistent with the CETA's lack of direct effect': paras 91–94.

[78]   Art 30.6 of Chapter 30 of the CETA, entitled 'Private Rights', reads as follows:
   1.   Nothing in this Agreement shall be construed as conferring rights or imposing obligations on persons other than those created between the Parties under public international law, nor as permitting this Agreement to be directly invoked in the domestic legal systems of the Parties.
   2.   A Party shall not provide for a right of action under its domestic law against the other Party on the ground that a measure of the other Party is inconsistent with this Agreement.

[79]   See *Opinion 1/17* (n 3), para 181, which deals with the second question that Belgium posed, and not with the first one regarding the effect on the autonomy of the EU's legal order.

very few instances whereby a CETA-related question could be dealt with by EU national courts, and hence by the Court of Justice itself. The only limited cases that one could imagine are those where an applicant questions whether an EU act complies with the CETA. But this can at most lead to an effort of 'taking account of' the CETA whilst interpreting an EU act or 'consistent interpretation' of the EU act with the CETA provisions and can never lead to the review of the legality of the EU act in the light of the CETA.[80]

One further, albeit rather limited possibility for the Court to deal (rather indirectly) with the CETA is the scenario in which EU institutions prepare or take decisions relating to acts by the Joint Committees established under CETA and this leads to inter-institutional litigation for example, relating to Article 218(9) or (10) TFEU. One cannot exclude, at least in theory, litigation before the Court regarding a dispute on EU internal procedures relating to the CETA, but such disputes will be unlikely to hand an individual a right of action under Article 263 or 265 TFEU. Equally, one cannot exclude entirely that infringement proceedings could be brought against an EU Member State by the Commission under Article 258 TFEU or by another Member State under Article 259 TFEU relating to (lack of) compliance with the CETA, but on the whole this seems rather theoretical. What limited jurisdiction the Court has over the CETA has probably already been exercised: it is its power to pronounce, pursuant to Article 218(11) TFEU, on whether (conclusion of) the CETA is compatible with the treaties.

There are other differences between the opinion of AG Bot and the Court's Opinion. For example, AG Bot accepted that CETA ICS tribunals are 'quasi-judicial'[81] – whereas the CJEU is comfortable with describing these bodies, although of a 'hybrid'[82] character, nonetheless as 'primarily judicial in nature'.[83] This leads to some further considerations. The Court of Justice itself has blessed the CETA ICS system, but the CETA has no 'primacy' over the ECHR. According to the consistent case law of the European Court of Human Rights in Strasbourg, the CETA will need to be regarded as a treaty subsequent to the ECHR. An EU Member State that concludes the CETA will be considered to retain liability under the ECHR in respect of any CETA commitments subsequent to the entry into force of the ECHR.[84] Whilst it is difficult to antic-

---

[80] *Commission v Germany* (n 61), para 72; *Intertanko* (n 61), paras 42–66.
[81] Opinion of AG Bot (n 14), para 165.
[82] *Opinion 1/17* (n 3), para 193.
[83] Ibid., para 190.
[84] This is consistent case law of the Strasbourg Court. In the *Boshporus* case, the Strasbourg Court held that Member States of the Union remain responsible under the Convention for measures which they adopt pursuant to international legal obligations, including where such obligations stem from their membership of an international

ipate hypotheses whereby a person could successfully bring a case against an EU Member State involving the CETA, experience shows that this cannot be entirely excluded. The answers given by the Court of Justice in response to Belgium's second and third questions, which are matters that are close related to and rely in part on the Strasbourg Court's case law, could sooner or later be subject to review by the latter court in proceedings brought by either foreign or EU investors.[85]

4.2   Judicial Outsourcing of a Class of Disputes Involving EU Law

Secondly, following Opinion 1/17 it is now clear that a class of disputes involving EU law can be carved out from the EU legal system and outsourced to external judicial fora that will have exclusive competence to deal with such disputes.[86] Opinion 1/17 thus stands in marked contrast to the line that the Court appears to have taken in Opinion 1/09 against outsourcing of patent law disputes to a multilateral court, and of course also in Opinion 2/13 regarding the question of CFSP-related disputes. It is instructive to read again what that Court of Justice said on this matter in Opinion 2/13:

> 256. The Court has already had occasion to find that jurisdiction to carry out a judicial review of acts, actions or omissions on the part of the EU, including in the light of fundamental rights, cannot be conferred exclusively on an international court which is outside the institutional and judicial framework of the EU (see, to that effect, *Opinion 1/09*, EU:C:2011:123, paras 78, 80 and 89).

A possible explanation for this u-turn in Opinion 1/17 can be found in what the Court decided in Opinion 2/15. As recalled above, in that Opinion the Court

---

organisation to which they have transferred part of their sovereignty: *Bosphorus Hava Yolları Turizm ve Ticaret Anonim Şirketi v Ireland* ECHR 2005-VI, paras 152–154.

[85]   Is there, e.g., scope for an individual to argue before the Strasbourg Court that by concluding the CETA and by giving its consent to the ISDS mechanism set out in CETA, an EU Member State acted in breach of its obligations under the ECHR insofar as it deprives foreign investors from resorting to the ordinary courts and obliges this investor to bring the proceeding exclusively before an ICS tribunal? Is there a possibility for an EU investor to argue before the Strasbourg Court that the CETA unlawfully discriminates between EU and Canadian investors in terms of judicial remedies? In other words, will the Strasbourg Court follow AG Bot and the Court of Justice in their response to Belgium's second and third questions and decide that the EU Member State that concludes CETA has not acted in breach of its obligations under the ECHR?

[86]   Leaving aside the uncertain possibility for parties to seek a review of an award in the enforcement phase, depending on the choice of arbitration rules. This is a possibility which the AG Bot alluded to in para 181 of his Opinion, and the Court itself referred to in para 135 of its Opinion.

stated that ISDS mechanism set out in the Singapore FTA, because it aims at removing from the jurisdiction of ordinary EU courts a category of disputes for which they would normally be competent, an EU-level ISDS mechanism requires the consent of every single EU Member State.[87] The Court did not explain why it considered that consent by each Member State is required but the result is clear: pursuant to Opinion 2/15, an agreement at EU level on an ISDS mechanism resembles an intergovernmental decision by EU Member States much like the EU Treaties themselves, which require that each individual Member State marks its consent to bound.

The overall result is that the CETA will be upon its conclusion by the EU and its MS part of the EU legal order, but only in a limited sense.

4.3 The Division of Labour between EU Courts and Outside Fora in Regard to the CETA

There is also a further question as regards the division of labour between the EU courts and the outside judicial fora insofar as dealing with EU law is concerned. If one disregards the distinction made by the Court in Opinion 1/17 between EU law set out in the agreement and the rest of EU law, the picture that emerges is interesting.

First, as regards jurisdiction to deal with disputes involving the CETA as a whole: not only is there no monopoly for EU courts to deal with the CETA's provisions, the jurisdiction of the EU Member States' courts and therefore, of the Court of Justice itself is substantially curtailed. The balance has been tilted towards arbitration (state-to-state, WTO). The same consequences apply of course to Canadian courts as well.

Secondly, as regards the investment protection provisions of the CETA: this class of disputes has been carved out from the jurisdiction of EU courts and has been exclusively outsourced to an outside judicial forum, without an obvious path back to the domestic jurisdictions. The same consequences apply of course to Canadian courts as well.

Thirdly, as regards EU law other than the provisions of the CETA itself (EU 'domestic' law): here the balance struck is very interesting. The ICS tribunals can deal with, consider and hence, for all practical purposes, also give an interpretation this domestic EU law, but whatever meaning or interpretation these tribunals give to this part of EU law, they cannot issue binding interpretations of this domestic EU law, even though they can of course issue awards that are binding on the EU on the basis of the meaning they give to this EU domestic law. The EU, however, will be able to give 'prevailing' interpretations of its

---

[87] Opinion 2/15 (n 35), para 292.

domestic law that will need to be followed by the ICS tribunals and there are a few corrective mechanisms included in the CETA that should assist with this endeavour.[88] The same applies of course also to Canadian domestic law.

5.   CONCLUSIONS

These days one is made all too painfully aware that the promotion of partnerships and a rule-based international legal order are not merely rhetorical endeavours. It is no secret that the Court of Justice's Opinions 1/09 (European Patent Court) and 2/13 (Accession to the ECHR) together with the *Achmea* judgment came as a disappointment to those who would like the see the EU to play its full part in the world: that of a confident international legal entity, open to and therefore also subject to international law, capable of using its role and weight to influence the development of international law. The Court's recent Opinion 1/17 (CETA) has confirmed that there remains room for such a role. There are several elements in Opinion 1/17 which appear remarkable and which appear to signal not only a change tone but also a change in substance. To give its legal blessing to the CETA's ICS system the Court had to be convinced that it was safe to remove some of the barbed wire installed in earlier case law *apropos* the autonomy of the EU legal order.

A closer examination reveals that Opinion 1/17 is a multi-layered and cleverly constructed judicial edifice. The outer layer is represented by what appears to be full-throated support given by the Court of Justice to the EU's common commercial policy and its drive for a rules-based international legal order. The second layer may be less obvious, but remains nonetheless discernible once the outer layer is removed: it is the close attention paid by the Court to the serious concerns consistently expressed by civil society against the EU signing up to ISDS, regardless of whether this takes the form of 'classic' ISDS as initially proposed for the TTIP negotiations, or whether it has evolved into a more modern version as proposed by the EU side for CETA and for a multilateral investment tribunal or court (MIC).

But on this point there may be more to Opinion 1/17 than meets the eye.

First, the Opinion fires a shot across the bow of the ISDS/ICS ship: it contains a stern warning to the CETA tribunals to refrain from interfering with the EU's internal decision-making on matters in the public interest. This red line is new and points towards yet another building block of the entirely judge- made *tableau* of the autonomy of the EU legal system. Yet untested, the prohibition for outside tribunals to meddle with 'choices democratically made by the EU'

---

[88]   See Art 8.31, paras 2 and 3 of ch 8, section F and point 6 (e) of the Joint Interpretative Instrument.

regarding a host of subject matters covering both primary and secondary EU law may or may not prove to be a credible sting in the ISDS/ICS/MIC's tail. Time will tell.

Secondly, Opinion 1/17 contains a subtle and almost hidden reminder of one of the noteworthy points that the Court made earlier in Opinion 2/15 (Singapore FTA): as far as the EU side is concerned, ultimately, the decision as to whether to bring the ISDS/ICS part of the CETA to life rests, not with the Commission, nor with the Council or the European Parliament, but with the EU's Member States, whose unanimous consent is needed for this purpose. This reminder can be found in paragraph 221 of Opinion 1/17, where the Court of Justice refers to Statement No 36 agreed with Canada, according to which '[...] the entry into force of the provisions of Section F of Chapter Eight of the CETA will not occur before the ratification of the CETA by all the Member States [...]'.

Thirdly, there is the question of what lessons can be drawn from Opinion 1/17 for other EU agreements where the legality of existing, agreed or proposed external dispute settlement remains a live subject. Unquestionably, at least from a scholarly perspective, Opinion 1/17 marks yet another important milestone in the evolving jurisprudence of the Luxemburg-based Court regarding the protection of the autonomy of the EU legal system. The answers given by the CJEU in Opinion 1/17 to the doubts expressed civil society should, consequently and logically, also serve as guidance for all other agreements and dossiers where such questions arise.

But the million-euro questions are these: does Opinion 1/17 now mark a genuine and definitive turning point in the judge-made bulwark against real or perceived threats to the autonomy of the EU legal order in the external sphere? Will the Luxembourg Court now warm up to the EU becoming a party to the ECHR, provided the necessary amendments and tweaks can be made to the draft accession agreement? And are there any useful hints that can be distilled from Opinion 1/17 as regards how the Luxembourg Court might judge the legality of the ISDS mechanism set out in the ECT, which is the sole existing international agreement which contains a long-standing operational ISDS mechanism that is now the basis of several investor-to-state disputes brought against the EU?

Or is a more sober assessment called for? Is Opinion 1/17 to be regarded as a one-off special case, one where on balance, the Court was persuaded that the safeguards set out in the CETA texts (and perhaps also the two caveats referred to above) mean that the CETA tribunals do not represent a real or substantial threat to its authority? If it is the latter, Opinion 1/17 should not be read as a case where the Luxembourg Court, unlike AG Bot, threw its full weight behind an external dispute settlement mechanism set out in an EU-level international agreement. Rather, it should then be read as a one-off instance where the Luxembourg Court found enough grounds to distinguish the CETA from other agreements which the Court has in the past found to be wanting on the question of the defence of the autonomy of the EU legal order. Seen in this light Opinion 1/17 might epitomise the clever *politique judiciare* the Luxembourg Court is known for: given the safeguards set out in the CETA texts the Court felt comfortable enough not to stand in the way of the EU's trade policy and hence not to take the blame for putting a spanner in the wheels of multilateralism. Ultimately, the ball can be returned to others, more in particular to the court of the EU Member States. And in the case of Belgium, back to its constituent regions.

4. Investment tribunals vis-à-vis national courts: Lessons on judicial dialogue from the EU

Urszula Jaremba and Giancarlo Piscitelli

1. INTRODUCTION

The exact boundaries of the constitutional relationship between investment tribunals and domestic courts are far from defined.[1] Domestic courts are increasingly critical of various aspects of international economic agreements and investor-state tribunals, occasionally referring preliminary questions to the Court of Justice of the European Union (CJEU) on the compatibility of these agreements with EU law. This is exemplified in the recent reference to the CJEU by the German Federal Court of Justice (*Bundesgerichtshof*) on the compatibility with EU law of the 1991 Bilateral Investment Treaty (BIT) between the Netherlands and the Czech and Slovak Republic.[2] Domestic courts also directly interfere with specific arbitral proceedings, while these are pending before arbitral tribunals and/or at the enforcement stage of arbitral awards. This was the case of the (in)famous *Yukos* saga before the Dutch courts, or the set-aside proceedings of the *Achmea* award before the *Bundesgerichtshof*.[3]

Investor-state tribunals are also, for their part, in tension with domestic courts, being increasingly called on to answer questions of constitutional

---

[1] See, inter alia, Stephan W Schill (ed), *International Investment Law and Comparative Public Law* (OUP 2010); Laurence Boisson de Chazournes and Brian McGarry, 'What Role Can Constitutional Law Play in Investment Arbitration?' (2014) 15 *Journal of World Investment & Trade* 862.

[2] Case C-284/16 *Slovak Republic v Achmea BV* [2018] ECLI:EU:C:2018:158.

[3] *Yukos Universal Limited (Isle of Man) v The Russian Federation*, PCA Case No AA 227, Final Award (2014), see Section III. See also Bundesverfassungsgericht (BVerfGE) in the procedure for the annulment of a domestic arbitral award (2016) I ZB 2/15. In this case, the court quashes an intra-EU investment arbitration award based on its incompatibility with Arts 344 and 267 TFEU.

relevance for the states, which normally rest within the national jurisdiction.[4] Issues related to national public law that go 'beyond the consideration of "facts"', are increasingly raised before investment tribunals.[5] Investment tribunals may consider key questions ranging from the scope of states' (regulatory) powers, to the implementation of national non-discrimination policies,[6] or human and fundamental rights,[7] to name just a few. '[V]irtually every aspect of public regulation' might be subject to review by investment tribunals,[8] creating a constitutional tension that Schill encapsulates in the term 'the constitutional frontiers of international economic law'.[9] Frictions between these judicial bodies have become manifest, in particular, on matters of constitutional importance, or in the context of, for instance, intra-EU Investor-State Dispute Settlement (ISDS), where the CJEU figures as an additional actor in the judicial tension. It is against this background of a fast-changing relationship between investment tribunals and domestic courts that it becomes essential to rethink their relationship in a form of judicial dialogue and cooperation, rather than dissonance, conflict or plain indifference.

This chapter aims to answer the question of how the tradition of judicial cooperation and dialogue between the CJEU and Member States' national courts can be instructive for facilitating the relationship between international investment tribunals and national courts. The starting point of this exercise is a conceptual parallel between the relationships of, respectively, the CJEU and investment tribunals with national courts. The European experience of judicial dialogue between the CJEU and national courts of the Member States – and

---

[4]   In particular, the focus is on investor-to-state dispute settlement bodies established in the investment chapters of free trade agreements or bilateral investment treaties. Investment protection, reportedly, has become 'a truly global phenomenon'. See Stephan W Schill, 'International Investment Law and Comparative Public Law – an Introduction' in Schill (n 1), 5.

[5]   From Boisson de Chazournes and McGarry (n 1), 864. The authors provide various examples of such disputes. See also Laurence Boisson de Chazournes, 'Fundamental Rights and International Arbitration: Arbitral Awards and Constitutional Law' in A J Van den Berg, *Arbitration Advocacy in Changing Times. ICCA Congress Series No 15* (Wolters Kluwer 2011) 309–324. For a more general discussion see Gus van Harten, 'Investment Treaty Arbitration, Procedural Fairness, and the Rule of Law' in Schill (n 1) 627–630.

[6]   Schill (n 4), 15.

[7]   Boisson de Chazournes (n 5), 310.

[8]   Jan Kleinheisterkamp, 'Investment Treaty Law and the Fear for Sovereignty: Transnational Challenges and Solutions' (2015) 78(5) *Modern Law Review* 793, 794.

[9]   Stephan W Schill, 'Editorial: The Constitutional Frontiers of International Economic Law' (2017) 18 *The Journal of World Investment and Trade* 1. The term indicates the evolving constitutional powers (and limits thereto) of the international economic legal order in its relation to nation states and the EU legal order.

particularly the preliminary reference procedure under Article 267 TFEU – is taken as an example to articulate and facilitate the relationship between investment tribunals and domestic courts (and, indirectly, the CJEU).[10] This chapter follows a functional comparative legal methodology.[11] It is, in fact, based on the presumption of a parallel between these two types of relationships, of a 'functional' similarity, in other words, along the lines described by Schill.[12] In that sense, this chapter's ultimate aim is to formulate ways to smooth judicial cooperation and dialogue between international investment tribunals and national courts. In order to conceptualize the mechanism of judicial dialogue between different courts we borrow, inter alia, from the Paunio's concept of dialogue, which is based on the elements of conflict, power but also mutual understanding.[13]

This chapter is structured as follows. Section 2 will begin by considering the framework of judicial cooperation and dialogue under EU law. Section 3 will define why and how the relationship between investor-state tribunals and domestic courts is problematic, with the inclusion of examples. In Section 4, the relationship of judicial cooperation and dialogue between the CJEU and national courts will be critically applied to the relationship between investor-state tribunals and national courts. Some concluding thoughts will follow.

---

[10]   This chapter is inspired by, and builds on, a thesis developed by Schill in 2017, who suggested a comparative legal analysis between the CJEU and investment tribunals in their relationship to domestic courts: Schill (n 9). As questions with constitutional relevance no longer remain within the discrete domains of national courts, a comparative analysis can contribute to learning about the constitutional boundaries constraining both national courts and international tribunals. The need for such comparative legal scholarship, which is aimed at improving the (constitutional) interplay between domestic courts and investment tribunals, has been acknowledged elsewhere in the academic literature. Beside Schill's suggestions, see Boisson de Chazournes and McGarry (n 1), 881 et seq; see also Montt, *State Liability in Investment Treaty Arbitration - Global Constitutional and Administrative Law in the BIT Generation* (Hart 2009) 293 et seq, who views comparative law as a useful methodology to prevent arbitral law-making by dispute settlement bodies. See also Duncan Kennedy, 'New Approaches to Comparative Law: Comparativism and International Governance' (1997) 2 *Utah Law Review*.

[11]   The 'functional method' followed is, essentially, that described by Van Hoeke, 'Methodology of Comparative Legal Research' (2015) Law and Method, 9 https://www.bjutijdschriften.nl/tijdschrift/lawandmethod/2015/12/RENM-D-14-00001.pdf, accessed 15 February 2019.

[12]   Schill (n 9), 4.

[13]   Elina Paunio, 'Conflict, Power, and Understanding – Judicial Dialogue between the ECJ and National Court' (2010) 4(7) *No Foundations: Journal of Extreme Legal Positivism*, 5.

2. JUDICIAL COOPERATION, DIALOGUE AND MUTUAL UNDERSTANDING BETWEEN THE CJEU AND NATIONAL COURTS

This section looks at the nature and dynamics of the judicial dialogue between the CJEU and national courts, addressing the tensions, forms of cooperation, and (shared) values that it entails. While the basis for this dialogue rests with the preliminary reference procedure under Article 267 TFEU, it clearly goes beyond the scope of the mechanism.

The preliminary ruling procedure enables a very specific form of judicial cooperation, in setting out a right, and sometimes an obligation, for national courts to request the CJEU to issue a ruling relating to the interpretation or validity of a point of EU law, necessary to deliver a judgment in a case pending before them. When deciding on matters of EU law, national judges are therefore EU judges, whose role is aided by the CJEU's rulings on the interpretation or validity of EU law. The procedure relies on a division of tasks: interpretation of EU law by the CJEU; and application of that interpretation to the national dispute by the domestic courts. The preliminary ruling procedure has proven to be one of the most vital mechanisms for the EU's legal system,[14] providing a communication channel between the supranational and national judges[15] that guarantees the coherence of the EU legal order.[16] The importance of dialogue and cooperation by means of the preliminary reference is further supported by national courts. In the *Maastricht* decision, the German Federal Constitutional Court emphasized the need for a 'relationship of cooperation' in the context of fundamental rights.[17]

Importantly, judicial dialogue in the context of the preliminary ruling procedure constitutes a form of indirect dialogue. The CJEU and national courts do not engage in a direct discussion about their ideas, possible, most appropriate, or desired interpretation of EU law. Instead, the dialogue is an intrinsic element of the reference sent to the CJEU and the final ruling given by it.[18] Indeed, the dialogue between the national courts and the CJEU 'have been

---

[14] Urszula Jaremba, 'Polish Civil Judiciary vis-à-vis the Preliminary Ruling Procedure: In search of a mid-range theory' in Bruno de Witte, Juan A Mayoral, Urszula Jaremba, Marlene Wind, and Karolina Podstawa, *National Courts and EU Law New Issues, Theories and Methods* (Edward Elgar 2016).

[15] Ibid.

[16] European Parliament resolution of 9 July 2008 on the role of the national judge in the European judicial system (2007/2027 (INI)) OJ C294E/27, point 24.

[17] Bundesverfassungsgericht (BVerfGE), Maastricht Decision of 12 October 1993, Az 2 BvR 2134, 2159/92, BVerfGE 89, 155.

[18] Paunio (n 13), 11.

mostly implicit, informal and indirect'.[19] The process of (indirect) dialogue can be enhanced through procedural tools, such as the possibility for the CJEU to request clarifications on the reference to the referring court set out in the Rules of Procedure of the CJEU.[20] The possibility is used by the CJEU mostly to request more background information regarding the legal or factual situation, but it can promote inter-court cooperation and better connections between both sides. The indirect dialogue can be further promoted by means of citations of the CJEU's case law by national courts, academic writings of the CJEU's judges and Advocates General, and direct meetings of national judges with the Luxembourg judges, organized since 1968.[21]

It needs to be emphasized that the dialogical relationship between the CJEU and national courts is sometimes conflictual rather than cooperative, especially where the questions raised before national courts are deemed to be of 'constitutional' importance.[22] The judicial interaction between the CJEU and the German Verwaltungsgericht in *the Solange I* and *Solange II* cases, are one of the most famous examples of this conflictual relationship.[23] These conflicts do not come as a surprise, and they are 'conceptually unavoidable because courts at both levels proclaim the ultimate supremacy of their constitutional

---

[19]   Monica Claes and Maartje de Visser, 'Are You Networked Yet? On Dialogues in European Judicial Networks' (2012) 8(2) *Utrecht Law Review* 100, 104.
[20]   Rules of Procedure of the Court of Justice of the European Union [2012] OJ L 265, as amended on 18 June 2013 (OJ L 173/65) and on 19 July 2016 (OJ L 217/69), Article 101 on the request for clarifications. There are no other formal possibilities for the referring national court to supplement the reference with new facts or developments. The CJEU does not accept that a referring court autonomously submit observations outside the request for clarification, see C-351/14 *Estrella Rodríguez Sánchez v Consum Sociedad Cooperativa Valenciana* [2016] ECLI:EU:C:2016:447. Nor is CJEU obliged to accept requests from the parties to hear from the referring court. The CJEU has the discretion to decide whether the information provided is sufficient to enable the judgment.
[21]   See Court of Justice, Press Release No 183/ 18.
[22]   Schill (n 9).
[23]   In both cases a tension occurred between the understanding of fundamental rights as protected by the German constitutional order, and that of the EU legal order. There are many other examples which illustrate that the Court was not ready to accept national constitutional identities or local understandings of fundamental rights: see Case C-399/11 *Stefano Melloni v Ministerio Fiscal* [2013] ECLI:EU:C:2013:107; Dimitry Kochenov and Matthijs van Wolferen, 'Dialogical Rule of Law and the Breakdown of Dialogue in the EU' (2018) 1 EUI working papers 1, 12 for a more detailed discussion on *Solange* and a critical analysis of the dialogue between the CJEU and national constitutional courts. The authors go as far as to call it 'the breakdown of the dialogue'. According to the authors the CJEU does not allow for actual dialogue, as 'there is no longer a dialogue between equals, in effect the ECJ sees itself now as a hegemon in a single legal order', at 15.

order'.[24] This conflictual dynamic is enhanced by the fact that in practice, the courts are not on a level playing field, i.e., it is the CJEU that ultimately rules on the interpretation of EU law, Member States' courts are sometimes obliged to refer questions, and they are also obliged to comply with the Court's judgments and apply them to the case at hand, under threat of the infringement procedure that can be triggered by the European Commission (Art 258 TFEU) and/or national actions for damages.[25] Nevertheless, it would not be entirely correct to say that this relationship is a strictly hierarchical one: the CJEU is wary of interfering with the (constitutional) identity of Member States. What is more, the judicial activity of the CJEU in the context of the preliminary ruling procedure is at the mercy of national courts' references, as the competence to refer questions to the CJEU is exclusively vested in national judges, who formulate the questions that will go before the Court, and decide themselves to stall national proceedings. Therefore, the success of the mechanism relies, to a large degree, on the willingness of national courts to accept the CJEU's authority as the highest interpreter of EU law and to cooperate accordingly.[26] From the foregoing, it follows clearly that there are points of tension and points of harmony in the relationship between the CJEU and national courts. On the one hand, there is a tension between the interpretative monopoly of the CJEU and the autonomy of national courts to refer questions. On the other hand, both Courts demonstrate considerable deference towards each other: national courts acknowledge, generally, the interpretative monopoly of the CJEU, and the CJEU accords some margin of appreciation for domestic courts to implement their constitutional values.[27] Approaching the topic of the preliminary reference procedure in conceptual and philosophical terms, this chapter abstracts the dialectical relationship between the CJEU and Member States' courts as a relationship that does contain elements of conflict and power, but also, as argued by Paunio, elements of agreement and mutual understanding between the courts, and, presumably, a shared value-based system across the spectrum.[28] At the same time, agreement and mutual understanding regarding the meaning of (EU) law can only be achieved by means of dialogue, communication and cooperation between both sides.[29]

---

[24]   Schill (n 9).
[25]   Paunio (n 13), 12. See also, Case 283/81 *Srl CILFIT and Lanificio di Gavardo SpA v Ministry of Health* [1982] ECR 3415; Case C-224/01 *Gerhard Köbler v Republik Österreich* [2003] ECR I-10239; Case C-160/14 *João Filipe Ferreira da Silva e Brito and Others v Estado português* [2015] ECLI:EU:C:2015:565.
[26]   Jaremba (n 14).
[27]   Kochenov and van Wolferen (n 23).
[28]   Paunio (n 13), 6.
[29]   Ibid., 8.

The process of finding a balance between conflict, power, and mutual understanding requires that in the communication between courts, emphasis is placed on common values, such as fundamental rights and the rule of law, since those values underscore a platform for mutual trust between the courts.[30] In the process of dialogue, the CJEU's interpretation of EU law is supposed to take into account the legal varieties in terms of normative traditions and cultures underpinning 'the pluralistic EU community',[31] to respect national legal traditions above and beyond its preferred legal solution among 28 national legal regimes.[32] The CJEU's respect and understanding of different legal cultures enhances the legitimacy of the interpretation of EU law and promotes the acceptance of the outcomes of its decisions by national courts, fostering dialogue and mutual understanding.[33]

3.   ARBITRAL TRIBUNALS VIS-À-VIS DOMESTIC COURTS: ISSUES OF JURISDICTION, PARALLEL PROCEEDINGS AND ENFORCEMENT

In this section, the discussion shifts to some of the most salient instances in which domestic courts and investment tribunals disagreed. The challenges of national courts to the multilateral trading system can be described as a symptom of this more general phenomenon, i.e., the slow-down of mega-regionalism in international trade.[34] The challenge of the German Constitutional Court (BVerfG) to the constitutionality of CETA was the first case in EU law in which the constitutional frontiers of international economic law were unilat-

---

[30]   Ibid.

[31]   Ibid., 14.

[32]   Miguel Maduro, 'Interpreting European Law: Judicial Adjudication in a Context of Constitutional Pluralism', (2007) 1(2) *European Journal of Legal Studies* 137. See Cases C-112/00 *Schmidberger v Republik Österreich* [2003] ECLI:EU:C:2003:333; C-36/02 *Omega Spielhallen- und Automatenaufstellungs-GmbH v Oberbürgermeisterin der Bundesstadt Bonn* [2004] ECLI:EU:C:2004:614; C-244/06 *Dynamic Medien Vertriebs GmbH v Avides Media AG* [2008] ECLI:EU:C:2008:85, where the CJEU appraised national constitutional values and admitted that there might be different levels of protection of fundamental rights within Member States. For more, Oreste Pollicino, 'The New Relationship between National and the European Courts after the Enlargement of Europe: Towards a Unitary Theory of Jurisprudential Supranational Law' (2010) 29(1) *Yearbook of European Law* 65.

[33]   Paunio (n 13), 21.

[34]   S W B Schill and G Vidigal, 'Reforming Dispute Settlement in Trade: The Contribution of Mega-Regionals' (2018) *International Centre for Trade and Sustainable Development*.

erally tested by a national court (though ultimately unsuccessfully).[35] Another contemporary instance of challenge to the constitutionality of the CETA agreement that came before the CJEU is the recently delivered Opinion 1/17.[36] The Kingdom of Belgium in late 2017 requested an opinion on the compatibility of CETA's Investment Chapter with EU law, and in particular the principle of autonomy of the EU legal order. In its recently delivered Opinion 1/17,[37] no such conflict was found.[38] Conflicts are especially likely in the context of intra-EU ISDS, where the CJEU acts as an actor in the tension between domestic courts and investor-state tribunals. The CJEU, in fact, in its *Achmea* judgment (March 2018), was adamant that ISDS are forbidden in an intra-EU setting.[39] However, the *Achmea* judgment has been routinely disregarded by investor-state tribunals, thereby leaving domestic courts with the following dilemma: should arbitral awards be enforced (thereby recognizing the jurisdiction of investor-state tribunals) or should the jurisdiction of the tribunals be rejected, based on a strict reading of the CJEU case law? Furthermore, investor-state tribunals themselves have also come to wrestle with legal questions that have a more or less immediate constitutional relevance to nation states, as will be outlined below.

There are numerous ways in which domestic courts may interfere over the course of the arbitral proceedings, from the appointment of arbitrators to the enforcement of arbitral awards. National courts' increased desire to be involved in arbitral proceedings is particularly evident in their invasive review of jurisdiction and arbitral awards of investor-state tribunals. For the sake of clarity, this tension is articulated below in two different scenarios: *before* or *during* arbitral proceedings, the jurisdiction of the investor-state may be challenged by domestic courts (often in parallel proceedings); and *after* the issuance of the arbitration award, the collection and enforcement of the award may be hindered by subsequent domestic courts' judgments.

---

[35] Bundesverfassungsgericht (BVerfGE), Rejection of an interim order according to the grounds of the Comprehensive Economic and Trade Agreement (CETA) between Canada and the European Union, 2 BvR 1369/16, 2 BvR 1444/16, 2 BvR 1482/16, 2 BvE 3/16 Pronounced on 13 October 2016.

[36] Opinion C-1/17 *EU-Canada CET Agreement* [2019] ECLI:EU:C:2019:341.

[37] Ibid.

[38] Ibid.

[39] *Achmea* (n 2).

3.1   The Tension Between Investor-State Tribunals and Domestic Courts: the Jurisdiction of Intra-EU Arbitral Tribunals

The relationship between investor-state tribunals and domestic courts is especially contentious in the context of intra-EU ISDS, due to the role the CJEU played in the debate. In the *Achmea* judgment,[40] the CJEU was adamant that such forms of investor-state dispute settlement are forbidden in an EU setting.[41] The ICSID tribunal in *UP v Hungary* (October 2018)[42] is just one of the latest instances in which an arbitral tribunal took a radically opposite approach, establishing its jurisdiction and issuing a final award.

In the *Achmea* decision, which was the result of a preliminary reference procedure by the German Bundesgerichtshof, the CJEU ruled that intra-EU BIT arbitration is incompatible with Articles 267 and 344 TFEU, in order to ensure the autonomy and full effectiveness of EU law.[43] In the arbitration of *UP v Hungary*, the claimants, who were in the business of meal vouchers, brought an indirect expropriation action against Hungary, the respondent, who introduced a legislative measure which included favourable low-cost vouchers that hurt the claimants' business – a measure allegedly in breach of the 1986 BIT between France and Hungary. The tribunal eventually asserted its jurisdiction under Article 25 ICSID Convention, in just under three pages, with the argument that 'this Tribunal is placed in a public international law context and not in a national or regional context',[44] and therefore, unlike *Achmea*, it lacked an intra-EU dimension.[45] Ultimately the tribunal found that Hungary was in breach of its obligations and required it to pay damages to the claimants for unlawful expropriation.[46]

The significance of this breed of awards for domestic courts is clear: whether the ICSID tribunal falls within the scope of *Achmea* can be argued both ways. If this or other arbitral awards were to be appealed in national pro-

---

[40]   Ibid.

[41]   Ibid.

[42]   *UP and CD Holding Internationale v Hungary*, ICSID Case No ARB/13/35, Final award (2018). The preliminary decision on the jurisdiction was issued on 3 March 2016.

[43]   *Achmea* (n 2), paras 52–56.

[44]   *Up v Hungary* (n 42), para 253.

[45]   McCarthy Tétrault, 'Jurisdiction is, well, Jurisdiction: in UP v Hungary the ICSID Arbitral Tribunal Refuses to Follow Achmea' (*The International Arbitration Blog*, 22 November 2018) https://www.lexology.com/library/detail.aspx?g=d519ceaa -e729-4a55-b20a-cccdfac7ff97, accessed 18 March 2019.

[46]   Kit Chong Ng and Mubarak Waseem, 'Moving on Up? Intra-EU investor-State dispute settlement following the decision in UP v Hungary' (*Wolters Kluwer Regulating for Globalization*, 9 November 2018).

ceedings before an EU domestic court on the ground of a lack of jurisdiction of the ICSID tribunal, domestic courts would face the dilemma of whether or not to acknowledge the jurisdiction of the investor-state tribunal. Even in the event of a preliminary reference to the CJEU, where the CJEU would interpret *Achmea* as applying to ICSID tribunals, domestic courts would still have to choose between entering into open disagreement with the ICSID tribunal or the CJEU. If they rejected the jurisdiction of ICSID tribunals, this would create great legal uncertainty for investors who rely on the finality of arbitral awards; if the CJEU interpretation were to be rejected, *Achmea* would have created a hollow obligation, and the effectiveness of EU law would be called into question. Clearly, the CJEU and ISDS tribunals in the circa 200 intra-EU BITs speak different languages, and this may translate (or already is translating) into considerable constitutional tensions between domestic courts and investor-state tribunals.

3.2   Parallel Proceedings: *Vattenfall v Germany* and (Possible) Divergent Rulings

Domestic courts are pivotal in fostering a debate around the constitutional frontiers of international economic law. However, questions raising constitutional concerns are also increasingly becoming the subject matter of tribunals established under international economic agreements.[47] The *Vattenfall* saga[48] exemplifies the constitutional issues arising out of parallel domestic and international proceedings.[49] The dispute, more specifically, took the shape of a jurisdictional contest between the German BVerfGE and, again, the ICSID investor-state tribunal.[50]

The Swedish state-owned energy company Vattenfall is incorporated in Germany, as well as being a foreign investor. This enabled it to bring parallel proceedings against Germany by using both the domestic (application to the German Federal Constitutional Court for a constitutional review) and the international forum (investment tribunal). The saga concerned the German

---

[47]   Boisson de Chazournes (n 5).

[48]   For the international proceedings, see *Vattenfall AB v Germany (I)*, ICSID Case No ARB/09/6 Award (2011) and *Vattenfall AB v Germany (II)* (Pending award), ICSID Case No ARB/12/12, Decision on the Achmea issue (2018). For the proceedings at the national level, see BVerfGE, Judgment of the First Senate [2016] 1 BvR 2821/11 ECLI: DE:BVerfG:2016:rs20161206.1bvr282111.

[49]   Boisson de Chazournes (n 5).

[50]   Steffen Hindelang and Marcus Krajewski (eds), *Shifting Paradigms in International Investment Law: More Balanced, Less, Less Isolated, Increasingly Diversified* (OUP 2016).

decision to expeditiously phase out nuclear power by 2022, which prompted Vattenfall to initiate ICSID, as well as domestic proceedings against Germany. The claimant sought damages for the change in its licences to operate nuclear power plants, based on Germany's obligations under the Energy Charter Treaty (ECT).

The German government, in the domestic proceedings, put forward an argument based on the above-discussed CJEU decision in *Achmea*,[51] and contended that investor-state dispute settlement mechanisms with an intra-EU dimension (irrespective of their bilateral or multilateral character) are incompatible with EU law. In particular, the autonomy of the EU legal system was endangered, as 'the disputes falling within the jurisdiction of the arbitral tribunal [...] may relate to the interpretation both of that [BIT] agreement and of EU law' and, therefore, 'the possibility of submitting those disputes to a body which is not part of the judicial system of the EU [...] is such as to call into question [...] the preservation of the particular nature of the law established by the Treaties', essentially repeating the CJEU's reasoning in *Achmea*.[52]

The ICSID tribunal, opposing the German position and similarly to the *UP* tribunal, asserted its jurisdiction in intra-EU arbitration disputes, on the grounds that the CJEU *Achmea* judgment solely applies to intra-EU investment agreements, while the ECT involves third states and the EU itself, as well as the Member States.[53] Therefore, this investor-state tribunal, headquartered in Washington DC, USA, determined its jurisdiction based on its very own (liberal) reading of a European case, opposing the view of the highest German court, and without a possibility of internal appeals. The implications are clearly enormous for judicial dialogue between investor-state tribunals and domestic courts. The issue of jurisdiction is, it is understood, merely a preliminary question as the final award is pending at the time of writing this chapter.[54] While the investor-state tribunal was unapologetically dismissive of the German argument of a lack of jurisdiction, it remains to be seen whether the final arbitral award of the ICSID tribunal will comply with the decision of the German

---

[51]   Case C-284/16 (n 2), para 60.
[52]   Ibid., para 58. For a summary, see Krzysztof Wierzbowski and Aleksander Szostak, 'The European View: The Decision on the Jurisdictional Objection in Vattenfall AB and Others v Federal Republic of Germany' (*CPR Speaks*, 9th November 2018) https://blog.cpradr.org/2018/11/09/the-decision-on-the-jurisdictional-objection -in-vattenfall-ab-and-others-v-federal-republic-of-germany/#_ftn7, accessed 11 March 2019.
[53]   *Vattenfall AB v Germany* (n 48), para 162.
[54]   Ibid. The proceedings are currently pending. The latest sign of activity was the dismissal of the ICSID tribunal of Germany's request to disqualify the members of the tribunal (6 March 2019) https://www.italaw.com/sites/default/files/case-documents/ italaw10405.pdf, accessed 28 June 2021.

Federal Court, which, in December 2016, already ruled in parallel proceedings on certain aspects of the substance of Vattenfall's claim against Germany.

For the time being, further uncertainties remain: for domestic courts, for the CJEU, for investment tribunals, and down the line for investors. The constitutional tension in the parallel proceedings of Vattenfall is two-fold: on the one hand, domestic courts and investor-state tribunals disagree on the issue of jurisdiction; on the other hand, the problem is likely to extend to award recognition and award enforcement. If presented with a question of award enforcement, (German) domestic courts will have to decide whether to fall in line with the CJEU and reject the award on jurisdictional grounds, or recognize intra-EU investment arbitration in this instance and therefore accept the award enforcement. Without a forum of conversation, or a conceptual basis for dialogue between the arbitral tribunal and domestic courts (in this case the BVerfG) not much seems to prevent opposing rulings in the parallel proceedings of Vattenfall against Germany – after all, the tribunal already opposed the German's court reading of *Achmea* and asserted its jurisdiction based on its own interpretation of EU law (which, arguably, is the core of what the CJEU tried to prevent). Could this tribunal, in its final award, cause further disagreement and contradict the judgment of the highest German court? The structural absence of judicial dialogue or cooperation between the mentioned courts adds up to the uncertainty of the situation.

3.3   After the Award: The *Yukos* Arbitration Saga and the Issue of Award Enforcement

Judicial dialogue and cooperation between national courts and ISDS tribunals are also necessary after an arbitral award has been rendered. The *Yukos* arbitrations saga certainly produced the most sizable awards ever issued to date, with cases still pending before Dutch courts at the time of writing this chapter.[55] The claim arose under the ECT between the then Russian oil giant Yukos against the Russian Federation, with the claim that the Russian government manipulated legislation to force Yukos into bankruptcy.[56] In July 2014, a PCA investor-state arbitral tribunal sitting in The Hague held unanimously that the Russian government, by unlawfully expropriating Yukos, breached its obliga-

---

[55]   The 'Yukos award' is a collective term that refers to three separate claims filed by shareholders of the OAO Zukos Oil Company, each brought by a branch of Yukos incorporated in the laws of two European states, two in Cyprus, one on the Isle of Man. See *Yukos arbitration* (n 3).

[56]   Lena U Serhan, 'Arbitration Unbound: How the Yukos Oil Decision Yields Uncertainty for International-Investment Arbitration' (2016) 95 *Texas Law Review* 101, 102.

tions under the ECT, and ordered the payment of damages in excess of USD 50 billion to the majority shareholders of Yukos.[57]

The arbitration award, however, set in motion numerous post-arbitration problems before the national courts of the seat of the arbitration, The Hague, and the courts of the places where the claimants attempted to enforce the awards.[58] Indeed, the difficulties connected to enforcing arbitral awards are illustrated excellently by the host of cases before European domestic courts, which severely undermined the collection of this award by the Yukos majority shareholders.

In the Netherlands, the District Court of The Hague overturned the arbitral award, after the Russian Federation successfully appealed against the award to Dutch domestic courts.[59] The Dutch court sided with the Russian argument that under the Russian Constitution and other domestic laws the tribunal lacked the jurisdiction to hear the case. This decision took a diametrically opposite approach to the jurisdiction of the investor-state arbitral tribunal compared to the arbitral award.[60] Also, the Paris Court of Appeal, in June 2017, declared void Yukos' seizure of the assets of the Russian space agency Roscosmos, on the grounds that Roscosmos, as a separate legal entity, was not liable to pay debts owed by Russia.[61] The Brussels Court of First Instance, similarly, unfroze Russian assets at the expense of Yukos and removed attachments on Russian real estate and bank accounts in Brussels, because Yukos lacked a valid enforcement title for such measures.[62]

The Yukos saga is an illustration that the tensions between investor-state tribunals and domestic courts extend to post-award enforcement, where an arbitral award may be practically rendered meaningless by being overturned by domestic courts on the basis of a lack of jurisdiction of the tribunal, or on specific enforcement measures by the claimants. This too is an articulation of

---

[57] *Yukos* arbitration (n 3).

[58] Boisson de Chazournes and McGarry (n 1), 878 et seq. See also Patrick Dumberry, 'State of Confusion: The Doctrine of "Clean Hands" in Investment Arbitration After the Yukos Award' (2016) 17 *The Journal of World Investment & Trade* 229, 237.

[59] The competence of the court to review the award was based on the fact that the investor-state tribunal was based in The Hague and gave resort to appeals in domestic proceedings.

[60] Boisson de Chazournes and McGarry (n 1), 868.

[61] Paris Court of Appeal, *La Federation Russe contre Yukos*, 27 June 2017, 15/11666.

[62] Brussels Court of First Instance, *La Federation Russe contre Yukos*, 8 June 2018, 15/8991/A.

a constitutional tension between investor-state tribunals and domestic courts, and this too necessitates new forms of judicial dialogue and cooperation.

4.   THE CONSTITUTIONAL FRONTIERS OF INTERNATIONAL ECONOMIC LAW: LESSONS FROM THE EU?

The intrusive forms of judicial interaction described above illustrate that international economic law and national (constitutional) law are, in a sense, gravitating closer and closer to each other. This increasing proximity between two fields that have 'so far kept in maximum distance to each other'[63] causes the more immediate problem of having to define which system has primacy over the other in the event of such conflict. More fundamentally, however, it can also serve as an opportunity to shape the 'constitutional frontiers' of international economic law, in terms of its relationship to domestic legal orders.[64] At present, there are no formal fora for judicial dialogue and/or cooperation between national courts and international investment tribunals.[65] Therefore, as the matters under dispute are becoming highly relevant and decisive to the constitutional integrity and coherence of both international economic law and domestic courts, it is imperative to define what type of relationship these judicial bodies envision to ensure legal certainty and the upholding of the rule of law.[66]

As illustrated, the frictions between investor-state tribunals and domestic courts can take numerous forms: often, they are merely a risk (as is the case in pending parallel proceedings), at other times they are very concrete conflicts, as is the case in reversed arbitral awards. It is these latter cases that, arguably, 'deter the effectiveness of international arbitration'.[67] The tense and conflictual relationship between investor-state tribunals and domestic courts calls for reviewing their tools of dialogue. To this end, the dialogue between the CJEU and national courts under the preliminary reference procedure may inspire solutions to such difficult relationships occurring between international investment tribunals and domestic courts. Arguably, both domestic courts and investor-state tribunals share an interest in making sure their judgments are

---

[63]   Schill (n 9), 4.
[64]   Ibid.
[65]   Boisson de Chazournes and McGarry (n 1).
[66]   The rule of law is a highly debated, 'popular and vague' concept – for more on this concept, applied in an EU setting, see: Dimitry Kochenov, 'The EU Rule of Law: Cutting Paths through Confusion' (2009) 2(1) *Erasmus Law Review* 6, 7 et seq.
[67]   Serhan (n 56), 101.

accepted and executed (i.e., that the rule of law is respected).[68] The relationship between the CJEU and national courts is not only an excellent illustration of a conflictual relationship – it predominantly exemplifies the cooperation underlying a judicial system that is ultimately aimed at ensuring common values such as the rule of law, democracy and fundamental rights.

The preliminary reference procedure, as a form of judicial dialogue, heavily relies, it is submitted, on a mutual interest of courts to make the system 'work', with national courts exercising their right (or duty) to refer questions, and the CJEU pledging respect for the constitutional traditions of the Member States. To achieve necessary convergence, the CJEU and national courts must cooperate in interpreting the concept of constitutional identity.[69] This peculiar interaction shapes a shared value-based system in which both levels of the judiciary will tolerate restrictions to their judicial powers in pursuit of higher goals, such as the rule of law. Similarly, it is submitted that it is also in the best interest of national judges and judges in international tribunals to adjudicate in a manner that creates consistency, coherence, avoids conflict and protects the rule of law. This chapter now turns to the question of how judicial dialogue and cooperation can be facilitated in the context of international tribunals and their relationship to domestic (constitutional) courts. We discuss some formal and informal mechanisms that, inspired by the preliminary reference procedure and the principles underpinning it, may foster judicial dialogue and coopera-tion between national courts and investment tribunals.

4.1 Formal or Institutional Path of Judicial Cooperation and Dialogue

Although somewhat unlikely and on a purely theoretical level, formal modes of cooperation and dialogue could be set up between national courts and investment tribunals, inspired by the relationship between national courts and the CJEU. Such solutions would entail setting up structural channels and opportunities for judges to communicate and share information, by means of creating procedural rules that allow for the stay of proceedings and referral of questions.

Under the direct inspiration of the preliminary reference procedure, a first option to enhance dialogue between national courts and investment tribunals would be establishing a mechanism similar to the preliminary ruling procedure that, along the lines of the procedure under Article 267 TFEU, would allow

---

[68] Schill (n 9).
[69] Tímea Drinóczi and Ágoston Mohay, 'The Preliminary Ruling Procedure and Identity Review' (2017) 1 *EU and Comparative Law Issues and Challenges* 192.

international investment tribunals to refer questions to national constitutional courts.[70] This suggestion was first proposed by Schill, as a possibility
of allowing international investment tribunals to refer questions to national
constitutional courts, or even the CJEU, where a given issue is deemed as
too sensitive and political to be determined by the tribunal itself.[71] The call
for what we refer to as a *'reverse* preliminary reference procedure' could
indeed facilitate judicial dialogue and cooperation. On a superficial level,
dialogue would be enhanced because such a formal mechanism would allow
for a channel of communication between the concerned judicial bodies (which,
at present, is lacking). On a deeper level, such procedural possibilities could
also articulate a more specific balance of power between the judicial bodies,
setting out, for instance, the types of questions that each judicial body would
have jurisdiction to answer. If investor-state tribunals were left the competence
to determine their own jurisdiction, while domestic courts were left the final
say on constitutionally relevant questions for their jurisdiction, the possibility
of diverging rulings would be limited, if not eliminated. In fact, investor-state
tribunals would be legally bound by the preliminary rulings of national constitutional courts, as is the case for domestic courts with respect to the CJEU
under Article 267 TFEU.

However, this formal proposal also raises a host of obvious practical and
procedural difficulties in terms of, for instance, the types of questions that
could be referred, access to courts, limitation and waiting periods, *locus
standi*, and the form of the reference for a ruling, to the more general problem
of how this would be integrated in the already convoluted system of judicial
protection in the EU. More specifically, the first hurdle would be to determine
whether such a mechanism should be created on a multilateral basis vis-à-vis
all the domestic legislative systems, or rather tailor them individually for each
state. The additional problem is how these rules would be integrated within
the specific legal systems: problems of this nature stem from the diversity of
legal systems, which may very well differ in terms of waiting times to issue
a ruling, limitation periods to lodge claims and, naturally, languages and
judicial cultures. In fact, while the CJEU and domestic courts have had nearly
half a century of history of preliminary rulings, investor-state tribunals are
as numerous as the treaties that set them up – perhaps establishing separate
procedural mechanisms allowing for a preliminary reference with each of
them is one step too far for each legal system to allow. The final issue is how
this would be integrated in the system of EU law as such – would a domestic
court handling a reference from an investor-state tribunal itself be allowed to

---

[70] Schill (n 9).
[71] Ibid.

refer a preliminary ruling on the concerned matter to the CJEU? Should rules be formulated to prevent or facilitate that? If so, procedures most likely would be mind-numbingly and unacceptably convoluted and long. Therefore, the proposal for such a *reverse* preliminary reference procedure is not only legally unlikely, but perhaps even undesirable.

4.2 Informal Paths of Judicial Cooperation and Dialogue

Even very efficient procedural rules allowing for judicial dialogue are only as good as the willingness of courts to welcome and enforce, in good faith, the judgments of other judicial bodies. Informal modes of cooperation and dialogue refer to the conceptual basis of the relationship between investor-state tribunals and national courts.[72] These include whether a court feels bound to follow another judicial body's rulings, the extent to which other judicial authorities exercise any gravity on its judgments, and whether courts are open to engage in judicial dialogue outside an institutional or formal/procedural setting. The functional similarity between the two types of judicial dialogue is clear: just like the CJEU and domestic courts do depend on each other (as explained in section 2), investor-state tribunals depend on national courts to enforce their arbitral awards, and domestic courts increasingly depend on investor-state tribunals to adequately interpret and apply provisions of domestic (and EU) law.

In light of this mutual interdependence, investor-state tribunals and domestic courts should be guided by the overarching goal of delivering a system of justice whereby both types of judicial bodies produce judgments that are consistent with each other, serve legal certainty and, ultimately, the rule of law. An informally cooperative relationship guided by this goal would also minimize the risk of conflicting judgments. This can be observed, in the best scenarios, in the EU setting where opposing judgments are typically prevented, although the CJEU and some domestic constitutional courts do raise the tone over time. The experience at the level of domestic courts and investor-state tribunals is quite different: there is very little verbal confrontation and exchange of opinions, and yet there are conflicting judgments, as is the case in *Vattenfall* or *Yukos*. By guaranteeing a better 'balance and mutual supportiveness' between these levels of the judiciary, the obligations of states, and the rights of investors can be better preserved in a 'dispute-preventive', rules-based system, ultimately catering to the shared principle of the rule of law.[73] Indeed, as rightly contended by Kochenov and van Wolferen 'Any rule of law-based

---

[72] Boisson de Chazournes and McGarry (n 1), 887.
[73] Ibid., 886.

system [...] implies the control of the applicable law through *dialogical* legal considerations, elevating such dialogue – should it play an effective systemic law-limiting function – to a necessary element of the rule of law.'[74]

Applying Paunio's understanding of judicial dialogue to investor-state tribunals and national courts, power contests and judicial conflicts would certainly still be expected as part of the theory – and somehow they would even be considered part of a healthy judicial dialogue, as is the case for the CJEU and domestic courts in the preliminary reference procedure. However, the emphasis would still be placed on mutual understanding and a shared value-based system, where the chief interest of investor-state tribunals and domestic courts alike is to uphold of the efficacy and stability of the international and domestic legal systems, to create consistent judgments, and to deliver legal certainty for investors, thereby avoiding conflicting outcomes.

As the tribunal in the *Himpurna California Energy* case famously claimed, '[t]he members of the Arbitral Tribunal do not live in an ivory tower. Nor do they view the arbitral process as one which operates in a vacuum, divorced from reality'.[75] The examples of *Vattenfall* and *UP v Hungary*, however, are evidence that investor-state tribunals often show no hesitation in the face of sensitive questions, causing conflict with national judgments or misinterpreting EU jurisprudence (which forms integral part of EU domestic legal systems). The reality, right now, is therefore an often-contradictory landscape of investor-state judicial protection, and a tangible conflict between investor-state tribunals and domestic courts. Judicial dialogue, in the words of Paunio, 'could be said to constitute a bargaining process where the result is a negotiated compromise between different legal cultures and traditions'.[76] Reformulating the relationship between these judicial bodies along the lines described by Paunio would still allow for vigorous debates, while ensuring that, above all, consistency is delivered in the case law of domestic courts and investor-state tribunals.

Quite obviously, such a mutually supportive understanding between judicial bodies,[77] a spirit of conciliation and compromise,[78] and discursive legal plural-

---

[74]   Kochenov and van Wolferen (n 23).
[75]   *Himpurna California Energy Ltd v PT (Persero) Perusahaan Listruik Negara* [2000] Final award UNCITRAL Ad Hoc-Award of 4 May 1999.
[76]   Paunio (n 13), 22.
[77]   Boisson de Chazournes and McGarry (n 1), 888.
[78]   Xavier Groussot, 'Spirit, Are You There? Reinforced Judicial Dialogue and the Preliminary Ruling Procedure' (2008) Eric Stein Working Paper No 4/2008 https://ssrn .com/abstract=1279367, or http://dx.doi.org/10.2139/ssrn.1279367, both accessed 28 June 2021.

ism,[79] cannot rise from nothing. It could however be initiated and generated by creating some sort of a judicial forum or network that would facilitate bringing national judges and international arbitrators together and getting to know each other.[80] Such a network would also facilitate direct contacts between domestic judges and adjudicators, cooperating with each other which could ultimately result in creating and enhancing mutual trust. Such informal cooperation may be further strengthened by a common website, (soft law) guidelines that judges and arbitrators pledge to adhere to, setting out rules of conduct, and due diligence obligations in taking into account each other's case law to the effect of delivering consistent judgments. Naturally, exchanges through academic publications, joint conferences and informal events would strengthen this outcome, as the EU judicial tradition testifies. Academic exposure could certainly be a vehicle to make the members of the respective judicial bodies better acquainted with each other's legal cultures and traditions.

5.   CONCLUSIONS

The tensions between investor-state tribunals and domestic courts described above inevitably result in a crippling uncertainty – for domestic courts and investment tribunals, and down the line for investors and states. The aim of this contribution is to explore how the EU tradition of judicial cooperation and dialogue between national courts and the CJEU could serve as an inspiration for facilitating dialogue between investor-state tribunals and national courts. The functional comparative approach of this work provides a novel perspective to explore the problem of judicial dialogue and constructively put forward proposals on how judicial dialogue may be facilitated by investor-state tribunals and national courts. Section 2 provided a conceptual understanding of judicial dialogue under the preliminary reference procedure. Section 3 sketched some instances of conflict between investor-state tribunals and domestic courts (and, indirectly, the CJEU). Section 4 formulated formal and informal suggestions to facilitate judicial dialogue between investor-state tribunals and domestic courts, based on the EU experience. In particular, it was found that a formal solution based on setting up a (reverse) preliminary reference procedure based on the EU formula is somewhat remote or nearly inconceivable. Nevertheless, reframing the conceptual basis along the lines described by Paunio, with the stimulus of judicial fora or networks, face-to-face informal meetings, and

---

[79]   Ibid.
[80]   See Claes and de Visser (n 19) for more on judicial networks, their purpose, organization and working methods.

academic exchanges, constitutes a better way forward to improve dialogue and cooperation between investor-state tribunals and domestic courts.

5. The relationship between the Court of Justice of the European Union and international courts after Opinion 1/17

Ewa Żelazna

1. INTRODUCTION

In *Opinion 1/17*,[1] the Court of Justice demonstrated a small degree of openness toward other systems of international law by accepting that investor-state tribunals can be compatible with EU law.[2] The *Opinion* came at the time, when the EU has been pursuing an ambitious international trade and investment agendas, which aim to broaden and deepen relationships with other countries in the world, as well as contribute toward the EU's economic growth.[3] The ruling of the Court of Justice has enabled the Commission to continue the implementation of the international trade and investment strategies on a bilateral basis and to engage in the multilateral negotiations on reforms of the investment protection regime.[4]

While the Commission was able to find a way to effectively manage jurisdictional overlap between the Court of Justice and investor- state tribunals in the Comprehensive Economic and Trade Agreement (CETA), it did not contemplate establishing a cooperation between the two dispute resolution bodies.

---

[1]   Opinion 1/17 *CETA* [2019] OJ C 220/2 (Opinion 1/17).
[2]   Cf: Opinion 2/13 *Accession of the European Union to the European Convention for the Protection of Human Rights and Fundamental Freedoms* [2014] OJ C 65/2 (Opinion 2/13).
[3]   Commission (EU), Trade for All: Towards a More Responsible Trade and Investment Policy, (Publication Office of the European Union, 2014); Commission (EU), Communication from the Commission to the European Parliament, the Council, the European Economic and Social Committee and the Committee of the Regions: Trade Policy Review – An Open, Sustainable and Assertive Trade Policy, COM(2021) 66 final.
[4]   Commission (EU), Concept Paper: Investment in TTIP and Beyond – the Path for Reform, https://trade.ec.europa.eu/doclib/docs/2015/may/tradoc_153408.PDF, accessed 21 August 2019 (TTIP Concept Paper).

In the light of this, it is argued in this chapter that *Opinion 1/17* reaffirms the Court's traditional approach toward international law that emphasises separate and self-contained nature of EU law.[5]

From a theoretical perspective, the discussion in this chapter adheres to the cosmopolitan global pluralism as advocated by Berman.[6] Although it is recognised that there are many versions of legal pluralism,[7] the objective of the analysis in this chapter is not to provide a summary of the literature on the subject. Instead, the theoretical insights are used in the analysis, to uncover possibilities for future development of the relationship between the EU legal order and the international investment protection regime. It is argued that the implementation of procedural tools enabling a structured dialogue between the Court of Justice and investor-state tribunals would contribute to the development of a coherent legal framework in the field of international economic law.

To that end, the first part of the chapter highlights that while in its decision on the compatibility of investor-state tribunals with EU law the Court of Justice displayed greater openness towards other systems of international law, its reasoning continued to accentuate separateness of the EU legal order. The second part, accounts for some possible negative consequences arising out of coexistence of the two systems without a mechanism that allows to refer questions about interpretation of EU law to the Court of Justice. The final part highlights that EU law does not preclude the possibility of establishing a closer cooperation between the two regimes, which would be desirable for future development of international economic law.

---

[5]   Joined cases C-402/05 P and C-415/05 P *Kadi and Al Barakaat International Foundation v Council and Commission* [2008] ECR I-06361 Opinion of Advocate General Poiares Maduro, para 24; Gráinne de Búrca, 'The European Court of Justice and the International Legal Order after *Kadi*' (2010) 51 Harv Int'l L J 1; Joris Larik, 'Two Ships in the Night or in the Same Boat Together: How the ECJ Squared the Circle and Foreshadowed Lisbon in its *Kadi* Judgment' (2019) 13 Y B Polish Eur Stud 149; Piet Eeckhout, 'Human Rights and the Autonomy of EU Law: Pluralism or Integration?' (2013) 66 CLP 169; Daniel Halberstam, '"It's the Autonomy, Stupid" A Modest Defence of *Opinion 2/13* on EU Accession to the ECHR, and the Way Forward' (2015) 16 German L J 105.

[6]   Paul Schiff Berman, *Global Legal Pluralism: A Jurisprudence of Law beyond Borders* (CUP 2012).

[7]   For a discussion on different versions of legal pluralism and how they compare to the constitutionalist approaches, see: Nico Krisch, 'The Case for Pluralism in Postnational Law' in Gráinne de Búrca and Joseph Weiler (eds), *The World of European Constitutionalism* (CUP 2011).

2.   COEXISTENCE BETWEEN THE COURT OF JUSTICE AND INVESTOR-STATE TRIBUNALS

Investor-state arbitration was an established part of the system of international investment protection before the EU became an actor in the field.[8] Therefore, in developing its comprehensive investment policy since the entry into force of the Treaty of Lisbon,[9] the Union decided to build on the legacy of its Member States and followed their approach to dispute resolution.[10] However, the negotiations of the EU's first investment protection treaties coincided with a public backlash against the system, which intensified after the EU opened talks with the US.[11] This led the Commission to introduce a number of changes to common substantive standards and procedural rules.[12] The amendments to the dispute resolution mechanism were intended to address issues concerning legitimacy and correctness of awards.[13] As observed by Advocate General Bot, this has put the Union at the forefront of the reform in the field of international investment law[14] and it was up to the Court to decide, in *Opinion 1/17*, whether the Union's action can continue.[15]

The stakes were high, as the CETA has been a blueprint of the EU's new approach to investment protection. Its provisions on dispute resolution were regarded as building blocks for the multilateral investment court[16] and have

---

[8]   Rudolf Dolzer and Christoph Schreuer, *Principles of International Investment Law* (OUP 2012).

[9]   The EU gained competence in foreign direct investment with the entry into force of the Treaty of Lisbon, which enabled it to develop a comprehensive policy on international investment: Article 207 of the Consolidated Version of the Treaty on the Functioning of the European Union [2016] OJ C202/47 (TFEU).

[10]   Commission, 'Towards a comprehensive European international investment policy' (Communication) COM (2010) 343 final, 9–10.

[11]   Alexia Chan and Beverly Crawford, 'The Puzzle of Public Opposition to TTIP in Germany' (2017) 19 *Business and Politics* 683.

[12]   TTIP Concept Paper (n 4); Comprehensive Economic and Trade Agreement (CETA) between Canada, of the one part, and the European Union and its Member States, of the other part [2017] OJ L11/23 (CETA), Chapter Eight.

[13]   Ibid.

[14]   Opinion 1/17 *EU-Canada CET Agreement* [2019] OJ C 220/2, Opinion of AG Bot, para 18.

[15]   Ibid., paras 18, 37.

[16]   Council (EU), Negotiating Directives for a Convention Establishing a Multilateral Court for the Settlement of Investment Disputes (2018) 12981/17 ADD 1; UNCITRAL, 'Possible Reform of Investor-State Dispute Settlement (ISDS): Submission from the European Union and Its Member States' (24 January 2019) A/CN.9/WG.III/WP.159/Add. 1; UNCITRAL, 'Possible Reform of Investor-State Dispute Settlement (ISDS): Note by Secretariat' (30 July 2019) A/CN.9/WG.III/WP.166; Art 8.29 CETA.

been implemented in a number of other new generation free trade agreements negotiated by the Union since the entry into force of the Treaty of Lisbon.[17] Furthermore, it was emphasised by Advocate General Bot, in his Opinion on the matter, that investor-state arbitration was a neutral and efficient system of dispute resolution that would benefit EU investors abroad, and its inclusion was a result of the democratic process in the EU and its Member States.[18] *Opinion 1/17* has, therefore, put the Court in the limelight, as finding that investor-state tribunals had not been compatible with EU law would have hindered not only the implementation of the EU's new comprehensive investment policy, but also its reform efforts at a global level, and could have been perceived as detrimental to EU investors by the Member States.

However, the Court of Justice has been known to vigilantly safeguard the EU legal order from potentially adverse external influences, notwithstanding pressure from the Member States or EU institutions.[19] Its traditionally cautious approach towards international law was regarded as an obstacle to incorporating investor-state dispute resolution mechanisms in the EU's agreements.[20] A reluctance towards establishing a close relationship with other systems of international law was particularly visible in the case law on external courts and tribunals,[21] in which the Court of Justice rejected an opportunity for cooperation with the ECtHR,[22] and prevented the establishment of the EEA Court[23] and the Unified Patents Court.[24] The past Opinions have raised doubts about

---

[17]   For example, in agreements with Mexico, Singapore, Vietnam, Chile, China, Indonesia, Japan, Malaysia, Myanmar, Philippines: Opinion of AG Bot (n 14), para 14.

[18]   Ibid., paras 12, 32, 33.

[19]   Opinion 2/13 is the primary example: Opinion 2/13 (n 2); Steve Peers, 'The EU's Accession to the ECHR the Dream Becomes a Nightmare' (2015) 16 *German Law Journal* 213.

[20]   Mauro Gatti, '*Opinion 1/17* in the Light of *Achmea:* Chronicle of an Opinion Foretold?' (2019) 4 European Papers 109; Marcus Burgstaller, 'Investor-State Arbitration in EU International Investment Agreements with Third States' (2012) 39 *Legal Issues of Economic Integration* 207; Burkhard Hess, 'The Fate of Investment Dispute Resolution after the *Achmea* Decision of the European Court of Justice' (2018) 3 MPILux Research Paper Series; Szilárd Gáspar-Szilágyi, 'It Is Not Just About Investor-State Arbitration: A Look at Case C-28416, *Achmea BV*' (2018) 3 European Papers 357.

[21]   Marco Bronckers, 'The Relationship of the EC Courts with Other International Tribunals: Non-committal, Respectful or Submissive?' (2007) 44 *Common Market Law Review* 601.

[22]   Opinion 2/13 (n 2).

[23]   Opinion 1/91 *Agreement on the European Economic Area* [1991] ECR 6099.

[24]   Opinion 1/09 *Creation of a Unified Patent Litigation System* [2011] ECR I-01137.

the EU ever adhering to a jurisdiction of an external court,[25] albeit such a possibility has always been acknowledged as a matter of principle.[26]

Notwithstanding its hesitant attitude towards international law,[27] the Court of Justice has appreciated that the EU legal order and its judicial system do not function in isolation.[28] As the guardian of the EU's constitutional integrity, the Court has used the idea of legal pluralism as a framework for the relationship between the EU legal order and international law. The approach has not always promoted systemic openness on the part of the EU, as manifested in *Kadi*[29] and the treatment of WTO law within the EU legal order.[30] Legal pluralism describes the world as a hybrid space where a multitude of normative systems coexist and frequently overlap with each other.[31] The theory accepts that clashes and competition occur among these distinct normative systems, as each of them possesses the same claim to authority.[32] Legal pluralism does not seek to provide an authoritative solution for determining which norms should prevail in a hybrid legal space or who should decide.[33] In opposition to legal

---

[25]   Panos Koutrakos, 'Editorial: More on Autonomy - Opinion 1/17 (CETA)' (2019) 44 *European Law Review* 293.
[26]   Opinion 2/13 (n 2), para 182; Opinion 1/91 (n 23), paras 40 and 70; Opinion 1/09 (n 24), para 74.
[27]   Federico Casolari, 'Giving Indirect Effect to International Law within the EU Legal Order: The Doctrine of Consistent Interpretation' in Enzo Cannizzaro, Paolo Palchetti and Ramses Wessel (eds), *Studies in EU External Relations: International Law as Law of the European Union* (Brill 2011) 395.
[28]   See, e.g., Joined Cases 21 to 24/72 *International Fruit Company NV and others* [1972] ECR 1219; Case 181/73 *Haegeman* [1974] ECR 00449; Case C-469/93 *Chiquita Italia SpA* [1995] ECR I-4533, paras 35 and 40; Case C-386/08 *Brita* [2010] ECR I-01289; Cases C-224/16 *Aebtri* [2018] OJ C 22 ECR; Case C-344/04 *IATA and ELFAA* [2006] ECR I-00403; Case 181/73 *Haegeman* [1974] ECR 00449, paras 5 and 6; Case C-386/08 *Brita* [2010] ECR I-01289, para 39; Case C-224/16 *Aebtri* OJ C 22/8, para 50; Allan Rosas, 'The European Court of Justice in Context: Forms and Patterns of Judicial Dialogue' (2007–2008) 1 *European Journal of Legal Studies* 121.
[29]   Joined Cases C-402/05 P and C-415/05 P *Kadi and Al Barakaat International Foundation v Council and Commission* [2008] ECR I-0636; Ramses Wessel, 'Reconsidering the Relationship between International and EU Law: Towards a Content-based Approach?' in Cannizzaro, Palchetti and Wessel (n 27).
[30]   Antonello Tancredi, 'On the Absence of Direct Effect of the WTO Dispute Settlement Body's Decision in the EU Legal Order' in Cannizzaro, Palchetti and Wessel, ibid.
[31]   Berman (n 6).
[32]   Paul Schiff Berman, 'Global Legal Pluralism as a Normative Project' (2018) 8 *UC Irvine Law Review* 149.
[33]   Berman (n 6), 15.

pluralism stands the constitutionalist approach, which advocates for some systemic unity in international law and favours hierarchy among its norms.[34]

The Court of Justice has manged interaction with international law and other legal regimes by establishing itself as the final authority responsible for deciding which norms of international law can permeate the EU legal order and determining their internal effect.[35] Its reasoning in *Kadi* was considered as 'robustly pluralist' and was criticised for being inward-looking and accentuating the separate nature of the EU legal order from other systems of international law.[36] The same approach, that emphasises clear dividing lines between sovereign spheres of authority, has been followed by the CETA drafters to manage jurisdictional overlap between the Court of Justice, its Canadian counterparts and investor-state tribunals.[37] The Court noted in *Opinion 1/17* that while all judicial bodies had the same authority over the interpretation of the CETA provisions, they could render normative interpretations binding, only within their respective legal systems.[38] In light of this, the Court of Justice was satisfied that the powers of investor-state tribunals were sufficiently delineated, to prevent any adverse effects on the constitutional integrity of the EU legal order, and permitted the inclusion of the dispute resolution mechanism in the EU agreements.[39]

The separation between investor-state tribunals and domestic courts is reinforced by the fact that the CETA expressly precludes its direct effect.[40] As foreign investors cannot invoke provisions of the CETA before courts of the Member States, the Court of Justice has limited opportunity to interpret them, which reduces occurrence of a clash with investor-state tribunals.[41] Nonetheless, since the CETA is an integral part of EU law, it could appear

---

[34]   Nico Krisch, *Beyond Constitutionalism: The Pluralist Structure of Postnational Law* (OUP 2010), ch 2.

[35]   Joined Cases C-402/05 P and C-415/05 P *Kadi and Al Barakaat International Foundation v Council and Commission* [2008] ECR I-06361, Opinion of AG Poiares Maduro, para 211; Armin von Bogdandy, 'Pluralism, Direct Effect and the Ultimate Say: On the Relationship between International and Domestic Constitutional Law' (2008) 6 *International Journal of Constitutional Law* 397.

[36]   De Búrca (n 5), 12; Katja Ziegler, 'Strengthening the Rule of Law, but Fragmenting International Law: The *Kadi* Decision of the ECJ from the Perspective of Human Rights' (2009) 9 *Human Rights Law Review* 288.

[37]   Opinion 1/17 (n 1), paras 116–118.

[38]   Ibid.

[39]   Ibid., paras 120–161.

[40]   Art 30.6.1 CETA.

[41]   Opinion of AG Bot (n 14), para 63; Beatrice Bonafé, 'Direct Effect of International Agreements in the EU Legal Order: Does It Depend on the Existence of an International Dispute Settlement Mechanism?' in Cannizzaro, Palchetti and Wessel (n 27).

before the Court of Justice in a different context.[42] In this instance, the jurisdictional overlap has been managed through ensuring that investment awards lack an *erga omnes* effect, therefore they cannot compel the Court to adopt a particular interpretation of applicable law.[43] In addition, overlap has been managed by granting investor-state tribunals limited powers that permit them to award only monetary compensation.[44]

Further limits to the effects of decisions of investment tribunals in adjacent jurisdictions have been emphasised in *Opinion 1/17,* with a comparison between the interaction of the EU with the WTO regime.[45] In *Opinion 1/17,* the Court of Justice notably distinguished the dispute resolution system established pursuant to the CETA from that of the WTO.[46] Whilst the decisions rendered against the EU pursuant to the WTO agreements have limited effects, which are controlled by the Court of Justice, they permeate the EU legal order, providing a standard for review of EU secondary legislation, albeit not determining its legality.[47] Limited competence for investor-state tribunals ensures that their awards exist completely outside the EU legal order. Therefore, when compared to WTO decisions, it is even less likely that investment awards will interact with EU law in a way that could adversely affect its essential character.

The strict jurisdictional divide established in the CETA, allowed the Court to find, in *Opinion 1/17,* that powers of investor-state tribunals did not undermine the integrity of the EU legal order.[48] The attitude that is more open to coexistence with other judicial bodies aligns more closely with the EU's identity, which presumes a close relationship with international law.[49] Nonetheless, there is scope for development in the EU's approach to its interaction with other regimes. It is apparent that in the drafting of the CETA, the EU legislature took due regard of the Court's preference for the pluralist approach and established clear boundaries between legal orders.[50] Legal pluralism has, however, started to progress in a normative direction, and the idea of developing procedural

---

[42] Art 19(3) TFEU; Opinion 1/17 (n 1), paras 116–117.
[43] Art 8. 41 CETA.
[44] Ibid., Art 8. 36.
[45] Opinion 1/17 (n 1), para 146.
[46] Ibid.
[47] Tancredi (n 30), 252; Adam Cygan, 'The European Court of Justice and External Relations: Internationalist Objectives or Integrationist Priorities?' in Jens-Uwe Wunderlich and David J Bailey, *The European Union and Global Governance: A Handbook* (Routledge 2011) 108.
[48] Opinion 1/17 (n 1).
[49] Art 3(5) TEU provides that the Union shall contribute to the 'strict observance and development of international law': Consolidated Version of the Treaty on the European Union [2016] OJ C 202/13; De Búrca (n 5), 45.
[50] Art 8.31 CETA.

mechanisms that enable 'productive interaction' among overlapping legal systems has appeared in the literature.[51] The EU has not embraced these ideas yet, but an evolution in the theoretical approach creates opportunities for the relationship between EU law and international law to evolve alongside it. A possible procedural innovation is to establish a preliminary ruling mechanism between investor-state tribunals and the Court of Justice, in order to ensure the correct application of EU law in all circumstances.

3.   CONSEQUENCES OF MAINTAINING A STRICT JURISDICTIONAL DIVIDE BETWEEN THE EU LEGAL ORDER AND INVESTOR-STATE TRIBUNALS

Allowing for a mere coexistence of investor-state tribunals alongside the Court of Justice is a pragmatic compromise that can produce effects within the internal market, notwithstanding the establishment of clear jurisdictional boundaries.[52] The objectives and nature of the investment protection chapter in the CETA make the interaction between the two legal systems inevitable.[53] In disputes brought against either the Union or its Member States, an investor-state tribunal will be required to evaluate EU measures and their compatibility with investment protection standards. This has been acknowledged in the drafting of the applicable law clauses in the CETA, which permit investor-state tribunals to take EU law into consideration, provided that it is only used as a matter of fact, and in accordance with the prevailing interpretation of the Court of Justice.[54] This interaction can affect the EU legal order in a number of ways.

First of all, repeated awards against the same EU legislation could force its amendment in order to limit the Union's financial liability.[55] This danger was considered in *Opinion 1/17* and the Court stressed that such a situation was not acceptable within the EU's constitutional framework.[56] However, the Court was satisfied that the EU democratic process, limited powers of investor-state tribunals, and express safeguards for states' rights to regulate contained in

---

[51]   Berman (n 6); Berman (n 32).
[52]   Steffen Hindelang, 'Repellent Forces: The CJEU and Investor-State Dispute Settlement' (2015) 53 Archiv des Völkerrechts 68.
[53]   Markus Burgstaller, 'European Law and Investment Treaties' (2009) 26 *Journal of International Arbitration* 181.
[54]   Art 8.31 CETA.
[55]   Council (EU), Regulation 912/2014 establishing a framework for managing financial responsibility linked to investor-to-state dispute settlement tribunals established by international agreements to which the European Union is a party [2014] OJ L 257/121.
[56]   Opinion 1/17 (n 1), paras 149–150.

the CETA, provided sufficient guarantees that such a problem was unlikely to arise.[57] This is one of the examples of the Court's more flexible attitude to the interaction with other legal orders, particularly when compared to *Opinion 2/13*.[58] In that Opinion, the Court was much more thorough in its evaluation, and denied the possibility of establishing a closer relationship with the ECtHR at the slightest hint of even a hypothetical incompatibility.[59]

Second, the current formulation of the applicable law clause in the CETA permits investor-state tribunals to use EU law, even where no interpretation by the Court of Justice exists.[60] Although it does not undermine the constitutional integrity of the EU, because of the strict jurisdictional separation, courts of the Member States may find it problematic to enforce awards that appear to contravene provisions of EU law.[61] Although national courts have an option to seek clarification from the Court of Justice through the preliminary ruling procedure in Article 267 TFEU, a reference would put the EU legal order on a direct collision course with the system of international investment, which the drafters of the CETA had been trying to avoid.[62] A similar conflict can arise in cases rendered against the EU that will be enforced before the Court of Justice.

Furthermore, enforced awards based on incorrect interpretations of EU law could create inequality of treatment between domestic and foreign investors. In the aftermath of *Achmea*,[63] recourse to courts of the Member States will become the only avenue available to EU firms, which operate in the internal market, to challenge a measure that has an unjustifiably adverse effect on their enterprise.[64] The possibility exists for the interpretation of EU legislation by the Court of Justice, particularly on novel points of law, to produce a less favourable outcome for a 'domestic' investor,[65] when compared to an already

---

[57]   Ibid., paras 151–161.

[58]   Opinion 2/13 (n 2).

[59]   Bruno de Witte and Šejla Imamovic, 'Opinion 2/13 on Accession to the ECHR: Defending the EU Legal Order Against a Foreign Human Rights Court' (2015) 40 *European Law Review* 683; Katja Ziegler, 'Beyond Pluralism and Autonomy: Systemic Harmonization as a Paradigm for the Interaction of EU Law and International Law' (2016) 35 *Yearbook of European Law* 667.

[60]   Art 8.31 CETA.

[61]   *Micula* is one of the examples that arose under the existing Member States' Bilateral Investment Treaties. A question on enforceability of the award due to its conflict with the EU state aid rules has been recently referred by the Belgian Court of Appeal: see Cour d'appel Bruxelles- 2016/AR/393 joint avec 2016/AR/394.

[62]   See analysis in the preceding section.

[63]   Case C-284/16 *Slovak Republic v Achmea BV* [2018] OJ C 296.

[64]   Commission, 'Communication from the Commission to the European Parliament and the Council: Protection of Intra-EU Investment' COM(2018) 547 final.

[65]   In this paragraph a 'domestic investor' includes all EU companies that invest in the internal market, e.g., a French firm that invests in Poland is regarded as a domestic investor.

enforced award rendered in favour of a foreign investor by an investor-state tribunal. At this point it should be noted that arbitration has traditionally favoured finality of awards over their correctness,[66] and in the light of its specific functions as an international dispute resolution mechanism, a level of inequality may be tolerated.

There are, however, ongoing efforts at the global level to improve predictability and correctness of investment awards, which is perceived by states as essential for enhancing confidence in the investment environment and legitimacy of the regime.[67] To that end, the EU was the first to introduce appeals tribunals in its investment protection treaties.[68] Nevertheless, the aim cannot be fully achieved unless tribunals are allowed to verify interpretation of EU law with the Court of Justice, which has been acknowledged by the Commission in its Communication that was released in the aftermath of *Achmea*.[69] The Commission unequivocally stated that arbitrators cannot 'properly apply EU law, in the absence of the indispensable judicial dialogue with the Court of Justice'.[70] The appellate mechanism has the capability of improving consistency only within the system of investment protection, which may also be limited in the absence of the rule of binding precedent. In order to improve coherence in international law, methods for constructive cooperation between the legal systems that coexist in the hybrid space should be contemplated.[71]

Finally, an acquiescence to the parallel existence of the investor-state tribunals without establishing a mechanism enabling cooperation, allows circumvention of the preliminary ruling procedure in Article 267 TFEU.[72] The CETA permits a foreign investor to bring a claim before an investor-state tribunal, pursuant to the agreement, after discontinuing domestic proceedings that may concern the same measure.[73] Therefore, as already acknowledged in *Opinion 2/15*, the investment protection treaties remove disputes from the jurisdiction

---

[66]   Christoph Schreuer et al, *The ICSID Convention: A Commentary* (2nd edn, CUP 2009), 903.

[67]   UNCITRAL, Report of Working Group III (Investor-State Dispute Settlement Reform) on the Work of Its Thirty-sixth Session (Vienna, 29 October–2 November 2018).

[68]   Art 8.28 CETA.

[69]   Commission, 'Protection of Intra-EU Investment' (n 64), 2.

[70]   Ibid.

[71]   August Reinisch, 'The Proliferation of International Dispute Settlement Mechanism: The Threat of Fragmentation vs. the Promise of a More Effective System? Some Reflections from the Perspective of Investment Arbitration' in Isabelle Buffard, James Crawford, Alain Pellet et al (eds), *International Law between Universalism and Fragmentation* (Martinus Nijhoff Publishers 2009) 121.

[72]   Hindelang (n 52), 76–80.

[73]   Art 8.22(g) CETA.

of the courts of the Member States.[74] Since the clauses on applicable law in the CETA do not permit investor-state tribunals to verify interpretation of novel aspects of EU legislation with the Court of Justice,[75] a possibility exists that these issues are only resolved outside of the judicial structure of the EU. While the decisions of the investor-state tribunals will not pose a threat to the integrity of the EU legal order, they will shape the investment environment in the internal market without the participation of the Court of Justice.[76]

4. A POSSIBILITY OF ESTABLISHING A DIALOGUE BETWEEN THE COURT OF JUSTICE AND INVESTOR-STATE TRIBUNALS

Although the option was not contemplated by the drafters of the CETA, there exists a possibility to establish a procedure for a dialogue between the Court of Justice and investor-state tribunals, which would resolve the aforementioned issues.[77] This was mentioned by Belgium, which in its request for an Opinion, sought a clarification on whether a preliminary ruling mechanism was necessary to safeguard the exclusive jurisdiction of the Court of Justice.[78] The Court was satisfied that the clear jurisdictional separation effectively protected the essential character of its function, and dismissed the need for closer cooperation with investor-state tribunals in a single paragraph.[79] Furthermore, lack of procedural rules enabling a dialogue between the courts was regarded as consistent with the international law principles applicable between the parties to the CETA.[80] The statement implies the Court's respect for the principle of institutional balance, and the decision of the EU legislature to establish a system for resolution of investor-state disputes, outside of domestic judiciaries.[81]

---

[74] Opinion 2/15 *Free Trade Agreement between the European Union and the Republic of Singapore* [2017] OJ C239, para 292.

[75] Art 8.31 CETA.

[76] In this context it is worth noting that treaty shopping is an accepted practice in international investment, see on the subject: Jorun Baumgartner, *Treaty Shopping in International Investment Law* (OUP 2016).

[77] Opinion 1/00 *Proposed agreement between the European Community and non-Member States on the establishment of the European Common Aviation Area* [2002] ECR I-03493, paras 19–20; Opinion 1/92 *Revised Agreement on the European Economic Area* [1992] ECR I-2821, para 32.

[78] Opinion of AG Bot (n 14), paras 43 and 44; Opinion 1/17 (n 1), para 50.

[79] Opinion 1/17 (n 1), para 134.

[80] Ibid.

[81] This point was raised by the Advocate General Bot, see Opinion of AG Bot (n 14), para 179.

The Court's brief and vague reasoning concerning the preliminary ruling mechanism in *Opinion 1/17* did not display enthusiasm for close cooperation with the system of international investment.[82] Nevertheless, it did not foreclose an option to develop a dialogue in the future. Unlike the Advocate General, the Court did not explicitly state that the system of prior involvement would have undermined the neutrality and autonomy of the dispute settlement mechanism in the CETA.[83] The Advocate General also warned of the need to grant reciprocal concessions that enable the possibility of engaging the domestic courts of the non-member country, which is a party to the EU agreement, on questions of the interpretation of its domestic law.[84] Whilst this obstacle could be overcome by recognising the *sui generis* nature of the EU legal order, the reasoning of Advocate General Bot highlights a lack of political will on the part of the EU to commit to a closer relationship with the system of international investment protection.[85]

Nevertheless, advantages of bridging jurisdictional divides through a preliminary ruling mechanism have been acknowledged in academic literature.[86] The procedural solution has been considered as an effective means for improving coherence and clarity in international law.[87] Schill observed that functionally, investor-state tribunals resemble domestic administrative or constitutional courts, as they evaluate matters that pertain to the exercise of public authority.[88] As such, these dispute resolution bodies contribute to the

---

[82]   Opinion 1/17 (n 1), para 134.
[83]   Opinion of AG Bot (n 14), para 182.
[84]   Ibid.
[85]   Ibid., paras 179–184.
[86]   See Urszula Jaremba and Giancarlo Piscitelli Chapter 4 in this volume; Reinisch (n 71); Christoph Schreuer, 'Preliminary Rulings in Investment Arbitration' (2007) 6 *Transnational Dispute Management*; Christian Tams, 'An Appealing Option? The Debate about an ICSID Appellate Structure' (2007) 5 *Transnational Dispute Management*; John Gaffney, 'Should Investment Treaty Tribunals be Permitted to Request Preliminary Rulings from the Court of Justice of the European Union' (2013) 2 *Transnational Dispute Management*; Renato Nazzini, 'Parallel Proceedings before the Tribunal and the Courts/ Competition Authorities' in Gordon Blanke and Phillip Landolt (eds), *EU and US Antitrust Arbitration: A Handbook for Practitioners* (Kluwer Law International 2011) 881; Stephan Schill, 'Arbitration Procedure: the Role of the European Union and the Member States in Investor- State Arbitration' in Catherine Kessedjian (ed) *Le droit européen et l' arbitrage d'investissement – European Law and Investment Arbitration* (Panthéon-Assas 2011); Konstanze von Papp, 'Clash of "Autonomous Legal Orders": Can EU Member State Courts Bridge the Jurisdictional Divide Between Investment Tribunals and the ECJ? A Plea for Direct Referral from Investment Tribunals to the ECJ' (2013) 50 *Common Market Law Review* 1039.
[87]   Schreuer (n 86), Reinisch (n 71).
[88]   Schill (n 86),144–145.

development of norms that govern the sphere of international economic relations not only between states, but also individual actors in the field. Therefore, a mechanism which ensures the correct application of different overlapping norms within this framework would certainly be desirable. The most effective tool of the Court of Justice for securing the uniform application of EU law within the internal market has been the preliminary ruling procedure in Article 267 TFEU.[89] The EU legislature should consider extending its use outside the EU legal order, to contribute to a coherent development of international economic law.

The cosmopolitan approach to global pluralism has proposed maximising interaction among various legal systems as an alternative way of managing the jurisdictional overlap in the hybrid legal space, in comparison to the traditional approach that insists on maintaining strict divisions between different sovereign spheres of authority.[90] Establishing a preliminary ruling mechanism between the Court of Justice and investor-state tribunals could spark a normative dialogue between the two systems, guaranteeing that in all contexts EU law is uniformly applied. It would also send a signal that the EU is interested in shaping the international legal space in a manner that is cooperative and embraces its plurality.[91] The ongoing development of the EU's policy on international investment and the bilateral manner through which it is implemented, provide good conditions to test any new solutions, keeping in mind the long-term ambition of creating a multilateral investment court.

The Court of Justice accepted, in its previous Opinions, that an international agreement entered into by the EU with non-Member States, may extend its powers to decide on questions referred to it in preliminary rulings, pursuant to the international agreement.[92] Such a procedure for a dialogue with external courts has been established in the Agreement on the European Economic Area (hereinafter EEA Agreement)[93] and the agreement establishing the European Common Aviation Area (ECAA).[94] Both of these agreements sought to extend

---

[89]   Tams (n 86), 46, 48.

[90]   Berman (n 6), 10–15.

[91]   Berman (n 32), 237.

[92]   Opinion 1/00 (n 77), paras 19–20; Opinion 1/92 (n 77), para 32; Opinion 1/09 (n 24); Opinion 1/91 (n 23).

[93]   Art 107, Protocol 34 of the Agreement on the European Economic Area [1994] L 1/3 (EEA Agreement). On the functioning of the preliminary ruling mechanism between the EFTA Court and the CJEU see Carl Baudenbacher, 'The EFTA Court: An Actor in the European Judicial Dialogue' (2005) 28 *Fordham International Law Journal* 351.

[94]   Art 20 of the Multilateral Agreement between the European Community and its Member States, the Republic of Albania, Bosnia and Herzegovina, the Republic of Bulgaria, the Republic of Croatia, the former Yugoslav Republic of Macedonia, the

the EU *acquis* to non-member countries,[95] hence it was recognised that incorporating a preliminary ruling mechanism was necessary for the attainment of these objectives.[96]

In addition, a procedure for dialogue between the Court of Justice and external courts was contemplated in other contexts.[97] It was proposed in the first agreement on the Unified Patent Court,[98] which was intended as a specialist court in the area of intellectual property law that encompassed within its jurisdiction EU Member States and non-member countries.[99] The solution was also included in the EU's accession agreement to the ECHR, providing a framework for cooperation between the Court of Justice and the ECtHR.[100] Although the agreements were found incompatible with EU law,[101] the Court's unwillingness to engage in a dialogue with other systems should not be treated as the reason behind these decisions. Neither agreement established a sufficiently clear jurisdictional divide, as they left open the possibility that decisions of external courts could produce effects within the EU legal order that would undermine its autonomy.[102] In relation, to the ECtHR, the Court of Justice was particularly concerned with the fact that an external court had the power to rule on the validity of provisions EU law.[103]

The aforementioned problem has been eliminated by the drafters of the CETA, who expressly excluded questions pertaining to the legality of domestic law from the scope of competence of investor-state tribunals.[104] Therefore, *Opinion 1/17* opens the possibility for further development of the relationship

---

Republic of Iceland, the Republic of Montenegro, the Kingdom of Norway, Romania, the Republic of Serbia and the United Nations Interim Administration Mission in Kosovo on the establishment of a European Common Aviation Area [2006] L 285/3 (ECAA Agreement).

[95]   Ibid., Art 1; Art 1 EEA Agreement.

[96]   Opinion 1/00 (n 77), paras 5–8.

[97]   Opinion 2/13 (n 2); Opinion 1/09 (n 24).

[98]   Opinion 1/09 (n 24), paras 78 and 79.

[99]   The agreement was subsequently revised, and the jurisdiction of the Unified Patents Court was limited. Now, it encompasses only EU Member States and includes a procedure for dialogue with the Court of Justice, see Jacopo Alberti, 'New Developments in the EU System of Judicial Protection: The Creation of the Unified Patent Court and Its Future Relations with the CJEU' (2017) 24 *Maastricht Journal of European and Comparative Law* 7.

[100]   Opinion 2/13 (n 2), paras 238–247.

[101]   Opinion 2/13 (n 2); Opinion 1/09 (n 24).

[102]   Ibid.

[103]   Opinion 2/13 (n 2), para 247; Piet Eeckhout, 'Opinion 2/13 on EU accession to the ECHR and Judicial Dialogue: Autonomy or Autarky?' (2015) 38 *Fordham International Law Journal* 955.

[104]   Art 8.31.2 CETA; Opinion 1/17 (n 1), para 121.

between the EU legal order and the system of international investment protection. The Court of Justice has, however, confirmed that it is only open to a dialogue if its decisions are treated as final and binding.[105] The first EEA agreement was considered incompatible with EU law, inter alia, because it stipulated that interpretations provided by the Court of Justice would be treated as merely advisory by the EEA Court.[106] The issue was rectified in the revised version, which was accepted by the Court of Justice.[107] The ruling was subsequently followed in the ECAA agreement.[108] The previous jurisprudence highlights that any international agreement that incorporates a preliminary ruling procedure must guarantee the essential function of the Court of Justice as the final arbiter of EU law.[109] The requirement applies even if the jurisdiction of an external court is kept separate, in a manner that precludes its decision from having any effect on the interpretation of EU law within the EU legal order, similar to the outcome achieved in CETA.[110]

Another aspect that was problematic in the past regarded the applicability of EU liability rules. In *Opinion 1/09,* the Court of Justice held that it was not enough that the proposed external court could request the interpretation of provisions of EU legislation, it was also necessary to provide the same guarantees for its correct application as those offered by the courts of the Member States.[111] In relation to this aspect, the jurisdictional separation between the Court of Justice and investor-state tribunals, which was repeatedly underlined in *Opinion 1/17,*[112] is likely to provide an effective solution.[113] As decisions of the CETA tribunals, unlike those of the Unified Patent Court, have no effect within the EU legal order, it is likely that there is no need for the liability rules to apply, and the Court did not insist on them in *Opinion 1/92*[114] and *Opinion 1/00.*[115]

---

[105] Opinion 1/91 (n 23), para 61.

[106] Ibid., paras 61 and 65.

[107] Art 108 EEA Agreement; Opinion 1/92 (n 77).

[108] Art 20 ECAA Agreement.

[109] Opinion 1/92 (n 77); Opinion 1/00 (n 77).

[110] Ibid.

[111] Opinion 1/09 (n 24); Thomas Jaeger, 'Back to Square One? An Assessment of the Latest Proposal for a Patent Court for the Internal Market and Possible Alternatives' (2012) 43 *International Review of Intellectual Property and Competition Law* 286.

[112] Opinion 1/17 (n 1), paras 113, 114, 118, 134, 199, 200, and 213.

[113] Bruno De Witte, 'A Selfish Court? The Court of Justice and the Design of International Dispute Settlement Beyond the European Union' in Marise Cremona and Anne Thies (eds), *European Court of Justice and External Relations Law: Constitutional Challenges* (Bloomsbury Publishing 2014).

[114] Opinion 1/92 (n 77).

[115] Opinion 1/00 (n 77), para 45.

As highlighted above, existing EU law keeps the door open to establishing a mechanism for preliminary rulings between the Court of Justice and investor-state tribunals in the future. The final point to emphasise is that the establishment of such a procedural innovation that bridges the jurisdictional divide would not necessarily be overly burdensome. Commentators have pointed out that the number of investment cases filed each year does not give a reason to think that the Court of Justice would be flooded with requests from investor-state tribunals to clarify points of EU law.[116] The investment tribunal in *Eastern Sugar* implied that it would only seek clarification on complex points of EU law.[117] After all, efficiency of proceedings is one of the defining characteristics of investment arbitration, which investor-state tribunals would want to preserve. For that reason, it has been suggested that a referral of a question to the CJEU should only be considered in exceptional cases.[118]

5.   CONCLUSIONS

The CETA and *Opinion 1/17* are important milestones in the evolution of the relationship between the EU legal order and international law. They both provide useful guidance on how a jurisdictional overlap with the Court of Justice can be managed, in order to ensure compatibility of an international agreement with EU law. In *Opinion 1/17*, the Court of Justice displayed greater flexibility, compared to its previous decision on a similar matter, in accepting the coexistence with investor-state tribunals, despite certain risks that could adversely affect the internal market. Therefore, by confirming that the EU's adherence to the jurisdiction of an external court is not just a mere theoretical possibility, *Opinion 1/17* breaks the trend in the case law that created an image of the EU as being isolationist and protectionist.[119] While the *Opinion*

---

[116]   Gaffney (n 86), 13; Schill (n 86).
[117]   *Eastern Sugar BV (Netherlands) v Czech Republic,* SCC Case No 088/2004 (27 March 2007), para 137.
[118]   Nazzini (n 86); von Papp (n 86).
[119]   Marise Cremona, 'A Reticent Court? Policy Objectives and the Court of Justice' in Marise Cremona and Anne Thies (eds) *Modern Studies in European Law, Vol 49: European Court of Justice and External Relations Law: Constitutional Challenges* (Bloomsbury Publishing 2014) 29; August Reinisch, 'The EU on the Investment Path – Quo Vadis Europe? The Future of EU BITs and other Investment Agreements' (2013–2014) 12 *Santa Clara Journal of International Law* 111, 152; Stephan E Schill, 'Luxembourg Limits: Conditions for Investor-State Dispute Settlement under Future EU Investment Agreements' in Marc Bungenberg, August Reinisch and Christian Tietje (eds), *EU and Investment Agreements* (Nomos 2013) 37–54; Daniel Halberstam, 'Local, Global, and Plural Constitutionalism: Europe Meets the World' in Gráinne De Búrca and Joseph Weiler, *The Worlds of European Constitutionalism*

contributes towards building an international space that promotes coexistence of distinct legal orders based on mutual respect, the interaction of the EU legal order with international investment regimes offers opportunities to develop closer cooperation between them.

The reasoning in *Opinion 1/17* accentuated the separate and self-contained nature of legal orders. Although the clear jurisdictional separation in the CETA provided sufficient safeguards for the constitutional integrity of the EU legal order, it did not contribute towards improving coherence in the international legal framework that governs economic relations between states, as well as individual actors. *Opinion 1/17* continues the same pluralist vision of international law as that found in *Kadi* and *Opinion 2/13*,[120] albeit demonstrating a more lenient attitude to the application of the principle of autonomy of EU law. Such an approach to the interaction of the EU with other legal systems is visible, not only in the reasoning of the Court, but also in the choices made by the EU legislature in designing provisions in the CETA.

There are, however, versions of global legal pluralism that call for maximising opportunities for productive interaction among legal orders, rather than focusing on protecting sovereign spheres of authority.[121] The evolution in theoretical thinking offers opportunities for the EU policy choices to develop alongside it. A mere coexistence of investor-state tribunals and the Court of Justice could be developed into cooperation, by establishing a preliminary ruling procedure that allows the former to clarify novel and complex points of EU law. The bilateral approach of the EU to the implementation of its comprehensive policy on international investment provides a possibility to test this innovative approach before considering its implementation multilaterally.

Although the CETA perpetuates the old models for interaction of legal systems in the international space, *Opinion 1/17* is welcomed from the perspective of the global reform of the system of international investment protection. The Court's decision is an important endorsement of the Commission's efforts and strengthens its position in the international scene. Nevertheless, a greater commitment from the EU to the systemic development of the inter-

---

(CUP 2012) 187; Katja Ziegler, 'International Law and EU law: between Asymmetric Constitutionalisation and Fragmentation' in Alexander Orakhelashvili, *Research Handbook on the Theory and History of International Law* (Edward Elgar 2011) 268.

[120] Giuseppe Martinico, 'Building Supranational Identity: Legal Reasoning and Outcome in *Kadi* and Opinion 2/13 of the Court of Justice' (2016) 8 *Italian Journal of Public Law* 235; Jean d'Aspremont and Frédéric Dopagne, '*Kadi:* the ECJ's Reminder of the Elementary Divide between Legal Orders' (2008) 5 *International Organizations Review* 371.

[121] Berman (n 6), 15.

national legal framework would align more closely with its identity as defined in the TEU.

6. Settling disputes on TSD Chapters of EU FTAs: Recent trends and future challenges in the light of CJEU Opinion 2/15

Susanna Villani

1. INTRODUCTION

During the past years, international trade agreements have not only increased in number but also enlarged their scope beyond the obligations of the 1994 WTO Agreement. Since 2005, the European Union (EU) itself has designed a wide strategy to conclude Free Trade Agreements (FTAs) outside the WTO framework, with more than 100 partners.[1] These new kinds of agreements include relatively novel fields such as sustainable development, investment and labour law, that are classified as WTO-plus and WTO-extra rules. Being outside the WTO system, they do not fall within the jurisdiction of the WTO when dealing with dispute settlement.[2] In this regard, therefore, the contracting parties to FTAs are free to decide the mechanisms and procedures devoted to

---

[1] For an overview of the FTAs concluded by the EU and their status of implementation: Commission Staff Working Document, Individual reports and info sheets on implementation of EU Free Trade Agreements, Accompanying the document Report from the Commission to the European Parliament, the Council, the European Economic and Social Committee and the Committee of the Regions on Implementation of Free Trade Agreements, 1 January 2019 – 31 December 2019, COM(2020) 705 final, 12 November 2020.

[2] This issue has been explored in depth: William J Davey, 'Dispute Settlement in the WTO and RTAs: A Comment', in Lorand Bartels, Federico Ortino (eds), *Regional Trade Agreements and the WTO Legal System* (OUP 2006) 343; Jennifer Hillman, 'Conflicts between Dispute Settlement Mechanisms in Regional Trade Agreements and the WTO – What Should WTO Do' (2009) 42 *Cornell International Law Journal* 194; Gabrielle Marceau, 'The Primacy of the WTO Dispute Settlement System' (2015) 23 *Questions of International Law* 3.

settling potential disputes concerning these kinds of provisions and making them enforceable at bilateral level.[3]

Against this background, this chapter focuses on the dispute settlement mechanism of the so-called Trade and Sustainable Development (TSD) chapters[4] included in the most recent FTAs concluded by the EU. These chapters require the respect of international labour and environmental standards and agreements as a condition for fully benefitting from enhanced market access and trade liberalisation. One of the most notable features of the TSD chapters is that the dispute settlement procedure envisaged therein is expressly separated from the general dispute settlement mechanism (DSM) of the FTAs, without providing for a system of sanctions in case of non-compliance. While TSD provisions have been analysed in depth in terms of content, the present chapter is aimed at exploring such a peculiar mechanism of dispute settlement and proposes new potential developments in the light of practice and the CJEU's jurisprudence. After first evaluating the structure and content of the TSD chapters, as well as the dispute settlement procedure (Sections 2–3), attention will be devoted to the passage of the notable CJEU Opinion 2/15,[5] concerning the nature of TSD provisions. Particular focus will be reserved in this respect to the argument by the Luxembourg judges, that conceives TSD substantive obligations as 'essential elements' of EU trade agreements (Section 4). By considering the recent calls for improvement of the enforcement of the TSD provisions, the ultimate goal of the present chapter is to explore whether the CJEU's perspective, adopted in the Singapore Opinion, could contribute to ensuring more enforceable solutions closer to those deriving from classical DSMs. In order to link the theoretical reasoning to practice, and to demonstrate the increasing interest in this topic at EU level, the chapter will consider the dispute between the EU and the Republic of Korea, activated on the basis of the bilateral FTA (KOREU agreement) and its major developments (Section 5).[6] Beginning in December 2018, it has represented the first ever procedure

---

[3]   For a comment on this, see Marie Claire Cordonier Segger, 'Sustainable Development in Regional Trade Agreements' in Bartels, Ortino, ibid., 313.

[4]   Virginie Barral, 'Sustainable Development in International Law: Nature and Operation of an Evolutive Legal Norm' (2012) 23 *European Journal of International Law* 377.

[5]   CJEU Opinion 2/15 *EU-Singapore Free Trade Agreement* [2017] ECLI:EU:C: 2017:376.

[6]   The KOREU agreement was the first deep and comprehensive FTA negotiated by the EU including chapters on trade and sustainable development and on protection of intellectual property rights. According to Art 1(1) of the KOREU agreement:

> [t]he objectives of the Agreement are: [...] g) to commit, in the recognition that sustainable development is an overarching objective, to the development of international trade in such a way as to contribute to the objective of sustainable

of dispute settlement activated for alleged violation of TSD provisions, and its outcome could have been affected by the reasoning proposed in Opinion 2/15. The analysis concludes with some general comments on the main findings of the chapter (Section 6).

2.   TSD CHAPTERS IN THE EU's 'NEW GENERATION' FTAs

The concept of sustainable development has been qualified as a policy-guiding principle of the EU legal system since the entry into force of the Maastricht Treaty, and further clarified by the Amsterdam Treaty.[7] The Lisbon Treaty has then consolidated the EU's commitment to work towards sustainable development both internally and externally. Indeed, even though the treaties do not provide a definition of the concept, they clearly bring sustainable development together with many different policy areas, especially in external relations. According to Article 21(2) TEU the Union should foster the sustainable economic, social and environmental advancement of developing countries. Moreover, it should help establish international measures to preserve and improve the quality of the environment and the sustainable management of global natural resources. Article 205 TFEU provides that the Union's action on the international scene shall be guided by the principles laid down in Article 21 TEU. The joint reading of Article 205 TFEU and Article 21(2) TEU therefore suggests that the Union is constitutionally required to integrate sustainable development interests into its external action.[8] In addition, the Charter of Fundamental Rights of the EU (hereinafter Charter) states, in its preamble, that the EU should promote sustainable development.[9]

---

development and strive to ensure that this objective is integrated and reflected at every level of the Parties' trade relationship.

[7]   For a deeper analysis on the evolution of the principle of sustainable development in the EU legal order: Bär Stefani, R. Andreas Kraemer, 'European Environmental Policy after Amsterdam' (1998) 10 *Journal of Environmental Law* 315; Sander R. W. van Hees, 'Sustainable Development in the EU: Redefining and Operationalising the Concept' (2014) 10 *Utrecht Law Review* 60.

[8]   For a general comment on the EU objectives of foreign policy aimed at fostering the protection of human rights and sustainable development, see Urfan Khaliq, *Ethical Dimensions of the Foreign Policy of the European Union: A Legal Appraisal* (CUP 2008).

[9]   The preamble to the Charter of Fundamental Rights of the European Union states: '[...] The Union [...] seeks to promote balanced and sustainable development and ensures free movement of persons, services, goods and capital, and the freedom of establishment'.

Such wide-ranging undertakings also apply to the field of international trade: since 2008, the EU has been implementing a broader approach to the promotion of sustainable development in its trade agreements. Over recent years, the support for including sustainability concerns in trade agreements has also been reflected in the position of most political parties represented in the European Parliament. The Commission's *Trade for All* strategy[10] commits the EU to a sustainable trade and investment policy. In addition, the recent Commission's *Reflection Paper on Harnessing Globalisation*[11] underlines the EU's commitment to a balanced, rules-based, and progressive trade and investment agenda that enhances global governance on issues like human rights, working conditions, food safety, public health, environmental protection and animal welfare, that are governed by specific provisions progressively elaborated at EU level. As a result, although not possessing an autonomous character, the EU notion of sustainable development is anchored to substantive and specific provisions concerning both the protection of the environment and the accomplishment of those labour standards clearly envisaged, inter alia, in the Charter.[12] Such a composite notion of sustainable development goes beyond the abstract paradigm that just combines the temporal and ideological perspective of inter-generational and intra-generational equity.[13]

In recent years, the interest in including non-trade values, such as labour rights and environmental protection, in trade agreements as concrete definitions of the concept of sustainable development has intensified. Earlier EU agreements containing labour or environmental provisions were mainly limited to rather general provisions regarding cooperation. Recent EU FTAs, negotiated or under negotiation, include a single TSD chapter characterised

---

[10]   European Commission, 'Trade for All: Towards a more responsible trade and investment policy' (14 October 2015) COM (2015) 497.

[11]   European Commission, 'Reflection Paper on Harnessing Globalisation' (10 May 2017) COM (2017) 240.

[12]   Many provisions which are at the heart of labour law and environmental law have been included throughout the Charter. Being incorporated into the Treaties by Art 6 TEU, the Charter can be now invoked in order to challenge the acts adopted by the EU institutions, including the international agreements concluded with third countries. For deeper insights on the impact of the Charter in the field of analysis: Brian Bercusson, *European Labour Law and the EU Charter of Fundamental Rights* (ETUI 2002); Valeria Bonavita, 'The EU Charter of Fundamental Rights and the Social Dimension of International Trade' in Giacomo Di Federico (ed), *The EU Charter of Fundamental Rights: From Declaration to Binding Instrument* (Springer 2011) 261; Samantha Velluti, 'The Promotion and Integration of Human Rights in EU External Trade Relations' (2016) 32 *Utrecht Journal of International and European Law* 43.

[13]   Barral (n 4).

with a distinctive structure.[14] Exceptionally, the Comprehensive Economic and Trade Agreement (CETA) between the EU and Canada does not contain a unique chapter dedicated to trade and sustainable development, but two separate chapters, one aimed at regulating the relationship between the environment and trade and another between labour and trade. Under the classical TSD chapters enclosed in the current EU FTAs, parties undertake to avoid a 'race to the bottom' in terms of labour and environmental standards, by committing themselves not to derogate from, and not to fail to effectively enforce, any of their domestic and international commitments in the field of labour and environmental protection. They also commit to encourage high levels of labour and environmental standards protection. TSD provisions therefore do not aim to create new substantive obligations concerning labour and environmental protection, but reaffirm certain existing commitments at international level, by referring to specific multilateral conventions. These include the core eight Conventions of the International Labour Organisation (ILO)[15] and the Multilateral Environmental Agreements (MEAs).[16] Contracting parties also reiterate their commitments to effectively ratify and implement international agreements covering core environmental and labour standards (i.e., freedom of association and right to collective bargaining; forced or compulsory labour; child labour; and non-discrimination in respect of employment and occupation). Finally, the TSD chapters stipulate that parties will cooperate in certain policy areas, such as engagement in multilateral fora, exchange of information and best practices on relevant topics such as corporate social responsibility. The added value of TSD chapters does not lie in the harmonisation of social and environmental standards between the partners, but rather in fostering dialogue and cooperation to achieve sustainable trade in the long run. In fact,

---

[14]   Interestingly, such a structure reflects that characterising the FTAs concluded by third States, such as the TTP, the FTA between the US and Singapore or the Agreement between the United States of America, the United Mexican States, and Canada.

[15]   The eight ILO fundamental Conventions are: the Forced Labour Convention (1930); the Abolition of Forced Labour Convention (1957); the Freedom of Association and Protection of the Right to Organise Convention (1948); the Right to Organise and Collective Bargaining Convention (1949); the Equal Remuneration Convention (1951); the Discrimination (Employment and Occupation) Convention (1958); the Minimum Age Convention (1973); and the Worst Forms of Child Labour Convention (1999).

[16]   The MEAs are: the Convention on Long-range Trans-boundary Air Pollution (1979); the Convention on Environmental Impact Assessment in a Trans-boundary Context (1997); the Convention on the Protection and Use of Trans-boundary Watercourses and International Lakes (1996); the Convention on the Trans-boundary Effects of Industrial Accidents (1992); the Convention on Access to Information, Public Participation in Decision-making and Access to Justice in Environmental Matters (1998).

these chapters do not stand in isolation but are integrated within the international network of protection by representing a positive signal of interaction between the different components of international law. Furthermore, even though TSD chapters do not introduce new labour and environmental standards to be added to the multilateral framework,[17] their legal relevance cannot be underestimated. Indeed, although it is unquestionable that further improvements are needed,[18] parties' commitments to ratify international instruments and to exchange information on the effective progress in improving labour and environmental standards do actually amount to substantive obligations.

The process of monitoring and enforcing the TSD obligations involves a variety of bodies framed in a well-established institutional structure designed to be inclusive and cooperative. Specifically, the Sub-Committee on Trade and Sustainable Development (TSD Committee) – comprised of senior officials from each party or their delegates – is tasked with the aim of reviewing the implementation of TSD chapters. The main innovation of TSD chapters is their systematic monitoring by two specialised bodies. In particular, the Joint Civil Society Dialogue and domestic advisory groups (DAGs) of both contracting parties can play a supporting and active role in overseeing the implementation of TSD provisions by submitting, inter alia, views or recommendations to the relevant party. Composed of civil society, business representatives, social partners, and other experts from relevant stakeholder groups, these groups are supposed to meet on a regular, typically annual, basis. The members of the relevant DAGs also meet in a 'joint forum' to discuss and produce a public report to be submitted to the TSD Committee. The intention of maximising the compliance with commitments through bilateral dialogue and cooperation is also reflected in case of dispute between the parties on the respect and implementation of these provisions. Interestingly, the TSD chapters envisage a special procedure of dispute settlement that is expressly separated from the general mechanism described in a different section of the FTAs.

---

[17]   Axel Marx, Franz Ebert, Nicolas Hachez and Jan Wouters, *Dispute Settlement in the Trade and Sustainable Development Chapters of EU Trade Agreements* (Leuven Centre for Global Governance Studies 2017).

[18]   In this regard: Axel Marx, Brecht Lein, Nicolas Brando, 'The Protection of Labour Rights in Trade Agreements. The Case of the EU-Colombia Agreement' (2016) 50 *Journal of World Trade* 587; Evgeny Postnikov, Ida Bastiaens, 'Does Dialogue Work? The Effectiveness of Labor Standards in EU Preferential Agreements' (2014) 21 *Journal of European Public Policy* 923.

3.   THE PROCEDURE OF DISPUTE SETTLEMENT
       UNDER TSD CHAPTERS: PATTERN AND
       LIMITS

The commitments and obligations provided under the TSD chapters are expressly excluded from unilateral enforcement and are not subject to the traditional DSM provided for in the FTAs.[19] Indeed, the general DSM of EU trade agreements typically includes binding decisions by an arbitral panel that can also result in the suspension of the trade benefits. Instead, TSD chapters are endowed with a self-contained DSM. That mechanism is initially based on the dialogue among the parties, carried out through government consultations. Parties are requested to make every attempt to arrive at a mutually satisfactory resolution of the matter by resorting also to the TSD Committee.

Should consultations not resolve the dispute, each party can refer the issue to a 'panel of experts'. With variations, the procedure appears to be articulated as follows. The TSD Committee shall set the rules of procedures for the panel of experts by referring to those that apply to the arbitration panels set out for other kind of disputes. Moreover, the TSD Committee shall establish a list of individuals who are willing and able to serve on the panel of experts.[20] This list shall be composed of three sub-lists: one sub-list for each party and one sub-list of individuals who are not nationals of either party and who shall act as chairperson of the panel of experts. The individuals selected must be independent and have a specialised knowledge of, or expertise in, labour or environmental law and the resolution of disputes arising under international agreements. Once a request for the establishment of a panel of experts is forwarded, it is set on the basis of the more traditional arbitral panel. It is, indeed, composed of three members and the parties shall consult in order to reach an agreement on its composition as soon as possible. The task of the panel of experts for dispute settling shall be to examine, in the light of the relevant provisions of the TSD chapter, the matter referred to in the request for its establishment and to issue an interim and a final report, setting out the findings of facts, the applicability of the relevant provisions and the basic rationale behind any findings and rec-

---

[19]   For a general overview on the mechanism of dispute settlement under the TSD chapters, see Marx, Ebert, Hachez and Wouters (n 17).

[20]   International courts and tribunals are increasingly facing scientific and technical issues in their case law, and international disputes have seen greater resort to expert opinion, both by parties and adjudicators. For insights on their role in dispute settlement mechanisms see, inter alia: Cherise Valles, 'Different Forms of Expert Involvement in WTO Dispute Settlement Proceedings' (2018) 9 *Journal of International Dispute Settlement* 367; Mohamed Bennouna, 'Experts Before the International Court of Justice: What For?' (2018) 9 *Journal of International Dispute Settlement* 345.

ommendations. In this phase, individuals, as well as groups of subjects as part of civil society, can participate as *amicus curiae* by submitting observations to the TSD Committee.

Besides the fact that the commencement of the procedure is obviously based on the discretional attitude of domestic authorities, for the purposes of the present analysis, another element deserves to be stressed. Notwithstanding the implementation of the final report is monitored by the TSD Committee, no instruments for mandatory enforcement exist. In particular, no real opportunity of adopting sanctions in the form of withdrawal or suspension of trade prefer-ences in the event of non-compliance is envisaged within the EU FTAs. The only exception to such a pattern is the EU-Cariforum Trade Agreement which allows the parties to submit disputes regarding labour and environmental pro-visions to regular dispute settlement by resorting to an arbitral panel. Should the panel find a breach of the agreement's provisions, the complaining party can take 'appropriate measures' including sanctions such as cuts in the area of development cooperation.[21] Apart from this case, the regular proceeding is therefore a fact-finding and non-sanction-based procedure, which concludes with non-binding recommendations, rather than a real dispute settlement procedure.

The choice not to subject TSD chapters to a sanction-based approach is due to the European Commission, that has always refrained from considering such an option for two main reasons.[22] First, by acknowledging that for most of the Union's FTA partners these provisions are still unfamiliar, there is a wide-spread belief that cooperation and dialogue between parties having different levels of protection are more adequate tools to address non-compliance with labour and environmental standards. On the contrary, imposing strict rules on them and envisaging economic sanctions would be counterproductive or likely not accepted by the trading partners thereby narrowing down the scope of the TSD chapters.[23] Second, also with reference to well-developed partners like Canada, such a system guarantees to be anchored to the international multi-lateral system, broad in scope, with an institutionalised involvement of civil

---

[21]   Martin Gallie, 'Le droit international du travail dans la coopération Européenne au développement. Le cas de l'Accord Cariforum-CE' (2009) 1 *Revue Belge de Droit International* 195.

[22]   For insights, Kateřina Hradilová, Ondřej Svobod, 'Sustainable Development Chapters in the EU Free Trade Agreements: Searching for Effectiveness' (2018) 52 *Journal of World Trade* 1025.

[23]   These arguments have been proposed again by the EU Trade Commissioner Malmström in her Speech on Trade and Sustainable Development (Brussels, 6 October 2017) https://trade.ec.europa.eu/doclib/docs/2017/october/tradoc_156137.pdf, accessed 29 June 2021.

society. By moving from these considerations, it does not come as a surprise that, also in case of evident non-compliance, for about a decade no case regarding EU trade agreements relating to labour or environmental standards has triggered the launching of formal – even soft – dispute settlement procedures. However, as proof of the increasing interest in this field, over the last two years some members of the European Parliament,[24] EU Member States[25] and stakeholders, including NGOs and civil society, have started to call for major efforts in detecting new instruments to further foster TSD enforcement, that still appears quite weak.[26] Particular focus was dedicated to the opportunity to extend trade sanctions to situations of non-compliance with TSD provisions. On the grounds addressed in the following sections, the CJEU's arguments in Opinion 2/15 could represent an instrument of support to relevant proposals in this regard.

4.   OPINION 2/15 OF THE CJEU: WHAT IMPLICATIONS FOR DISPUTE SETTLEMENT IN THE FIELD OF TSD PROVISIONS?

On 16 May 2017, the CJEU issued its Opinion 2/15 on the requisite competence of the EU to conclude the EU-Singapore Free Trade Agreement (EUSFTA) without additional ratification by the Member States' parliaments. As is well known, the decision has produced implications that necessarily extend beyond the specific EU-Singapore relationship, by further enlarging the scope of the exclusive EU competence of the Common Commercial Policy (CCP) under Article 207(1) TFEU.[27] It resulted in a gencrous reconstruction of its EU exclu-

---

[24]   European Parliament resolution of 5 July 2016 on the implementation of the 2010 recommendations on social and environmental standards, human rights and corporate responsibility (2015/2038(INI)), http://www.europarl.europa.eu/sides/getDoc .do?pubRef=-%2f%2fEP%2f%2fTEXT%2bTA%2bP8-TA-2016-0298%2b0%2bDOC %2bXML%2bV0%2f%2fEN&language=EN, accessed 29 June 2021.

[25]   In May 2017, the trade ministers of Belgium, Sweden, Luxemburg, Finland and The Netherlands sent a letter to Commissioner Malmström calling for improving the implementation of TSD provisions in EU trade policy: Letter to EU trade Commissioner   Cecilia   Malmström   http://www.politico.eu/wp-content/uploads/ 2017/06/20170511155157994.pdf?utm_source=POLITICO.EU&utm_campaign= e95ace0190-EMAIL_CAMPAIGN_2017_06_27&utm_medium=email&utm_term=0 _10959edeb5-e95ace0190-189774485, accessed 29 June 2021.

[26]   European Commission, 'Trade and Sustainable Development (TSD) chapters in EU Free Trade Agreements (FTAs)', 11 July 2017. https://trade.ec.europa.eu/doclib/ docs/2017/july/tradoc_155686.pdfhttps://trade.ec.europa.eu/doclib/docs/2017/july/ tradoc_155686.pdf, accessed 29 June 2021.

[27]   Marise Cremona, 'Shaping EU Trade Policy post-Lisbon: Opinion 2/15 of 16 May 2017' (2018) 14 *European Constitutional Law Review* 231; Nicolas Pigeon,

sive competence. Among others, Opinion 2/15 has introduced some new and interesting elements with regard to the nature of TSD chapters. The decision brings the sustainable development provisions under the umbrella of the CCP when linked to trade and investment.[28] While the reasoning of the Court has been widely analysed in relation to the extension of the Union's competence in the field of CCP, the present chapter intends to propose that it might also have significant implications with regard to the mechanism of dispute settlement under the TSD chapters illustrated above.

According to the CJEU, trade liberalisation cannot be separated from the objectives of sustainable development of which the social protection of workers and environmental protection are mutually reinforcing components. On the contrary, they are functional to contemporary international trade and investment.[29] By combining Article 21 TEU and Articles 9, 11, 205 and 207 TFEU,[30] the Court therefore demonstrates that the TSD chapters have direct and immediate effect on trade. Indeed, the provisions on TSD reduce the risk of major disparities between the costs of producing goods and supplying services to be then traded between the partners. At the same time, they avoid environmental and labour standards being lowered to attract trade and investment, or used in a protectionist manner. However, the effects of TSD provisions on trade are even broader. Indeed, the respect of their content conditions the imports into the EU under trade agreements to the compliance with key international labour and environmental standards, which become a *conditio sine qua non* for trading with the EU.[31] Accordingly, the Court concludes that

---

'Droit primaire et compétences externes implicates. Réflexions à partir de l'avis 2/15 de la Cour de justice de l'Union européenne' in Eleftheria Neframi and Mauro Gatti (eds) *Constitutional Issues of EU External Relations Law* (Nomos 2018) 167; David Kleimann and Gesa Kübek, 'The Signing, Provisional Application, and Conclusion of Trade and Investment Agreements in the EU: The Case of CETA and Opinion 2/15' (2018) 45 *Legal Issues of Economic Integration* 13.

[28]   CJEU Opinion 2/15 (n 5), paras 147, 166. For a comment on this point, see Joris Larik, 'Trade and Sustainable Development: Opinion 2/15 and the EUs Foreign Policy Objectives' (*Europe and the World: A Law Review Blog,* 2017) www.blogs.ucl.ac.uk/europe-and-the-world-journal/, accessed 10 October 2017; Giovanni Gruni, 'Towards a Sustainable World Trade Law? The Commercial Policy of the European Union After Opinion 2/15 CJEU' (2018) 13 *Global Trade and Customs Journal* 4.

[29]   CJEU Opinion 2/15 (n 5), para 157. This expression was first used in the *Daiichi case*: CJEU Case C414/11 *Daiichi Sankyo and Sanofi-Aventis Deutschland* [2013] ECLI:EU:C:2013:520, paras 52–53.

[30]   CJEU Opinion 2/15 (n 5), paras 144–146.

[31]   Ibid., para 166:

   It follows from all of those factors that the provisions of Chapter 13 of the envisaged agreement are intended not to regulate the levels of social and environmental protection in the Parties' respective territory but to govern trade between the

the provisions embodied within the TSD chapters 'play an *essential role* in the envisaged agreement'.[32]

The reasoning proposed by the Court in Opinion 2/15 is supported by a wider interpretation of the text and, above all, of the preamble of the new EU FTAs, according to Article 31(2) of the Vienna Convention on the Law of the Treaties (VCLT). Indeed, preambles, despite not having the function of laying down legal obligations, are part of the *narratio* of the agreement and may have a strong legal significance if both the motives and the aims of the treaty are mentioned in specific terms. In addition to the primarily interpretative function, preambles may also have an incorporative function by including clauses that aim at explicitly taking into account another treaty or a part of another treaty when applying the provisions.[33] That said, two main elements in the preamble of the EUSFTA may justify the CJEU's position. First, recital 4 underlines the determination of the contracting parties to strengthen and to promote trade and investment according to internationally recognised standards and agreements in the field of environment and labour to which they adhere. Second, the very first recital of the preamble refers to the Partnership and Cooperation Agreement between the EU and Singapore.[34] Such an agreement, which represents the general legal framework of the bilateral cooperation, explicitly sets respect of international human rights as an essential element of the agreement.[35] Even more importantly, in the mentioned framework agreement, the sustainable development objectives are explicitly listed within the general principles and among the basis for cooperation.[36] Bilateral trade cannot therefore disregard the respect of TSD provisions that explicitly shape and give substance to the obligations enshrined in the framework agreement. A comprehensive reading of the preamble might, therefore, justify the interpretation given by the Court in relation to the definition of the TSD provisions as essential elements of the agreement.

European Union and the Republic of Singapore by making liberalisation of that trade subject to the condition that the Parties comply with their international obligations concerning social protection of workers and environmental protection.

[32]   Ibid., para 162.

[33]   Makane Moïse Mbengue, 'Preamble' *The Max Planck Encyclopedia of Public International Law* (2006).

[34]   The Partnership and Cooperation Agreement (PCA) between the EU, its Member States, and Singapore provides a general framework on issues such as health, environment, climate change, energy tax, education and culture, labour, employment and social affairs, science and technology, and transport. The agreement was signed on 19 October 2018 and is now waiting for ratification by all EU Member States before entering into force.

[35]   Art 1(1) of the PCA between the EU, its Member States, and Singapore.

[36]   Ibid., Art 1(3).

In rendering such an interpretation, the Court has responded to the necessity of ensuring an adequate and uniform application of EU law requiring, inter alia, the integration of the objectives enshrined in the treaties within the EU policies. More specifically, it has recalled the obligation for the EU to abide by and pursue non-commercial objectives within the field of trade. Besides that, as anticipated, it is reasonable to think that the Court's interpretation might have important consequences with regard to the enforcement phase of the dispute settlement procedure envisaged in the TSD chapters. As recalled by the Court itself, the rule of customary international law codified in Article 60(1) VCLT provides that the violation of essential provisions of a treaty can amount to a material breach, therefore justifying the suspension or termination of the operation of the treaty. In the case of trade agreements, the violation of the essential clauses could imply the suspension of liberalisation of trade or other countermeasures that are proportionate to the violation. Accordingly, the attribution of an essential role to the TSD provisions of the FTA could have not just a theoretical relevance: their breach can potentially trigger the termination or suspension of the liberalisation of bilateral trade.[37]

By keeping in mind the structure of the recent FTAs, even though Opinion 2/15 concerns just the EUSFTA, the Court's reasoning can be generalised and applied to all the new generation FTAs. Therefore, in theory, it could greatly influence the practice of the enforcement of the TSD provisions. Indirectly, it could reshape the final outcome of the dispute settlement procedure envisaged in the TSD chapters that, as reported in the previous section, is based on a non-sanction approach. In the light of this new scenario, should the counterpart persistently fail to comply with those provisions that are deemed as essential prerequisites for bilateral trade, sanctions or other appropriate measures could be adopted.

In this regard, it is appropriate to reflect on one point. Until Opinion 2/15, such an essential role was reserved to the respect for human rights and democratic principles generally acknowledged in the preamble of the agreements. By way of illustration, the 2013 EU-Colombia/Peru Free Trade Agreement reads as follows: 'respect for democratic principles and fundamental human rights, as laid down in the Universal Declaration of Human Rights, and for the principle of the rule of law, underpins the internal and international policies of the Parties. Respect for these principles constitutes an essential element of this Agreement'. The 'essential elements clause' enshrined in that treaty was therefore intended to flank trade agreements with hard 'human rights conditionality' consequently reflecting the Union's tendency to use trade as

---

[37]   CJEU Opinion 2/15 (n 5), para 161.

an instrument for promoting the respect of human rights and global values.[38] Admittedly, considering that the EU has a right to adopt appropriate measures but not an obligation to do so,[39] essential elements clauses on human rights have often met a weaker application in practice.[40] Moreover, it is interesting to note that in the more recent FTAs, including that with Singapore, there is no longer any explicit reference to the respect of human rights and related international instruments as essential elements of the agreement.

By the TSD provisions being comprised in the essential elements of the trade agreements, the Court has *de facto* reopened the doors to the essential element clause. However, in comparison to the classical clause on human rights, two main issues contribute to suggest hard TSD enforcement as more likely in terms of feasibility. First of all, when dealing with TSD provisions, the essential element clause is anchored to an entire chapter of the FTA comprising clear obligations for the parties and not just to a single and generic recital of the preamble. Alongside a well-established institutional structure of monitoring, this contributes to give more substance to the content of the clause at stake. The second argument is that, for the reasons reported by the Court, TSD provisions have a direct and immediate effect on trade flows.

---

[38] The first operative human rights clause was inserted in Art 1(1) of the 1990 Framework Agreement for trade and economic cooperation between the European Economic Community and the Argentine Republic. More recently, Art 8(3) of the 2012 EU–Colombia/Peru Trade Agreement provides that 'any Party may immediately adopt appropriate measures in accordance with international law in case of violation by another Party of the essential elements referred to in Articles 1 and 2 of this Agreement'. Similarly, the 2012 EU-Central America agreement explicitly states (Art 1) that:

> [t]he respect for democratic principles and fundamental human rights, as laid down in the Universal Declaration of Human Rights, and for the principle of the rule of law, underpins the internal and international policies of both Parties and constitutes an essential element of this Agreement.

[39] CJEU Case C-581/11 P *Mugraby v Council and Commission*, Order of 12 July 2012 ECLI:EU:C:2012:466, para 70.

[40] For example, since 2000 the Council has suspended development aids to Fiji (2000, 2007), Zimbabwe (2002), the Central African Republic (2003), Guinea-Bissau (2004, 2011), Togo (2004) and Madagascar (2010) on the basis of Art 96 of the Cotonou Agreement regulating the relations between the EU and the African, Caribbean and Pacific (ACP) countries. However, the Council applies the conditionality policies in an inconsistent way and according to a double standard as deplored more than once by the European Parliament (European Parliament resolution on the human rights and democracy clause in European Union agreements (2005/2057(INI)), 14 February 2006, OJ C290E/107). For insights, see Lorand Bartels, *The Application of Human Rights Conditionality in the EU's Trade Agreements and Other Trade Arrangements with Third Countries European Parliament Directorate for External Relations* (European Parliament 2008).

Products imported and exported under trade agreements must respect key international labour and environmental standards. The persistent violation of TSD provisions cannot therefore be tolerated, because it risks jeopardising not only international labour and environmental protection requirements, but also the process of bilateral trade liberalisation. To comply with TSD standards is not just an ambitious value-related objective, but a concrete trade-related challenge.

It is evident that such a perspective can only reinforce the position of those pushing towards the introduction of more assertive enforcement solutions envisaging also trade sanctions when actions are not satisfactory and compliance concerns persist. However, starting from the Court's conclusion, further clarification with regard to some critical points would be needed. *In primis*, without a clear reference to such eventuality in the text of the agreements and contextual discussions among the parties, it is necessary to carefully explore the typology and the temporal extent of the measures to be effectively adopted. In particular, it should be determined whether to envisage either the total suspension of trade benefits or other measures other than trade sanctions, as in the case of the EU-Cariforum agreement. Moreover, for requiring compensation there would be the need to quantify the economic damage resulting from a breach of social or environmental standards, without undermining their effective and lasting improvement on the ground.

Against this background, in the coming years it will have to be seen whether and how the interpretation adopted by the Court on the essential nature of the TSD provisions will be reconciled with these practical concerns. At this stage, the dispute between the EU and the Republic of Korea, to which the following section is devoted, has not only represented a step forward in testing TSD enforcement but also, hopefully, triggered a new debate on the potential implications of the Court's orientation for the DSM envisaged in the TSD chapters.

5. THE FIRST EVER BILATERAL CONSULTATIONS UNDER THE TSD CHAPTER OF A FREE TRADE AGREEMENT

The KOREU agreement was the first of the 'new generation' comprehensive EU FTAs and it was concluded as mixed agreement by the EU and its Member States. As a new generation agreement, it also contains a TSD chapter structured according to the general model reported in the previous sections. The provisions contained therein must be read in conjunction with the bilateral

Framework Agreement,[41] which includes the promotion of sustainable development among the basis for cooperation between the parties. The Committee on Trade and Sustainable Development (CTSD) of the KOREU agreement was constituted in 2012 in order to exchange the reciprocal commitments taken under the agreement.

On occasion of the various CTSD's meetings, Union representatives have often underlined the shortcomings concerning labour policy and urged Korea to move to the appropriate level of engagement for making progress on the implementation of shared labour standards. However, for some time, the former Trade Commissioner, Karel De Gucht, refrained from initiating formal consultations with the Korean Government on this matter,[42] preferring to deal with the issue through informal discussions.[43] Tensions escalated with the imprisonment of the President of the Korean Confederation of Trade Unions, the statement of the EU-Korea Civil Society Forum,[44] and the report of the Special Rapporteur of the human rights council.[45] In 2016, the chair of the EU-Korea Domestic Advisory Group wrote to Trade Commissioner Malmström, recalling the major concerns related to the weakening of the freedom of association and labour rights and recommending the opening of formal consultations under Article 13 of the KOREU agreement.[46] The European Parliament has also constantly expressed its concerns about the lack of progress in the area of labour rights in Korea. In 2017, both the European Parliament in its

---

[41] Framework Agreement between the European Union and its Member States, on the one part, and the Republic of Korea, on the other part (Brussels, 10 May 2010).

[42] Thomas Jenkins, Chair of the EU-Korea Domestic Advisory Group, 'Serious Violations of Chapter 13 of the EU-Korea FTA' Letter to Karel de Gucht (13 January 2014).

[43] Lore Van den Putte, 'Involving Civil Society in Social Clauses and the Decent Work Agenda' (2015) 6 *Global Labour Journal* 229.

[44] Conclusions by the EU-Korea Civil Society Forum on occasion of the 4th meeting held in Seoul, 10 September 2015, https://www.eesc.europa.eu/resources/docs/eu-korea-csf-conclusions_september-2015_en_final-version.pdf, accessed 29 June 2021.

[45] Report of the Special Rapporteur on the rights to freedom of peaceful assembly and of association on his mission to the Republic of Korea (15 June 2016) UN Doc. A/HRC/32/36/Add.2.

[46] Letter on Government Consultations Pursuant to the EU-Korea FTA issued by Georgi Stoev, Thomas Jenkins and Gaelle Dusepulchre to Commissioner Cecilia Malmström (Brussels, 16 December 2016) http://ec.europa.eu/carol/?fuseaction=download&documentId=090166e5af1bf802&title=EU_DAG%20letter%20to%20Commissioner%20Malmstrom_signed%20by%20the%20Chair%20and%20Vice-Chairs.pdf, accessed 10 October 2017.

Resolution[47] and the European Economic and Social Committee (EESC) in its Opinion, highlighted these areas as unsatisfactory.[48]

On 17 December 2018, the EU activated the formal dispute settlement procedure under Article 13.14, para 1, of the KOREU agreement, regarding labour commitments. In its communication to the Korean authorities,[49] the Union has challenged a number of provisions of the Korean Trade Union Act[50] and of the Korean Criminal Code.[51] In particular, the EU questioned the excessively narrow scope of the 'worker' concept in the Trade Union Act, which excluded individuals in 'special employment' categories; the denial of legal recognition to trade unions admitting members who are not workers; the arbitrary operation of a trade union establishment reporting system and judicial practices punishing peaceful strikes as criminal 'obstruction of duties'. Therefore, according to the EU, the contested provisions violated Article 13.4, para 3, of the KOREU agreement, under which the parties commit to respect, promote and realise the principles concerning fundamental rights in accordance with the obligations deriving from their membership to the ILO.[52] A number of legislative and administrative reforms on labour in South Korea were therefore necessary. The Union also complained that Korea's efforts towards ratifying the four fundamental ILO Conventions, after more than seven years from the entry into force of the KOREU agreement,[53] remained inadequate. The conventions to be ratified generally concerned the strengthening of basic labour rights, such as guaranteeing the rights of individuals to organise a group to represent themselves and to take action to defend such rights. The persistent

---

[47]   European Parliament resolution of 18 May 2017 on the implementation of the Free Trade Agreement between the European Union and the Republic of Korea (2015/2059/INI), para 5.

[48]   European Economic and Social Committee opinion of 17 October 2017 on EU-Korea Free Trade Agreement – Trade and Sustainable Development Chapter (REX/479-EESC-2017-2894), para 6.

[49]   The official document adopted by the EU on the request for consultations is available at http://trade.ec.europa.eu/doclib/docs/2018/december/tradoc_157586.pdf, accessed 29 June 2021.

[50]   Korean Trade Union and Labour Relations Adjustment Act, Act No. 5310, adopted on 13 March 1997.

[51]   Criminal Code of the Republic of Korea, adopted on 3 October 1953.

[52]   The Follow-up of the ILO Declaration on Fundamental Principles and Rights at Work was adopted by the ILO at its Eighty-sixth Session held in Geneva on 18 June 1998 and was revised in 2010.

[53]   The EU refers to four Conventions adopted within the framework of the ILO that are the Convention on the Freedom of Association and Protection of the Right to Organise (1948); the Convention on the Right to Organise and Collective Bargaining (1949); the Convention on Forced Labour (1930) and the Convention on the Abolition of Forced Labour (1957).

delay in ratifying the ILO Conventions represented a violation of the KOREU agreement.

On the basis of such allegations, the EU promoted the opening of the government consultations with the Korean domestic authorities. The Korean President Moon was confirmed as being committed on the implementation of priority tasks for building a society where labour is respected and on the pursuit of the ratification of the ILO's core conventions. Despite such promises, after the period of 90 days following the request of government consultations, Commissioner Malmström recognised that the Korean Government failed to produce substantive evidence of concrete steps to address the above EU concerns.[54] The government consultations were not therefore satisfactory. As a result, on 4 July 2019, the Commission requested the convening of a panel of experts under Article 13.15 of the KOREU agreement.[55] On 20 January 2021, the panel issued the report confirming the EU's concerns that Korea has not acted consistently with its trade and sustainable development obligations under the EU-Korea trade agreement. The independent Panel concluded that Korea needs to adjust its labour laws and practices and to continue swiftly the process of ratifying four fundamental ILO Conventions in order to comply with the agreement, and in particular with the principle of freedom of association. Finally, the panel confirmed the EU's arguments that the two commitments at issue are legally binding and have to be respected regardless of their effect on trade.[56]

At the moment, it is premature to speculate on the possible outcomes of the procedure and of the reasoning proposed by the panel of experts. So far, the European Commission has refrained from addressing options of hard enforcement and the parties have not discussed potential consequences in the case of persistent non-compliance. However, since Korea is still tackling serious problems in compliance with labour standards, by taking into account the CJEU's orientation, it is not unreasonable to expect change. In particular, should the Korean Government not properly align with the final report of the panel of experts, it cannot be totally excluded that the Union could decide to take proportionate countermeasures against Korea, as instruments of last resort,

---

[54] Letter of Commissioner Cecilia Malmström to the Korean Minister of Trade (Brussels, 4 March 2019) http://trade.ec.europa.eu/doclib/docs/2019/march/tradoc_157723.pdf, accessed 29 June 2021.

[55] Republic of Korea – compliance with obligations under Chapter 13 of the EU – Korea Free Trade Agreement, Request for the establishment of a Panel of Experts by the European Union (Brussels, 4 July 2019) http://trade.ec.europa.eu/doclib/docs/2019/july/tradoc_157992.pdf, accessed 29 June 2021.

[56] Panel of experts proceeding constituted under Article 13.15 of the EU-Korea Free Trade Agreement, Report of the Panel of Experts, 20 January 2021.

because of the violation of essential elements of the agreement. The EU/South Korea has therefore become a major test case for evaluating the effectiveness of the DSM concerning violations of labour conditions under a FTA. However, the next steps will also be crucial for verifying whether, and how, the theory addressed in the present chapter can be reflected in reality.

6.   CONCLUSIONS

In the aftermath of the entry into force of the Lisbon Treaty, the growing presence of the EU within the international trading system, accompanied by the progressive extension of the material scope of the CCP due to the jurisprudence of the CJEU, has resulted in a considerable reshaping of the content of trade agreements. The 'new generation' FTAs now embody well-developed and integrated provisions and chapters aimed at fulfilling new objectives, including sustainable development in the field of trade, that is strictly linked to the respect of environmental and labour standards. By going beyond the classical analysis of the substantial content of the so-called TSD chapters, the present contribution has intended to present an overview of the main elements that characterise the procedure for settling disputes arising from the non-compliance with TSD provisions.

The model of dispute settlement envisaged in the TSD chapters can be compared to conciliation as, after a first phase based on political dialogue, the panel of experts convened by the parties is required to investigate and produce a report on the facts surrounding the dispute. In comparison to arbitration, the report is not binding and the parties involved may freely decide whether or not to give it any effect. As a result, no opportunity of adopting sanctions in the case of non-compliance with the final report of the panel of experts is apparently envisaged. This chapter was aimed at proposing a different outcome by applying a wider reading of Opinion 2/15, wherein the CJEU has defined the content of the TSD chapters as essential elements of the FTAs concluded by the EU. According to this perspective, should the counterparty persistently fail to comply with those provisions that are deemed as essential prerequisites for bilateral trade, sanctions or other appropriate measures could be adopted. Hence, the essential character of the TSD provisions would indirectly reinforce the recommendations issued by the panel of experts, thereby partially impinging on the soft outcome of the dispute settlement procedure.

In recent times, the partially unsatisfactory state of affairs concerning the compliance with labour and environmental standards has invoked a renewed debate within the EU. The European Commission has demonstrated itself to be ready to follow the Court's orientation by paving the way for a more effective application of the DSM enshrined in the TSD chapters. As a result of multiple calls, in February 2018, the Commission services issued a non-paper for improving implementation and enforcement of TSD chapters in EU FTAs.[57] Interestingly, the non-paper stresses that, should the results of these proceedings not be satisfactory, 'the Commission might explore ways to learn from them to keep ensuring compliance'.[58] Regarding the enforcement phase, the non-paper reports the Commission's intentions to step up the monitoring and analysis of compliance with TSD commitments, by sending letters to partner countries setting out concerns and measures to be taken. The action against the Republic of Korea falls exactly into this perspective, and it will be quite interesting to see what steps (possible) future dispute settlement procedures under a TSD chapter will take.

---

[57] European Commission Services, 'Feedback and way forward on improving the implementation and enforcement of Trade and Sustainable Development chapters in EU Free Trade Agreements' (26 February 2018).
[58] Ibid., 8.

PART II

Promoting dialogue in the EU external
economic relations. Dialogue by treaty drafting

7. The price for a seat at the ISDS reform table: CJEU's clearance of the EU's investment protection policy in Opinion 1/17 and its impact on the EU constitutional order

Steffen Hindelang[1]

1. INTRODUCTION

In 2009, the European Union's (EU) Common Commercial Policy was explicitly extended to foreign direct investment. Since then, the EU has expanded its increasingly ambitious agenda on negotiating investment agreements with major trading partners and reforming the prevalent investment law regime and its encrusted structures.

The EU's policy approach has undergone remarkable development. At the beginning, the EU largely sought to adhere to and to perpetuate the protection regime essentially created in the course of decolonisation after the Second World War,[2] as evidenced by the 2013 and 2014 drafts of the Comprehensive Economic and Trade Agreement (CETA) with Canada.[3] Public pressure forced

---

[1] I wish to thank Niels Lachmann for helpful comments on and editing of earlier drafts. Thanks are also due to Jane Kvist Poulsen for her editorial support. Errors remain my own.

[2] The first 'modern' bilateral investment agreement which contained essentially the same substantive protection standard found in the majority of today's bilateral investment agreements was the Germany-Pakistan Treaty for the promotion and protection of investments (with protocol and exchange of notes) (25 November 1959) 457 UNTS 23. Arguably, the first bilateral investment agreement with a bifurcated consent to arbitrate was the Netherlands-Indonesia Agreement on economic cooperation (with protocol and exchanges of letters) (7 July 1968) 799 UNTS 13. See Love Rönnelid, 'The Emergence of Routine Enforcement of International Investment Law' (PhD dissertation, Uppsala University 2018) 130 and 135.

[3] See Steffen Hindelang, 'Study on Investor-State Dispute Settlement (ISDS) and Alternatives of Dispute Resolution in International Investment Law' in Pieter Jan

the EU to explore different avenues. Investment agreements, such as the CETA,[4] or those with Singapore and Vietnam respectively, have brought about the so-called 'Investment Court System' (ICS).[5] The ICS is a hybrid form of arbitration with, inter alia, a government-appointed roster of arbitrators and an appeals mechanism. Even more ambitiously, the EU in the United Nations Commission on International Trade Law (UNCITRAL) Working Group III is

---

Kuijper, Ingolf Pernice, Steffen Hindelang, Michael Schwarz and Martin Reuling, *Investor-State Dispute Settlement (ISDS) Provisions in the EU's International Investment Agreements. Volume 2 – Studies* (European Parliament 2014), 51–114.

[4]   Comprehensive Economic and Trade Agreement (CETA) between Canada, of the one part, and the European Union and its Member States, of the other part [2017] OJ L11/23 (CETA). In October 2019, the European Commission presented its procedural proposals for the so-called Investment Court System contained in the Comprehensive Economic and Trade Agreement: European Commission, 'Proposal for a Council Decision on the position to be taken on behalf of the European Union in the CETA Joint Committee established under the Comprehensive Economic and Trade Agreement (CETA) between Canada, of the one part, and the European Union and its Member States, of the other part as regards the adoption of a decision setting out the administrative and organisational matters regarding the functioning of the Appellate Tribunal' COM (2019) 457 final; 'Proposal for a Council Decision on the position to be taken on behalf of the European Union in the CETA Joint Committee established under the Comprehensive Economic and Trade Agreement (CETA) between Canada, of the one part, and the European Union and its Member States, of the other part as regards the adoption of a decision on the procedure for the adoption of interpretations in accordance with Articles 8.31.3 and 8.44.3(a) of CETA as Annex to its Rules of Procedure' COM (2019) 458 final; 'Proposal for a Council Decision on the position to be taken on behalf of the European Union in the Committee on Services and Investment established under the Comprehensive Economic and Trade Agreement (CETA) between Canada, of the one part, and the European Union and its Member States, of the other part as regards the adoption of a code of conduct for Members of the Tribunal, the Appellate Tribunal and mediators' COM (2019) 459 final; 'Proposal for a Council Decision on the position to be taken on behalf of the European Union in the Committee on Services and Investment established under the Comprehensive Economic and Trade Agreement (CETA) between Canada, of the one part, and the European Union and its Member States, of the other part as regards the adoption of rules for mediation for use by disputing parties in investment disputes' COM (2019) 460 final.

[5]   Steffen Hindelang and Carl-Philipp Sassenrath, *The Investment Chapters of the EU's International Trade and Investment Agreements in a Comparative Perspective* (European Parliament 2015); Steffen Hindelang and Teoman Hagemeyer, *In Pursuit of an International Investment Court. Recently Negotiated Investment Chapters in EU Comprehensive Free Trade Agreements in Comparative Perspective* (European Parliament 2017); Steffen Hindelang, Teoman M Hagemeyer and Simon Richtmann, *Study on Free Trade Agreement between the EU and the Socialist Republic of Vietnam submitted to the European Parliament* (unpublished 2018). Somewhat problematic – at least from a capital export perspective – is the fact that substantive investment protection standards saw a significant reduction of its protective scope.

currently pressing for the establishment of a multilateral investment court[6] to eventually replace the widely used arbitration model to settle investor-state disputes.

All of these developments could have been brought to an abrupt halt, perhaps even to an end, if the Court of Justice of the European Union (CJEU) had decided differently in its Opinion 1/17 on the CETA.[7] The CJEU, however, concluded that the CETA's investment provisions are in compliance with the EU Treaties; this judgment is not just of considerable political importance, but also has significant consequences for the EU constitutional order. This chapter will explore the said consequences – or the price to be paid – of clearing the way for investor-state dispute settlement (ISDS) in EU agreements with third countries. In order to do so, this chapter will first briefly present the CJEU's analysis of the CETA, focusing on the principle of autonomy of EU law, which proved again to be one of the major touchstones of dispute settlement in international agreements (below 2).[8] On this basis, the chapter then proceeds

---

[6] See UNCITRAL, Submission of the European Union and its Member States to UNCITRAL Working Group III: establishing a standing mechanism for the settlement of international investment disputes [2019].

[7] Opinion 1/17 *EU-Canada CET Agreement* [2019] ECLI:EU:C:2019:341; see the assessments by: Nikos Lavranos, 'CJEU *Opinion 1/17*: Keeping International Investment Law and EU Law Strictly Apart' (2019) 4 *European Investment Law and Arbitration Review* 240; Christian Riffel, 'The CETA Opinion of the European Court of Justice and its Implications – Not that Selfish After All' (2019) 22 *Journal of International Economic Law* 503; Patricia Sarah Stöbener de Mora and Stephan Wernicke, 'Riskante Vorgaben für Investitionsschutz und Freihandel – Das CETA-Gutachten des EuGH' (2019) 30 *Europäische Zeitschrift für Wirtschaftsrecht* 970; Panos Koutrakos, 'More on Autonomy – Opinion 1/17 (CETA)' (2019) 44 *European Law Review* 293; Simas Grigonis, 'Investment Court System of CETA: Adverse Effects on the Autonomy of EU Law and Possible Solutions' (2019) 5 *International Comparative Jurisprudence* 127.

[8] Developed in a series of opinions and judgements, most recently in Case C-284/16 *Slovak Republic v Achmea BV* [2018] ECLI:EU:C:158. See also Opinion 1/91 *Draft agreement between the Community, on the one hand, and the countries of the European Free Trade Association, on the other, relating to the creation of the European Economic Area* [1991] ECLI:EU:C:1991:490, para 35; Opinion 1/00 *Proposed agreement between the European Community and non-Member States on the establishment of a European Common Aviation Area* [2002] ECLI:EU:C:2002:231, paras 11–12; Opinion 1/09 *Draft agreement – Creation of a unified patent litigation system – European and Community Patents Court – Compatibility of the draft agreement with the Treaties* [2011] ECLI:EU:C:2011:123, para 77; Opinion 2/13 *Draft international agreement – Accession of the European Union to the European Convention for the Protection of Human Rights and Fundamental Freedoms – Compatibility of the draft agreement with the EU and FEU Treaties* [2014] ECLI:EU:C:2014:2454; and Case C-196/09 *Paul Miles and Others v Écoles Européennes* [2011] ECLI:EU:C:2011: 388.

to highlight three dimensions in which Opinion 1/17 will possibly impact (the further development of) the EU constitutional order (below 3). First, the CJEU might find itself more often involved in judicial conflicts with adjudicative bodies that have been established on the basis of EU agreements. This may eventually lead to ISDS's '*Kadi* moment' (below 3.1). Second, by allowing different standards when reviewing the exercise of sovereign powers inside and outside the EU judicial system,[9] Opinion 1/17 essentially gave the green light to a reshaping of the EU's rule of law (below 3.2). Third, the EU constitutionality of both the Member States' bilateral investment agreements (BITs) with third countries and the application of the Energy Charter Treaty (ECT)[10] in disputes with non-EU investors must be reassessed in light of the CJEU's reading of the principle of autonomy of EU law in Opinion 1/17 and the clarity gained in that respect (below 3.3). The chapter closes with a summary assessment of the observed impacts (below 4).

2. THE REQUIREMENTS STIPULATED BY THE PRINCIPLE OF AUTONOMY OF EU LAW FOR A DISPUTE SETTLEMENT BODY ADJUDICATING DISPUTES BETWEEN PRIVATE ENTITIES AND THE EU AND ITS MEMBER STATES

In order to secure the uniform interpretation and equal application of EU law, the EU Treaties in Article 19 of the Treaty on European Union (TEU) as well as Articles 251 through 281 and 344 of the Treaty on the Functioning of the European Union (TFEU) have vested in the CJEU a monopoly in authoritatively determining the content and meaning of EU law and controlling its lawful application. The CJEU has secured this monopoly by developing the principle of autonomy of EU law.[11] Over time, this principle has morphed into

---

[9]   The EU judicial system relates to the CJEU and the EU Member State courts and tribunals: see Case C-192/18 *Commission v Poland (Independence of the ordinary courts)* [2019] ECLI:EU:C:2019:924, paras 98–106.

[10]   The Energy Charter Treaty (1994) 2080 UNTS 95.

[11]   See most recently: Niamh Nic Shuibhne, 'What is the Autonomy of EU Law, and Why Does that Matter' (2019) 88 *Nordic Journal of International Law* 9; Panos Koutrakos, 'The Autonomy of EU Law and International Investment Arbitration' (2019) 88 *Nordic Journal of International Law* 41; Violeta Moreno-Lax, 'The Axiological Emancipation of a (Non-)Principle: Autonomy, International Law and the EU Legal Order' in Inge Govaere and Sacha Garben (eds), *The Interface Between EU and International Law: Contemporary Reflections* (Hart Publishing 2019) 45–71.

a comprehensive concept of EU self-assertion that limits the effects of public international law on EU law.[12]

While the CJEU applied the principle to an intra-EU context in *Achmea*,[13] in Opinion 1/17, it stipulated a two-pronged test for assessing the constitutionality of a dispute settlement body that adjudicates disputes between *third country* private entities and the EU and its Member States. The opinion held, first, that courts or tribunals that have been established on the basis of an agreement between the EU, its Member States, and third countries, may not interpret or apply EU law. They shall treat it as fact only (below 2.1). Second, activities of the aforesaid courts or tribunals may not produce (significant) spill-over effects on the operation of the EU constitutional order (below 2.2).

2.1 Jus Nostrum: No Outsourcing of the Definitive Determinations on the Application and Interpretation of EU Law

The CETA constitutes an agreement between a third country, Canada, on the one hand, and the EU and its Member States, on the other. An adjudicative body[14] established on the basis of the agreement may decide a dispute by applying and interpreting the CETA, other rules and principles of international law applicable between the parties to the agreement.[15] EU law may be taken into consideration as fact only.[16]

From an international investment law perspective, the CETA's applicable law clause is not an unusual means – though not a compelling one[17] – of excluding the respective 'local law' of the parties to the agreement from the spectrum of applicable law.[18] From an EU law angle, it is – to follow the

---

[12]   Opinion 1/17 (n 7), paras 106–111; see the assessments in: Steffen Hindelang, 'Conceptualisation and Application of the Principle of Autonomy of EU law – the CJEU's Judgment in Achmea Put in Perspective' (2019) 44 *European Law Review* 383; Steffen Hindelang, 'Repellent Forces: the CJEU and Investor-State Dispute Settlement' (2015) 53 *Archiv des Völkerrecht* 68.

[13]   *Achmea* (n 8); see Hindelang, 'Conceptualisation and Application of the Principle of Autonomy of EU Law' (n 12).

[14]   The CETA in Art 8.27 refers to 'Tribunal' and in Art 8.28 to an 'Appellate Tribunal', while according to Art 8.29, eventually this arbitration solution shall be replaced by a permanent international court.

[15]   Ibid., Art 8.31.1.

[16]   Ibid., Art 8.31.2.

[17]   See the CJEU's considerations on applicable law in relation to the BIT underpinning the arbitration in the *Achmea* judgment: *Achmea* (n 8), paras 39–60.

[18]   According to a report by the Organisation for Economic Cooperation and Development, in the early 2010s, about 32 per cent of the sample investment treaties contained language on the applicable law, and 23 per cent of sample investment treaties referenced domestic law: Organisation for Economic Co-operation and Development,

CJEU – not just an option, but a constitutional *conditio sine qua non* to prevent a 'non-EU court', given that it is unable to refer questions for preliminary ruling to the CJEU in accordance with Article 267 of the TFEU, from applying EU law as law; to secure a uniform interpretation and application of EU law, the EU Treaties through Article 19 of the TEU have vested the CJEU with *exclusive* jurisdiction to render *definite* decisions in this respect.[19] For the sake of maintaining 'the power of the Union in international relations',[20] however, an adjudicative body that is outside the EU judicial system, established on the basis of an international agreement with a third country is allowed to render binding decisions upon the EU (and its Member States) by the way of applying and interpreting the respective *agreement*.[21]

To avoid the EU being an outsider on the international scene, the Court's further development of the principle of autonomy of EU law in Opinion 1/17 may appear sensible and balanced. It was, however, neither compelling nor necessarily expected when considering the CJEU's previous jurisprudence.[22] According to this, an international agreement in which the EU is a party forms an integral part of EU law.[23] If the CJEU had emphasised this perspective on the CETA, it could well have concluded that its jurisdictional monopoly extended to the said international agreements, thereby excluding essentially any dispute settlement mechanism external to the EU judicial system. This step was seemingly too daring even for the CJEU to take. Thus, the interpretation and application of EU law – as a kind of *jus nostrum* – is the exclusive domain of the CJEU, bound together with the courts and tribunals of the EU Member States in the 'judicial dialogue' enshrined in Article 267 of the TFEU.[24] International agreements with third countries such as the CETA are not perceived as *jus nostrum,* but rather law 'shared' among the EU and the

---

'Dispute settlement provisions in international investment agreements: A large sample survey' (Organisation for Economic Co-operation and Development 2012), paras 80–81   www.oecd.org/investment/internationalinvestmentagreements/50291678.pdf, accessed 11 February 2020.

[19]   Opinion 1/17 (n 7), para 111.

[20]   Ibid., para 117.

[21]   Ibid., para 118.

[22]   Cf Jacob Grierson, 'The Court of Justice of the European Union and International Arbitration' [2019] 2 *b-Arbitra – Belgian Review of Arbitration* 309.

[23]   See Case C-240/09, *Lesoochranárske zoskupenie VLK v Ministerstvo životného prostredia Slovenskej republiky Slovak Ministry* [2011] ECLI:EU:C:2011:125, paras 29–36 and the cases cited therein.

[24]   The EU Member States by virtue of the EU Treaties have chosen to have their relationship inter se 'governed by EU law to the exclusion [...] of any other law', if EU law so requires: Opinion 2/13 (n 8), para 212.

third country parties in the agreement, in which no claim to jurisdictional exclusivity is made.

Furthermore, the CJEU in Opinion 1/17 notes in this context[25] that its 'exclusive jurisdiction […] to give rulings on the division of powers between the Union and its Member States' is preserved in the agreement, as CETA-based adjudicative bodies do not enjoy:

> the power to determine, when a Canadian investor seeks to challenge measures adopted by a Member State and/or by the Union, whether the dispute is, in the light of the rules on the division of powers between the Union and its Member States, to be brought against that Member State or against the Union.[26]

The CJEU, seeking to justify this very statement against the backdrop of its earlier jurisprudence, limited itself to the brief declaration that the CETA, in this respect, is different from the draft agreement on the accession of the EU to the Convention for the Protection of Human Rights and Fundamental Freedoms, known as the European Convention on Human Rights (ECHR) that was the subject of Opinion 2/13.[27] A closer look at both CJEU opinions reveals, however, that such an assertion may be motivated more by legal policy rather than prudent comparative analysis. In fact, both agreements, the CETA and the ECHR, allow a determination on the division of powers in the EU's constitutional order, binding both the EU and its Member States, *without* recourse to the CJEU.[28] This is due to the fact that, according to CETA, the investor is given a residual right to determine the proper respondent in case the EU fails to do so. In exercising this right, amongst others, the investor must establish whether it was adversely affected 'exclusively [by] measures of a Member State' or also by 'measures of the European Union'.[29] The two phrases are not further defined in the CETA, and thus leave the investor with complicated questions regarding attribution and division of competences between the EU and its Member States. Investors therefore appear to be given considerable leeway – and margin for error – in assessing whether a measure qualifies as being attributable to either the EU or to a Member State, especially when it comes to acts of the EU Member States implementing EU law. In Opinion 2/13 on the ECHR, the CJEU was not prepared to accept the alloca-

---

[25] That the CJEU mentions this issue in the context of discussing the applicable law question is a bit surprising as it actually relates to the factual spill-over effects on the EU constitutional order to which the Court turns later in its analysis.

[26] Opinion 1/17 (n 7), para 132.

[27] Referring to Opinion 2/13 (n 8), paras 224–231.

[28] For a closer analysis, see Hindelang, 'Repellent Forces: the CJEU and Investor-State Dispute Settlement' (n 12), 80–83.

[29] Art 8.21.4 CETA.

tion of any such competence to the recognised international adjudicative body of the European Court of Human Rights (ECtHR).[30] With regard to the CETA, however, the CJEU seems to have considerably more faith in the legal abilities of the investor (and its advisors). Coming as somewhat of a surprise perhaps, the CJEU in Opinion 1/17 indeed teaches us that handing over such powers to a disputing party, i.e., the investor – and this is indeed the difference between the CETA and the ECHR, where the ECtHR would make such determinations – does little to threaten the principle of autonomy of EU law.

2.2   Autonomy also from those not Formally Applying and Interpreting EU Law – the CJEU's Spill-Over Test

Even if an international adjudicative body does not apply and interpret EU law as law, but treats it as fact,[31] its decisions can nonetheless lead to an adverse factual impact – i.e., spill-over effects[32] – on the EU legal order and its autonomy from international law. Indeed, Opinion 1/17 outlines that if an adjudicative body, such as one formed on the basis of the CETA:

> were to have jurisdiction to issue awards finding that the treatment of a Canadian investor is incompatible with the CETA because of the level of protection of a public interest established by the EU institutions, this could create a situation where, in order to avoid being repeatedly compelled by the CETA Tribunal to pay damages to the claimant investor, the achievement of that level of protection needs to be abandoned by the Union.[33]

Already, the mere possibility that 'the Union – or a Member State in the course of implementing EU law – has to amend or withdraw legislation' as a consequence of such an adjudicative body's findings is deemed unacceptable.[34] The CJEU's statement makes it abundantly clear that the principle of autonomy of EU law is not formalistic, but rather one of effect. Inapplicability or deselection of EU law as applicable law in a dispute based on an EU agreement with a third country does by no means save the respective dispute settlement

---

[30]   Opinion 2/13 (n 8), paras 223–225.
[31]   Opinion 1/17 (n 7), paras 120–136.
[32]   Hindelang, 'Repellent Forces: the CJEU and Investor-State Dispute Settlement' (n 12), 74–76. Already in the opinion on the accession of the EU to the ECHR, the CJEU established a violation of the principle of autonomy of EU law based on mere factual impact on the EU legal order as the ECtHR does not apply EU law as law, but as facts: Opinion 2/13 (n 8), paras 187–189.
[33]   Opinion 1/17 (n 7), para 149; see also Hindelang, 'Repellent Forces: the CJEU and Investor-State Dispute Settlement' (n 12), 75.
[34]   Opinion 1/17, ibid., para 150.

mechanism from falling foul of the principle of autonomy of EU law.[35] Rather, the principle of autonomy of EU law prohibits referring jurisdiction to the respective adjudicative bodies if those bodies might:

> in the course of making findings on restrictions on the freedom to conduct business challenged within a claim, *call into question the level of protection of a public interest that led to the introduction of such restrictions by the Union* with respect to all operators who invest in the commercial or industrial sector at issue of the internal market.[36]

In Opinion 1/17, the CJEU specifically points to several safeguards[37] that allegedly preclude 'call[ing] into question the level of protection of public interest that led to the introduction of such restrictions by the Union'. The opinion stressed that, first, in accordance with Article 28.3.2. of the CETA,

---

[35] With regard to the EU Member States internally as well as in their dealings among each other, EU law is always the applicable law. Irrespective of whether there is an express stipulation in domestic law that EU law is applicable law, 'every national court must, in a case within its jurisdiction, apply [EU] law in its entirety ... and must accordingly set aside any provision of national law which may conflict with it, whether prior or subsequent to the [EU] rule': Case 106/77 *Administrazione delle Finanze dello Stato v Simmenthal SpA* [1978] ECLI:EU:C:1978:49, para 21. The same holds true when the EU Member States resort to public international law in their dealings between them. There is no 'contracting-out' of the EU Treaties by deselecting EU law as applicable law. The CJEU made the point clear that 'the very nature of EU law ... requires that relations *between the Member States be governed by EU law to the exclusion, if EU law so requires, of any other law*'. (emphasis added): Opinion 2/13 (n 8), para 212. See also Case C-402/05 P and C-415/05 P, *Kadi and Al Barakaat International Foundation v Council of the European Union and Commission of the European Communities* [2008] ECLI:EU:C:2008:461, para 285. Investment tribunals display a remarkable 'creativity' in ignoring the aforesaid CJEU's jurisprudence by developing arguments impossible to square with very basic legal rules of the EU constitutional order and general public international law. This ignorance allows them to preserve their jurisdiction – *honi soit qui mal y pense*. A case in point is the statement by the tribunal in the ICSID Case No ARB/15/50, *Eskosol s.p.a. in liquidazione v Italian Republic, Decision on Italy's Request for Immediate Termination and Italy's Jurisdictional Objection based on Inapplicability of the Energy Charter Treaty to Intra-EU Disputes* [2019], para 175 www.italaw.com/sites/default/files/case-documents/italaw10512.pdf, accessed 11 February 2020: 'it appears that EU Member States may bring arbitral tribunals into being for the purposes of deciding treaty disputes under general principles of international law, but are no longer allowed to authorize such disputes to apply EU law in addition'. It is difficult not to characterise this statement as a purpose-driven misconstruction in light of the CJEU's standing case law cited above and general public international law.

[36] Opinion 1/17 (n 7), para 137 (emphasis added).

[37] Ibid., para 148.

the rules regarding the non-discriminatory treatment of an investment[38] shall not be construed in a way that prevents the adoption or enforcement of measures necessary to protect public security or public morals, to maintain public order, or to protect human, animal or plant life or health.[39] Second, the CJEU referred to provisions of the CETA on regulatory measures.[40] These contain, first, a reaffirmation of the CETA parties' 'right to regulate' and then they outline that the mere fact that a CETA party regulates, including through a modification to its laws, in a manner which negatively affects an investment or interferes with an investor's expectations, including expectations of profit, does not amount to a breach of the (absolute) standards of protection of an investment ensured by the agreement's section on investment.[41] Third, the opinion referred to Point 1(d) (Preamble) and Point 2 (Right to regulate) of the Joint Interpretative Instrument on the CETA between Canada and the EU and its Member States.[42] There, the CETA parties declared that they will interpret the agreement in a way that does not 'lower [the treaty parties'] [...] respective standards and regulations' and that they will preserve 'the ability of the European Union and its Member States and Canada to adopt and apply their own laws and regulations that regulate economic activity in the public interest, to achieve legitimate public policy objectives' regarding the right to regulate.[43] Last, but not least, fourth, the CJEU referred to Point 3 of Annex 8-A of the CETA on expropriation and to Article 8.10.2 of the CETA on fair and equitable treatment.[44] Both provisions specifically circumscribe and limit the said protection standards regarding the grave abuse of sovereign power so that adjudicative bodies 'cannot call into question the level of protection of public interest determined by the Union following a democratic process'.[45]

On the basis of the analysis sketched above, the CJEU concluded that an adjudicative body established on the basis of CETA has 'no jurisdiction to declare incompatible with the CETA the level of protection of a public interest established by an EU measure'[46] and, thus, found the investment chapter compatible with the principle of autonomy of EU law.

---

[38]   Arts 8.6–8.8 CETA.
[39]   Opinion 1/17 (n 7), para 152.
[40]   Ibid., para 154.
[41]   Arts 8.9.1. and 8.9.2 CETA.
[42]   Opinion 1/17 (n 7), para 155.
[43]   Joint Interpretative Instrument on the Comprehensive Economic and Trade Agreement (CETA) between Canada and the European Union and its Member States [2017] OJ L 11/3, point 1(d) and 2.
[44]   Opinion 1/17 (n 7), para 156.
[45]   Ibid., paras 155–157.
[46]   Ibid., para 153; see also paras 156 and 160.

It is therefore apparent that policing the level of protection of public interests established by EU legislation is essentially a task reserved for the CJEU.[47] By expressly referring to the EU legislator and to the 'democratic process',[48] the Court of Justice seeks to carve-out *legislative* acts from the jurisdiction of adjudicative bodies standing outside the EU judicial system. Such a carve-out, however, is not comprehensive. Legislative acts which, for example, are applied 'in a manner that would constitute a means of arbitrary or unjustifiable discrimination between the Parties where like conditions prevail, or a disguised restriction on trade between the Parties'[49] can be scrutinised by adjudicative bodies standing outside EU judicial system. Although the CJEU is concerned with the 'application', not 'adoption' of such acts, it can be safely assumed that a measure which, for example, has already been adopted as 'a means of arbitrary or unjustifiable discrimination' would also be applied in such a defective way.[50] This, in turn, opens up a (back-)door to an external review of EU legislative acts; albeit an indirect one.[51] Hence, the safeguards contained in the CETA do not in fact preclude, but *merely restrict,* the potential of an adjudicative body established on the basis of the said agreement to 'call into question the level of protection of public interest that led to the introduction of such restrictions by the Union'.[52]

3. THE IMPACT OF THE CJEU's OPINION 1/17 ON THE EU CONSTITUTIONAL ORDER

One could almost hear the gasp of relief at the European Commission's *Berlaymont* headquarters after the CJEU had rendered its Opinion 1/17. The EU could go on with its treaty-making activities. It was also allowed to continue along its chosen path in the current policy debate on reforming the international investment protection regime. In particular, in the current UNICTRAL Working Group III policy process,[53] Opinion 1/17 provides the

---

[47]   Ibid., paras 148–151.

[48]   Ibid., para 151.

[49]   Art 28.3.2 CETA.

[50]   CETA's provision on fair and equitable treatment, for example, seems also to restrict a comprehensive review of administrative acts in its provision on fair and equitable treatment: ibid., Art 8.10.2. This, however, appears necessitated by the principle of autonomy of EU law which the CJEU in Opinion 1/17 expressly links to legislative acts.

[51]   Laws which are self-executing might in fact be carved-out.

[52]   Opinion 1/17 (n 7), para 148.

[53]   UNCITRAL Working Group III (Investor-State Dispute Settlement Reform), 'Possible reform of investor-state dispute settlement (ISDS): Appellate and multilateral court mechanisms' (Note by the Secretariat) A/CN.9/WG.III/WP.185 2020.

European Commission with a valuable bargaining chip: essentially, any accord struck through a new ISDS model can, at least politically, hardly fall short of the one contained in the CETA.[54] However, the CJEU's decision to allow the EU to take part in the current reform debate will not be without consequences for the EU constitutional order. In the remainder of this chapter, three facets in which the Court's Opinion 1/17 impacts its further development are identified and explored. First, the CJEU may be confronted more often with judicial conflicts in the future, which could eventually lead to ISDS' *'Kadi* moment' (below 3.1). Second, by allowing different standards for reviewing the exercise of sovereign power, Opinion 1/17 paves the way for a reshaping of the current state of the EU's rule of law (below 3.2). Third, the EU constitutionality of the EU Member State BITs with third countries and the ECT relied on in disputes with non-EU investors has become questionable (below 3.3).

3.1   Looming Judicial Conflicts and Investor-State Dispute Settlement's *'Kadi* Moment'

It is hard to resist the impression that this time, the CJEU was clearly concerned with not creating further obstacles for the EU's international treaty-making agenda. Whether it was the ideal moment to strike a more moderate chord, only time can tell. In light of both the predominantly expansive interpretation of the protective scope of investment agreements by arbitral tribunals[55] and

---

[54]   Whether Opinion 1/17 also prescribes an EU constitutional minimum standard with regard to the autonomy of EU law for transferring jurisdiction up on an international adjudicative body is up for discussion. See for an argument in favour of this view: Stöbener de Mora and Wernicke (n 7), 977; and Markus Krajewski, 'Ist CETA der "Golden Standard"?: EuGH hält CETA-Gericht für unionsrechtskonform' (*Verfassungblog.de*, 30 April 2019) verfassungsblog.de/ist-ceta-der-golden-standard -eugh-haelt-ceta-gericht-fuer-unionsrechtskonform/, accessed 11 February 2020. The CJEU simply states that the safeguards provided in CETA – as a whole – are satisfactory to preserve the autonomy of EU law: Opinion 1/17 (n 7), para 132. Whether a different quality of safeguards or different means would have been insufficient is speculative.

[55]   Cf, Gus Van Harten, 'Leaders in the Expansive and Restrictive Interpretation of Investment Treaties: A Descriptive Study of ISDS Awards to 2010' (2018) 29 *European Journal of International Law* 507; and Katherine Jonckheere, 'Practical Implications of an Expansive Interpretation of Umbrella Clauses in International Investment Law' (2015) 11 *South Carolina Journal of International Law and Business* 143. Of a different view and disputing that arbitrators are activists and tend to exceed their authority is Andrea K. Bjorklund, 'Are Arbitrators (Judicial) Activists?' (2018) 17 *The Law & Practice of International Courts and Tribunals* 49. The decision in ICSID Case No ARB/98/2 *Victor Pey Casado and President Allende Foundation v Republic of Chile: Decision on Provisional Measures* [2001] may provide an example for an expan-

their outright hostility towards the EU legal order in intra-EU ISDS disputes,[56] the CJEU's assessment must be perceived to be a particularly generous gesture that seeks to foster co-existence with adjudicative bodies operating outside the EU's judicial system despite potential judicial conflicts on the horizon.

The question of how generous this opening-up to outside adjudication may be is likely to become somewhat clearer when it is considered that adjudicative bodies established on the basis of the CETA can in fact call into question the 'democratic choice' by the EU legislature made with regard to the level of protection of public interests vis-à-vis the freedom to conduct business. It is

---

sive interpretation. The wording of the ICSID Convention is that tribunals can 'recommend' provisional measures: Art 47 of the Convention on the settlement of investment disputes between States and nationals of other States (18 March 1965) 575 UNTS 579. The tribunal reasoned however that provisional measures indicated by ICSID tribunals were binding. According to Fuad Zarbiyev, 'Judicial Activism in International Law – A Conceptual Framework for Analysis' (2012) 3 *Journal of International Dispute Settlement* 247, 273 fn 153, this reasoning built essentially on the one by the International Court of Justice in the *LaGrand Case (Germany v United States of America),* Judgment of 27 June 2001, [2001] ICJ Rep 466, paras 92–110, where the court asserted its authority to order provisional measures on account of the 'power to indicate' them mentioned in its statute: Art 41 of the Statute of the International Court of Justice [1945]. The significance of the two most recent decades' development of arbitral tribunals holding that they actually can order provisional measures, regardless of the wording of the ICSID Convention, is discussed by Tarcisio Gazzini and Robert Kolb, 'Provisional Measures in ICSID Arbitration from "Wonderland's Jurisprudence" to Informal Modification of Treaties' (2017) 16 *The Law & Practice of International Courts and Tribunals* 159.

[56] See, e.g., *Eskosol SpA. in liquidazione v Italian Republic,* ICSID Case No. ARB/15/50 (n 34), paras 112–123 for a rather 'creative' interpretation of the applicable law clause of Art 26(6) of the Energy Charter Treaty (n 10) which, by its terms, includes all 'applicable rules of international law', meaning not only international law binding between all Contracting Parties, but international law applicable to 'the issues in dispute'. This is not the place to provide a comprehensive analysis of the tribunal's argument, and, therefore, this chapter limits itself to a note: It is at least surprising that, in the course of interpreting the ECT's applicable law clause about what constitutes 'applicable rules and principles of international law', the international commitments created among the EU Member States by the EU Treaties did not come into the picture. Furthermore, the reliance on the Permanent Court of International Justice (PCIJ) case in *SS Lotus (France v Turkey)* [1927] PCIJ Ser A No 10, 16–17, seems to take the PCIJ's reading on the applicable law clause in that case completely out of its specific context and arbitrarily imposes this reading on the ECT. This dubious interpretive practice – estranged from the Vienna Convention on the Law of Treaties rules on treaty interpretation – is witnessed ever more often in arbitral awards and entails the danger that the will of the state parties to the agreement (i.e., here the ECT) gets confused with the will of the arbitrators in the course of the interpretative exercise. See on this Hindelang, 'Study on Investor-State Dispute Settlement (ISDS) and Alternatives of Dispute Resolution in International Investment Law' (n 3), 69–71.

only the extent to which an adjudicative body can do so which the CETA seeks to limit to only grave situations of abuse of sovereign power, as shown above.[57] The CETA even allows, in exceptional situations, for an outside determination of the division of powers in the EU constitutional order by choice of the investor.[58]

It remains the CJEU's secret as to why it placed the draft agreement on the EU's accession to the ECHR and the ensuing role for the ECtHR under the microscope and ultimately met these prospects with rejection,[59] all the while endowing investment tribunals with trust in respecting and preserving the CETA's envisaged jurisdictional limits and with it the autonomy of EU law. Investment tribunals do not have the best track record of upholding such limits, recalling the non-compliance with the CJEU's *Achmea* judgment[60] and the misrepresentation of EU law as not being part of the relevant international law applicable to an intra-EU dispute.[61] Furthermore, the above-discussed safeguards in CETA,[62] intended to prevent an adjudicative body established on the agreement's basis from 'second-guessing' the balance between private and public interests struck in EU legislation, are phrased quite openly. It will be for the CETA adjudicative body to establish the meaning of terms such as 'manifestly excessive', 'arbitrary or unjustifiable discrimination', or 'disguised restriction on trade'. Seemingly, the CJEU in its Opinion 1/17 hopes for judicial constraint.

In the event that this hope will be disappointed, arbitral practice with regard to Article 1105(1) of the NAFTA on fair and equitable treatment reveals how challenging it can be to keep the genie in the bottle. Despite repeated efforts by all three NAFTA treaty parties to ensure that fair and equitable treatment meets

---

[57]   See above 2.2. and Simon Lester, 'CETA ISDS Upheld by CJEU' (*International Economic Law and Policy Blog*, 30 April 2019) ielp.worldtradelaw.net/2019/04/ceta-isds-upheld-by-cjeu.html, accessed 11 February 2020.

[58]   See above 2.2.

[59]   Opinion 2/13 (n 8).

[60]   *Achmea* (n 8). See for an, e.g., *Eskosol SpA in liquidazione v Italian Republic*, ICSID Case No. ARB/15/50 (n 35), para 175 and the cited arbitral awards therein.

[61]   Beyond *Eskosol SpA in liquidazione v Italian Republic*, ibid., paras 115, 121 and 130, this point of view has been recently taken by the arbitral tribunals in *Greentech Energy Sys A/S v Italy*, SCC Case No. 2015/095, Final Award (2019), para 397 www.italaw.com/sites/default/files/case-documents/italaw10291.pdf, accessed 11 February 2020; *Cube Infrastructure Fund SICAV v Spain*, ICSID Case No. ARB15/20, Decision on Jurisdiction, Liability and Partial Decision on Quantum (2019), paras 129–130 and 158 www.italaw.com/sites/default/files/case-documents/italaw10692.pdf, accessed 11 February 2020; *Rockhopper Italian SpA v Italy*, ICSID Case No. ARB/217/14, Decision on the Intra-EU Jurisdictional Objection (2019), para 174 www.italaw.com/sites/default/files/case-documents/italaw10646_0.pdf, accessed 11 February 2020.

[62]   See above 2.2.

the international minimum standard,[63] NAFTA arbitral tribunals nonetheless largely converge towards a fair and equitable treatment standard that is in line with other investment agreements that do not contain NAFTA-like restrictions on the standard.[64] Arbitral tribunals have achieved such a result by an 'unorthodox' interpretation of the international minimum standard, that they found to be rapidly evolving,[65] and by employing a means of interpretation alien to the Vienna Convention on the Law of Treaties' rules on treaty interpretation: 'de facto precedents'.[66]

In light of these experiences, it may not be a completely theoretical exercise to consider the question of what to do if adjudicative bodies established on the basis of the CETA 'trespass' on the CJEU's exclusive jurisdiction to determine 'the [appropriate] level of protection of a public interest established by an EU measure'.[67] The CETA itself provides an instrument of binding authoritative interpretation.[68] The CJEU has diminished the instrument's effectiveness by restricting it to future disputes.[69] Its operation in practice can also be burdened with significant uncertainties, as the above NAFTA example has shown.

In the event of the binding authoritative interpretation failing to keep tribunals at bay, ISDS may face its '*Kadi* moment': should the CJEU be confronted with an award at the stage of enforcement[70] that does not comply with the EU constitutional limits stipulated in Opinion 1/17, it might frustrate any such enforcement efforts within the EU. This situation would be similar to the sit-

---

[63] See NAFTA Free Trade Commission, 'Notes of Interpretation of Certain Chapter 11 Provisions (Article 1105 and the Availability of Arbitration Documents)' (31 July 2001) http://www.sice.oas.org/TPD/NAFTA/Commission/CH11understanding_e.asp, accessed 11 February 2020.

[64] Andrew Paul Newcombe and Lluís Paradell, *Law and Practice of Investment Treaties: Standards of Treatment* (Walters Kluwer 2009) 27.

[65] Arbitrators reacted in a 'flexible' manner to the perceived 'challenge' by holding that 'both customary international law and the minimum standard of treatment of aliens it incorporates, are constantly in a process of development': *ADF Group v United States of America,* ICSID Case No. ARB (AF)/00/1, Award (2003), para 179 http://www.italaw.com/sites/default/files/case-documents/ita0009.pdf, accessed 11 February 2020.

[66] On the potential 'power-grabbing' effects of non-compliance with the Vienna rules on treaty interpretation, see Hindelang, 'Study on Investor-State Dispute Settlement (ISDS) and Alternatives of Dispute Resolution in International Investment Law' (n 3), 66–68.

[67] Opinion 1/17 (n 7), paras 153; see also paras 156 and 160.

[68] Art 8.13.3 CETA.

[69] Opinion 1/17 (n 7), para 153; and paras 235–237.

[70] That even ICSID awards may face a stay on the enforcement stage in an EU Member States court is, e.g., evidenced by *Micula and Others v Romania* [2018] EWCA Civ 1801.

uation in *Kadi*, where an EU regulation that implemented an act of the United Nations Organisation was annulled.[71] Thus, we may see a residual control over adjudicative bodies established on the basis of the CETA and similar EU investment agreements. Its effectiveness, however, will be limited. The CJEU has no authority to declare the 'trespassing award' itself invalid. The award remains enforceable outside the EU.

However, when considered from a policy perspective, such limited effectiveness in shielding the EU legal order from outside influence may just be tolerable for the CJEU. With its Opinion 1/17, it avoided the criticism of being a 'spoilsport' again, leading the EU into 'isolationism' in international economic relations.[72] Should the judicial activities of adjudicative bodies established on the basis of the CETA and similar agreements indeed produce unwanted spill-over effects on the EU constitutional order, contrary to the CJEU's assumption, the CJEU can hardly be blamed, except maybe for its endless optimism and good will.[73] Any attempts to force the genie back into the bottle – as the experiences with the intra-EU investment arbitration saga and the NAFTA's 'elevated minimum standard' show[74] – will possibly be met with some robust resistance by adjudicative bodies if they are determined to expand their jurisdiction. If one assumes that the CJEU was aware of the incentive structures inherent in an ISDS mechanism relying on non-tenured adjudicators,[75] perhaps the CJEU took a gamble that 'all will play out just fine' with the establishment of a multilateral investment court and/or a permanent appeals mechanism mentioned in the CETA[76] and currently under negotiation in the UNCITRAL Working Group III. Indeed, if the EU does succeed in the

---

[71]   *Kadi* (n 35).

[72]   Cf Riffel (n 7). For a viewpoint to the contrary, see Stöbener de Mora and Wernicke (n 7), 972–973.

[73]   By not comprehensively ruling out the review of EU legislative acts, the CJEU also, at least on principle, did not close the door for an accession of the EU to the ECHR. However, whether other members of the Council of Europe would be prepared to accept such a carefully circumscribed jurisdiction of the ECtHR is open to question.

[74]   See the references above (nn 55 and 64).

[75]   Regarding the debate on the incentive structure issue, see Hindelang, 'Study on Investor-State Dispute Settlement (ISDS) and Alternatives of Dispute Resolution in International Investment Law' (n 3), 100–104. The CJEU, in Opinion 1/17 (n 7), paras 239–244, seems to be of a different view, as it held that attached risks would be mitigated by following the guidelines provided by the International Bar Association, 'IBA Guidelines on Conflicts of Interest in International Arbitration adopted by resolution of the IBA Council on Thursday 23 October 2014' (International Bar Association 2014) acica.org.au/wp-content/uploads/IBA_Guidelines/IBA-Guidelines-on-Conflict -of-Interest.pdf, accessed 11 February 2020.

[76]   Art 8.29 CETA.

talks, a permanent mechanism will possibly be staffed with tenured, full-time judges.[77]

3.2 The Rule of Law and Alternative Standards of Review of Sovereign Power

Potential judicial conflicts, however, may not be the only price to be paid for the EU's participation in the ISDS reform debate. Tacitly, the CJEU gave its blessings to a bypass of its most important sparring partner in upholding the rule of law within the EU, the domestic courts of the EU Member States, which are entrusted with 'the responsibility for ensuring the full application of EU law […] and the judicial protection that individuals derive from EU law'.[78]

According to provisions of the CETA, if a Canadian investor submits a claim to a CETA adjudicative body, it needs to withdraw or discontinue ongoing proceedings in the CJEU or in the EU Member State courts, or it needs to waive its right to initiate such proceedings.[79] In *Achmea*,[80] and also in *Commission v. Poland*[81] and in *Associação Sindical dos Juízes Portugueses*,[82] the CJEU was eager to uphold the role and to secure the proper functioning of the EU Member State courts as the prime guardian of the rule of law and

---

[77] Submission of the European Union and its Member States to UNCITRAL Working Group III (n 5), point 16.

[78] *Commission v Poland (Independence of the ordinary courts)* (n 9), para 98. An issue to be separated is the one of whether the domestic courts and tribunals actually live up to their envisaged role, which has been waged as a criticism against the CJEU's position on arbitration tribunals in both intra-EU BITs and the CETA: see Stöbener de Mora and Wernicke (n 7), 974. However, factual deficiencies in certain EU Member States currently addressed by the Commission, even if they may require further attention in the years to come and, in fact, also an even more robust EU intervention into these EU Member States, do not call into question the constitutional conceptualisation of an, in principle, full reviewability and accountability of the exercise of sovereign power enshrined in Arts 2 and 19 of the TEU.

[79] Arts 8.22.1 (f) and (g) and 8.23 CETA.

[80] *Achmea* (n 8).

[81] *Commission v Poland (Independence of the ordinary courts)* (n 9), paras 98–107. See also C-619/18, *European Commission v Republic of Poland (Independence of the Supreme Court)* [2019] ECLI:EU:C:2019:531, paras 47–50; and Case C-216/18, *PPU Minister for Justice and Equality (Deficiencies in the system of justice)* [2019] ECLI: EU:C:2018:586.

[82] Case C-64/16 *Associação Sindical dos Juízes Portugueses v Tribunal de Contes* [2018] ECLI:EU:C:2018:117, paras 29–37. For the link between the principle of autonomy of EU law and the constitutional role of the courts and tribunals of the EU Member States, see Hindelang, 'Conceptualisation and application of the principle of autonomy of EU law' (n 12), 391–392.

the entry point for the 'judicial dialogue' between them and itself.[83] This is not the case, however, in Opinion 1/17: with the CETA, the very same courts were relegated to a mere alternative to ISDS when it comes to reviewing the exercise of sovereign power in the EU towards Canadian – that is, *third country* – investors.

Providing a separate dispute settlement venue on the basis of the CETA entails an alternative standard of review of sovereign power. While the CJEU or an EU Member State court reviews an EU or Member State measure in light of the entire EU legal order, a CETA adjudicative body reviews the same measure in light of a very small number of generically phrased substantive protection standards contained in the said agreement. Interestingly, the alternative standard of review of the exercise of sovereign power has not attracted the CJEU's attention in Opinion 1/17.

Arguably, to the extent that investors move from domestic courts to the CETA adjudicative bodies, the EU and its Member States may evade – either unintendedly or in collusion with the investor – sanctions for violations of EU law, as not all breaches of EU law amount to breaches of the CETA.[84] Put differently, by 'switching' from a 'comprehensive review' of legality, especially of administrative conduct, in light of the whole EU legal order[85] to a 'minimal review' in light of the CETA, the bond of compliance with the EU legal order is loosened. This is not without consequence for the principle of legality of administration (*Gesetzesbindung der Verwaltung, principe de légalité*) as part of the rule of law, which seeks exactly to prevent an administration from loosening 'the chains of law' which ties it back to the legislature and, ultimately, to the will of the people.[86] The principle is recognised as a general principle of

---

[83]   Cf Art 267 of the Consolidated Version of the Treaty on the Functioning of the European Union [2016] OJ C326/47 (TFEU).

[84]   This is at least the declared intention of the parties to the CETA as they wish to limit the review to grave abuses of sovereign power, see, e.g., the specification of what amounts to a breach of the obligation of fair and equitable treatment: Art 8.10 CETA. See, in contrast, the jurisdiction of the CJEU which extends to 'lack of competence, infringement of an essential procedural requirement, infringement of the Treaties or of any rule of law relating to their application, or misuse of powers': Art 263(2) TFEU.

[85]   It is important to stress that the degree to which administrative conduct is reviewable by courts varies from EU Member State to EU Member State due to different traditions, which is not without problem when it comes to EU law: Ulrich Stelkens, 'Paneuropäische allgemeine Rechtsgrundsätze guter Verwaltung zum Ermessen und ihre Bedeutung für die georgische Verwaltung' [2018], 6 www.researchgate .net/publication/323759368_Paneuropaische_allgemeine_Rechtsgrundsatze_guter _Verwaltung_zum_Ermessen_und_ihre_Bedeutung_fur_die_georgische_Verwaltung, accessed 11 February 2020.

[86]   While the question of how strictly the administration is bound to legislative programming or to what degree it can exercise its own discretion defines the relationship

EU law,[87] and as such, it contributes to the protective scope of the autonomy of EU law.[88]

The degree to which the just-described band can be loosened, while still being perceived as satisfying the principle of legality of administration, varies not only among the EU Member States according to their constitutional traditions, but also according to EU law, where there currently seems, as of yet, to be no clear position on this point.[89] Within an internal-EU context, the CJEU, arguably, does not seem to demand an extremely tight judicial control of the administration. Rather, it advocates in favour of a margin of appreciation which is governed by the 'reasonableness' of a respective administrative decision.[90]

---

between executive and legislative branch, the intensity of judicial review of an administrative measure defines the relationship of administration and judiciary. Both are equivalent expressions of the principle of legality.

[87] Recognised as general principles of EU law, see Jörg Philipp Terhechte, 'Europäisches Verwaltungsrecht und europäisches Verfassungsrecht' in Jörg Philipp Terhechte (ed), *Verwaltungsrecht der Europäischen Union* (Nomos 2011), 288–289, with reference to *Kadi* (n 34) and Cases 38/70 *Deutsche Tradax GmbH v Einfuhr- und Vorratsstelle für Getreide und Futtermittel* [1971] ECLI:EU:C:1971:24; and 113/77 *NTN Toyo Bearing Company Ltd and others v Council of the European Communities* [1979] ECLI:EU:C:1979:91.

[88] Opinion 1/17 (n 7), para 110.

[89] On principle:

The Treaties set up a system for distributing powers among the different Community institutions, assigning to each institution its own role in the institutional structure of the Community and the accomplishment of the tasks entrusted to the Community. Observance of the institutional balance means that each of the institutions must exercise its powers with due regard for the powers of the other institutions.

Case C-70/88 *European Parliament v Council of the European Communities. Capacity of the European Parliament to bring an action for annulment* [1990] ECLI:EU:C:1990: 217, paras 21 and 22. For a general account of the principle of constitutional balance in the Common Commercial Policy, see Jörg Philipp Terhechte, 'Im Dienste der Demokratie? - Das institutionelle Gleichgewicht in der gemeinsamen Handelspolitik der EU' (Europa-Kolleg Hamburg, Institute for European Integration 2019) europa -kolleg-hamburg.de/wp-content/uploads/2019/08/Das-institutionelle-Gleichgewicht .pdf, accessed 11 February 2020.

[90] Case 55/75 *Balkan-Import Export GmbH v Hauptzollamt Berlin-Packhof* [1976] ECLI:EU:C:1976:8, para 8; Case C-120/97 *Upjohn Ltd v The Licensing Authority established by the Medicines Act 1968 and Others* [1999] ECLI:EU:C:1999:14, paras 27 and 32–37; Case C-55/06 *Arcor AG & Co KG v Bundesrepublik Deutschland* [2008] ECLI:EU:C:2008:244, paras 160–170. The CJEU stresses the necessity to adhere strictly to the administrative procedure in order to make decisions reviewable by the judiciary: Case C-269/90 *Technische Universität München v Hauptzollamt München-Mitte* [1991] ECLI:EU:C:1991:438, paras 13–14; Case C-405/07 P, *Kingdom of the Netherlands v Commission of the European Communities* [2008] ECLI: EU:C:2008:613, para 55. Courts of the EU Member States can however employ

Concluding from the CJEU's non-addressal of the issue in Opinion 1/17, where judicial control is transferred to an international adjudicative body with the view to allow the EU a meaningful foreign policy in general and a common commercial policy in particular, the principle of legality cannot mean that the CETA review standard must equal the EU domestic review standard.[91] At a minimum level, however, a review standard must not be so minimal that an encroachment upon the essence – the *Wesensgehalt* – of the EU fundamental rights by the administration cannot be remedied.[92] According to the jurisprudence of the CJEU, the essence of rights is encroached upon if the 'right as such' is called into question.[93] This level of review seems to still be guaranteed by the substantive standards provided for in the CETA. For example, the provision on fair and equitable treatment of the CETA renders a fundamental breach of due process compensable, including a fundamental breach of transparency, in administrative proceedings or manifest arbitrariness.[94]

---

a stricter standard of review, see BVerwG 6 C 13.12 [2013] ECLI:DE:BVerwG:2013: 250913U6C13.12.0, para 33.

[91]   Opinion 1/17 (n 7), paras 106 and 117.

[92]   See Art 52(1), 1st sentence of the Charter of Fundamental Rights of the European Union [2016] OJ C 202.

[93]   See Case C-73/16 *Peter Puškár v Finančné riaditeľstvo Slovenskej republiky and Kriminálny úrad finančnej správy* [2017] ECLI:EU:C:2017:725, para 64; Case C-18/16 *K. v Staatssecretaris van Veiligheid en Justitie* [2017] ECLI:EU:C:2017:680, para 35; Case C-601/15 *JN v Staatssecretaris van Veiligheid en Justitie (PPU N)* [2016] ECLI: EU:C:2016:84, para 52; Case C-524/15, *Criminal proceedings against Luca Menci* [2018] ECLI:EU:C:2018:197, para 43; Case C-129/14 *Zoran Spasic (PPU Spasic)* [2014] ECLI:EU:C:2014:586, paras 58–59; Case C-528/13 *Geoffrey Léger v Ministre des Affaires sociales, de la Santé et des Droits des femmes and Établissement français du sang* [2015] ECLI:EU:C:2015:288, para 54; Case C-650/13 *Thierry Delvigne v Commune de Lesparre Médoc and Préfet de la Gironde* [2015] ECLI:EU:C:2015:648, para 48.

[94]   Art 8.10 CETA.

What is more, while advanced domestic administrative law systems,[95] the EU legal system,[96] and general public international law[97] prioritise restitution[98] over pecuniary remedies, the CETA provides for essentially the opposite: that is, that an adjudicative body may *only* award pecuniary damages (and interest), with the exception of restitution of property, under certain conditions.[99]

Prioritising restitution is, first, an expression of the idea that property is protected in its integrity, not just in its value. Second, and more importantly for our discussion, giving priority to restitution emphasises the primacy of the legislator in shaping the social function of both property and fundamental rights, and is therefore a specific expression of the principle of legality of administration with an emphasis on the role of parliament. This is because an administrative act that does not reflect the legislator's choice expressed in a given law is declared void, rather than being compensated for violating the law, but with the law otherwise persisting.

With the CETA, the EU legislator and the legislators of the EU Member States[100] retreat to some degree from prioritising restitution over pecuniary

---

[95]   David Gaukrodger and Kathryn Gordon, 'Investor-State Dispute Settlement: A Scoping Paper for the Investment Policy Community' (Organisation for Economic Co-operation and Development 2013), 79–87 www.oecd-ilibrary.org/docserver/ 5k46b1r85j6f-en.pdf?expires=1581448044&id=id&accname=guest&checksum=2B F3471DB7A493185100659B7E43C8DC, accessed 11 February 2020.

[96]   Cf Arts 263 and 264 TFEU.

[97]   See ILC, 'Articles on State responsibility', Annex to UNGA Res 56/83 (12 December 2001) UN Doc A/RES/56/83, Arts 34–39. Restitution is said to conform 'most closely to the general principle of the law on responsibility according to which the author State is bound to "wipe out" all the legal and material consequences of its wrongful act by re-establishing the situation that would exist if the wrongful act had not been committed': Gaeteno Arangio-Ruiz, 'Preliminary Report on State Responsibility', in International Law Commission (ed), *Yearbook of the International Law Commission, Volume II* (United Nations Publications 1988), UN Doc A/CN.4/416 & Corr. 1 & 2 and Add.1 & Corr.1, para 114. In fact, the question of whether investment tribunals are or should be allowed to order restitutio in rem is contentious, see Steffen Hindelang, 'Restitution and Compensation – Reconstructing the Relationship in International Investment Law', in Rainer Hofmann and Christian J Tams (eds), *International Investment Law and General International Law: From Clinical Isolation to Systemic Integration* (Nomos 2011) 161-199; possibly of a different view James Crawford, 'The ILC's Articles on Responsibility of States for Internationally Wrongful Acts – A Retrospective' (2002) 96(4) *American Journal of International Law* 874, 881; and Irmgard Marboe, 'State Responsibility and Comparative State Liability for Administrative and Legislative Harm to Economic Interest' in Stephan W Schill (ed), *International Investment Law and Comparative Public Law* (OUP 2010) 377–411.

[98]   For example (the order) to repeal a challenged administrative act or law or to restore property previously taken.

[99]   Art 8.39 (1) CETA.

[100]   CETA is a so-called mixed agreement.

remedies. This choice, together with the 'minimal review' discussed above, further softens the compliance pressure on the administration, although admittedly, pecuniary damages also exercise some of this pressure. Nonetheless, it could enable an administration, by colluding with the investor, to 'buy' its way out of a situation that is illegal under EU law if the investor chooses the remedies available under the CETA. While a domestic court, on the basis of domestic law that includes EU law, or the CJEU, on the basis of EU law, would possibly void the administrative act and demand restitution, a CETA adjudicative body, on the basis of Article 8.39 of the CETA, would only award pecuniary damages. The illegal administrative act would persist. Whether the CETA, in prioritising pecuniary damages and opting for 'minimal review', actually infringes the principle of legality of the administration is still somewhat doubtable in view of the limited overall scope of the CETA agreement. However, the more that EU agreements actually allow for an opt-out of domestic courts (including the CJEU), and the more accessible ISDS becomes in EU agreements,[101] more palpable is the decline of comprehensive judicial control over administrative conduct.

3.3　Reassessing the EU Constitutionality of the EU Member State BITs with Third Countries and the Application of ECT in Disputes with Non-EU Investors

With Opinion 1/17, the Court provided another piece to the puzzle that is understanding the EU constitutional principle of autonomy of EU law. Beyond the CETA, the Court's findings have implications for other investment agreements of the EU and its Member States, most prominently the ECT and the bilateral investment agreements of the EU Member States with third countries.

Regarding the ECT, Opinion 1/17 made it abundantly clear that the contained ISDS mechanism violated the principle of autonomy of EU law. The intra-EU scenario was already conclusively addressed by the Court in *Achmea.*[102] Opinion 1/17 reconfirms this finding and, as will be discussed

---

[101] Recalling the CJEU's petition in Opinion 1/17 (n 7), paras 205–219 for proper financial assistance of natural persons and small- and medium-sized investors in order to make use of the respective investor-state dispute settlement mechanism, Canada could make similar assistance available to its own investors.

[102] See Steffen Hindelang, opinions in support of the Kingdom of Spain in US District Court for the District of Columbia, *Novenergia II – Energy & Environment (SCA) v The Kingdom of Spain*, No. 1:18-cv-1148; *Eiser Infrastructure Ltd and Energia Solar Luxembourg SARL v The Kingdom of Spain*, No. 1:1818-cv-114801686-CKK; *Infrastructure Services Luxembourg SARL and Energia Termosolar BV v The Kingdom of Spain*, No. 1:18-cv-1753 (EGS); *Masdar Solar & Wind Cooperatief UA v The Kingdom of Spain*, No. 1:18-cv-02254-JEB, *NextEra Energy Global Holdings BV and*

shortly, adds further weight to the argument that any existing intra-EU ISDS mechanism, irrespective of whether it is based on a bilateral or multilateral investment protection agreement, is contrary to EU law in general[103] and the principle of autonomy in particular.[104]

An investor-state dispute settlement *in a third-country scenario,* whereby a third-country investor brings a claim against the EU or an EU Member State based on a 'pre-CETA' ISDS model, like the one contained in the ECT, would also be in violation of the principle of autonomy of EU law. The ECT lacks – to a large extent – safeguards intended to preserve the autonomy of EU law in a third-country scenario, as identified in Opinion 1/17. Functional equivalent safeguards to ensure that an investment tribunal established on the basis of the ECT declares when the level of protection of public interests determined by the EU legislature are insufficient are not contained in the said treaty.

For example, the substantive standards on indirect expropriation in Article 13 of the ECT and fair and equitable treatment in Article 10(1) of the ECT are not specifically circumscribed. They catch situations which go beyond the grave abuse of sovereign power to which the CETA has been limited to in Point 3 of Annex 8-A of the CETA on expropriation and Article 8.10.2 of the CETA on fair and equitable treatment. Thus, the aforesaid protection standards in the ECT allow for – or at least do not rule explicitly out – calling 'into question the level of protection of public interest that led to the introduction of such restrictions by the Union'.[105]

The general clause that governs exceptions from the substantive standards in Article 28.3.2 of the CETA appears to be broader than the corresponding provision in Article 24 of the ECT. Moreover, Article 28.3.2 of the CETA does

---

NextEra Energy Spain Holdings BV v The Kingdom of Spain, No. 19-cv-01618-TSC; *9REN Holding SARL v Kingdom of Spain,* No. 19-cv-1871-TSC; US District Court for the Southern District of New York, *Foresight Luxembourg Solar 1 SARL v The Kingdom of Spain,* No. 1:19- cv-3171. See also Steffen Hindelang, opinion in support of the Republic of Poland in Högsta Domstolen (the Swedish Supreme Court), *Republiken Polen (Republic of Poland) v PL Holdings SARL,* Case No. T 1569-19.

[103] It can also be doubted that the ISDS mechanism in the ECT fulfils the criteria formulated in Opinion 1/17 (n 7), paras 189–222 in regard to the right of access to an independent tribunal (see Art 47 of the Charter).

[104] Of a different view is Nikos Lavranos, 'Court of Justice approves CETA Investment Court System' (*Thomson Reuters Arbitration Blog,* 14 June 2019) arbitrationblog.practicallaw.com/court-of-justice-of-the-eu-approves-ceta-investment -court-system/, accessed 27 January 2020, who suggests that the 'analysis of the Vattenfall and most recently *Ekosol* tribunals contain particularly convincing reasons why the Achmea judgment is not relevant and applicable in intra-EU ECT disputes'. However, as explained above (n 35), the finding that in an intra-EU dispute EU law does not form part of the applicable law in the arbitration is fundamentally flawed.

[105] Opinion 1/17 (n 7), para 156.

not apply to substantive protection standards of the CETA Investment Chapter (Section D). This indicates that a CETA adjudicative body, in the course of assessing whether a host state has violated the substantive protection standards contained,[106] shall, on principle, *not* begin to second-guess the *balance* between interests of the common good and the interests of the investor. A violation of the substantive protection standard – at least so it seems when conceptualised – requires such an outrageous act of abuse of sovereign power that no public interests could possibly justify such conduct. Article 24 of the ECT, in contrast, provides for a balancing test and, thus, does not rule out such 'second-guessing' by the tribunal.

Furthermore, a similarly comprehensive pronouncement[107] of the so-called right to regulate and its interpretative safeguarding in the CETA,[108] is lacking in the ECT. Article 8.9(2) of the CETA prevents a tribunal from second-guessing the level of protection of public interests determined by the Union following a democratic process. The provision reads: 'the mere fact that a [treaty] Party regulates, including through a modification to its laws, in a manner which negatively affects an investment or interferes with an investor's expectations, including its expectations of profits, does not amount to a breach of an obligation under this Section'. The ECT, in contrast, merely acknowledges state sovereignty and refers to a right to regulate in the environmental and safety spheres, both exercised *in accordance with and subject to the rules of international law.*[109] In comparison to the CETA, any such reference to state sovereignty and the right to regulate, seem to be largely declaratory.

In an intra-EU scenario – that is, an investor from an EU Member State bringing a claim against another EU Member State, *argumentum a fortiori* – the fact that the ECT falls short of the safeguard requirements described in Opinion 1/17 only underlines and reconfirms that its ISDS provisions are in violation of the principle of autonomy of EU law, especially in such a scenario. This is because considerations 'of the reciprocal nature of international agreements [with third countries] and the need to maintain the powers of

---

[106] In particular, fair and equitable treatment and full protection and security, see Art 8.10 CETA.

[107] Ibid., Art 8.9.

[108] See Joint Interpretative Instrument on the CETA (n 43), point 2.

[109] See Arts 18(1) and (3) of the Energy Charter Treaty (n 10):
The Contracting Parties recognize state sovereignty and sovereign rights over energy resources. They reaffirm that these must be exercisedin accordance with and subject to the rules of international law.[...] Each state continues to holdin particularthe rights to [...] regulate the environmental and safety aspects of such exploration, development and reclamation within its Area [...], and to participate in such exploration and exploitation, inter alia, through direct participation by the government or through state enterprises (emphasis added).

the Union in international relations' which guided the CJEU's reasoning in Opinion 1/17[110] and led to a 'softening' of the prerequisites that flowed from the principle of the autonomy of EU law, are misplaced in an intra-EU context. Therefore, if Opinion 1/17 supports one conclusion, then it is this one: namely that the ISDS provisions in the ECT are, in any scenario, in obvious conflict with the principle of the autonomy of EU law.

With regard to the EU Member States' BITs with third countries, they have been grandfathered by Regulation 1219/2012 establishing transitional arrangements for bilateral investment agreements between Member States and third countries.[111] Such grandfathering extends, however, only to the BITs' non-compliance with the allocation of competences between the EU and the Member States contained in the EU Treaties.[112] However, the EU cannot discretionarily dispense the EU Member States from other EU obligations in the EU Treaties. While a number of EU Member State BITs have already been found to violate the TFEU provisions on free movement of capital,[113] many, if not all, are likely to fall foul of the principle of autonomy of EU law as interpreted in Opinion 1/17. Just like an EU agreement, EU Member State agreements can be:

> capable of having the consequence [...] [that] a Member State in the course of implementing EU law [...] has to amend or withdraw legislation because of an assessment made by a tribunal standing outside the EU judicial system of the level of protection of a public interest established, in accordance with the EU constitutional order, by the EU institutions.[114]

Opinion 1/17 found such danger to be unacceptable, violating the principle of autonomy of EU law. Since most of the EU Member State BITs lack safeguards equivalent to those in the CETA, tribunals can 'call into question

---

[110] Opinion 1/17 (n 7), para 117.
[111] Regulation (EU) No 1219/2012 of the European Parliament and of the Council establishing transitional arrangements for bilateral investment agreements between Member States and third countries [2012] OJ L 351/40.
[112] See the most recent list of the bilateral investment agreements published in accordance with ibid., Art 4(1): List of the bilateral investment agreements referred to in Art 4(1) of Regulation (EU) No 1219/2012 of the European Parliament and of the Council establishing transitional arrangements for bilateral investment agreements between Member States and third countries [2019] OJ C 198.
[113] See Case C-205/06 *Commission of the European Communities v Republic of Austria* [2009] ECLI:EU:C:2009:118; Case C-249/06 *Commission of the European Communities v Kingdom of Sweden* [2009] ECLI:EU:C:2009:119; Case C-118/07 *Commission of the European Communities v Republic of Finland* [2009] ECLI:EU:C:2009:715.
[114] Opinion 1/17 (n 7), para 150.

the level of protection of a public interest that led to the introduction of such restrictions by the Union with respect to all operators who invest in the commercial or industrial sector at issue of the internal market'.[115]

Overall, Opinion 1/17 replaces what one may refer to as 'strategic ambiguity' with clarity over the unconstitutionality of a large number of existing EU legal instruments protecting EU investments abroad. In terms of the rule of law, this clarification should be welcomed. However, clarity increases the political pressure to come forward with some lawful instrument which, at the same time, sufficiently secures the economic interests of EU businesses abroad – something which could prove challenging in the current political climate that no longer unreservedly embraces globalisation.[116]

4.   CONCLUSIONS

Opinion 1/17 allows for a ratification of the CETA and frees the Commission's present investment protection policy from the shadow of illegality. At the same time, three facets – (1) looming judicial conflicts and the CJEU's limited effectiveness in shielding the EU legal order from outside influence, (2) alternative standards of reviewing sovereign power and the reshaping of the rule of law in the EU, and (3) the unavoidable revaluation of a large number of existing investment protection agreements in light of the further specification of the EU constitutional principle of autonomy of EU law – show that Opinion 1/17 is also significantly impacting the EU constitutional order. Whether it is worth paying this 'price' for allowing the EU to take a seat at the ISDS reform table can ultimately only be judged over time, as adjudicative practice on the basis of the CETA (and similar agreements) can then be included in the equation.

On a positive note, a continuing EU engagement in the ISDS reform process might indeed help overcome the weaknesses identified in the traditional forms of ISDS.[117] Equally, or perhaps even more importantly, such engagement

---

[115] Ibid., para 137.

[116] Cf, the Netherlands' new model BIT: Ministerie van Buitenlandse Zaken, Netherlands model investment agreement (2019) www.rijksoverheid.nl/binaries/rijksoverheid/documenten/publicaties/2019/03/22/nieuwe-modeltekst-investerings akkoorden/nieuwe+modeltekst+investeringsakkoorden.pdf, accessed 11 February 2020. The work on the model investment agreement predates Opinion 1/17. Due to the fact that the text was modelled closely to the CETA provisions, it seems to address at least some of the EU constitutional deficits of EU Member State BITs with third countries. It is, however, beyond the scope of this chapter to analyse whether the safeguards provided therein are indeed sufficient in terms of the principle of autonomy of EU law.

[117] On these weaknesses, see Hindelang, 'Study on Investor-State Dispute Settlement (ISDS) and Alternatives of Dispute Resolution in International Investment Law' (n 3), 56–113.

allows EU businesses to take advantage of a *legal* mechanism that provides protection – albeit on a lower level than previous agreements of the EU Member States – against the realisation of political risk when they engage in investment activities in third countries.

One possibly encounters mixed feelings when reflecting on the clarity gained regarding both the incompatibility of EU law with a large number of existing EU Member State agreements and the ECT protection of EU investments abroad. It is high time that lawful instruments that sufficiently secure the economic interests of EU businesses abroad are deployed.

Turning to the more challenging parts of the CJEU's Opinion 1/17, accepting that an investor can choose between domestic courts, including the CJEU, and CETA's ICS, is not unproblematic. Each forum comes with different standards for reviewing the exercise of sovereign power as well as different legal remedies. While the courts and tribunals of EU Member States and the CJEU provide in principle for a 'comprehensive review' of the exercise of sovereign power, the ICS – if operating as envisaged by the parties to the agreement – only provides for a 'minimal review'. A 'minimal review' diminishes the overall judicial control of administrative conduct and reshapes the specific expression of the principle of legality of administration in the EU constitutional order to the detriment of the legislature. This reshaping, however, seems to be still *within* the spectrum of political choices available to the EU legislator. Nonetheless, it is a victory for an errant ideology that domestic courts are distrusted to the extent that they may not even receive a single opportunity to get it right. It is, moreover, a choice against subsidiarity, one of the core building principles of the EU.[118] It is also a choice that rejects a close tying of administration to the democratic will of parliament. A flexible, ECHR-like[119] local remedies rule[120] could have addressed the competing interests at stake in a more nuanced fashion. Not this time, though.

---

[118] Cf Arts 5(1) and (3) of the Consolidated Version of the Treaty on European Union [2012] OJ C 326/13.

[119] See Art 35(1) of the Convention for the Protection of Human Rights and Fundamental Freedoms (1950) 87 UNTS 103, which requires, in principle, the exhaustion of local remedies before turning to the ECtHR. However, the requirement is not an absolute one. If the local remedies are not to be considered accessible or effective, the applicant may turn to the ECtHR directly, see: William Schabas, *The European Convention of Human Rights: A Commentary* (OUP 2015) 764–769; David J Harris, Michael O'Boyle, Ed P Bates and Carla M Buckley, *Harris, O'Boyle and Warbrick: Law of the European Convention on Human Rights* (4th edn, OUP 2018) 60–62 and the cases referred to therein.

[120] Hindelang, 'Study on Investor-State Dispute Settlement (ISDS) and Alternatives of Dispute Resolution in International Investment Law' (n 3), 91–92.

8. Draft EU-Swiss institutional agreement: Towards a new institutional paradigm?

Adam Łazowski[1]

1. INTRODUCTION

The EU-Swiss relations are without a shadow of the doubt an ideal laboratory for study of various legal, political, and economic phenomena.[2] They are continuously characterised by contrapuntal tendencies. On the one hand, Switzerland remains deeply integrated with the EU and its Member States. On the other hand, it has a well-deserved reputation of being a reluctant European.[3] As aptly put by Christine Kaddous, the relationship between the EU and Switzerland is 'dense, intense and in constant evolution'.[4] This is reflected, for instance, in the

---

[1]   The author is grateful to Dr Anna Łabędzka for her comments to the earlier drafts of the chapter. The usual disclaimer applies.

[2]   For a comprehensive overview see, inter alia: Marius Vahl and Nina Grolimund, *Integration without Membership. Swizterland's Bilateral Agreements with the European Union* (CEPS 2006); Clive H Church (ed) *Switzerland and the European Union. A Close, Contradictory and Misunderstood Relationship* (Routledge 2007); René Schwok, *Switzerland – European Union. An Impossible Membership?* (P.I.E. Peter Lang 2009); Matthias Oesch, *Switzerland and the European Union. General Framework. Bilateral Agreements. Autonomous Adaptation* (Nomos 2018); Paolo Dardanelli and Oscar Mazzoleni (eds), *Switzerland-EU Relations. Lessons for the UK after Brexit?* (Routledge 2021). For a more general perspective, see Magdalena Bernath, Laurent Goetschel and Daniel Schwarz, *Swiss Foreign Policy. Foundations and Possibilities* (Routledge 2005).

[3]   See, for instance, Sandra Lavenex and René Schwok, 'The Swiss Way. The Nature of Switzerland's Relationship with the EU' in Erik O Eriksen and John Erik Fossum (eds), *The European Union's Non-Members. Independence under Hegemony?* (Routledge 2015) 37.

[4]   Christine Kaddous, 'Switzerland and the EU. Current Issues and New Challenges under the Draft Institutional Framework Agreement' in Sieglinde Gstöhl and David Phinnemore (eds), *The Proliferation of Privileged Partnerships between the European Union and its Neighbours* (Routledge 2019) 68.

idiosyncratic fashion in which the bilateral legal framework has been evolving since 1956, when the first agreement was concluded by the High Authority of the European Steel and Coal Community and the Swiss Federation.[5] A quick *tour de table* of EU relations with its neighbours demonstrates that traditionally a legal backbone for bilateral relations materialises in the shape of a comprehensive association, or co-operation agreement.[6] Textbook examples are legal frameworks bringing together the EU and the Eastern Partnership *avant garde*: Ukraine;[7] Moldova;[8] and Georgia.[9] Comprehensive association agreements[10] are supplemented by sectoral treaties dealing with, for instance, visa facilitation,[11] readmission[12] or air transport.[13] In this respect the bilateral EU-Swiss framework stands out as it comprises over 120 sectoral agreements, however – thus far – it is shy of a *chapeau* agreement. Consequentially, the EU-Swiss framework is very patchy and hard to navigate. The practical chal-

---

[5]   Accord de Consultation entre la Confédération Suisse et la Haute Autorité de la Communauté Européenne du Charbon et de l'Acier [1958] JO 7/85.

[6]   For an overview see, inter alia, Steven Blockmans and Adam Łazowski (eds), *The European Union and Its Neighbours. A Legal Appraisal of the EU's Policies of Stabilisation, Partnership and Integration* (Asser Press 2006); Roman Petrov, *Exporting the Acquis Communautaire through European Union External Agreements* (Nomos 2011); Peter Van Elsuwege, 'The EU and its Neighbours' in Ramses A Wessel and Joris Larik (eds) *EU External Relations Law. Text, Cases and Materials* (Hart Publishing 2020).

[7]   Association Agreement between the European Union and the European Atomic Energy Community and its Member States, of the one part, and Ukraine, of the other part [2014] OJ L 161/3.

[8]   Association Agreement between the European Union and the European Atomic Energy Community and their Member States, of the one part, and the Republic of Moldova, of the other part [2014] OJ L 260/4.

[9]   Association Agreement between the European Union and the European Atomic Energy Community and their Member States, of the one part, and Georgia, of the other part [2014] OJ L 261/4.

[10]   See further Guillaume Van der Loo, *The EU-Ukraine Association Agreement and Deep and Comprehensive Free Trade Area. A New Legal Instrument for EU Integration without Membership* (Brill Nijhoff 2016); Michael Emerson and Veronica Movchan (eds), *Deepening EU-Ukrainian Relations: What, why and how?* (2nd edn, CEPS 2018); Michael Emerson and Denis Cenuşa (eds), *Deepening EU-Moldovan Relations: What, why and how?* (2nd edn, CEPS 2018); Michael Emerson and Tamara Kovziridze (eds), *Deepening EU-Georgia Relations: What, why and how?* (2nd edn, CEPS 2018).

[11]   See, for instance, Agreement between the European Community and Ukraine on the facilitation of the issuance of visas [2007] OJ L 332/68.

[12]   Agreement between the European Union and Georgia on the readmission of persons residing without authorisation [2011] OJ L 52/47.

[13]   Common Aviation Area Agreement between the European Union and its Member States, of the one part, and Georgia, of the other part [2012] OJ L 321/3.

lenges are exacerbated by the lack of a horizontal institutional set-up facilitating regular and general dialogue between the parties. The existing EU-Swiss Agreements offer tailor-made arrangements, making the system unnecessarily varied and complex. The crux of the problem is inextricably linked with all these factors but lies elsewhere. Several agreements concluded between the EU and Switzerland in the past decade envisage the market access and consequential development of a common regulatory space. The present author, in one of the earlier contributions to the debate, has referred to this model of integration without membership as enhanced bilateralism.[14] The system created by the bilateral agreements is, with a few exceptions, static. To put it differently, Switzerland is not required to follow any new EU *acquis*. Consequentially, the homogeneity of the joint legal space has been strained, with the EU-Swiss Agreement on Free Movement of Persons being the prime culprit.[15] Not surprisingly, the EU has become increasingly vocal about its concerns, calling for recalibration of the bilateral framework, in particular for creation of a new institutional arrangement.[16] The latter has materialised in the Draft Agreement, the negotiations of which – not without political dramas – have been concluded in 2018.[17] When this chapter was completed, the Draft Agreement had yet to be signed and ratified. Alas, no cast iron plan as to the future steps was in sight as Switzerland, in May 2021, effectively withdrew from it. The political shenanigans were not accidental. *Au contraire*, the way in which the Draft Agreement was negotiated, frozen, and then effectively shelved, symbolises rather well the current mood and crisis in EU-Swiss relations.[18]

The aim of this contribution is to put the Draft Agreement under the microscope with the view of fleshing out the main parameters of the new institutional arrangement. However, as the starting point, the author will reach for the telescope and take a brief look at the big picture, that is the existing EU-Swiss relations and, in particular, the Bilateral I package (section 2). This will set the scene for the analysis of the Draft Agreement and its potential (section

---

[14]   Adam Łazowski, 'Enhanced Bilateralism and Multilateralism: Integration without Membership' (2008) 45 *Common Market Law Review* 1433.

[15]   Agreement between the European Community and its Member States, of the one part, and the Swiss Confederation, of the other, on the free movement of persons [2002] OJ L 114/6.

[16]   See, inter alia, Council (EU), Council conclusions on EU relations with the Swiss Confederation, No 116/19, 19 February 2019, paras 9 and 13.

[17]   Accord facilitant les relations bilatérales entre l'Union européenne et la Confédération suisse dans les parties du marché intérieur auxquelles la Suisse participe https://www.eda.admin.ch/dam/dea/fr/documents/abkommen/Acccord-inst-Projet-de -texte_fr.pdf, accessed 30 November 2020.

[18]   See René Schwok, 'Switzerland-EU Relations: The Bilateral Way in a Fragilized Position' (2020) 25 *EU Foreign Affairs Review* 159.

3). As the next step, the author will pursue the argument that some features of the Draft Agreement have a potential to become a new institutional paradigm for upgrades to existing agreements between the EU and its most integrated neighbours.[19] In particular, this may be appealing to Ukraine, Moldova, and Georgia, whose authorities have already called for upgrades in their relations with the EU. Interestingly enough, the EU-UK Withdrawal Agreement, a *de facto* and *de iure* a vehicle for de-integration, is also built on the same institutional paradigm, proving that it may be used in non-Swiss context (section 4).[20]

2.   EU-SWISS BILATERAL FRAMEWORK: A LARGE-SCALE FRAGMENTATION

2.1   Introduction

As already alluded to, the EU-Swiss framework is characterised by high levels of complexity, both in terms of the sheer number of bilateral agreements but also their substance. The two sets of bilateral agreements dating back to, respectively 1999 and 2002, are textbook examples.[21] Yet, in recent years the

---

[19]   On the current state of affairs, see Guillaume Van der Loo, 'The Institutional Framework of the Eastern Partnership Association Agreements and the Deep and Comprehensive Free Trade Areas' in Gstöhl and Phinnemore (n 4), 102.

[20]   Agreement on the withdrawal of the United Kingdom of Great Britain and Northern Ireland from the European Union and the European Atomic Energy Community [2020] OJ L 29/7. For an academic appraisal see, inter alia: Federico Fabbrini (ed), *The Law and Politics of Brexit. Volume II The Withdrawal Agreement* (OUP 2020); Michael Dougan, 'So long, farewell, auf wiedersehen, goodbye: The UK's Withdrawal Package' (2020) 57 *Common Market Law Review* 631.

[21]   The Bilateral I is composed of, inter alia: Agreement between the European Community and its Member States, of the one part, and the Swiss Confederation, of the other, on the free movement of persons [2002] OJ L 114/6; Agreement between the European Community and the Swiss Confederation on Air Transport [2002] OJ L 114/73; Agreement between the European Community and the Swiss Confederation on the Carriage of Goods and Passengers by Rail and Road [2002] OJ L 114/91; Agreement between the European Community and the Swiss Confederation on trade in agricultural products [2002] OJ L 114/132; Agreement between the European Community and the Swiss Confederation on mutual recognition in relation to conformity assessment [2002] OJ L 114/369; Agreement between the European Community and the Swiss Confederation on certain aspects of government procurement [2002] OJ L 114/430.

The main components of Bilateral II are: Agreement between the European Union, the European Community and the Swiss Confederation on the Swiss Confederation's association with the implementation, application and development of the Schengen *acquis* [2008] OJ L 53/52; Agreement between the European Community and the Swiss Confederation concerning the criteria and mechanisms for establishing the

co-operation between the two sides has gone much further, even despite the already mentioned political crisis. A fitting proof of the former is, for instance, linking of the EU and Swiss greenhouse emissions in a tailor-made agreement aiming at meeting the objectives of the Paris Agreement.[22] In reality, though, there is more than meets the eye. The legal integration of Switzerland goes well beyond what is required by the EU-Swiss treaties as for decades the authorities in Bern have been keen to model the national law on EU *acquis*. This is referred to as an autonomous adaptation,[23] which – one may argue – is a very good example of 'Brussels Effect'.[24] While the latter is based on a voluntary decision and leads to adoption of legal transplants,[25] the challenges to homogeneity of the joint legal space arise in the areas where Switzerland is under the obligation to follow EU law, or, as the case may be, when some provisions are modelled on EU law. This has been causing concerns of the EU and, eventually, has led to the negotiations of the Draft Agreement. Against this backdrop, the centre of gravity in the next paragraph will be on the Bilateral I package,

---

state responsible for examining a request for asylum lodged in a Member State or in Switzerland [2008] OJ L 53/5; Agreement between the European Community and the Swiss Confederation providing for measures equivalent to those laid down in Council Directive 2003/48/EC on taxation of savings income in the form of interest payments [2004] OJ L 385/30; Agreement between the European Community and the Swiss Confederation amending the Agreement between the European Economic Community and the Swiss Confederation of 22 July 1972 as regards the provisions applicable to processed agricultural products [2005] OJ L 23/19; Agreement between the European Community and the Swiss Confederation concerning the participation of Switzerland in the European Environment Agency and the European Environment Information and Observation Network [2006] OJ L 90/37; Agreement between the European Community and the Swiss Confederation on cooperation in the field of statistics [2006] OJ L 90/2. Agreement for scientific and technological cooperation between the European Union and European Atomic Energy Community and the Swiss Confederation associating the Swiss Confederation to Horizon 2020 — the Framework Programme for Research and Innovation and the Research and Training Programme of the European Atomic Energy Community complementing Horizon 2020, and regulating the Swiss Confederation's participation in the ITER activities carried out by Fusion for Energy [2014] OJ L 370/3.
[22]   Agreement between the European Union and the Swiss Confederation on the linking of their greenhouse gas emissions trading systems [2017] OJ L 322/3.
[23]   The origins of this pro-EU drive go back to a decision of the Federal Council taken in 1988. See Oesch (n 2), 139–153; Kaddous, 'Switzerland and the EU' (n 4), 72.
[24]   See further Anu Bradford, *The Brussels Effect. How the European Union Rules the World* (OUP 2020). See also on export of EU law qua EU agreements with third countries, inter alia, Roman Petrov, *Exporting the Acquis Communautaire through European Union External Agreements* (Nomos 2011).
[25]   See further on the notion of legal transplants: Beata Kviatek, *Explaining Legal Transplants. Transplantation of EU Law into Central Eastern Europe* (Wolf Legal Publishers 2015); Helen Xanthaki, 'Legal Transplants in Legislation: Defusing the Trap' (2008) 57 *International and Comparative Law Quarterly* 659.

which is where the main challenges arise. With ample literature in place, the agreements forming the Bilateral I need no detailed rehearsing.[26] However, some of the key points merit attention as they will set the scene for assessment of the Draft Agreement.

2.2   Bilateral I Package: Homogeneity Under Strain

The genesis of Bilateral I package (and, in equal measure of Bilateral II) goes back to the early 1990s when Switzerland took steps aiming at closer integration with the emerging EU. To begin with, since 1984 it was deeply involved in creation of the European Economic Area (EEA).[27] Furthermore, in 1992 Switzerland formally submitted its application for membership of the EU. However, courtesy to a nationwide referendum on the EEA, neither participation in the EEA, nor the EU membership ever materialised.[28] The end result was an immediate pull out from the EEA project.[29] Not surprisingly, the EU

---

[26]   For a detailed assessment see: Stephan Breitenmoser, 'Sectoral Agreements Between the EC and Switzerland: Contents and Context' (2003) 40 *Common Market Law Review* 1137; René Schwok, 'Switzerland's Approximation of its Legislation to the EU *Acquis*: Specificities, Lessons and Paradoxes' (2007) *IX European Journal of Law Reform* 449; Christine Kaddous, 'The Relations Between the EU and Switzerland' in Alan Dashwood and Marc Maresceau (eds), *Law and Practice of EU External Relations. Salient Features of a Changing Landscape* (CUP 2008) 227, 231–243.

[27]   Agreement on the European Economic Area [1994] OJ L 1/1. Further on the negotiations of the EEA Agreement see, inter alia, Sven Norberg and Martin Johansson, 'The History of the EEA Agreement and the First Twenty Years of Its Existence' in Carl Baudenbacher (ed), *The Handbook of EEA Law* (Springer 2015) 3.

[28]   More on the domestic factors behind Swiss attitude to the EU see, inter alia: Goetschel, Bernath and Schwarz (n 2), 63–78; Joachim Blatter, 'Bilateralism's Polarising Consequences in a Very Particular/ist Democracy', in Eriksen and Fossum (n 3).

[29]   This took place even before the EEA Agreement entered into force. The withdrawal of Switzerland caused procedural challenges and forced the remaining EEA parties to negotiate a tailor-made protocol. Ultimately, this delayed entry into force of the EEA Agreement, and the launch of the EEA, to 1 January 1994. See further Bertil Cottier and Alexandra Gerber, 'Some Problems Regarding Ratification and Implementation of the European Economic Area Agreement in the EFTA Member States' (1993) 20 *Polish Yearbook of International Law* 253.

application was frozen in turn.[30] Eventually, the shenanigans of 1992 plebiscite paved the way for the negotiations and conclusion of the Bilateral I package.[31]

From the start this exercise had features of a legal experiment as a series of separate, yet inextricably linked, agreements negotiated simultaneously by the EU with a single neighbouring country had been previously unheard of. In order to make sure that Switzerland does not approach the agreements forming the Bilateral I package in *à la carte* fashion, the European Commission already before the talks commenced envisaged that the agreements would be bound by a guillotine clause. In simple terms, only the entire package could enter into force and, should one of the agreements be terminated in the future, the remaining ones would share the fate.[32] This idea turned into reality and the guillotine clauses have been inserted into each and every agreement.[33] In hindsight, such a *modus operandi* has been a blessing and a curse. On the one hand, it potentially stopped the Swiss authorities (and Swiss voters) from cherry picking. On the other hand, the guillotine clause remains a risky endeavour, particularly when one takes into account the resentment in parts of Swiss population to the continuation of free movement of persons. For instance, had the referendum of 27 September 2020 delivered a different result, the entire Bilateral I package would have faced the risk of termination.[34] Despite its hazardous nature, the

---

[30]   Another twist in the EU membership saga could have come from a referendum on immediate start of accession negotiations, which took place in 2001. However, this idea failed to gain the momentum and led to overwhelmingly negative outcome of this plebiscite. Switzerland eventually withdrew its application for EU membership in 2016. See further on that referendum René Schwok and Nicolas Levrat, 'Switzerland's Relations with the EU after the Adoption of the Seven Bilateral Agreements' (2001) 6 *European Foreign Affairs Review* 335, 351–352.

[31]   For a detailed account of the negotiations see, inter alia, Cédric Dupont and Pascal Sciarini, 'Back to the Future. The First Round of Bilateral Negotiations with the EU' in Church (n 2).

[32]   Commission, 'Future relations with Switzerland' (Communication) COM (93) 486 final, para 12 and Annex VI.

[33]   See Art 25 EU-Swiss Agreement on Free Movement of Persons; Art 36 EU-Swiss Agreement on Air Transport; Art 58 EU-Swiss Agreement on Road and Railway Transport; Art 17 EU-Swiss Agreement on Trade in Agricultural Products; Art 21 EU-Swiss Mutual Recognition Agreement; Art 18 EU-Swiss Public Procurement Agreement; Art 14 EU-Swiss Scientific and Technological Cooperation Agreement. The latter has been modified, for instance, by Article 13 of the EU-Swiss Scientific and Technological Cooperation Agreement of 2014. The guillotine clause covered only the Agreement on Free Movement of Persons. Furthermore, a failure to ratify a Protocol to the latter, resulting from Croatia's accession to the EU, would have triggered the termination of the Scientific and Technological Cooperation Agreement itself.

[34]   On that day Switzerland held a referendum on 'moderate immigration' initiative, which was triggered by a proposal of the populist Swiss People's Party (SVP). At the end of the day, over 60 per cent of voters cast negative ballots, thus – at least for

guillotine clause, which is a piece of political weaponry, is likely to stay for the foreseeable future and play the role of the Chekhov's gun, causing a degree of insecurity as it may be used at any point in time.

What is more, the intention of negotiators was to offer piecemeal access to benefits of the EU Internal Market. Consequentially, this triggered a plethora of key questions. First, which sections of the EU Internal Market were on offer. Secondly, how to guarantee that the final package would cover dossiers of interests for both sides, not only those on the radars of the Swiss or the EU authorities. As the European Commission aptly put in its Communication of 1993, the early advances made by the Swiss authorities, right after the failed EEA referendum, 'should [be] considered on a strict basis of mutual advantage and without undermining the EEA'.[35] A compromise was eventually reached, however the negotiations were not easy by any stretch of imagination. In terms of the levels of tension and disagreement, two dossiers stood out: the free movement of persons as well as the road and rail transport. The first was high on the agenda of the EU and, at the same time, it was the least welcome addition to the negotiations for authorities in Bern. The second proved to be tricky as different priorities in the negotiations had to be addressed. Overall, as part of this round of negotiations, seven agreements were finalised. To placate concerns and trepidation, a transitional regime was envisaged in relation to the free movement of persons, which allowed a gradual phasing in of the Internal Market principles.[36] Similar arrangements applied also to the road and rail transport.[37] With such safeguards in place, the Bilateral I package was signed in 1999 and entered into force on 1 June 2002.[38]

One of the main features of the Bilateral I Agreements is the market access, allowing Switzerland to benefit from chunks of the EU Internal Market. This, however, had to come at a price, a phenomenon which reflects the well-known rule of thumb: the closer the integration, the higher levels of regulatory convergence are required. Consequentially, several Bilateral I Agreements contain lists of EU *acquis* that Switzerland has the obligation to comply with. Furthermore, some provisions of the Agreements are modelled on respective

---

now – free movement of persons is destined to stay in relations between the EU and Switzerland. See further on the background of the referendum Schwok (n 18), 167–170.

[35]   Commission, 'Future relations with Switzerland' (Communication) (n 32), 3.

[36]   Art 10 of the EU-Swiss Agreement on Free Movement of Persons. For a detailed account, see Adam Łazowski, 'Switzerland' in Blockmans and Łazowski (n 6), 177.

[37]   Art 8 of the Road and Rail Transport Agreement. See further on the negotiations of this Agreement, Dupont and Sciarini (n 31), 203–204.

[38]   It was followed by negotiations of Bilateral II package. See further: Alexandre Afonso and Martino Maggetti, 'Bilaterals II. Reaching the Limits of the Swiss Third Way?' in Church (n 2), 215; Kaddous (n 26), 243–255.

provisions of EU law.[39] Not surprisingly, it has been a matter of major concern for the EU how to secure the homogeneity of the joint legal space, both in the law book and in the courtrooms. It was clear from the start that the dynamic system for updates of EU *acquis* – modelled on the EEA – was not on the cards.[40] Hence, the fundamental question was whether a static *modus operandi*, that is not requiring automatic updates, would suffice. Almost two decades of implementation have demonstrated that concerns about the homogeneity of the EU-Swiss legal space, raised by the EU during the negotiations, were justified. This has been particularly visible in the free movement of persons area, where – due to insistence of authorities in Bern – no update to the EU-Swiss framework has been made following the adoption of Directive 2004/38/EC on rights of EU citizens.[41] Furthermore, EU *acquis* has come a long way since the concept of EU citizenship and the Charter of Fundamental Rights became beacons for navigation for the Court of Justice. Neither of the two is a part of the EU-Swiss Agreement on Free Movement of Persons, which can be disruptive for the homogeneity of the legal space.[42] Last but not least, the institutional system of the Bilateral I has proven to be low key, patchy and difficult to navigate.[43] This may be to the liking of authorities in Bern, however the

---

[39]   See, for instance, Arts 8–9 EU-Swiss Air Transport Agreement, which are almost carbon copies of Arts 101–102 TFEU. See also Art 10 EU-Swiss Free Movement Persons Agreement, which although modelled on Art 45(4) TFEU (providing for public service exception from free movement of workers) is shaped in fashion reflecting interpretation of the latter by the Court of Justice and the European Commission.

[40]   On the EEA see, inter alia: Dag Wernø Holter, 'Legislative Homogeneity' in Carl Baudenbacher (ed), *The Fundamental Principles of EEA Law. EEA-ities* (Springer 2017) 1; Georges Baur, 'Decision-Making Procedure and Implementation of New Law' in Carl Baudenbacher (ed), *The Handbook of EEA Law* (Springer 2016) 45.

[41]   Directive 2004/38/EC of the European Parliament and of the Council of 29 April 2004 on the right of citizens of the Union and their family members to move and reside freely within the territory of the Member States amending Regulation (EEC) No 1612/68 and repealing Directives 64/221/EEC, 68/360/EEC, 72/194/EEC, 73/148/ EEC, 75/34/EEC, 75/35/EEC, 90/364/EEC, 90/365/EEC and 93/96/EEC [2004] OJ L 158/77. For a detailed account, see Elspeth Guild, Steve Peers and Jonathan Tomkin, *The EU Citizenship Directive: A Commentary* (2nd edn, OUP 2019).

[42]   This is problematic not only for the EU-Swiss framework but also for the European Economic Area. See, inter alia: Johanna Jonsdottir, *Europeanization and the European Economic Area. Iceland's Participation in the EU's Policy Process* (Routledge 2013), 96–112; Matthew Jay, 'Homogeneity, the Free Movement of Persons and Integration Without Membership: Mission Impossible?' (2013) 8 *Croatian Yearbook of European Law and Policy* 78, 100–113.

[43]   It largely hinges upon joint committees composed of civil servants. Each agreement falling under the Bilateral I package envisages such joint EU-Swiss Institutions. See Art 14 EU-Swiss Agreement on Free Movement of Persons; Arts 21–22 EU-Swiss Agreement on Air Transport; Art 51 EU-Swiss Agreement on Road and Railway

same cannot be said about the EU, which – rightly – pays particular attention to the coherence and integrity of its legal order. It is hardly surprising that the EU supported the initiative to negotiate and conclude a *chapeau* institutional agreement, tackling the weaknesses of the existing procedural regime.

3. DRAFT EU-SWISS INSTITUTIONAL AGREEMENT: AN OVERVIEW

3.1 Introduction

Despite its uncertain future the Draft Agreement merits a closer look.[44] Even if it does not enter into force in its current shape, it may surely be a point of reference during future talks between the EU and Switzerland, or – as argued later in the present chapter – in the EU negotiations with other third countries. The Agreement in question is interesting for several reasons. First, its centre of gravity is on tackling the threats to the homogeneity of the EU-Swiss joint legal space. It provides for enhancement of the *modus operandi* for adoption of updates to selected agreements falling under the Bilateral I umbrella. Furthermore, the Draft Agreement acknowledges the importance of jurisprudence of the Court of Justice of the European Union (CJEU) for the uniform interpretation of EU law. It also lays down the foundations for the enhanced joint institutional structure and guarantees more open access for Swiss officials to the EU comitology procedure.[45] Finally, the Draft Agreement provides a set of comprehensive rules governing the dispute settlement. They are all presented in turn.

Transport; Art 6 EU-Swiss Agreement on Trade in Agricultural Products; Art 10 EU-Swiss Mutual Recognition Agreement; Art 11 EU-Swiss Public Procurement Agreement; Art 5 EU-Swiss Scientific and Technological Cooperation Agreement (2014).

[44] The centre of gravity in the analysis that follows is on the institutional arrangements. However, one should note that the scope of the Draft Agreement goes beyond the matters in question and also extends to, inter alia, state aid rules applicable to aviation (see Annex X).

[45] Regulation (EU) No 182/2011 of the European Parliament and of the Council of 16 February 2011 laying down the rules and general principles concerning mechanisms for control by Member States of the Commission's exercise of implementing powers [2011] OJ L 55/13. See further, inter alia, Carl Fredrik Bergström and Dominique Ritleng (eds) *Rulemaking by the European Commission: The New System for Delegation of Powers* (OUP 2016).

3.2   Scope of Application

As noted earlier, the current EU-Swiss legal framework comprises over 120 agreements. However, the scope of the Draft Agreement is, for now, rather limited. In accordance with Article 2(2) Draft Agreement, it extends to five market access agreements falling under the Bilateral I umbrella. This includes agreements on free movement of persons, air transport, rail and road transport, trade in agricultural products, mutual recognition of technical standards. In accordance with Article 17, the Draft Agreement does not affect the scope, objectives and contents of the Bilateral I package, however, in case of inconsistencies, it will have primacy.[46] In an interesting move, the drafters also envisaged a solution *pro futuro*. As per Article 2(1), the Draft Agreement will also apply to future EU-Swiss treaties facilitating the market access. According to Schwok, it may extend to the Agreement on Electricity, which is currently on the negotiation table.[47]

3.3   Homogeneity of the Law Book

One of the main challenges posed by the agreements forming the Bilateral I package is ensuring homogeneity of the EU-Swiss legal space. As already mentioned, back at the time of negotiations, making the system static was a *conditio sine qua non* for the Swiss delegation.[48] Thus, changes to the EU *acquis* do not automatically trigger revisions of Bilateral I package as Switzerland is permitted to pick and choose. Consequentially, the reality offers a mixed bag and, as the example of the EU-Swiss Agreement on Free Movement of Persons demonstrates, the existing *modus operandi* may backfire and, in turn, undermine the homogeneity of the legal space and the legal certainty. To address this, Article 5 Draft Agreement aims at bringing some dynamic flavours into the equation. While it is shy of automatic incorporation of new EU *acquis* into the respective agreements forming the Bilateral I, it does provide that any relevant development in EU secondary legislation should be incorporated into the EU-Swiss bilateral framework, and consequentially the Swiss legislation, as quickly as possible. This, however, is subject to the procedural requirements laid down in Articles 13–14 Draft Agreement. In a nutshell, the decisions on adaptations of relevant Bilateral I Agreements will remain in the hands of the

---

[46]   At the same, it gives the two sides the freedom to decide otherwise: Art 17(2) Draft Agreement.

[47]   Schwok (n 18), 163.

[48]   The only EU-Swiss Agreements, which establish a dynamic system for updates are EU-Swiss Agreement on Association with Schengen *Acquis* (Art 7), EU-Swiss Agreement on Asylum (Art 4) and EU-Swiss Agreement on Customs (Art 22).

bilateral bodies established therein. While the *raison d'être* behind the new solutions is to facilitate prompt adaptations, the Draft Agreement is tailored in such a fashion as to accommodate the well-established Swiss model of direct democracy.[49] Should Switzerland oppose an update, the EU will have the right to trigger the dispute settlement procedure envisaged in Article 10 Draft Agreement and Protocol 3 (see section 3.6 below).

Two matters related to the updates of the relevant Bilateral I Agreements merit further attention. First, the Swiss authorities managed to secure exemptions in relation to several contentious dossiers. This, arguably, was the price that the EU had to pay in order to reach a compromise. As per Protocols 1 and 2 to the Draft Agreement, they extend to selected matters covered by the EU-Swiss Agreement on Free Movement of Persons, the EU-Swiss Agreement on Road and Rail Transport as well as the EU-Swiss Agreement on Trade in Agricultural Products. Furthermore, the proverbial elephant in the room: the Directive 2004/38/EC on free movement of persons has been kept at bay. Irrespective of that, a set of tailor-made arrangements for rules on, inter alia, posting of workers, has been agreed to in Protocol 1 to Draft Agreement.[50]

Secondly, the Draft Agreement facilitates for a more in-depth institutional engagement in development of EU *acquis*. One of the main features of the Bilateral I package is a very limited involvement of Swiss officials in the EU decision-making. As things currently stand, they may participate in meetings of a handful of committees, and only in capacity of observers without voting rights.[51] Similarly to the EEA framework, this amounts to

---

[49]   Still, however, the new arrangement may fall short of the desired democratic standard.

[50]   This covers the controversial Directive 96/71/EC of the European Parliament and of the Council of 16 December 1996 concerning the posting of workers in the framework of the provision of services [1997] OJ L 18/1. On the EU regulatory regime applicable to posting of workers see, inter alia, Piet Van Nuffel and Sofia Afanasjeva, 'The Revised Posting of Workers Directive: Curbing or Ensuring Free Movement?' in Nathan Cambien, Dimitry Kochenov and Elise Muir (eds), *European Citizenship under Stress. Social Justice, Brexit and Other Challenges* (Brill Nijhoff 2020) 271.

[51]   For a list of committees see: Declaration on Swiss Attendance of Committees, annexed to the Agreement on Free Movement of Persons [2002] OJ L 114/72; Declaration on Swiss Attendance of Committees, annexed to the Air Transport Agreement [2002] OL L 114/89; Declaration on Swiss Attendance of Committees, annexed to Road and Railway Transport Agreement [2002] OJ L 114/130; Declaration on Swiss Attendance of Committees, annexed to Agreement on trade in agricultural products [2002] OJ L 144/368; Declaration on Swiss Attendance of Committees, annexed to Agreement on mutual recognition in relation to conformity assessment [2002] OJ L 114/429; Declaration on Swiss Attendance of Committees, annexed to Agreement on public procurement [2002] OJ L 114/467; Article 6 of the Agreement for Scientific and Technological Cooperation [2014] OJ L 370/3. A similar arrangement

contribution to decision-shaping, making Switzerland a norm taker, not a norm maker. Bearing in mind the already discussed *modus operandi* for updates to the respective Bilateral I Agreements, which is envisaged in the Draft Agreement, it should not come as a surprise that the Swiss involvement in the EU decision-shaping is destined for enhancement. In this respect, the Draft Agreement brings no breakthrough solutions but rather replicates the solutions already known from the existing EU-Swiss Agreement on Association with Schengen *Acquis*,[52] EU-Swiss Agreement on Asylum[53] and the EU-Swiss Agreement on Customs.[54] First, proposals for EU secondary legislation coming from the European Commission, falling within the scope of the respective Bilateral I Agreements, will be shared and informally consulted with Swiss authorities along the lines of standard procedures applicable to the Member States. The sectoral committees established on the basis of the relevant Bilateral I Agreements will serve as an institutional outlet for the bilateral consultations ahead of proceedings within the Council of the European Union. Article 12(4–6) Draft Agreement envisages involvement of Swiss authorities in the work of committees established for the purposes of adoption of implementing and delegated acts. Again, this extends to the right to participate and to contribute to the discussions, but it is shy of the right to vote.

3.4   Homogeneity in the Court Rooms

As well-known and documented in the literature, EU law continuously develops not only through the actions of the legislature but also thanks to the active role played by the CJEU.[55] Hence, the discussion on exportability of its jurisprudence to countries seeking deeper integration with the EU Internal

---

is also provided in Bilateral II package. See, for instance, Agreement in the form of an Exchange of Letters between the Council of the European Union and the Swiss federation on the committees that assist the European Commission in the exercise of its executive powers [2008] OJ L 53/77. Furthermore, a more recent Agreement on Customs follows suit (see Art 23) [2009] OJ L 199/31.

[52]   Arts 5–6 EU-Swiss Agreement on Association with Schengen.
[53]   Art 2 EU-Swiss Agreement on Asylum.
[54]   Art 22 EU-Swiss Customs Agreement.
[55]   For a legal and political account see, inter alia: Sabine Saurugger and Fabien Terpan, *The Court of Justice of the European Union and the Politics of Law* (Palgrave 2016); Dorte Sindbjerg Martinsen, *An Ever More Powerful Court? The Political Constraints of Legal Integration in the European Union* (OUP 2015); Alan Rosas, Egils Levits, Yves Bot (eds), *The Court of Justice and the Construction of Europe: Analyses and Perspectives on Sixty Years of Case-law* (Asser Press 2013); Karen J. Alter, *The European Court's Political Power. Selected Essays* (OUP 2009); Thomas Horsley, *The Court of Justice of the European Union as an Institutional Actor. Judicial Lawmaking and its Limits* (CUP 2018).

Market is traditionally part of the game. The negotiations of Bilateral I package were no exception, yet they ended with modest results. Only two Agreements forming Bilateral I require taking account of case-law of the CJEU, which – however – is limited to jurisprudence predating the Bilateral I.[56] What has since happened at Kirchberg needs only to be brought to the attention of Swiss authorities.[57] In this respect the solutions in question partly reflect Article 6 EEA Agreement, which also brings into the equation the Luxembourg jurisprudence, but limits that to case-law predating creation of the EEA.[58] As evidence proves, neither in the case of Switzerland nor in the EEA-EFTA states has it stopped the national courts from engaging, in varying degrees and depth, with the subsequent jurisprudence of the CJEU. In case of the Swiss courts this was particularly visible in relation to the EU-Swiss Agreement on Free Movement of Persons, where – not surprisingly – the tensions between the old and new CJEU case-law became acutely visible.[59] But, as a matter of fact, the references spread also to other areas covered by the EU-Swiss bilateral framework as well as to dossiers to which the autonomous adaptation extends. The areas where such EU-inspired jurisprudence is most prolific include immigration, private international law, social security, and public procurement.[60] At the same time, occasional frictions are visible too; as noted by Christa Tobler,[61] some of the Swiss courts experience trepidation and troubles in following such controversial developments as the very creative jurisprudence of the Court of Justice on

---

[56] A different arrangement is provided in EU-Swiss Agreement on Association with Schengen (Art 8) and EU-Swiss Agreement on Asylum (Art 5) whereby bilateral EU-Swiss joint committees keep under regular review the developments at the Court of Justice of the European Union.

[57] See Art 16(2) EU-Swiss Agreement on Free Movement of Persons and Art 1(2) EU-Swiss Air Transport Agreement.

[58] Philipp Speitler, 'Judicial Homogeneity as a Fundamental Principle of the EEA' in Carl Baudenbacher (ed), *The Fundamental Principles of EEA Law. EEA-ities* (Springer 2017) 19.

[59] Francesco Maiani, 'CJEU Citations in the Case Law of the Swiss Federal Supreme Court. A Quantitative/Qualitative Analysis' in Arie Reich and Hans-W Micklitz (eds), *The Impact of the European Court of Justice on Neighbouring Countries* (OUP 2020) 81, 98–101.

[60] Ibid., 107.

[61] Christa Tobler, 'One of Many Challenges after "Brexit". The Institutional Framework of an Alternative Agreement – Lessons from Switzerland and Elsewhere?' (2016) 23 *Maastricht Journal of European and Comparative Law* 583.

Regulation 261/2004,[62] in particular the *Sturgeon* case.[63] Overall, a fair degree
of voluntarism has raised concerns on the EU side. Quite understandably, they
were exacerbated by the lack of a bridging EU-Swiss judicial authority, akin
of the EFTA Court serving the EEA.[64]

With the above in mind, Article 4(2) Draft Agreement should not come as
a surprise. It provides that relevant parts of the Bilateral I, as well as the Draft
Agreement itself, should be interpreted and applied as per jurisprudence of
the CJEU, irrespective of whether it was delivered prior or post conclusion of
a relevant agreement. It logically follows from the general obligation stemming
from Article 4(1) Draft Agreement to uniformly interpret relevant Bilateral
I Agreements and the relevant EU *acquis*. In order to secure the homogeneity,
Article 11 Draft Agreement creates a legal basis for regular dialogue between
the CJEU and the Swiss Federal Court.

Regardless of the new solutions, the question still remains whether the new
rules will make much of a difference. The fact of the matter is that not all, *prima
facie* relevant, case-law coming from Kirchberg may be fit for purpose for the
EU-Swiss framework. Once again, a good example may be the jurisprudence
on the free movement of persons. In the EU context it is strongly anchored in
the EU citizenship as well as the Charter of Fundamental Rights.[65] The trouble
is that neither of the two is applicable to the EU-Swiss framework, even though
the Swiss courts occasionally refer to the Charter when dealing with Schengen
related cases.[66] Furthermore, some of the jurisprudential output of the Court of

[62]   Regulation (EC) No 261/2004 of the European Parliament and of the Council of
11 February 2004 establishing common rules on compensation and assistance to passengers in the event of denied boarding and of cancellation or long delay of flights, and
repealing Regulation (EEC) No 295/91 [2004] OJ L 46/1.

[63]   Joined Cases C-402/07 and C-432/07 *Christopher Sturgeon, Gabriel Sturgeon
and Alana Sturgeon v Condor Flugdienst GmbH* (C-402/07) *and Stefan Böck and
Cornelia Lepuschitz v Air France SA* (C-432/07) ECLI:EU:C:2009:716. For a comprehensive appraisal see, inter alia, Michal Bobek and Jeremias Prassl (eds), *Air
Passengers Rights. Ten Years On* (Hart Publishing 2016).

[64]   See further, inter alia, Carl Baudenbacher, 'The EFTA Court: Structure and
Tasks' in Carl Baudenbacher (ed), *The Handbook of EEA Law* (Springer 2016) 139.

[65]   Above all, under the Polydor doctrine, provisions contained in international
agreements even if carbon copies of their EU law equivalents not always merit the
same interpretation. See, inter alia, Christa Tobler, 'Context-related Interpretation of
Association Agreements. The Polydor Principle in a Comparative Perspective: EEA
Law, Ankara Association Law and Market Access Agreements between Switzerland
and the EU' in Daniel Thym and Margarite Zoeteweij-Turhan (eds), *Rights of
Third-Country Nationals under EU Association Agreements. Degrees of Free Movement
and Citizenship* (Brill Nijhoff 2015) 101.

[66]   Adam Łazowski, 'Exporting Cherries for the Cakes: The Charter of Fundamental
Rights in Domestic Courts of the EU's Neighbourood' in Michal Bobek and Jeremias

Justice may prove to be too bitter a pill to swallow for the Swiss judges. Time will tell as to what extent the desiderata behind Article 4 Draft Agreement will turn into reality. The question is whether a formal requirement to interpret the relevant Agreements forming Bilateral I *in sync* with jurisprudence of the Court of Justice will persuade the Swiss judges to follow suit.

3.5 EU-Swiss Institutional Framework

The EU-Swiss institutional framework is patently patchy. A brief overview of the Bilateral I and Bilateral II packages proves that each and every agreement has its own institutional framework with joint committees at the heart of the procedural *modi operandi*. In order to address that deficiency, the Draft Agreement provides for creation of the Horizontal Joint Committee, composed of representatives of the EU and Switzerland.[67] It is destined to serve as the main institutional platform for the bilateral EU-Swiss co-operation. The main functions of the Horizontal Joint Committee will include ensuring the overall vision of the EU-Swiss relations, co-ordination between the committees established on the basis of the respective Bilateral I Agreements (referred to as sectoral committees) and supervision of implementation of the Draft Agreement when/if it enters into force. The Horizontal Joint Committee will be empowered, as per Article 15(2–3) Draft Agreement, to adopt non-binding recommendations as well as binding decisions.

Furthermore, in Article 16, the Draft Agreement lays down the foundation for creation of the Joint Parliamentary Committee. On the one hand, the latter solution fills an important gap and adds democratic credentials to the existing framework. On the other hand, it is not an original idea by any stretch of imagination. It follows the model well-known from the EU association agreements with other EU neighbours, including the EEA[68] and the agreements with the ENP *avant garde*.[69] Should the Draft Agreement enter into force, the Committee in question will be composed of representatives of the European

---

Adams-Prassl (eds), *The EU Charter of Fundamental Rights in the Member States* (Hart Publishing 2020) 499, 517.

[67] Art 15 Draft Agreement leaves it open how the representatives will be appointed and at what political level.

[68] Art 95 EEA Agreement.

[69] The Association Agreements with Ukraine, Moldova, and Georgia envisage creation of the Parliamentary Association Committees, composed of MEPs and members of respective parliaments of the ENP countries. See Arts 467–468 EU-Ukraine Association Agreement; Arts 440–441 EU-Moldova Association Agreement; Arts 410–411 EU-Georgia Association Agreement.

Parliament and the Swiss Parliament. It will serve as a vehicle for regular dialogue between the representatives of both legislatures.

Last but not least, the Draft Agreement does not bring ground-breaking changes to the institutional design for supervision of the implementation of the respective Bilateral I Agreements. It confirms that in this respect, the first point of call are the sectoral joint committees. Furthermore, as per Article 7(3) Draft Agreement, the European Commission and the Swiss authorities are empowered to monitor application of agreements by the other party. Should it demonstrate unsatisfactory results, the dispute settlement procedure discussed in the next section of this chapter could be triggered.

3.6   Dispute Settlement

One of the main features of the Draft Agreement is the comprehensive *modus operandi* for settlement of disputes.[70] It constitutes a considerable upgrade from the existing regimes laid down separately in each and every Bilateral I Agreement.[71] While it builds on the sectoral joint committees envisaged in the latter, it adds new layers with the possibility of appointment of the Arbitration Tribunal and even a reference for preliminary ruling to the CJEU.[72] It should be noted that in accordance with Article 9 Draft Agreement, no other dispute settlement mechanisms may be employed by the parties as far as the respective Bilateral I Agreements are concerned.

The dispute settlement procedure laid down in the Draft Agreement will be available, should the two sides experience difficulties in arriving at the same

---

[70]   Art 10 Draft Agreement and Protocol No 3. For a commentary see, inter alia, Kaddous, 'Switzerland and the EU' (n 4), 76–77.

[71]   See Art 19 EU-Swiss Agreement on Free Movement of Persons; Art 29 EU-Swiss Agreement on Air Transport; Art 54 EU-Swiss Agreement on Road and Railway Transport; Art 7 EU-Swiss Agreement on Trade in Agricultural Products; Art 14 EU-Swiss Mutual Recognition Agreement; Art 10 EU-Swiss Public Procurement Agreement; Art 5 EU-Swiss Scientific and Technological Cooperation Agreement (2014).

[72]   A possible engagement of the CJEU is not a novelty as it is already envisaged in several multilateral and bilateral agreements concluded by the European Union. See Art 16 and Annex IV to European Common Aviation Area Agreement (Multilateral Agreement between the European Community and its Member States, the Republic of Albania, Bosnia and Herzegovina, the Republic of Bulgaria, the Republic of Croatia, the former Yugoslav Republic of Macedonia, the Republic of Iceland, the Republic of Montenegro, the Kingdom of Norway, Romania, the Republic of Serbia and the United Nations Interim Administration Mission in Kosovo on the establishment of a European Common Aviation Area [2006] OJ L 285/3); Art 322 EU-Ukraine Association Agreement; Art 403 EU-Moldova Association Agreement; Art 267 EU-Georgia Association Agreement; Art 174 EU-UK Withdrawal Agreement.

interpretation of the relevant Bilateral I Agreements and/or EU secondary legislation listed therein. As already brought up, the same *modus operandi* will also apply should Switzerland refuse to update the respective Bilateral I Agreements in order to reflect developments in EU law. In the first instance, such matters should be resolved *qua* consultations in a relevant sectoral committee. If that does not bring the required results, the matter in question may be formally put to a resolution by a sectoral committee. If within three months a solution is not found, either of the sides may request settlement of the dispute by the Arbitration Tribunal. Logistical support services would be provided by the Permanent Court of Arbitration in the Hague.[73] Protocol No 3 attached to the Draft Agreement regulates the appointment and functioning of the Arbitration Tribunal. It is essential to note, that in case of doubts regarding interpretation of a provision of EU law, the Arbitration Tribunal shall proceed with a reference to the Court of Justice.[74] The judgment of the Court of Justice will be binding for the Arbitration Tribunal, whose decisions will be – in turn – binding for the EU and for Switzerland. Should they be not followed, either party would have a recourse to compensatory measures, the compliance of which with the principle of proportionality could be challenged at the sectoral joint committee, or further at the Arbitration Tribunal.

3.7   Where Do We Go From Here?

The analysis presented above gave the readers an insight into the Draft Agreement. The negotiations took five years to accomplish and were concluded in 2018. Alas, due to the 'policy of procrastination',[75] employed by the authorities in Bern, the Draft Agreement waited for 3 years to be initialled, signed, and ratified.[76] When this chapter was completed, it stood very little chance of entering into force. The public consultations, in which the Swiss authorities engaged in 2019, demonstrated that not all aspects of the agreed text were plausible to the members of the Swiss public. At the same time, the pro-EU result of the referendum on future of the EU-Swiss Agreement on Free Movement of Persons, held on 27 September 2020, gave the authorities in Bern a political mandate to return to the contentious Draft Agreement. They

---

[73]   Art 1.2 of Protocol 3 to the Draft Agreement.
[74]   See further Art III.9 of Protocol 3 to the Draft Agreement.
[75]   I borrow this apt characterisation of the Swiss Governments' policy from René Schwok (n 18), 162.
[76]   For the historical account of negotiations and the current state of affairs, see: Schwok, ibid., 161–163; Matthias Oesch, 'Switzerland-EU Bilateral Agreements, the Incorporation of EU Law and the Continuous Erosion of Democratic Right' (2020) 39 *Yearbook of European Law* 1, 26–35.

did so in November 2020 and, as already noted, pulled the plug in May 2021.[77] While the Draft Agreement was facing uncertain future, some of its main solutions were becoming an exportable commodity. For instance, the dispute settlement *modus operandi*, laid down in the EU-UK Withdrawal Agreement, was largely a carbon copy of the Draft Agreement. Furthermore, it has the potential to serve as a model for upgrades to several integration agreements concluded between the EU and its closest neighbours. In this respect, the Draft Agreement seems to be an emerging institutional paradigm, a phenomenon that is worth exploring in greater depth.

4.   TOWARDS A NEW INSTITUTIONAL PARADIGM?

4.1   *Tour de Table*: EU Agreements with its Neighbours

Over the past decades the EU has squared a ring of friends. It negotiated and concluded a plethora bilateral and multilateral agreements with almost all of its close, and more remote, geographical neighbours. The agreements in question result from the EU's drive to establish itself as a global player and, by the same token, its desire to pursue the deep trade agenda.[78] A brief *tour de table* shows that EU agreements with neighbours vary in their nature, scope and overall aims. As highlighted in the introduction to this chapter, traditionally the bilateral relations are based on the framework agreements, which – in many instances – take the shape of association agreements.[79] Frequently they are supplemented by flanking agreements of sectoral kind. In some cases the framework agreements are full of integration flavours, aimed at either *rapprochement* without EU membership or deep and comprehensive relations, with the EU accession on the horizon (even if remote). The first category includes the EEA Agreement as well as the EU-Swiss framework (even though it does not follow the pattern of a horizontal agreement, supplemented by sectoral treaties). By the looks of it, the forthcoming Association Agreement

---

[77]   See information available at the website of the Swiss Federal Council https://www.fdfa.admin.ch/europa/en/home.html, accessed 19 July 2021.

[78]   See further Billy A Melo Araujo, *The EU Deep Trade Agenda. Law and Policy* (OUP 2016); Isabelle Bosse-Platière and Cécile Rapoport (eds), *The Conclusion and Implementation of EU Free Trade Agreements. Constitutional Challenges* (Edward Elgar 2019).

[79]   See further Peter Van Elsuwege and Merijn Chamon, *The meaning of 'association' under EU law. A study on the law and practice of EU association agreements* (European Parliament 2019), https://www.europarl.europa.eu/RegData/etudes/STUD/2019/608861/IPOL_STU(2019)608861_EN.pdf, accessed 30 November 2020.

with Andorra, Monaco, and San Marino will also fall into this category.[80] As far as the second category is concerned, it definitely comprises the Association Agreements with Ukraine, Moldova, and Georgia and, to a lesser extent, the Enhanced Partnership Agreement with Armenia.[81] The framework agreements concluded with other EU neighbours are less integration oriented, even though in some cases they may ultimately serve as the vehicles for accession. Good examples in this respect are the Stabilisation and Association Agreements with the Western Balkans[82] as well as the Ankara Agreement, which serves as the backbone for the EU-Turkey relations.[83] One should also mention the Euromed Agreements with selected countries of the Mediterranean, which lay down the foundations for creation of free trade areas but which have, under no circum-

---

[80]   See further, inter alia, Francesco Maiani, 'Unique, yet Archetypal. Relations between the European Union and Andorra, Monaco and San Marino' in Gstöhl and Phinnemore (n 4), 84.

[81]   Comprehensive and enhanced Partnership Agreement between the European Union and the European Atomic Energy Community and their Member States, of the one part, and the Republic of Armenia, of the other part [2018] OJ L 23/4.

[82]   Stabilisation and Association Agreement between the European Communities and their Member States, of the one part, and the Former Yugoslav Republic of Macedonia, of the other part OJ 2004 L 84/1; Stabilisation and Association Agreement between the European Communities and their Member States, of the one part, and the Republic of Albania, of the other part [2009] OJ L 107/116; Stabilisation and Association Agreement between the European Communities and their Member States, of the one part, and the Republic of Montenegro, of the other part [2010] OJ L 108/3; Stabilisation and Association Agreement between the European Communities and their Member States, of the one part, and the Republic of Serbia, of the other part [2013] OJ L 278/14; Stabilisation and Association Agreement between the European Communities and their Member States, of the one part, and Bosnia and Herzegovina, of the other part [2015] OJ L 164/2; Stabilisation and Association Agreement between the European Union and the European Atomic Energy Community, of the one part, and Kosovo*, of the other part [2016] OJ L 71/3. See further on this family of association agreements, inter alia, David Phinnemore, 'Stabilisation and Association Agreements: Europe Agreements for the Western Balkans' (2003) 9 *European Foreign Affairs Review* 77.

[83]   Agreement creating an association between the European Economic Community and Turkey [1964] OJ 217/3687. For an academic appraisal see, inter alia, Nicola Rogers, *A Practitioners' Guide to the EC-Turkey Association Agreement* (Kluwer Law International 2000). See further on the institutional aspects of EU-Turkey relations, inter alia, Tamás Szigetvári, 'EU-Turkey Relations: Customs Union and More ... or Less?' in Sieglinde Gstöhl (ed), *The European Neighbourhood Policy in a Comparative Perspective. Models, challenges, lessons* (Routledge 2016) 107; Özlem Terzi 'The EU–Turkey Customs Union: Shortcomings and Prospects for Modernization' in Gstöhl and Phinnemore (n 4), 121.

stances, the capacity to become the tools for EU accession.[84] As it is clear from the example of Morocco, neither of these countries would meet the geographical criterion for the EU membership laid down in Article 49 TEU.[85] Last but not least, it is fitting to mention the Partnership and Co-operation Agreement with Russia[86] and similar agreements in force with several neighbours of the EU neighbours, which were established on the ashes of the Soviet Union.[87]

---

[84]   Euro-Mediterranean Agreement establishing an association between the European Communities and their Member States, of the one part, and the Kingdom of Morocco, of the other part [2000] OJ L 70/2; Euro-Mediterranean Agreement establishing an Association between the European Community and its Member States, of the one part, and the Republic of Lebanon, of the other part [2006] OJ L 143/2; Euro-Mediterranean Agreement establishing an Association between the European Community and its Member States, of the one part, and the People's Democratic Republic of Algeria, of the other part [2005] OJ L 265/2; Euro-Mediterranean Agreement establishing an Association between the European Communities and their Member States, of the one part, and the Arab Republic of Egypt, of the other part [2004] OJ L 304/39; Euro-Mediterranean Agreement establishing an Association between the European Communities and their Member States, of the one part, and the Hashemite Kingdom of Jordan, of the other part [2002] OJ L 129/3; Euro-Mediterranean Interim Association Agreement on trade and cooperation between the European Community, of the one part, and the Palestine Liberation Organization (PLO) for the benefit of the Palestinian Authority of the West Bank and the Gaza Strip, of the other part [1997] OJ L 187/3; Euro-Mediterranean Agreement establishing an association between the European Communities and their Member States, of the one part, and the State of Israel, of the other part, [2000] OJ L 147/3; Euro-Mediterranean Agreement establishing an association between the European Communities and their Member States, of the one part, and the Republic of Tunisia, of the other part [1998] OJ L 97/2. See further Karolien Pieters, *The Integration of the Mediterranean Neighbours into the EU Internal Market* (Asser Press 2010).

[85]   See further Susanna Fortunato, 'Article 49 TEU' in Hermann-Josef Blanke and Stelio Mangiameli (eds), *The Treaty on European Union (TEU). A Commentary* (Springer 2013) 1357. On the history of EU enlargements and the evolution of accession clause see, inter alia, Allan F Tatham, *Enlargement of the European Union* (Wolters Kluwer 2009).

[86]   Agreement on Partnership and Cooperation establishing a Partnership between the European Communities and their Member States and the Russian Federation [1997] OJ L 327/3.

[87]   Partnership and Co-operation Agreement between the European Communities and their Member States and the Republic of Kazakhstan [1999] OJ L 196/3; Partnership and Co-operation Agreement between the European Communities and their Member States, of the one part, and the Republic of Azerbaijan, of the other part [1999] OJ L 246/3; Partnership and Co-operation Agreement establishing a partnership between the European Communities and their Member States, of the one part, and the Kyrgyz Republic, of the other part [1999] OJ L 196/48; Partnership and Co-operation Agreement establishing a partnership between the European Communities and their Member States, of the one part, and the Republic of Uzbekistan, of the other part [1999] OJ L 229/3; Partnership and Co-operation Agreement establishing a partnership

As is well known, moving forward is part of the EU's DNA. This applies to both, its internal policies as well as external relations. In case of the latter, a good example of constant flux are the upgrades to bilateral frameworks with its neighbours. For instance, in the past decade the EU has negotiated and concluded the already mentioned agreements with Ukraine, Moldova, Georgia, and Armenia. Without a doubt all four agreements constituted considerable upgrades to the respective Partnership and Co-operation Agreements signed with these countries back in the 1990s.[88] When this chapter was completed, the EU was also busy negotiating new and more ambitious frameworks not only with the three micro states (Andorra, Monaco, and San Marino), but also with Tunisia and Azerbaijan (to name a few).[89] Last but not least, one should also remind the readers that the circumstances required the EU to negotiate, for the very first time, an agreement aiming downgrade of bilateral relations from the membership to a new framework of sorts.

Proceeding on from the current state of affairs, the question is to what extent the arrangements envisaged in the EU-Swiss Draft Agreement may, as argued earlier in this chapter, serve as the paradigm for the future. The answer is in the positive. In this respect, a reminder is fitting that this has already materialised in the EU-UK Withdrawal Agreement as its institutional provisions, including the dispute settlement *modus operandi*, are largely modelled on the Draft Agreement.[90] It, above all, proves that this emerging new paradigm is flexible and universal enough to serve successfully for the upgrades of bilateral relations as well as for their downgrades from the EU membership.

---

between the European Communities and their Member States, of the one part, and the Republic of Tajikistan, of the other part [2009] OJ L 350/3.

[88] Partnership and Co-operation Agreement between the European Communities and their Member States and Ukraine [1998] OJ L 49/3; Partnership and Co-operation Agreement between the European Communities and their Member States and the Republic of Moldova [1998] OJ L 181/3; Partnership and Co-operation Agreement between the European Communities and their Member States and the Republic of Georgia [1999] OJ L 205/3; Partnership and Co-operation Agreement between the European Communities and their Member States, of the one part, and the Republic of Armenia, of the other part [1999] OJ L 239/3.

[89] In November 2020 the negotiations of Deep and Comprehensive Free Trade Area with Tunisia were on-going. The pace slowed down following a change of government in Tunis and criticism of the DCFTA with the EU on side of civil society. The negotiations of Comprehensive Agreement with Azerbaijan were near completion. See Commission, 'Overview of FTA and other trade negotiations' https://trade.ec.europa .eu/doclib/docs/2006/december/tradoc_118238.pdf, accessed 30 November 2020.

[90] See further, inter alia, Alan Dashwood, 'The Withdrawal Agreement: Common Provisions, Governance and Dispute Settlement' (2020) 45 *European Law Review* 183; Joris Larik, 'Decision-Making and Dispute Settlement' in Federico Fabbrini (ed), *The Law and Politics of Brexit. Volume II The Withdrawal Agreement* (OUP 2020) 191.

However, with no future EU exits on the horizon, this paradigm *in spe* has the potential to be employed as a vehicle to intensify bilateral relations with some of the EU's neighbours. For instance, it could be the way forward for future *rapprochement* with the EU by the ENP *avant garde*: Ukraine, Moldova, and Georgia. All three countries are well advanced in implementation of their respective Association Agreements and, quite inevitably, questions are asked about the next steps. As evidenced by one of the policy documents published by the Georgian Government, it keeps the EU membership on its horizon.[91] Therefore, the time is apt to investigate the exportability of some of the institutional solutions offered by the Draft Agreement to other EU legal frameworks with its neighbours. This is further attended to in turn.

4.2   ENP Avant Garde: Is the New Paradigm a Way Forward?

The Association Agreements with Ukraine, Moldova, and Georgia can be classified as integration agreements as they envisage a good dose of the market access. This comes at the price of regulatory alignment, which – in respective Association Agreements – is referred to in a rather inconsistent fashion as law approximation, alignment or adoption of elements of the EU *acquis*.[92] While this linguistic cacophony should be attributed to poor drafting, it leaves no doubts that in the case of all three Association Agreements, the EU legal acts listed in the annexes need to be reflected in the Ukrainian, the Moldovan, and the Georgian legal orders. This triggers the well-rehearsed questions of legal homogeneity in the law books and in the courtrooms.

As far as the law book is concerned, it is worth starting with the Association Agreement with Ukraine. According to Article 463(3) EU-Ukraine Association Agreement, the Association Council may revise relevant parts of the Agreement. Thus, it is a general and static *modus operandi*, leaving the Association Council a wide discretion when it comes to the revision of annexes. A different solution is envisaged in Article 418 EU-Georgia Association Agreement as the language employed by the drafters is more imperative. It obliges the Association Council to revise the annexes on regular basis. It should be added, though, that the *modus operandi* applicable to the DCFTA part of the EU-Georgia Association Agreement indicates that dynamism is part of its DNA.[93] The same applies to the EU-Moldova Association Agreement,

---

[91]   'Georgia's European Union Integration Roadmap: RoadMap2EU. Better Integration for New Opportunities!' text on file with the author.

[92]   See further Van der Loo (n 10), 321.

[93]   As per Art 274(1) EU-Georgia Association Agreement: 'Georgia shall ensure the effective implementation of the domestic law approximated under Title IV (Trade and Trade-related Matters) of this Agreement and undertake any action necessary to reflect

where the law approximation clauses (Arts 410(1) and 449) mirror those of the EU-Georgia Association Agreement. Furthermore, unlike the EU-Ukraine Association Agreement, both the Georgian and Moldovan Agreements use the notion of 'dynamic approximation'. The practice demonstrates, however, that the dynamism is merely figurative as the respective Association Agreements are not updated often enough to catch up with the ever-evolving EU *acquis*.[94]

An area where one can easily see a potential for improvement, is the currently non-existent institutional engagement of the Ukrainian, Moldovan, and Georgian authorities in the EU decision-shaping. Neither of the three Association Agreements envisages access to the EU committees, akin to the EEA scenario, or options laid out in the EU-Swiss Draft Agreement. Mere information mechanisms are in place, obliging the European Commission to inform the three respective states of its proposals as they appear on the EU negotiating table. This, however, is short of participation in relevant committees, which are at the heart of the EU decision-making process.

The final question remains whether the jurisprudence of the CJEU is of any relevance. All three Association Agreements leave homogeneity in this respect at bay. To put it differently, the associated countries are not, with a very few exceptions, under the obligation to take into account the jurisprudence of the CJEU.[95] Hence, if they do so in course of law drafting or law application, it would be largely on a voluntary basis. As compilations of the relevant CJEU judgments prove, this is of particular importance in such areas as employment, equality, VAT tax or consumer protection, where the jurisprudence of the Court at Kirchberg is particularly prolific.[96] On the one hand, for anyone *au courant* with EU law, it is hard to imagine that law approximation would be limited merely to copy-pasting of listed EU regulations or EU directives into

---

the developments in Union law in its domestic law, in accordance with Article 418 of this Agreement.'

[94] So far, the EU-Ukraine Association Agreement has been amended seven times; the same applies to EU-Georgia Association Agreement. EU-Moldova Association Agreement has been amended ten times. See further, inter alia, Guillaume Van Der Loo and Tinatin Akhvlediani, *Catch me if you can: Updating the Eastern Partnership Association Agreements and DCFTAs* (CEPS 2020).

[95] See however Arts 153 and 264 EU-Ukraine Association Agreement; Arts 273 and 340 EU-Moldova Association Agreement; Art 146 of EU-Georgia Association Agreement.

[96] See, inter alia, the manuals on jurisprudence of the Court of Justice relevant for the Ukrainian and Georgian authorities: Огляд прецедентного права Суду Європейського Союзу у сферах, що регулюються Угодою про асоціацію між Україною та ЄС (Association 4U, 2018); *EU Case Law Relevant to Law Approximation* (Facility for the Implementation of the EU-Georgia Association Agreement–II, 2020). Both documents on file with the author.

Ukrainian, Georgian, and Moldovan laws. On the other hand, while such a desideratum is plausible for legal purists, it fails to take into account the reality on the ground. One needs to be aware of the pressures faced by the law drafters in the associated countries and a simple fact that frequently they operate in an environment, which is not a fertile ground for such a generous approach to law approximation. With ever pressing deadlines for domestication of EU laws an opportunity to venture into case-law of the Court, to make sure that the approximation effort is properly done, is simply an intellectual luxury that only a few can afford. At the same time, some of the Ukrainian,[97] Moldovan,[98] and Georgian[99] courts seem to embrace excursions into EU law and jurisprudence of the CJEU. It would potentially benefit them, and, by the same token, add legitimacy to their pro-EU law peregrinations, if the revised Association Agreement contained a clause explicitly requiring interpretation of relevant legal acts in light of the Luxembourg jurisprudence.

When this chapter was completed, the implementation of the respective Association Agreements was in full swing. This was the case despite the precarious political and economic background. As already mentioned, all three ENP countries were contemplating their next steps on the path to *rapprochement* with the EU. In this respect, some of the solutions envisaged in the Draft Agreement could have been considered as desirable way forward. Alas, the most recent review of the Eastern Partnership demonstrates that the EU is not yet ready to make this kind of commitment.[100] Yet, as argued in this chapter, the institutional solutions envisaged in the EU-Swiss Draft Agreement are an exportable material for future upgrades of the Association Agreements with the Eastern Partnership *avant garde*.

---

[97]   Roman Petrov, 'Legislative approximation and application of EU law in Ukraine' in Peter Van Elsuwege and Roman Petrov (eds), *Legislative Approximation and Application of EU Law in the Eastern Neighbourhood of the European Union. Towards a Common Regulatory Space?* (Routledge 2014) 137; Roman Petrov, 'The Impact of the EU-Ukraine Association Agreement on Constitutional Reform and Judicial Activism in Ukraine' (2018) 43 Review of Central and East European Law 99; Roman Petrov, 'The Impact of the Court of Justice of the European Union on the Legal System of Ukraine', in Arie Reich and Hans-W Micklitz (eds), *The Impact of the European Court of Justice on Neighbouring Countries* (OUP 2020) 173.

[98]   See, inter alia, Adam Łazowski (n 66), 509–511.

[99]   See Gaga Gabrichidze, 'The Impact of the Court of Justice of the European Union on the Georgian Legal System' in Arie Reich and Hans-W Micklitz (eds), *The Impact of the European Court of Justice on Neighbouring Countries* (OUP 2020) 241.

[100]   See, inter alia, Adam Łazowski, 'Where do we go from here? EU relations with the Eastern Partnership avant garde' in Wybe Douma, Christina Eckes, Peter Van Elsuwege, Eva Kassoti, Andrea Ott, Ramses A. Wessel (eds.) *The Evolving Nature of EU External Relations Law* (Springer/Asser Press 2021) 231.

5.   CONCLUSIONS

The EU-Swiss Draft Agreement carried the potential to open a new era in EU-Swiss relations This chapter demonstrates that despite the geographical, the economic and the legal proximity the EU-Swiss relations are fraught with trepidation and uneasiness. On the one hand, the existing bilateral agreements seem to serve the purpose, at least as the authorities in Bern are concerned. On the other hand, the EU has been, for quite a while now, raising concerns about the homogeneity of the EU-Swiss legal space. The example of updates to the EU-Swiss Agreement on Free Movement of Persons proves that this solicitude is not an abstract proposition, but it reflects the troubling reality on the ground. With prevalent risks to the homogeneity of EU-Swiss legal space, both sides embarked on the negotiations of the *chapeau* agreement solving, at least in some areas, the main problems caused by deficiencies of Bilateral I Agreements. The end result is the Draft Agreement, which faced big hurdles not only in course of the negotiations but also following their completion. This, quite obviously, has repercussions going way beyond the Draft Agreement itself. As it is made clear by the EU, the ratification and entry into force of the Draft Institutional Agreement is a *conditio sine qua non* for further negotiations and development of bilateral relationship.[101] Irrespective of where the EU-Swiss relations proceed in the future, the Draft Agreement contains solutions which can be offered to other non-EU countries that aim at closer economic and legal integration with the EU. As demonstrated in this chapter, while the solutions proposed in the Draft Agreement may never become operational in the EU-Swiss relations, they may serve as the paradigm for gradual *rapprochement* with other EU neighbours.

---

[101]   See, inter alia, Council (EU), Council conclusions on EU relations with the Swiss Confederation, No 116/19, 19 February 2019, para 9.

9. The role of treaty drafting in ensuring the binding nature and enforcement of international rulings handed down against States or international institutions: A comparison of EU and US case-law

Quentin Declève

1. INTRODUCTION: ENSURING THE BINDING NATURE AND ENFORCEMENT OF INTERNATIONAL RULINGS IN THE US AND THE EU: A MATTER OF SELF-EXECUTION, DIRECT EFFECT AND AUTONOMY

Decisions of international courts and tribunals are frequently enforced in both the United States (US) and in the European Union (EU). Such rulings relate, principally, to disputes between: (i) private parties (such as international commercial arbitral awards); (ii) a private party and a sovereign entity (such as international investment arbitral awards); or (iii) different sovereign States.

This chapter discusses how rulings falling within categories (ii) and (iii), particularly those that recognise the rights of individuals or that individuals may rely upon, are binding in the US and in the EU legal orders. With this aim in mind, this chapter will focus on the case-law of the US Supreme Court and that of the Court of Justice of the European Union (CJEU).

The chapter first examines the approach followed by the US Supreme Court with respect to the acceptance of judgments handed down by international courts, in particular by the International Court of Justice (ICJ). It will become apparent that for an international tribunal to render decisions that an individual will be able to enforce or rely upon before US courts, the treaty providing for that dispute resolution mechanism must include clear wording and language emphasising the intent of the US treaty drafters to conclude a 'self-executing treaty'. In the absence of such clear wording or language in the treaty, the decisions handed down by the relevant international court or tribunal will be deemed to be non-binding by US courts. Individuals will therefore not be able to rely upon such decisions in a domestic setting, unless Congress has adopted a law specifically making those decisions handed down by that international court or tribunal enforceable within the US legal order.

The chapter then moves on to analyse the situation in the EU. In most cases, the binding nature or the enforcement of international rulings by EU Member States' courts does not raise EU law questions. Indeed, in most cases, the EU Member States' domestic courts are asked to enforce or recognise the binding nature of international rulings that fall outside the scope of EU law (either because EU law does not apply in those disputes or because neither the EU nor its institutions are parties to the dispute at hand). Such international rulings are therefore exclusively enforced (or binding) according to the rules in place in the specific EU Member State concerned.

However, the binding nature and the enforcement of an international ruling may raise specific EU law questions, if such ruling is handed down against the EU, or if EU law is relevant to the dispute.

In particular, we will see that an individual – who was not a party to an international dispute initiated against the EU – will only be able to *rely*, before the domestic courts of the EU Member States, on the ruling handed down by an international court against the EU, if the underlying treaty, providing for the jurisdiction of the international court or tribunal, has direct effect.

In addition, this chapter will demonstrate that – irrespective of whether the underlying treaty has (or does not have) direct effect – the *enforcement*, by the EU domestic courts, of an international ruling, will only be possible if such enforcement does not interfere with the autonomy of the EU legal order. In light of the recent case-law of the CJEU, we will see how the drafting of specific clauses in the treaties concluded by the EU (but also potentially by its Member States) has become a key factor in whether the decisions made by international courts or tribunals under those treaties affect the autonomy of the EU legal order.

Ultimately, it will become apparent that the positions expressed by both the US Supreme Court and the CJEU illustrate a willingness to keep control and sovereignty over the influence of international rulings.

The scope of this chapter is however limited to the binding nature, or the enforceability, of decisions handed down by international courts and tribunals (in particular decisions which have recognised specific rights of individuals). The chapter therefore does not discuss the effect, in the US or EU legal systems, of foreign judgments (i.e., judgments handed down by the domestic courts in foreign jurisdictions) or of decisions adopted by international institutions. Nor does it discuss the issue of judicial dialogue between international courts or tribunals, on one hand, and courts in the US or in the EU, on the other hand.

2. THE US SUPREME COURT'S APPROACH TO THE EFFECTS OF DECISIONS DELIVERED BY INTERNATIONAL TRIBUNALS: THE NECESSITY FOR TREATY DRAFTERS TO CONCLUDE '*SELF-EXECUTING TREATIES*'

2.1   The Notion of '*Self-Executing Treaties*'

The effects of decisions handed down by an international court or tribunal on the US domestic legal order depend upon the nature of the treaty providing for the jurisdiction of that international court or tribunal, namely whether the treaty is self-executing (i.e., it takes effect automatically as a matter of domestic law), or non-self-executing (i.e., it only takes effect if Congress has enacted a law making this treaty part of US domestic law).

The distinction between 'self-executing' and 'non-self-executing' treaties is not new. In 1829, the US Supreme Court was asked to rule on a case in which two plaintiffs sought to recover a parcel of land in Louisiana, which the Spanish Governor had granted to them. The person in possession of the land at the time, however, argued that the grant made by the Spanish Governor was invalid because it had been made at a time when the territory on which the land was situated was being claimed by both the United States and Spain. The Spanish Governor was therefore not entitled to grant the land in question and the US' courts could not recognise such grant since the US disputed the sovereignty over that piece of land when the grant was afforded. In order to contest that argument, the plaintiffs relied on an 1819 US-Spain treaty which solved the territorial dispute between the two countries and which stipulated that all grants of lands made by Spain during the disputed period would be ratified by the US. Therefore, according to the plaintiffs, the US was obliged to recognise the effect of the grant made by the Spanish Governor in their favour. The US Supreme Court rejected that interpretation. It ruled that when the terms of a treaty require a legislative act (which was the case in the dispute at hand), the treaty as such cannot be considered as law until the terms of the treaty have been ratified.[1]

---

[1]   *Foster v Neilson* 27 US 253 (1829). Other cases have also dealt with issues surrounding the distinction between self-executing treaties and non-self-executing treaties. Such as *Whitney v Robertson* 124 US 190 (1888) and *Edye v Robertson* 112 US 580 (1884).

That case therefore highlights that, in the US legal order, some provisions of international treaties are 'self-executing', in that they take effect and have the force of domestic law without any intervention from the US Congress, while other treaty provisions require further implementing legislation to enter the US legal order (and are thus called 'non-self-executing').

Although the distinction between self-executing and non-self-executing treaties was originally applied when assessing the effects of international treaties in the US legal order, the US Supreme Court has later used that distinction to consider the binding nature and domestic enforceability of a judicial decision made by an international court. The relevant US Supreme Court's opinions in this regard have hinged on the question of the self-executing or non-self-executing nature of the underlying treaty establishing the court that issued the decision. These cases have also raised additional questions, such as what recourse, if any, exists when a sovereign party to a decision by an international court or tribunal – here, the United States – refuses to comply with the decision. They have also looked at to what extent an individual, on whom an international judiciary confers rights, can directly rely on that decision, or seek its enforcement, in a US court. These questions were at the centre of two ICJ cases, *LaGrand*[2] and *Avena*,[3] on the implications of which the US Supreme Court was later called on to decide in *Sanchez-Llamas v Oregon*[4] and *Medellín v Texas*.[5]

2.2 Case Study: Binding Nature and Enforcement of Decisions of the International Court of Justice – the US Supreme Court's Approach

The *LaGrand* case concerned two German brothers (Karl and Walter LaGrand) who had been arrested in Arizona in 1982 on suspicion of armed robbery and murder. They were subsequently convicted and sentenced to the death penalty.

The *Avena* case concerned 51 Mexican nationals who had been tried and convicted of murder in nine different States. They had also been sentenced to death.

In both cases, the LaGrand brothers and the Mexican nationals had not been made aware, following their arrest, of their right to obtain assistance from their respective German or Mexican consuls pursuant to Article 36 of the Vienna

---

[2]   *LaGrand Case* (*Germany v United States of America*), Judgment of 27 June 2001, [2001] ICJ Rep 466.
[3]   *Avena and Other Mexican Nationals* (*Mexico v United States of America*), Judgment of 31 March 2004, [2004] ICJ Rep 12.
[4]   *Sanchez-Llamas v Oregon* 548 US 331 (2006).
[5]   *Medellín v Texas* 552 US 491 (2008).

Convention on Consular Relations (the Vienna Convention).[6] Article 36 of the Vienna Convention (to which the US is a party) indeed provides that 'any person detained in a foreign country has the right to notify the consulate of his home country of his detention'. In addition to this procedural failure, a specific US criminal law provision (called the '*procedural default*' rule) further precluded the LaGrand brothers and the Mexican nationals from raising, on appeal, a claim based on the violation of their Vienna Convention right.

Dissatisfied with how the US had violated the rights of some of their nationals, Germany (in the *LaGrand* case) and Mexico (in *Avena*) brought the matter before the ICJ, alleging that the US had violated the Vienna Convention by failing to notify the persons involved of their right to communicate with their respective German or Mexican consuls. The ICJ ruled against the US in both cases.

In the 2001 *LaGrand* case, the ICJ explicitly found that the procedural default rule had made it impossible for the accused persons to effectively raise the issue of lack of consular notification after they had at last learned of their rights.[7] Unfortunately, the ICJ decision came too late for the LaGrand brothers: they were executed while the ICJ proceedings were on-going. Nevertheless, the ICJ added that if, in future cases, US authorities were to deprive defendants of their Vienna Convention rights, the US would have to provide 'review and reconsideration' of the defendant's conviction and sentence.[8]

Three years later, in *Avena*, the ICJ reached a similar conclusion and ruled that the 51 Mexican nationals who had been deprived of their Vienna Convention right and who – in contrast to the LaGrand brothers – were still alive when the decision of the ICJ was handed down, were entitled to 'review and reconsideration' of their convictions and sentences.

In *Sanchez-Llamas v Oregon* and *Medellín v Texas*, the US Supreme Court was later asked to examine the legal consequences and implications in US domestic law of the two ICJ decisions, and in particular of the ICJ's decision in *Avena*.

In *Sanchez-Llamas v Oregon*, two citizens from Mexico and Honduras had been convicted of murder in, respectively, Oregon and Virginia. In this case, neither of these men had been informed of their rights under the Vienna Convention.

---

[6]   Vienna Convention on Consular Relations (Vienna, 24 April 1963).
[7]   One commentator refers to the procedural default rule as 'the graveyard of so many article 36 claims': Howard S Schiffman, 'Breard and Beyond: The Status of Consular Notification and Access Under the Vienna Convention' (2000) 8 *Cardozo Journal of International and Comparative Law* 27.
[8]   *LaGrand* (n 2), para 128.

Although the case came after the ICJ's rulings in *LaGrand* and *Avena*, the US Supreme Court blatantly ignored those rulings. Even though the Supreme Court admitted that ICJ decisions merit 'respectful consideration',[9] they were nonetheless not binding.[10] The Supreme Court refused to depart from its previous decision in *Breard v Greene*[11] (a case decided before the ICJ rulings in *LaGrand* and *Avena*), in which it found that the procedural default rule precluded consideration and redress for a Vienna Convention violation just like any other procedural rules (such as statutes of limitations). According to the Court, 'absent a clear and express statement to the contrary, the procedural rules of the forum State govern the implementation of the treaty in that State'.[12] Quoting the Statute of the ICJ, the Supreme Court, in *Sanchez-Llamas*, found that the ICJ's decisions have no binding force except between the parties and in respect of that particular case, and that 'any interpretation of law the ICJ renders in the course of resolving particular disputes is thus not binding precedent even as to the ICJ itself'.[13]

In *Medellín*, the issue was somewhat different. José Medellín, the defendant in that case, was one of the 51 Mexican nationals whom Mexico had represented before the ICJ in *Avena*. By virtue of the ICJ's ruling, Mr Medellín was therefore entitled to full 'review and reconsideration' of his conviction and sentence. He therefore sought to obtain such review and consideration of whether, regardless of the procedural default rule, the police's failure to inform him of his Vienna Convention rights had caused prejudice in his criminal trial.

However, the Supreme Court rejected Medellín's claim. In reaching its decision, the Court relied on the distinction between self-executing treaties (i.e., treaties that take effect automatically as a matter of domestic law) and non-self-executing treaties (i.e., treaties that only take effect if Congress has enacted a law making those treaties part of US domestic law). According to the Supreme Court, the language of the applicable treaty in question – i.e., Article 94 of the United Nations (UN) Charter[14] – indicated that the treaty was a non-self-executing treaty. The Supreme Court indeed examined the exact wording of the UN Charter and concluded that decisions of the ICJ were not

---

[9]   *Sanchez-Llamas v Oregon* (n 4), 355.
[10]   Aloysius P Llamzon, 'Jurisdiction and Compliance in Recent Decisions of the International Court of Justice' (2007) 18 *European Journal of International Law* 815, 843.
[11]   *Breard v Greene* 523 US 371(1998), 375.
[12]   *Sanchez-Llamas v Oregon* (n 4).
[13]   *Sanchez-Llamas v Oregon* (n 4).
[14]   Article 94(1) of the UN Charter reads as follows: 'Each Member of the United Nations undertakes to comply with the decision of the International Court of Justice in any case to which it is a party.'

binding and enforceable in US courts. Therefore, the Supreme Court concluded that the US was not required to follow the ICJ's decision in *Avena* by granting 'review and reconsideration' to the 51 Mexican nationals represented by Mexico in *Avena*. Medellín was therefore prevented from appealing his conviction.

2.3   Binding Nature and Enforcement of International Rulings in the US: Take-Aways from *Sanchez-Llamas* and *Medellín* and the Role of Treaty Drafting

The thrust of the *Medellín* case is that, for an international tribunal to render decisions that are binding upon US courts, the treaty providing for that dispute resolution mechanism must include clear wording and language emphasising the will of the US treaty drafters to conclude a self-executing treaty. Without such language, the decisions handed down by that dispute resolution body will not be binding upon US courts, and individuals therefore cannot rely upon them in a domestic setting, unless Congress has adopted a law to that end.

For instance, in *Medellín*, the US Supreme Court paid careful attention to the particular phrasing of Article 94 of the UN Charter and found that the words 'undertakes to comply' in that provision did not send a sufficiently strong 'directive to domestic courts'.[15] In particular, the US Supreme Court read that provision as 'a commitment on the part of UN members to take future action through their political branches to comply with an ICJ decision'.[16] The Supreme Court therefore adopted a text-centred approach in order to determine the intent of the US treaty drafters.[17]

The Medellín Court's apparent requirement – that a treaty providing for a dispute resolution mechanism must do so in clear and express language showing the intent of the US treaty drafters to conclude a self-executing treaty – has been taken to heart by some US legislative bodies. For example, the US Senate Foreign Relations Committee has interpreted *Medellín* by including an explicit declaration in every treaty it proposes to the Senate regarding whether the treaty is self-executing or non-self-executing.[18]

---

[15]   *Medellín v Texas* (n 5), 508.
[16]   Ibid.
[17]   Curtis A Bradley, 'Intent, Presumptions, and Non-Self-Executing Treaties' (2008) 102 *American Journal of International Law* 540.
[18]   John Quigley, 'A Tragi-Comedy of Errors Erodes Self-Execution of Treaties: Medellín v. Texas and Beyond' (2012) 45 *Case Western Reserve Journal of International Law* 403, 420. The author also notes that such approach is imperfect though as a treaty may contain some self-executing provisions and others that are non-self-executing.

Finally, it is important to highlight that the conclusions of the US Supreme Court in *Medellín* do not concern the enforcement, within the US legal order, of awards handed down by international arbitral tribunals. The US Supreme Court in *Medellín* indeed expressly found that its decision did 'not call into question the ordinary enforcement of foreign judgments or international arbitral agreement'.[19] With respect to the enforcement of international arbitral awards, the US Congress had actually passed laws guaranteeing the enforcement of such awards handed down under the Convention of the International Centre for Settlement of Investment Disputes (the ICSID Convention) or[20] under the 1958 New York Convention on the Recognition and Enforcement of Foreign Arbitral Awards (the New York Convention).[21]

3.   THE CJEU's APPROACH TO DECISIONS OF INTERNATIONAL COURTS AND TRIBUNALS: A MATTER OF DIRECT EFFECT AND AUTONOMY

3.1   The Notions of 'Direct Effect' and 'Autonomy of the EU Legal Order'

The binding nature or the enforcement of an international ruling in the EU is first and foremost a question of national law in the country where enforcement is sought or where the international ruling is relied upon. Indeed, the enforcement of international rulings by the domestic courts within the EU depends upon the rules and formalities in place in the specific Member State where enforcement is sought. For instance, the possibility of enforcing an international arbitral award in a particular EU Member State will primarily depend on whether that State has ratified and given domestic effect to the New York Convention or to the ICSID Convention.

The binding nature or the enforcement of an international ruling may, however, raise specific EU law questions if (i) such ruling is handed down against the EU (or its institutions) pursuant to an international treaty to which the EU is a party or (ii) if EU law has been relevant in solving that dispute.

In particular, when an individual seeks to rely on a ruling handed down against the EU pursuant to a treaty to which the EU is a party, the question of whether such ruling may be relied upon by the domestic courts in the EU

---

[19]   *Medellín v Texas* (n 5), 519.
[20]   22 USC para 1650(a).
[21]   9 USC paras 201–202.

Member States depends on whether the underlying treaty on the basis of which the ruling was made provided for direct effect (Section 3.1.1).

The *enforcement*, by the EU domestic courts, of an international ruling will, however, only be possible if such enforcement does not interfere with the autonomy of the EU legal order (Section 3.1.2).

3.1.1   The requirement for direct effect

The notion of direct effect of international treaties is a fundamental element in assessing whether an individual may immediately invoke the provisions of an international treaty before a national or European court. Broadly speaking, this concept corresponds to the notion of self-executing effect of international treaties in US law.[22]

Like the US Supreme Court in *Medellín* regarding the notion of self-executing treaties, the CJEU has found that an individual – who was not a party to an international dispute initiated against the EU – will only be able to *rely*, before the domestic courts of the EU Member States, on the ruling handed down by an international court against the EU, if the underlying treaty, providing for the jurisdiction of the international court or tribunal, has direct effect.

In *FIAMM and Others*,[23] a case which concerned the right of two EU traders to rely on a decision of the World Trade Organisation (WTO) Dispute Settlement Body (DSB) to invoke the EU's non-contractual liability and obtain compensation for the loss that resulted from the EU's failure to comply with WTO law, the CJEU found that, since individuals were not entitled to rely directly upon WTO law before the EU courts, 'a decision of the DSB [...] cannot have the effect of requiring a party to the WTO agreements to accord individuals a right which they do not hold by virtue of those agreements in the absence of such a decision'.[24] In short, since WTO agreements do not confer direct effect, individuals may not rely upon decisions made pursuant to those agreements either.

3.1.2   The obligation not to violate the autonomy of the EU legal order

Irrespective of whether an international ruling has been handed down on the basis of a treaty which does (or does not) confer direct effect, the enforcement process of that ruling may still trigger EU law issues, in particular, if this ruling can potentially have adverse effects on the autonomy of the EU legal order.

---

[22]   Francesca Martines, 'Direct Effect of International Agreements of the European Union' (2014) 25 *European Journal of International Law* 131.

[23]   Joined Cases C-120/06P and C-121/06P *FIAMM and Others v Council and Commission* [2008] EU:C:2008:476.

[24]   Ibid., para 130.

The principle of autonomy of the EU legal order is a cornerstone of EU institutional law. According to that principle, 'it is for the national courts and for the CJEU to ensure the full application of EU law in all Member States and to ensure judicial protection of an individual's rights under that law'.[25] The autonomy of the EU legal order is therefore based to a great extent on the exclusive jurisdiction of the CJEU to have the final say on the interpretation and application of EU law. The principle of the autonomy of the EU legal order requires that this integrity is not undermined.[26]

The autonomy of the EU legal order has played a significant role in the establishment or accession of the EU to other international treaties and institutions. For instance, the interference of the European Convention on Human Rights (ECHR) (and the concurrent jurisdiction of the European Court of Human Rights) with this autonomy was the primary reason why the CJEU refused that the European Union accede to the ECHR.[27] Similarly, the interference of the unified patent litigation system with the same principle prompted the CJEU's objections to the creation of the European Patent Court.[28]

3.2   Case Study: The CJEU's Approach in *Achmea* and *Opinion 1/17*

In *Achmea*, Slovakia challenged, before the German courts, an arbitral award which ordered that country to pay EUR 22 million to Achmea (a Dutch investor) pursuant to the 1991 Czechoslovakia-Netherlands bilateral investment treaty (BIT). In its challenge, Slovakia argued that the arbitral award was invalid on the ground that the arbitration clause in the Czechoslovakia-Netherlands BIT violated certain provisions of the Treaty on the Functioning of the European Union (TFEU).

In its judgment of 6 March 2018,[29] the CJEU ruled that Articles 267 and 344 TFEU precluded Member States from concluding intra-EU investment treaties (i.e., treaties between EU Member States) which granted the possibility to investors in a Member State of initiating arbitration proceedings against the other EU Member State party to that treaty.

---

[25]   Opinion 2/13 *Accession of the European Union to the European Convention for the Protection of Human Rights and Fundamental Freedoms* [2014] OJ C 65/2, para 175.

[26]   Opinion 1/17 *EU-Canada CET Agreement* [2019] OJ C 220/2, Opinion of AG Bot, para 59.

[27]   Opinion 2/13 (n 25).

[28]   Opinion 1/09 *Creation of a Unified Patent Litigation System* [2011] ECR I-01137.

[29]   Case C-284/16 *Slovak Republic v Achmea BV* [2018] ECLI:EU:C:158.

The CJEU's reasoning in *Achmea* focused more particularly on an assessment of the choice of law clause in Article 8.6 of the Czechoslovakia-Netherlands BIT. According to the CJEU, the Article provided that the law to be applied in resolving disputes between a contracting party and an investor included 'the law in force of the Contracting Party concerned' and 'other relevant agreements between the Contracting Parties'. Given that EU law was in force in every EU Member State, the CJEU concluded that an arbitral tribunal established pursuant to the Czechoslovakia-Netherlands BIT could potentially apply and interpret EU law. However, because the arbitral tribunal did not form part of the EU judicial system, the CJEU considered that the potential interpretation and application of EU law by this tribunal affected the autonomy of the EU legal order.[30] The CJEU thus concluded that the arbitration clause contained in the Czechoslovakia-Netherlands BIT was contrary to EU law and violated the autonomy of the EU legal order. In addition, the CJEU in *Achmea* also recalled that the preliminary ruling procedure provided for in Article 267 TFEU was the keystone of the EU judicial system and could be used to safeguard the autonomy of EU law.[31]

In *Opinion 1/17*, the CJEU was asked to assess the compatibility, under EU law, of the Investment Court System (ICS). The ICS is a novel adjudicatory body established under the European Union-Canada Comprehensive Economic and Trade Agreement (CETA) in order to adjudicate on investment disputes initiated (i) by a Canadian investor against the EU or its Member States or (ii) by a European investor against Canada.

Therefore, although CETA did not provide for direct effect and private parties were precluded from directly invoking the provisions of CETA in courts, that treaty provided for the possibility that an investor from Canada could initiate a dispute against the EU or against one of its Member State before the ICS. The EU and its Member States can therefore potentially be found liable for breaches of their obligations under CETA.

In conducting its analysis, the CJEU confirmed that the principle of autonomy of EU law played a crucial role in assessing the compatibility with EU law of the ICS and its ability to hand down rulings with binding effects within the EU.

The CJEU examined the specific provisions contained in CETA and concluded that the power of the ICS did not violate the principle of the autonomy of EU law.

---

[30]   As mentioned above, the autonomy of the EU legal order is based, to a great extent, on the exclusive jurisdiction of the CJEU to have the final say on the interpretation and application of EU law.

[31]   *Achmea* (n 29), para 37.

More particularly, the CJEU found, first, that – unlike the case in, for example, *Opinion 1/09*[32] or *Achmea*[33] – the ICS under CETA did not have the power to interpret or apply EU law since the ICS (i) only had the power to interpret and apply the provisions of CETA and (ii) did not have jurisdiction to decide on the legality of a measure alleged to constitute a breach of CETA, under the domestic law of a party to CETA.

Second, the CJEU also noted that Article 8.31 of CETA made it explicitly clear that EU law and the law of the EU Member States had to be considered as a question of fact in investment disputes[34] and that the ICS would need to accept the prevailing interpretation given to domestic law by national courts or tribunals, and any interpretation of domestic law by the ICS would not bind national courts.[35]

Third, the CJEU found the ICS to be expressly precluded from annulling a contested national or EU measure.[36]

3.3 Binding Nature and Enforcement of International Rulings Within the EU: Take-Aways from *FIAMM*, *Achmea* and *Opinion 1/17* and the Role of Treaty Drafting

The findings of the CJEU in *FIAMM*, *Achmea* and in *Opinion 1/17* provide useful guidance on how to design dispute resolution clauses in future international agreements concluded by the EU or its Member States in order to rely on, or enforce, within the EU, decisions handed down by international courts or tribunals.

First, following the decision of the CJEU in *FIAMM*, it is clear that if the EU treaty drafters wish to grant the possibility to an individual – who is not a party to an international dispute initiated against the EU – to *rely*, before the domestic courts of the EU Member States or the European courts, on rulings handed down against the EU by an international court or tribunal pursuant to that treaty, the treaty drafters will need to express, as clearly as possible, their intention to confer a direct effect to the treaty at hand.

Second, in order to avoid the enforcement of international rulings interfering with the principle of autonomy of the EU legal order, it now seems clear, following *Achmea*, that applicable law clauses in future international agreements concluded by the EU or its Member States will need to avoid any reference to the domestic law of the parties. Such safeguards could be reinforced through

---

[32] Opinion 1/09 (n 28).
[33] Opinion 1/17 (n 26), paras 122 and 133.
[34] Ibid., para 130.
[35] Ibid., para 131.
[36] Ibid., para 144.

an express requirement in the future treaties that EU law and the law of the EU Member States must be considered as a question of fact by the international court or tribunal in question.

Third, if a treaty does contain an applicable law clause allowing an international court or tribunal to interpret and apply the domestic law of the parties, it may be useful (for the sake of avoiding any interference between the international ruling and the principle of autonomy of the EU legal order) to add a clause allowing that international court or tribunal to refer preliminary questions to the CJEU when deciding on the application and interpretation of EU law. This is, for instance, the case of Article 322(2) of the EU-Ukraine Association Agreement,[37] which envisages that international tribunals constituted to hear state-to-state disputes between the contracting parties may request a ruling on a question of interpretation of a provision of EU law from the CJEU. The Draft EU-UK Withdrawal Agreement[38] provides for a similar mechanism.

Fourth and finally, following the CJEU's findings in *Opinion 1/17*, if an international treaty concluded by the EU or its Member States contains clauses that ensure that the international tribunal (i) will not be in a position to decide on the legality of a contested EU law; (ii) will only apply and interpret the underlying treaty at issue and other rules and principles of international law, but not EU law; or (iii) will not be able to provide, to EU institutions (including the CJEU) binding interpretations, then such clauses could be additional guarantees safeguarding the principle of the autonomy of EU law.

4.   CONCLUSIONS

In the US, the question regarding the binding nature or enforceability of decisions issued by international courts or tribunals is linked to the issue of how international agreements are incorporated into US law. More particularly, the effects of decisions handed down by an international court or tribunal on the US domestic legal order depend upon the nature of the treaty providing for the jurisdiction of that international court or tribunal itself, namely whether the treaty is self-executing or non-self-executing.

---

[37]   Art 322(2) of the Association Agreement between the European Union and its Member States, of the one part, and Ukraine, of the other part [2014] OJ L161.
[38]   Art 174 of the Draft Agreement on the withdrawal of the United Kingdom of Great Britain and Northern Ireland from the European Union and the European Atomic Energy Community [2018] https://ec.europa.eu/commission/sites/beta-political/files/draft_withdrawal_agreement_0.pdf, accessed 1 July 2021. At the time of this chapter's drafting, the EU-UK Withdrawal Agreement has yet to gain the approval of the UK Parliament.

In the EU, the enforcement of an international ruling may raise specific EU law questions if the ruling is handed down against the EU (or its institutions) pursuant to an international treaty to which the EU is a party, or if EU law has been relevant in solving that dispute. When an individual – who was not a party to an international dispute initiated against the EU – seeks to *rely*, before the domestic courts of the EU Member States or the European courts, on a ruling handed down by an international court or tribunal against the EU, this will only be possible if the underlying treaty, providing for the jurisdiction of that international court or tribunal, has direct effect (which, broadly speaking, corresponds to the notion of self-executing effect of international treaties in US law). In addition, this chapter has demonstrated that the *enforcement*, by the EU domestic courts, of an international ruling, will only be possible if such enforcement does not interfere with the autonomy of the EU legal order.

This chapter further highlighted the role played by treaty drafting in considering whether decisions made by international courts and tribunals may enter the US and EU legal orders.

While the US Supreme Court adopted a text-centred approach in order to determine whether US treaty drafters intended, when drafting a particular treaty, to grant US domestic courts the power to enforce an international ruling made pursuant to that treaty, the recent case-law of the CJEU suggests that in negotiating future international agreements, EU treaty drafters will need to apply particular care to the wording of the clause on applicable law. In particular, any reference to the domestic law of the parties concerned should be avoided. It might also be advisable to clarify that EU law and the law of the EU Member States should be considered as a question of fact by the international court or tribunal adjudicating a future dispute. In addition, EU treaty drafters can always consider including a preliminary ruling mechanism to allow international courts or tribunals established under their drafted agreement to refer questions to the CJEU. Doing so preserves a level of respect, formally, for the CJEU's jurisdiction over EU law, and informally, for its caution in giving effect to any decision rendered by an international judicial body.

10. The phasing-out of intra-EU BITs and the risk for the rule of law

Raymundo Tullio Treves[1]

1. INTRODUCTION

This chapter explores the negative impacts on the rule of law of the implementation of the political decision to phase-out the system of intra-EU investment protection based on intra-EU bilateral investment treaties (BITs) and the intra-EU application of the Energy Charter Treaty (ECT). The reason for such negative effects on the rule of law is identified by the fact that the integration process which led to the decision of necessarily phasing-out intra-EU bilateral investment agreements is based exclusively on the principles of autonomy and of the primacy of EU law. These principles, however, transform problems of conflicts between legal orders into issues of conflicting competences and not into issues of conflicting rights of individuals. This chapter suggests adding the rule of law, alongside autonomy and primacy, as a principle of integration.

This chapter will argue that the overlap of legal orders offering protections to intra-EU-cross-border investors is a natural consequence of the EU integration process (2); suggest that the political decision to phase-out intra EU BITs and the intra-EU application of the ECT is a consequence of the principle of autonomy of EU law being the driving principle of the integration process (3). This chapter will then describe the consequences on the rule of law of an approach that focuses exclusively on autonomy: defining the rule of law (4); highlighting the creation of a climate of legal uncertainty surrounding intra-EU investments (5); and describing the menace against due process and the rights of intra-EU investors (6). This chapter will conclude by arguing that the principle of autonomy should at least be complemented by other principles or values of the EU, such as the rule of law (7).

---

[1]   This chapter was last updated in July 2019. Since then, there have been important developments regarding the EU's phasing-out of intra-EU BITs.

The views expressed in this chapter are those of the author alone. This chapter was drafted by the author in his academic capacity, prior to joining Three Crowns LLP.

2. THE OVERLAP OF LEGAL ORDERS PROTECTING INTRA-EU INVESTORS IS A NATURAL CONSEQUENCE OF THE EU INTEGRATION PROCESS

The hotly debated issue of the protection of intra-EU investments arises from a matter of fact: the coexistence of two different sets of norms regulating cross-border investment protection in the EU, i.e., EU law norms and international law norms, arising primarily from BITs.

BITs are created according to classical notions of international law: state sovereignty; sovereign equality of states; the freedom for each state to enter into treaties; the possibility for each state to agree on dispute settlement mechanisms for their disputes.[2] The EU is a *sui generis* system, different from both national legal systems and international law. It originates from international law treaties, it maintains within itself sovereign states, yet it has competences which used to belong to the sovereign states, it has its own governing bodies, legislative body and judicial system.[3] The Union is a 'space'.[4]

The fact of the coexistence of two different sets of norms regulating intra-EU investments is a natural consequence of the fact that the EU is not a static organisation, but a dynamic one. The EU is the product of a process of European integration that started with the creation of the European Communities. European integration has led to a Union that grows and aims at growing by expanding the competences of the Union, the geographical area of the Union and the cultural and value ties of the people of the Union. Such process of integration implies, in and of itself, potential conflicts of legal orders. For example, treaties between non-EU Member States could become intra-EU treaties, as is the case of intra-EU BITs.

It is not unlikely, and indeed it is hopeful, that a healthy Union will continue its process of integration and of expansion.[5] Integration will probably lead to new possible overlaps between the EU legal system and legal systems that originate from classical international law.

---

[2]   R Dolzer and C Schreuer, *Principles of International Investment Law* (2nd edn, OUP 2012) 1–27.
[3]   *Vattenfall AB v Germany (II)*, ICSID Case No. ARB/12/12, Decision on the Achmea issue (31 August 2018), para 146.
[4]   Art 3(2) TEU: 'The Union shall offer its citizens an area of freedom, security and justice without internal frontiers [...].'
[5]   In general, on the EU's evolution and process of integration, see R Adam and A Tizzano, *Manuale di Diritto dell'Unione Europea* (Giappichelli Editore 2014) 3–8.

3.   THE CONSEQUENCES OF THE PRINCIPLE
      OF AUTONOMY OF EU LAW DRIVING THE
      PHASING-OUT OF INTRA-EU BITS AND THE
      INTRA-EU APPLICATION OF THE ECT

It is not surprising that the institutions of the Union interpret the coexistence
of two different systems of protection of investment within the EU space as
problematic.

What is surprising is the way in which the EU has focused exclusively on
eliminating the non-EU system of investment protection:[6] aiming primarily at
protecting the autonomy of EU law.[7] Other interests appear disregarded, such
as the interests of investors which have invested in reliance on the protections
offered by BITs, or that have already initiated arbitrations, or of future investors to have a clearer law regarding their protection.

Having, as a principal aim, the protection of the autonomy and primacy of
EU law, has led the EU and arbitral tribunals to describe the issue of intra-EU
investment protection as an 'anomaly' within the EU's integration process,[8]
and an issue of systemic 'conflict': an issue of conflicting treaties; conflicting
substantive rights; conflicting jurisdiction; and an issue of discrimination.

Such characterisations reveal a static interpretation of the status of investment protection within the EU, a Union which is, and should be, intrinsically
dynamic. They reveal a static view because they focus on the fact that today
there are two overlapping systems of investment protection.

A dynamic approach would, instead, take into consideration the origins of
the intra-EU BITs and the potential usefulness for the future of the EU of the
BITs, or at least of their positive characteristics.

As regards the origin of the intra-EU BITs, it should be recalled that the
majority, if not all, of the BITs that are today intra-EU, were originally
between Member States and non-Member States. Their ratification was
required by the EU to secure the entry of the non-Member States in the EU.[9]

---

[6]   See D Simoes, 'A Guardian and a Friend? The European Commission's
Participation in Investment Arbitration' (2017) *Michigan State International Law
Review* 233; European Commission, 'Commission asks Member States to terminate
their intra-EU bilateral investment treaties' (Press Release, 18 June 2015).
[7]   Case C-284/16 *Slovak Republic v Achmea BV* [2018] ECLI:EU:C:158, paras
32–33.
[8]   L Fumagalli, 'Meccanismi ISDS negli intra-EU BITs: la Corte di Giustizia pone
fine a un lungo dibattito. E ora?' (2018) vol CI *Rivista di Diritto Internazionale* 896,
899.
[9]   H Wehland, 'Intra-EU Investment Agreements and Arbitration: Is European
Community Law an Obstacle?' (2009) 58 *International and Comparative Law
Quarterly* 297, 297–298; J Dahlquist, H Lenk and L Rönnelid, 'The Infringement

The BITs were seen as creators and enforcers of the rule of law and as such they had the implicit role of helping to transform the non-Member States into states more similar to the democratic values to the Members of the EU. They created an investment environment that EU investors could trust.[10] BITs had the role of preparing these states for a relationship of mutual trust with the Member States. It could be said that BITs were originally considered by the EU as vehicles of integration. An integration based on the rule of law as a unifying principle and not on the principle of autonomy of EU law exclusively.

The potential usefulness of BITs, or of a BIT-like EU regulation, for the future of the EU appears once the role of BITs as promoters of the rule of law is recognised. It should be considered, as it had been in the Non-Paper by five Member States, that BITs have certain characteristics that make them effective and highly appreciated by investors, as is testified by the ample use of them:[11] they are concise; and substantive rights, legal remedies and dedicated dispute resolution avenues are all indicated in the same text.[12] Consequently, the mere abolition of BITs may result in a loss of rights and protection for EU investors. Such loss could be avoided through the creation of a Union-wide regulation or agreement that incorporates at least the positive aspects of the BITs, or through the encouragement to sign intra-EU BITs with most-favoured-nation (MFN) clauses and the possibility of referral to the CJEU on issues of EU law. The inclusion of MFN clauses would eliminate the risk of discriminations within the EU.[13] The possibility of referral to the CJEU would eliminate the risk for the CJEU's monopoly of interpretation of EU law.

Proceedings over Intra-EU Investment Treaties – An Analysis of the Case Against Sweden' (2016) *Swedish Institute for European Policy Studies* 1–2.

[10] European Commission Press Release (18 June 2015) (n 6):
Many of these intra-EU BITs were agreed in the 1990s, before the EU enlargements of 2004, 2007 and 2013. They were mainly struck between existing members of the EU and those who would become the 'EU 13'. They were aimed at reassuring investors who wanted to invest in the future 'EU 13' at a time when private investors – sometimes for historical political reasons – might have felt wary about investing in those countries. The BITs were thus aimed at strengthening investor protection, for example by means of compensation for expropriation and arbitration procedures for the settlement of investment disputes.

[11] By 31 July 2018, 174 intra-EU investment arbitrations had been registered: UNCTAD, 'Fact Sheet on Intra-European Union Investor-State Arbitration Cases' (December 2018) IIA Issues Note – International Investment Agreements, Issue 3.

[12] Non-paper on intra-EU Investment Treaties, from Austria, Finland, France, Germany and the Netherlands, 7 April 2016.

[13] See S W Schill, 'MFN Clauses as Bilateral Commitments to Multilateralism – A Reply to Simon Batifort and J. Benton Heath' (2018) Amsterdam Law School Legal Studies Research Paper no 2018-01, 10–14.

Despite the existence of the principles of mutual trust and of sincere cooperation, the EU is made up of different sovereign states that have different approaches to the rule of law.[14] The TEU foresees a mechanism in case of breaches of the rule of law by a Member State (Art 7). The Commission introduced a New Framework for the rule of law, according to which it works together with a Member State in order to restore the rule of law, and is now implementing a stronger rule of law policy.[15] Instead of the elimination of all BITs, the creation of a Union-wide investment treaty or EU regulation with the better characteristics of BITs, could aid in the promotion of the rule of law.

So far, the EU has focused exclusively on the elimination of the intra-EU BIT system and this approach has had negative impacts on the rule of law, as will now be illustrated.

4.   THE RULE OF LAW AS A VALUE OF THE EU

The rule of law is a value of the EU included in Article 2 of the TEU. The Commission has defined the rule of law as being primarily a 'dominant organisational model of modern constitutional law and international organizations […] to regulate the exercise of public powers'.[16]

The core content of the rule of law can be defined as including a variety of other principles:

> […] **legality**, which implies a transparent, accountable, democratic and pluralistic process for enacting laws; **legal certainty; prohibition of arbitrariness of the executive powers; independent and impartial courts; effective judicial review**

---

[14]   Cf European Commission Press Release (18 June 2015) (n 6):
   Since enlargement, such 'extra' reassurances should not be necessary, as all Member States are subject to the same EU rules in the single market, including those on cross-border investment (in particular the freedom of establishment and the free movement of capital). All EU investors also benefit from the same protection thanks to EU rules. (e.g.,) non-discrimination on grounds of nationality). By contrast, intra-EU BITs confer rights on a bilateral basis to investors from some Member States only: in accordance with consistent case law from the European Court of Justice, such discrimination based on nationality is incompatibility with EU law.

[15]   European Commission, 'Communication from the Commission to the European Parliament and the Council – A New EU Framework to Strengthen the Rule of Law' (11 March 2014) COM(2014) 158 final; European Commission, 'Further Strengthening the Rule of Law within the Union' (Communication) (3 April 2019) COM(2019) 163 final.

[16]   European Commission Communication (11 March 2014), ibid., 3–4.

including respect for fundamental rights; and equality before the law.[17] [emphasis original]

Considering the EU as a particular form of international and constitutional organisation, with executive, legislative and judicial power, and composed of states which are by their nature constitutional organisations, respecting the rule of law should be a guiding force within the Union. However, the handling of the existence of intra-EU BITs has undermined the rule of law: there is a lack of legal certainty surrounding intra-EU investment protection; there are risks for arbitration as a form of adjudication based on the rule of law alternative to national courts and there is a risk of undermining the rights of EU investors.

5. THE IMPACT ON THE RULE OF LAW OF THE PHASING OUT OF INTRA-EU BITS: LACK OF LEGAL CERTAINTY

The main consequence of the phasing-out of intra-EU BITs is a general lack of legal certainty.

Intra-EU BITs have yet not been terminated (except for the Italian and Irish BITs).[18] It is yet unclear whether the ECT may or may not be used in intra-EU arbitrations.[19] There are numerous intra-EU BIT and ECT arbitrations

[17] Ibid., 4.
[18] *Eskosol SpA in Liquidazione v Italian Republic*, ICSID Case No. ARB/15/50, Decision on Italy's Request for Immediate Termination and Italy's Jurisdictional Objection based on Inapplicability of the Energy Charter Treaty to Intra-EU Disputes (7 May 2019), para 227.
[19] Compare arbitral awards upholding jurisdiction and declaring *Achmea* inapplicable to the ECT and the annulment proceeding before Swedish Courts: *Masdar Solar & Wind Cooperatief UA v Kingdom of Spain*, ICSID Case No. ARB/14/1, Award (16 May 2018), paras 669–676; *Vattenfall II*, Decision on the Achmea Issue (n 3); *Greentech Energy Systems A/S, NovEnergia II Enegy & Environment (SCA) SICAR, and NovEnergia II Italian Portfolio SA v The Italian Republic*, SCC Arbitration V (2015/095), Final Award (23 December 2018), paras 356–402; *Eskosol SpA in Liquidazione v Italian Republic*, Decision on Italy's Request for Immediate Termination and Italy's Jurisdictional Objection based on Inapplicability of the Energy Charter Treaty to Intra-EU Disputes, ibid., paras 207–227; *9REN Holding SARL v The Kingdom of Spain*, ICSID Case No. ARB/15/15, Award (31 May 2019), paras 152–158; *Rockhopper Italia SpA, Rockhopper Mediterranean Ltd, and Rockhopper Exploration Plc v Italian Republic*, ICSID Case No. ARB/17/14, Decision on the intra-EU Jurisdictional Objection (26 June 2019), paras 142–151. All news related to the annulment proceedings of the *NovEnergia v Kingdom of Spain* arbitration may be found on Global Arbitration Review and on Investment Arbitration Reporter, in particular: 'Spain asks for ECJ to rule on Energy Charter Treaty' (2018) 13 *Global Arbitration*

still ongoing;[20] EU law contains protections for EU investors, however, such protections are spelt differently from the protections contained in BITs, they are scattered throughout the Treaties, secondary EU legislation, the Charter of fundamental rights and the dispute settlement avenues do not always grant an investor the possibility of directly initiating an action against a state.[21] The CJEU's preliminary ruling in the *Achmea* case has not put a clear end to intra-EU investment arbitration.[22] Numerous arbitral tribunals in post-*Achmea* cases have found that the CJEU's decision is not applicable. The communication of the Commission in July 2018, and the three declarations by Member States of January 2019, offer partially diverging interpretations of the CJEU's decision and it is unclear from the Member States' declarations what they intend to do.

5.1   The Uncertainty Created by the CJEU's *Achmea* Judgment

The judgment by the CJEU in the *Achmea* case has not put a definitive end to the intra-EU investment treaty discussion.[23] The judgment has quite a wide grey area and the reasoning of the Court is difficult to translate into a rule, as has been pointed out in the *Vattenfall II* arbitration Decision on *Achmea*.[24]

The CJEU seems to reason that Article 8 of the BIT is in contrast with Articles 344 and 267 of the TFEU, because it challenges the principles of autonomy, mutual trust and sincere cooperation, which underly the two TFEU Articles.[25] The Court finds that Article 8 of the BIT breaches the EU principles, because the BIT investment dispute could potentially regard EU law,[26] arbitral tribunals are not courts or tribunals of a Member State and therefore do not have access to the CJEU's preliminary ruling mechanism,[27] and the BIT arbitral awards are subject only to limited review depending on the seat of the arbitration and on the applicable law to the enforcement and annulment issue.[28]

Review 4; Damien Charlotin, 'Spain Secures Stay of Enforcement of Energy Charter Treaty Award in Swedish Court' (*Investment Arbitration Reporter*, 18 May 2018).
   [20]   UNCTAD Fact Sheet (n 11).
   [21]   See T Fecák, *International Investment Agreements and EU Law* (Kluwer Law International 2016) 54–110.
   [22]   Cf Fumagalli (n 8).
   [23]   *Achmea* (n 7); R T Treves, 'The *Achmea* Judgment and Mutual Mistrust – Toward a Complete Transition of the Intra-EU Investment Protection System' in A Biondi and G Sangiuolo (eds) LAwTTIP Working paper 2018/3 75-91, 75–76.
   [24]   *Vattenfall II*, Decision on the Achmea Issue (n 3), para 159.
   [25]   *Achmea* (n 7), paras 31–35.
   [26]   Ibid., paras 39–42.
   [27]   Ibid., paras 43–49.
   [28]   Ibid., paras 50–55.

5.1.1   Unclear scope of application of the judgment

The scope of application of the CJEU's decision is unclear. The *dispositif* states that investor-state dispute settlement (ISDS) clauses 'such as' Article 8 in the Dutch/Slovak BIT are in conflict with Articles 344 and 267 of the TFEU. To answer the question of which ISDS clauses are comparable to the one in the Dutch/Slovak BIT it is necessary to discern from the reasoning of the Court the characteristics of Article 8, which made it incompatible with the TFEU.[29]

The reasoning by the CJEU reveals that the finding of the Court is modelled around the characteristics of the BIT under consideration.

The Court refers to treaties *between Member States* and distinguishes treaties in which the EU is a party.[30] Moreover, an important part of the Court's incompatibility finding is not based exclusively on the fact that arbitral awards are subject to a limited review. This would have led to considering incompatible with EU law all arbitrations, including commercial arbitrations. The Court sustains, instead, that the limited review of an investment award renders an ISDS clause incompatible with EU law when the Member States have 'removed from their own courts, and hence from the system of judicial remedies which the second subparagraph of article 19(1) TEU requires them to establish in the fields covered by EU law [...] disputes which may concern the application or interpretation of EU law'.[31]

The Court seems to argue that an ISDS clause is incompatible with EU law if it removes investment disputes entirely from the national court system. Arbitration should 'originate in the freely expressed wishes of the parties'.[32] It would appear, therefore, that ISDS clauses which grant an investor the option of solving its investment disputes in national courts or through arbitration are compatible with EU law. By including such option, the Member States are not removing investment disputes, which may potentially touch upon EU law,

---

[29]   See *Rockhopper*, Decision on the intra-EU Jurisdictional Objection (n 19), para 159:

> The Tribunal notes that, having set out a number of general considerations (which are of general application in EU law), the CJEU then discusses the precise circumstances of the Achmea BIT. This analysis of the Achmea BIT is particularly important as it informs the exact rationale for the answers given by the CJEU to the Bundesgerichtshof.

And para 167:

> The Tribunal makes two observations which arise from this conclusion of the CJEU. The reasoning stems entirely from the specific circumstances of the Achmea BIT, and is not based on any other BIT or a wider ISDS enquiry (particularly, not the ECT) [...].

[30]   *Achmea* (n 7), para 57.

[31]   Ibid., para 55.

[32]   Ibid.

from the national court system. They are creating new rights (the BIT protection standards) and granting their courts new jurisdiction, *ratione materiae*. The investor would have the free choice between national courts or arbitration. Such a choice, following the Court's reasoning regarding commercial arbitration, would seem to be compatible with EU law.

It appears, therefore, unclear whether the Court's decision should apply to ECT intra-EU arbitrations for two main reasons: (i) because the ECT is a multilateral treaty, in which the EU is a Party and also non-EU states are Parties;[33] and (ii) because Article 26(2) of the ECT includes arbitration and national court proceedings as alternative dispute settlement avenues at the investor's disposal. All of the *post-Achmea* arbitral decisions in ECT intra-EU arbitrations have, in fact, distinguished the ECT from a BIT and upheld jurisdiction.[34]

In the same manner, the CJEU's decision seems not to apply to BITs such as the Spain/Croatia or the Spain/Slovenia BITs that contain ISDS clauses with the alternative between national courts and arbitration.[35]

5.1.2   Lack of practical guidance for the implementation of the judgment

Furthermore, the CJEU's decision does not offer practical guidance as to *how it has to be implemented* by ongoing arbitral tribunals and by the referring national court.[36]

The language chosen by the Court does not allow an easy interpretation of the effects of the judgment. The Court states in the English version of the

---

[33]   See in particular *9REN Holding*, Award (n 19), paras 150–158.

[34]   *Masdar Solar*, Award (n 19), paras 669–676; *Vattenfall II*, Decision on the Achmea Issue (n 3); *NovEnergia*, Final Award (n 19), paras 356–402; *Eskosol*, Decision on Italy's Request for Immediate Termination and Italy's Jurisdictional Objection based on Inapplicability of the Energy Charter Treaty to Intra-EU Disputes (n 18), paras 207–227; *9REN Holding*, Award (n 19), paras. 152–158; *Rockhopper*, Decision on the intra-EU Jurisdictional Objection (n 19), paras 142–151.

[35]   Art XI(2) of the Agreement between The Republic of Croatia and The Kingdom of Spain on the Promotion and Reciprocal Protection of Investments, Madrid, 15 July 1997; Art 9(2), Acuerdo para la promoción y protección recíproca de inversiones entre el Reino de España y la Republica de Exlovenia, Madrid, 15 July 1998.

[36]   See e.g., *Eskosol*, Decision on Italy's Request for Immediate Termination and Italy's Jurisdictional Objection based on Inapplicability of the Energy Charter Treaty to Intra-EU Disputes (n 18), para 215:

> Finally, and most importantly, the *Achmea* Judgments was restricted to a discussion of EU law, [...] It certainly did not explain, as a matter of either VCLT conflicts analysis or VCLT rules on invalidity of treaty provisions, that intra-EU arbitration clauses are 'inapplicable' and 'would have to be disapplied,' with the effect that an 'arbitral tribunal established on the basis of [such] clauses lacks jurisdiction, due to a lack of a valid offer to arbitrate'.

judgment that Articles 267 and 344 of the TFEU 'preclude' dispute settlement provisions in BITs. However, the German word that had been used by the referring Bundesgerichtshof (BGH) and which is used by the CJEU in the German version of the decision is '*entgegenstehen*' which should be translated as 'to conflict with' or is 'opposed to'. The French version of the judgment reflects such meaning and states '*s'opposer*'. In the same manner, the Spanish version of the judgment reads '*se opone*'. The Italian version, however, reads '*preclude*'. The Italian version is quite relevant considering that the judge *rapporteur* was Judge Tizzano. Therefore, it may well be that the intention of the Court was to use a word with the meaning of 'precludes' and not an open-ended word such as 'to be in conflict with'. However, the fact remains that the Court chose a non-technical word, which consequently leaves space for different interpretations.

Moreover, the CJEU did not address explicitly the issue of the applicability of its judgment by arbitral tribunals, while it stated that it does not consider arbitral tribunals as courts or tribunals of Member States. It remains, therefore, unclear how a tribunal that is not obliged by the Treaties to refer questions to the CJEU should nonetheless apply as binding the interpretations of the CJEU.

In this regard, the fact that intra-EU BITs normally do not directly foresee the applicability of EU law, but that at least one BIT does (the Croatia/Austria BIT) should carry considerable weight in answering the question of the applicability of the CJEU's judgments.[37] Article 11(2) of the Croatia/Austria BIT states: 'The Contracting Parties are not bound by the present Agreement insofar as it is incompatible with the legal *acquis* of the European Union (EU) in force at any given time.' In an arbitration based on this BIT, the CJEU's *Achmea* judgment would seem to have to be applied by a tribunal as part of the *acquis* of the EU by following common notions of what is considered part of the *acquis*, which includes the interpretations of EU law by the CJEU. On the contrary, if a BIT does not foresee the applicability of EU law, the opposite conclusions should be reached.

Despite the referring BGH having motivated the decision to refer the questions to the CJEU, also because of the number of intra-EU investment treaties still in force and of the number of pending and potential intra-EU investment arbitrations, and therefore because of the significance that a potential CJEU decision would have,[38] the CJEU appears not to have taken it upon itself to prevent negative effects on ongoing arbitral proceedings, nor has it considered the impact of its decision on the substantive protections of EU investors.

---

[37]   Agreement between the Republic of Austria and the Republic of Croatia for the Promotion and Protection of Investments, Vienna, 19 February 1997.

[38]   *Achmea* (n 7), para 14.

An unfortunate illustration of the potential negative effects of not having addressed these issues and of the consequent legal uncertainty which surrounds intra-EU investment protection is represented by the numerous arbitral awards that have followed the CJEU's judgment and have decided that the judgment is not applicable in their proceedings.[39] There has been no dialogue between the CJEU and the tribunals: these tribunals have not had to answer to the Court's reasoning of applicability, because such reasoning was missing in the Court's judgment.

5.1.3   The *Achmea* judgment was centred around the autonomy of EU law and not the rule of law

The CJEU's decision was mainly motivated around the principle of the autonomy of EU law. By motivating its decision around the principle of autonomy, the entire decision refers to the Member States and focuses on their breach of EU law and of the principle of autonomy through the inclusion of an arbitration clause in their BITs. The CJEU, therefore, treated the issue before it as an issue of allocation of powers and constitutional structure, instead of dealing with the case as a question of rights and of investment protection.

Had the CJEU based its decision also on the principle of the rule of law, it might have managed to reach the same policy decision (a push towards the termination of the intra-EU BITs) while protecting the interests of EU citizens at the same time, for example, by rendering a more articulated decision and explicitly taking other interests into consideration.

It is interesting to note, in this regard, that in paragraph 34 of its decision, the CJEU recognises that the Union is based on a set of common values 'as stated in Article 2 TEU'. However, the Court does not put such common values at the basis of its judgment. Instead, it transforms the common values themselves into a question of constitutional structure. The Court, in fact, cites the common values not as principles to be taken into consideration when solving a conflict between legal systems, but as the reason for the existence of the principle of mutual trust. Mutual trust, however, is a principle that governs the relationships between the Member States and not the relationships between the Member States and their citizens.

5.2   The Uncertainty Created by the Arbitral Tribunals

The responsibility for the legal uncertainty surrounding the protection of EU investors cannot be entirely attributed to the CJEU's *Achmea* decision. Arbitral

---

[39]   See all the ECT intra-EU arbitrations cited above and *UP and CD Holding Internationale v Hungary*, ICSID Case No. ARB/13/35, Award, 9 October 2018.

tribunals share some responsibility. The *Achmea* decision was the first chance for the CJEU to intervene on intra-EU investment protection. Before the preliminary ruling request in the *Achmea* case, arbitral tribunals had already heard and decided numerous intra-EU arbitrations.[40]

A contribution of arbitral tribunals to the legal uncertainty may seem to derive from a certain reluctance to engage in a dialogue with the CJEU. Since the first intra-EU arbitrations the sole EU interlocutor of the arbitral tribunals has been the Commission, requesting to act and acting as *amicus curiae*.[41] The Commission, however, is not the judicial body of the EU, it is instead a political body and, in such role, it is the guardian of the EU Treaties.[42] The Commission is not the ultimate interpreter of EU law. That role is reserved to the CJEU. And to preserve such role, the CJEU in *Achmea* decided on the incompatibility of ISDS clauses in intra-EU BITs.

Arbitral tribunals never referred questions to the CJEU and always dealt with jurisdiction by applying general international law and not principles and concepts of EU law.[43] Therefore, for example, arbitral tribunals would solve arguments regarding conflicts of treaties by applying the Vienna Convention on the Law of Treaties (VCLT) and specific Articles in the BITs regarding conflicts with other provisions. Arbitral tribunals would not instead solve these issues by accepting the applicability of, and by applying, principles of EU law, such as autonomy and primacy.[44]

The reasons why arbitral tribunals did not proceed in this manner are understandable. For an arbitral tribunal to refer a question to the CJEU or to apply the principles of autonomy or of primacy of EU law would mean acceptance that EU law is applicable to the issue of jurisdiction. This acceptance would immediately insert the arbitral tribunal within the sphere of competence of EU courts. The whole argument by arbitral tribunals according to which there was

---

[40]   For an overview, see UNCTAD Fact Sheet (n 11).

[41]   See E Levine, 'Amicus Curiae in International Investment Arbitration: The Implications of an Increase in Third-Party Participation' (2011) 29 *Berkeley Journal of International Law* 200.

[42]   See Art 17 TEU.

[43]   Consider, e.g., *Eureko BV v The Slovak Republic*, PCA Case No. 2008-13, Award on Jurisdiction, Arbitrability and Suspension (26 October 2010), paras 148–149, 292, in which the arbitral tribunal was requested to make a preliminary ruling and instead decided not to. The tribunal did not comment on the possibility of a preliminary ruling, it only stated, in para 292, that it was premature to stay the proceedings allowing the CJEU to decide the infringement case that had been initiated in parallel with the BIT arbitration.

[44]   See, e.g., and recently, *Vattenfall II*, Decision on the Achmea Issue (n 3), in which the tribunal mentions autonomy and primacy also because referred to by the respondent and the Commission, but exclusively considers the VCLT.

no conflict with EU law was based on the fact that they were not called upon to interpret and apply EU law.[45] Arbitral tribunals have consistently founded their jurisdiction in a treaty, which granted them independence from all other courts or court systems to solve the dispute before them. As the CJEU has decided that BIT arbitral tribunals are not courts of Member States, so have arbitral tribunals never acted as such by applying EU law or the interpretations of the CJEU.

The same considerations may apply to the argument that suggests that comity would require arbitral tribunals to stay their proceedings while the CJEU dealt with the issue of the compatibility of intra-EU BITs with EU law.[46] An independent adjudicatory body, created on the basis of an international treaty has no reason to spontaneously decide to stay its proceedings and decide to be bound by a decision of a court of another legal system. This would imply having already determined that jurisdiction should be decided by EU law, and that the tribunal is part of the EU judicial system. Arbitral tribunals, therefore, appear to have their hands tied.

Arbitral tribunals' hands appear tied, however, by the particular interpretation of autonomy given by the Court. The CJEU's interpretation of its own role as master of the interpretation of EU law, which solves issues of conflicting systems through the one way road of primacy of EU law, creates paradoxes in cases in which there are more courts, deriving their jurisdiction from different treaties, competent on the same subject matter.

The legal uncertainty surrounding the protection of EU investors has been accentuated by the fact that arbitral tribunals in intra-EU BIT cases or intra-EU ECT cases that were pending when the *Achmea* decision was rendered have decided not to take into consideration the CJEU decision and instead retain jurisdiction and decide on the merits.[47] The situation that has arisen is again one of a lack of judicial dialogue. Arbitral tribunals have argued: that EU law is not applicable to the dispute settlement clause of the BIT;[48] that the ECT is distinguishable from the Dutch/Slovak BIT;[49] that the CJEU decision does not apply to ICSID arbitration;[50] and so on.

---

[45]   For a particularly clear applicable law analysis to the question of jurisdiction, *Vattenfall II*, Decision on the Achmea Issue, ibid., paras 108–168.

[46]   See G M Vallar, 'L'arbitrabilità delle controversie tra un investitore di uno Stato membro ed un altro Stato membro: alcune considerazioni a margine del caso Eureko/ Achmea v. The Slovak Republic' (2014) 4 *Rivista di Diritto Internazionale Privato e Processuale* 849.

[47]   See all the ECT intra-EU arbitration awards and Decision cited above and the intra-EU BIT awards cited.

[48]   For example, *Vattenfall II*, Decision on the Achmea Issue (n 3).

[49]   For example, *NovEnergia*, Final Award (n 19), para 398.

[50]   *UP CD Holding Internationale v Hungary*, Award (n 39), para 253.

These decisions certainly do not help to create legal certainty. They grant investors the hope or even the expectation of being able to pursue the BIT arbitration route, while it is possible that the awards will be annulled or not enforced in EU national courts. The respondent state and the Commission would try at least to challenge the award and, if necessary, to address the CJEU.[51]

In such a situation, lawyers advising clients seeking to initiate new intra-EU arbitrations have a heightened responsibility as to how to proceed.

5.3   The Uncertainty Created by the Commission

The Commission itself has contributed to the uncertainty surrounding the legal protections afforded to intra-EU investors, primarily because of the dual role that the Commission is playing: interpreter of EU law; and political arm interested in eliminating overlapping systems of investment protection.

In fact, on the one hand, the Commission acts as an *amicus curiae* in intra-EU BIT arbitrations, affirming the incompatibility of BITs with the EU Treaties as a matter of settled EU law. On the other hand, and in parallel, the Commission sets the political goal to eliminate all intra-EU BITs and enforces such political decision, for example, by discussing opening infringement proceedings against Member States that do not terminate their intra-EU BITs.[52]

The Commission's communication of July 2018 is particularly revealing of this conflicting dual role.[53] The communication, in fact, appears to set out as a political objective ending all intra-EU BITs, while it states as a matter of settled law the incompatibility of BITs with EU law because both systems of law provide for overlapping protections to EU investors.

---

[51] Spain is seeking annulment of the award in *NovEnergia v Kingdom of Spain*, SCC Case No. 063/2015 before the Swedish courts. All news related to the annulment proceedings of the *NovEnergia v Kingdom of Spain* arbitration may be found on Global Arbitration Review and on Investment Arbitration Reporter: (n 19). The investor in that case is seeking enforcement in DC Courts: see Damien Charlotin, 'Hungarian State-Owned Investor, MOL, Intervenes in Court in support of another Investor seeking to enforce an intra-EU ECT Award against Spain; MOL insists that ECT remains viable for intra-EU disputes-As it waits for award in its own case' (*Investment Arbitration Reporter*, 18 January 2019) https://www-iareporter-com.peacepalace.idm.oclc.org/articles/hungarian-state-owned-investor-mol-intervenes-in-court-in-support-of-another-investor-seeking-to-enforce-an-intra-eu-ect-award-against-spain-mol-insists-that-ect-remains-viable-for-intra-eu-dispute/, accessed 15 February 2019.

[52] European Commission Press Release (18 June 2015) (n 6).

[53] European Commission, 'Communication from the Commission to the European Parliament and the Council – Protection of intra-EU investment' (19 July 2018) COM(2018) 547 final.

By pursuing the underlying intent of arguing that EU law already offers all of the protections included in BITs and more, the Commission in reality reveals the contrary. EU law protections are scattered in different sources of EU law,[54] are to a large extent the product of the CJEU's interpretation of EU primary or secondary sources, do not offer exactly the same or all of the rights offered by BITs and do not offer a clear and compact document including rights and remedies.

In its communication, the Commission expands the scope of the CJEU's *Achmea* decision to cover all forms of ISDS clauses in all intra-EU BITs and also, in particular, to the intra-EU application of the ECT ISDS clause.[55]

By pursuing this dual role, the Commission runs the risk of creating more legal confusion than clarity, in particular, because it is not the Commission's institutional role to be the ultimate interpreter of EU law.

This has come up front and centre in the *Micula* case.[56] The Commission argued in different *fora* that Romania should not pay an arbitral award to the Micula brothers because payment would amount to state aid. Recently, instead, the General Court of the EU decided that the underlying case and therefore the payment of the award was not a case of illegal state aid, because Romania was not a Member of the EU when it took the relevant measures and therefore it was not bound by the prohibitions on state aid.[57] Of course, this judgment may still be appealed before the CJEU. However, it reveals that the Commission, although it applies EU law and it triggers infringement proceedings, is not the ultimate interpreter of EU law: the EU courts are, and in particular the CJEU.

Other than acting as the ultimate interpreter of EU law, the Commission had other instruments at its disposal to pursue the phasing-out of intra-EU BITs, for example: initiating infringement proceedings; and initiating and conducting a dialogue for the drafting of an EU wide investment treaty or regulation. The consequence of the Commission's equivocal role is, instead, again a lack of legal clarity and a heightening of the polarisation between institutional communities, the EU institutional community and the arbitration community, instead of heightening the protection of EU investors.

---

[54]   Also Fecák (n 21), 54–110.

[55]   European Commission Communication (19 July 2018) (n 53), 3–4.

[56]   *Ioan Micula, Viorel Micula, SC European Food SA, SC Starmill SRL and SC Multipack SRL v Romania*, ICSID Case No. ARB/05/20, Award, 11 December 2013. For an overview of the case, see P Bertoli, *Diritto Europeo dell'arbitrato internazionale* (Giuffrè editore 2015) 252–253.

[57]   Cases T-624/15, T-694/15 and T-704/15 *Ioan Micula and Others v European Commission*, [2019].

5.4   The Uncertainty Created by the Declarations of the Member States

The January 2019 declarations by Member States[58] seem to widen the legal uncertainty surrounding the protection of intra-EU investments.

First, Member States extend the application of the CJEU's judgment to sunset clauses, although the judgment does not mention such clauses.[59]

Second, Member States do not offer a unanimous interpretation of the applicability of the *Achmea* judgment to intra-EU ECT arbitrations – 22 Member States declare that the CJEU's decision does apply.[60] Six Member States disagree. Hungary declares that the CJEU's judgment is not directly applicable to the ECT because the CJEU does not mention the ECT expressly.[61] Finland, Malta, Luxembourg, Slovenia and Sweden declare that they should not prejudge the issue due to ongoing proceedings.[62]

Third, Member States' positions with respect to pending intra-EU investment arbitrations is unclear. All Member States indicate that they will 'inform' arbitral tribunals of the consequences of the *Achmea* judgment.[63] The use of the verb 'inform' leads to different interpretations. It could mean that Member States consider the declarations similar to *amicus curiae* briefs: for arbitral tribunals' consideration. Or, to 'inform' arbitral tribunals could mean that Member States consider that they are simply bringing to the tribunals' attention the inevitable consequence that tribunals must decline their jurisdiction because of an invalid offer to arbitrate as stated by the CJEU.[64]

---

[58]   Declaration of the Representatives of the Governments of the Member States on the Legal Consequences of the Judgment of the Court of Justice in *Achmea* and on Investment Protection in the European Union, 15 January 2019 (22 Member States signed this declaration: Belgium, Bulgaria, Czech Republic, Denmark, Germany, Estonia, Ireland, Greece, Spain, France, Croatia, Italy, Cyprus, Latvia, Lithuania, Netherlands, Austria, Poland, Portugal, Romania, Slovakia and the United Kingdom) ('Majority Declaration'); Declaration of the Representatives of Finland, Luxembourg, Malta, Slovenia and Sweden on the Enforcement of the Judgment of the Court of Justice in *Achmea* and on Investment Protection in the European Union, 16 January 2019; Declaration of the Representative of the Government of Hungary on the Legal Consequences of the Judgment of the Court of Justice in Achmea and on Investment Protection in the European Union, 16 January 2019 https://ec.europa.eu/info/publications/190117-bilateral-investment-treaties_en, accessed 15 February 2019.

[59]   See all three 15 January 2019 Member States' Declarations, ibid.

[60]   Majority Declaration, ibid., 2 and action-point 9.

[61]   Hungary's Declaration, ibid., 3, point 8.

[62]   Declaration by five Member States, ibid., 3.

[63]   See all three 15 January 2019 Member States' Declarations, ibid., action-point 1.

[64]   States acting as Respondents appear to be interpreting the Declarations in such manner, see, e.g. Italy's requests that led to a recent decision in the *Rockhopper* arbitra-

The interpretation of 'inform' should consider that Member States declare that they 'will ensure effective legal protection pursuant to the second subparagraph of Article 19(1) TEU under the control of the Court of Justice against State measures that are the object of pending intra-EU investment arbitration proceedings'.[65] This could be read as an attempt of taking into consideration the interests of EU investors in ongoing arbitrations by ensuring that ongoing arbitral proceedings will carry on until an award or until Member States provide for an alternative means of protection.

The arbitral tribunal in the *Eskosol v Italy* ECT arbitration considered the above referenced declaration by 22 Member States, amongst which were Belgium (home state of the investor) and Italy, to be a political statement supported by no particular legal analysis that went beyond the scope of the CJEU's judgment. The tribunal could not accept an interpretation of the Declaration that implied an interruption of ongoing proceedings.[66]

The difficulty for Member States of binding themselves to a particular strategy following the *Achmea* decision may be explained considering the many hats they wear: home states of investors; respondent states; Member States; and parties to treaties. As a result, their actions and inactions accentuate the legal uncertainty surrounding the protection of intra-EU investors.

6.   THE IMPACT ON THE RULE OF LAW OF THE PHASING OUT OF INTRA-EU BITS: RISKS FOR DUE PROCESS AND RISK OF UNDERMINING SUBSTANTIVE INVESTMENT PROTECTION RIGHTS

The implementation of the decision to phase out intra-EU BITs may also undermine, more significantly, the rule of law by interfering with due process rights of parties in ongoing arbitral proceedings and by reducing investors' substantive protections.

As regards the due process risks, requiring arbitral tribunals to automatically apply the *Achmea* judgment and decline jurisdiction may lead to a breach of the *competence de la competence* principle. Moreover, if the Member States' January 2019 declarations were sufficient to interrupt ongoing proceedings,

---

tion and in the *Eskosol* arbitration: *Rockhopper*, Decision on the intra-EU Jurisdictional Objection (n 19), paras 176–196; *Eskosol*, Decision on Italy's Request for Immediate Termination and Italy's Jurisdictional Objection based on Inapplicability of the Energy Charter Treaty to Intra-EU Disputes (n 18), paras 207–227.
[65]   See all three 15 January 2019 Member States' Declarations (n 58), action-point 6.
[66]   Ibid., paras 207–227.

this would violate the principle of equality of arms.[67] It would signify that states can decide whether and when to revoke their consent to arbitration, even during pending proceedings and independently of the will of the claimant investor.[68]

Admitting the possibility for states to interrupt ongoing proceedings would also undermine one of the distinctive features of foreign investment law: that BITs grant rights directly to the investor.[69] If the states can unilaterally decide whether an ongoing arbitration should continue, it would mean that BITs actually grant rights exclusively to the states and that investors only have a procedural right to initiate an arbitration: a right that is subdued to the will of the states.

Finally, phasing-out intra-EU BITs may undermine the substantive rights of intra-EU investors. EU law investment protection is scattered amongst primary and secondary legislation. EU law has no unique instrument, concise and user-friendly as BITs, for investment protection. EU law does not offer the same possibilities of redress directly against a state as BITs. Investors may directly initiate national court proceedings against a state, with the inevitable potential bias problems that BITs tried to avoid foreseeing arbitration. For certain breaches, however, investors must request the Commission to intervene and have no direct redress against the state.

7. CONCLUSIONS: THE RULE OF LAW AS A PRINCIPLE OF INTEGRATION

As has been argued throughout this chapter, the implementation of the political decision to phase-out all intra-EU BITs and the intra-EU application of the ECT is undermining the rule of law.

This is not to say that granting investors solely the protection offered by EU law implies a risk for the rule of law. What is being argued, instead, is

---

[67] See T Waelde, 'Procedural Challenges in Investment Arbitration under the Shadow of the Dual Role of the State' (2010) 26 *Arbitration International* 3.

[68] *Eskosol*, Decision on Italy's Request for Immediate Termination and Italy's Jurisdictional Objection based on Inapplicability of the Energy Charter Treaty to Intra-EU Disputes (n 18), para 226. Compare to the debate surrounding the interpretations by the Free Trade Commission and their impact on ongoing NAFTA arbitrations: G Kaufmann-Kohler, 'Interpretive Powers of the Free Trade Commission and the Rule of Law' in E Gaillard (general ed) and F Bachard (ed), *Fifteen Years of NAFTA Chapter 11 Arbitration* (Jurispub, IAI 2011) 175–194.

[69] See Z Douglas, *Investment Claims* (CUP 2009) para 6-575. Cf J Crawford, 'Treaty and Contract in Investment Arbitration' The 22nd Freshfields Lecture on International Arbitration (London, 29 November 2007), (2009) 6 TDM 5.

that the process of integration that requires the elimination of the BIT system undermines the rule of law.

The process of integration conflicts with the rule of law because the rule of law is not at the centre of this process. The unmoved mover of EU integration appears to be the principles of autonomy and of primacy of EU law. These principles, however, aim at protecting not the individual, but the EU as an institution. These principles transform every conflict between the EU legal system and other legal systems, even those that aim exclusively at granting and protecting the rights of individuals, into conflicts of competences: inexorably accentuating the democratic deficit that the EU fears and tries to close.[70]

For a Union based on the rule of law and on the protection of human rights, it is a paradox to aim at the outright elimination of treaty systems that grant rights and protections to EU investors.[71] It is, however, an unavoidable paradox as long as the EU focuses entirely on preserving and expanding its jurisdiction.

The Union must be preserved, but its common foundational values as well. To achieve a lasting and dynamic Union, autonomy and primacy could, and should, be complemented by the rule of law. A process of integration based on autonomy, primacy *and* the rule of law puts the individual back at the centre of the Union and the debate on integration may finally shift from one of conflicts of competences to one of rights and protections of the individual.

---

[70]   Alerting to the risk that founding principles of the EU run the risk of crystallising and accentuating a democratic deficit within the Union, see J H H Weiler, 'Van Gend en Loos: The Individual as Subject and Object and the Dilemma of European Legitimacy' Jean Monnet Working Paper 10/14.

[71]   See P Eeckhout, 'Opinion 2/13 on EU accession to the ECHR and Judicial Dialogue – Autonomy or Autarky?' Jean Monet Working Paper No. 01/15, 16:

> Moreover, from the perspective of the autonomy of EU law, it is not clear at all that the principle of mutual trust, as a 'specific characteristic' of EU law, trumps the protection of fundamental rights. It is true that the principle is a cornerstone of the AFSJ [Area of Freedom Security and Justice], and that the relevant TFEU provisions make several references to mutual recognition. But the protection of fundamental rights is a foundational EU value (see Art. 2 TEU), and the TFEU's opening provision on the AFSJ predicates the area on 'respect for fundamental rights' [Art 67(1)] – such respect is also a 'specific characteristic' of EU law. Surely, that means that in the event of a conflict between mutual trust and human rights, the latter must prevail, as a matter of EU law?

11. Unleash the liger: The nature of the investment court system and its impact on enforcement

Simon Weber

1. INTRODUCTION

In 2009, the European Member States added the terms 'foreign direct invest-ment' to Article 207(1) TFEU. In the field of Common Commercial Policy, this amendment confers to the EU the competence to negotiate and conclude agreements protecting foreign direct investments. In addition to substantive provisions on the protection of investment, these agreements normally also provide for different means of investor State dispute resolution (ISDR).[1] ISDR mechanisms enable foreign investors, or their home States, to take legal action against the investors' host States. One of the dispute resolution mechanisms, called 'investment arbitration', allows for the investor to initiate proceedings against the contracting parties to an international investment agreement, before an international tribunal, to uphold the standards of protection provided therein.

The latest version of the free trade agreements (FTAs) between the EU and Vietnam (EUVFTA), as well as the FTAs with Canada (CETA), Mexico and Singapore, introduce a new investment dispute resolution mechanism with a standing investment tribunal and an appellate body. The new body is called 'investment court system' (ICS) and was not created for one single FTA, but is supposed to be included in all future FTAs of the EU. It therefore constitutes the start of a new era of ISDR. This chapter will refer to EUVFTA and CETA as the two most prominent FTAs, but could have also used the remaining two FTAs. While the compatibility of the ICS with EU law has been ascertained

---

[1] The author refrains from using the term 'ISDS – investor State dispute settle-ment' as the term is misleading. A court or tribunal does not 'settle' an international dispute but 'resolves' it by rendering a binding decision. 'Settlements' do not happen in courtrooms, where judicial resolution of the dispute takes place.

by the CJEU in Opinion 1/17, it remains unclear to what extent the institution of a new standing investment tribunal measures up, when subjected to critical examination and scrutiny, in light of principles of investment arbitration and international adjudication.

This chapter discusses the nature of the ICS and its implications on the enforcement of ICS decisions. It is argued that the ICS combines features of classic international arbitration and international adjudication, which make it a 'hybrid tribunal'. The chapter sets out the objective implications of the hybrid nature of the ICS's features on the credibility of the investment protection system, and on the coherence and correctness of its decisions, also addressing the difficulties and complications that this change in nature will entail. It will be concluded that the hybrid ICS introduces promising changes that are likely to make the system of investor-State dispute resolution more accessible and to strengthen the rule of law. Positive changes include improved access for small- and medium-sized enterprises, and more coherence in the decisions, leading to more legal correctness. However, the ICS uses the same procedure as investment tribunals, resulting in no solution for issues such as high costs and the efficiency of the system.

In section 2, the chapter performs a comparative normative analysis of the provisions on dispute resolution of two prominent European free trade agreements, comparing them with the provisions of the ICSID Convention and the ICJ Statute. The comparator used to represent investment arbitration is the ICSID Convention, as it constitutes the most frequently used basis for investment arbitrations. As for international adjudication, the ICJ Statute is the most prominent forum used for the resolution of State- State disputes, and therefore the relevant reference. This section has a descriptive character, aiming to provide the reader with an overview of the two different types of dispute resolution.

Finally, in section 3, the objective implications of the ICS's hybrid nature on the enforcement mechanism will be laid out. Given that the ICS is not an arbitral tribunal but a hybrid, its attempt to use the New York Convention as an enforcement mechanism constitutes a dead end. Moreover, any comparison with the Iran-US Claims Tribunal, which is often argued to be a 'standing arbitral body', shows the difficulties that will arise when ICS decisions will be enforced.

2.   THE HYBRID CHARACTER

Have you ever heard of a liger? Most people have not. How about a mule? That should ring a bell. A mule is a cross between a female horse and a male donkey.[2] It is infertile and known for its kindness. You might have a lead now on what a liger is. It is a cross between a female tiger and a male lion.[3] These two examples are in line with the definition of 'hybrid' under the *Oxford Dictionary*, which defines the term as something 'of mixed character – composed of different elements'.

This chapter argues that the ICS also is a 'hybrid' species, this time of dispute resolution body, as it combines elements of two different concepts: classic international investment arbitration and classic international adjudication.[4] Indeed, EU Commissioner for Trade Malmström, herself stated, in relation to investment protection in a similar free trade agreement with the US, the Transatlantic Trade and Investment Partnership (TTIP), that it was the intention of the Commission to move away from international arbitration, to create 'a very different animal'.[5] Hence, a third 'species' was born.

To compare the three systems, five institutional features will be compared. First, the appointment mechanism is of interest. This is to find out who has the right to appoint the decision makers. Second, the qualification of the decision makers will be addressed, to see who can be appointed. Third, the provisions on the procedural rules will be evoked, to find out if they are predetermined or to be freely chosen. Fourth, an eventual appeal mechanism allows us to find out if the decision of the dispute resolution forum is final and binding or, in case an appellate body exists, if it is not. Finally, the enforcement mechanism will be laid out.

---

[2] 'What Is a Mule?' (*The Donkey Sanctuary*) https://www.thedonkeysanctuary.org .uk/what-we-do/knowledge-and-advice/about-donkeys/mule, accessed 3 October 2018.

[3] Michael Riley, 'Liger' (*Big Cat Habitat*) https://bigcathabitat.org/meet-the -animals/liger/, accessed 3 October 2018; 'Liger Facts' (*Big Cat Rescue*, 23 January 2018) https://bigcatrescue.org/liger-facts/, accessed 3 October 2018.

[4] The term 'hybrid' has already been used in the sphere of international courts and tribunals, namely when it comes to international criminal tribunals. Better known under the term 'mixed criminal tribunals' they are 'criminal courts of law that have features of both international and domestic criminal jurisdictions' and 'are composed of international and local staff (judges, prosecutors and other personnel) and apply a compound of international and national substantive and procedural law'. Good examples are the Special Panels for Serious Crimes in East Timor, the Mixed Panels in the Courts of Kosovo, the Special Courts for Sierra Leone, the War Crimes Chamber of the Court of Bosnia-Herzegovina, the Extraordinary Chambers in the Courts of Cambodia and the Special Tribunal for Lebanon. However, in the criminal context the term hybrid has only been used to describe specific features of the courts like their composition and not the court as a whole. The more common term is 'Mixed Criminal Tribunals'.

[5] Cecilia Malmström, Commissioner for Trade, European commission – Press Release – Discussion on Investment in TTIP at the Meeting of the International Trade Committee of the European Parliament' Brussels, 18 March 2015 http://europa.eu/ rapid/press-release_SPEECH-15-4624_en.htm, accessed 3 October 2018.

2.1   The Nature of Investment Tribunals

How can 'arbitration' be defined? It is a private dispute resolution mechanism, which allows the parties to decide on their own decision makers. It is 'an effective way of obtaining a final and binding decision on a dispute [...] without reference to a court of law'.[6] Both legal and natural persons can be parties to arbitration, just as States. Hence, arbitration is an often-used way to resolve an international dispute: there are contractual disputes, investment disputes, State- State disputes, sport disputes, and other fields that use arbitration as means of dispute resolution. In ICSID disputes, generally three 'arbitrators' hear a dispute.[7] The ICSID Convention contains only few mandatory provisions, leaving a vast freedom of choice to the parties. One of the few mandatory provisions regarding the set-up of the tribunal is the uneven number of arbitrators, which is designed to avoid a stalemate if the tribunal is evenly divided.[8] Consequently, the most important feature of arbitration is party autonomy.

In commercial arbitration, the parties do not only decide to submit their dispute to an arbitral tribunal, they also decide on their arbitrators, the seat of arbitration, the procedural rule and the applicable law. In investment arbitration, the source of the arbitral tribunal's competence, i.e., a BIT, an FTA, an investment contract, or national legislation, limits the disputing parties' choice as to the procedural rules and the applicable law, but nonetheless keeps a large part of party autonomy when it comes to choosing the arbitrators or submitting the dispute. Arbitration is an ad hoc dispute settlement mechanism and based on the parties' voluntary submission.[9] 'A distinctive feature of investment arbitration is its ad hoc nature: each tribunal is specifically constituted for the particular dispute'.[10] It is a private mechanism, as the arbitrators

---

[6]   Nigel Blackaby et al, *Redfern and Hunter on International Arbitration* (6th edn, OUP 2015) para 1.04.

[7]   Ibid., para 4.29.

[8]   Christoph Schreuer, *The ICSID Convention: A Commentary: A Commentary on the Convention on the Settlement of Investment Disputes between States and Nationals of Other States* (2nd edn, CUP 2009) 478.

[9]   Blackaby et al (n 6), para 1.40; Gabrielle Kaufmann-Kohler and Michele Potesta, 'Can the Mauritius Convention serve as a model for the reform of investor-State arbitration in connection with the introduction of a permanent investment tribunal or an appeal mechanism? Analysis and roadmap', Center for International Dispute Settlement, Research Paper, 3 June 2016, 36, at https://uncitral.un.org/sites/uncitral.un.org/files/media-documents/un-citral/en/cids_research_paper_mauritius.pdf.

[10]   Cesare Romano, Karen J Alter and Yuval Shani (eds), *The Oxford Handbook of International Adjudication* (First published in paperback, OUP 2014) 297.

are not State-appointed judges, but appointed by the parties to the dispute themselves.[11]

Finally, the outcome is binding on the parties. The ad hoc character of arbitral tribunals stems from their creation for the very dispute at stake. They are not permanent and finish their functions once the final award has been rendered.[12] This constitutes an important feature of the relevant rules of the New York Convention on the Recognition and Enforcement of Foreign Arbitral Awards: the decision must be binding to be enforceable under Article V (1) (e) of the New York Convention. In accordance with said provision, the award needs to be binding on the parties to be enforceable. This excludes interim measures and orders, which can neither be enforced nor set aside.[13] Even the arbitrators do not have any power of coercion on the parties and cannot force them to enforce the order in case they refuse to do so.[14] The award, however, is final and binding, and renders the arbitral tribunal *functus officio*. Hence, the tribunal has done its job and ceases to exist. The issue decided by the tribunal then has *res iudicata* effect and cannot be re-adjudicated anymore.

Exigencies of space preclude a detailed analysis of all available investment arbitration rules. This chapter uses the ICSID Convention as a comparator. This is because ICSID is the most prominent forum used for investment disputes.

2.1.1   ICSID's appointment mechanism – an ad hoc tribunal

The system of appointment of an arbitrator for an investment arbitration dispute under the ICSID Convention is rather simple. The arbitrators shall be appointed as the parties agree.[15] Whereas the ICSID Secretariat holds a list of arbitrators, the so-called 'panel of arbitrators' to facilitate the choice, the crucial appointment is the appointment as an actual arbitrator to hear a dispute. The parties to the investment dispute do not have to choose an arbitrator from the panels and have the right to choose any individual that complies with the

---

[11]   Ibid.

[12]   Andrew Tweeddale and Keren Tweeddale, *Arbitration of Commercial Disputes: International and English Law and Practice* (OUP 2007) para 10.46.

[13]   Blackaby et al (n 6), para 7.19.

[14]   Chartered Institute of Arbitrators, 'Application for Interim Measure' International Arbitration Practice Guideline (2015), 11, http://www.ciarb.org/docs/ default-source/ciarbdocuments/guidance-and-ethics/practice-guidelines-protocols-and -rules/international-arbitration-guidelines-2015/2015applicationinterimmeasures.pdf ?sfvrsn=16, accessed 28 August 2018. Most arbitral institutions provide for provisions on emergency arbitrators, e.g., Art 29 of the ICC Arbitration Rules 2017. These arbitrators do not render awards but non-enforceable orders. Hence the parties need to rely on each other's goodwill.

[15]   Art 37(2)(a) ICSID Convention.

requirements of Article 14 of the ICSID Convention.[16] Pursuant to Article 15 of the ICSID Convention, panel members shall serve for renewable periods of six years and can be renamed panel members as often as possible. They are designated by the contracting parties of the ICSID Convention, which have the right to appoint four persons to the panel of arbitrators,[17] or by the Chairman.[18]

To actually sit on an arbitral tribunal, the actual appointment by a party to the dispute is of importance.[19] The ICSID Convention leaves a large amount of freedom to the parties on how the tribunal shall be constituted. The same is true in regard to the method of appointment of the arbitrators. Article 37(2)(a) ICSID Convention only stipulates that the arbitrators are appointed 'as the parties shall agree'. It poses the principle that an agreement of the parties is sufficient.[20] This can be either an agreement prior to the dispute or an ad hoc agreement. There are three methods that can be envisaged: (i) pursuant to Article 37(2)(b) ICSID Convention each party has the right to appoint one arbitrator and the remaining third arbitrator will be appointed by agreement of the parties – a method of appointment that reflects perfectly one of the main features of arbitration, the freedom of the parties to decide on the composition of the dispute settlement body; (ii) by agreement of the two party-appointed arbitrators;[21] (iii) appointment by a neutral third party, a so-called 'appointing authority'.[22]

2.1.2   Qualifications – ICSID's flexibility

Under the ICSID Convention, the panellists are supposed to be of high moral character, possess a recognised competence in the fields of law, commerce, industry or finance, and shall be relied upon to exercise independent judgement.[23] These three criteria are expressly mentioned in the Convention. There are many more considerations the parties may take into account.[24]

---

[16]   Art 40(1) and (92) ICSID Convention.

[17]   Art 12(1) ICSID Convention.

[18]   Art 12(2) ICSID Convention.

[19]   Please note that arbitral institutions exist that provide for the institutions sole power to appoint the arbitrators: see Art 11 CAS Arbitration or Art 8 BAT Arbitration Rules.

[20]   Schreuer (n 8), 478.

[21]   See Art 10(3) Germany-Philippines BIT [1997].

[22]   Schreuer (n 8), 481.

[23]   Art 14(1) ICSID Convention.

[24]   The ICSID website goes a step further and clarifies what criteria the parties should pay attention to, when selecting an arbitrator. This includes knowledge of international investment law, public international law, international arbitration as well as the ability to speak at least one of the Centre's official languages (English, French and Spanish), availability to accept appointments in cases as of the date of designa-

If an arbitrator appears not to possess the qualifications of Article 14(1) ICSID Convention, he or she will likely be challenged on the ground of incapacity, a manifest lack of the requirements of Article 14 ICSID Convention, or ineligibility for appointment under the relevant provisions of the Convention,[25] 'The most frequently alleged ground for disqualification [...] is manifest lack of the qualities required by Article 14 (1) of the ICSID Convention, in particular, lack of reliability to exercise independent judgement.'[26]

Moreover, the Convention provides for a nationality requirement in Article 39, stating that the majority of the arbitrators shall be nationals of States other than the two parties. Nonetheless, the Convention gives a lot of freedom to the parties, as the nationality requirement can be waived by mutual agreement of the parties.[27]

2.1.3   The procedural rules

For the functioning of courts and tribunals, an established procedure is needed to organise the conduct of the proceedings. Under ICSID, the tribunals follow the Rules of Procedure for Arbitration Proceedings, a detailed text that sets out 56 provisions that need to be respected.[28] However, international investment arbitration generally allows the parties to a dispute to have recourse to a myriad of other rules. Most arbitral institutions have drafted their own set of procedural rules, each having their own advantages and disadvantages. Even national legal systems contain provisions regulating the arbitral procedure. If the dispute resolution clause on which a dispute is based allows for the parties to freely choose the procedural rules, any option is possible.

2.1.4   No appeal in investment arbitration

Not only the current ICSID system, but investment arbitration as a whole, does not know any form of appeal. Yet, under ICSID, the parties can seek annulment of any award on the basis of five grounds, including: a wrongly constituted tribunal, a manifest excess of powers, corruption, a serious departure from a fundamental rule of procedure, or a failure to state the reasons on which

---

tion and the availability and willingness to travel for case proceedings: 'Selection and Appointment of Tribunal Members – ICSID Convention Arbitration' https://icsid .worldbank.org/en/Pages/process/Selection-and-Appointment-of-Tribunal-Members -Convention-Arbitration.aspx, accessed 4 October 2018.

[25]   Arts 37–40, 56, 57 ICSID Convention.

[26]   'Disqualification of Arbitrators – ICSID Convention Arbitration' https://icsid .worldbank.org/en/Pages/process/Disqualification-of-Arbitrators.aspx,   accessed   4 October 2018.

[27]   Art 39 ICSID Convention.

[28]   Other arbitral institutions also have rules on procedure that are only slightly different such as UNCITRAL, the PCA, LCIA or the ICC and many more.

the award is based.[29] The case is heard by an ad hoc committee, appointed from the panel of arbitrators by the Chairman.[30] Their mandate is only to decide on whether an award should be annulled on one of the above-mentioned grounds: '[i]t has no power to revise an award on the merits or to reopen the tribunal's decision on the evidence'.[31] Pursuant to Article 52(6) ICSID Convention, if the award is annulled, in whole or in part, either party may resubmit the dispute to a new ICSID tribunal.

However, this does not come as a surprise and is, in general, normality in investment arbitration. It lies in the nature of arbitration that the decision of an arbitral tribunal is final and binding and no second instance revisits the findings of the appointed tribunal. Furthermore, domestic courts have the possibility to deny enforcement of the decision to which I turn.

2.1.5   Enforcement – Article 53 ICSID Convention
By signing the ICSID Convention, every State has consented to recognise and enforce any award rendered by an ICSID tribunal.[32] In Article 53, the Convention states that awards are binding on the parties without any right of appeal. Furthermore, the award has the same power as a final judgment of a court in the State where enforcement is sought.[33] Consequently, the domestic law of that very State at stake governs the enforcement procedure.[34]

Furthermore, as there are also investment awards not being rendered under the ICSID Convention, another mechanism exists. The New York Convention on the Recognition and Enforcement of Foreign Arbitral Awards states, at Article III, that all awards that comply with the requirements of the Convention shall be binding and enforced.[35]

2.2   The Nature of International Courts

In a second step, this section now turns to the nature of international courts and tribunals (ICTs). ICTs possess various features. They are standing bodies, established by a statute, composed of tenured judges that have the competence to apply international law following a predefined procedure, and render binding

---

[29]   Art 52(1) ICSID Convention.
[30]   Art 52(3) ICSID Convention.
[31]   Maximilian Szymanski and Harriet Tolkien, 'Annulment of Awards in ICSID Arbitration' [2018] *UK Practical Law* 25.
[32]   Rudolf Dolzer and Christoph Schreuer, *Principles of International Investment Law* (2nd edn, OUP 2012) 310.
[33]   Art 54 ICSID Convention.
[34]   Dolzer and Schreuer (n 32), 310.
[35]   Art V New York Convention.

decisions. Brower remarks that '[f]ormally, the chief difference between arbi-tration and judicial settlement lies in the character of the tribunals to which the parties submit their disputes'.[36] Whereas arbitral tribunals are instituted on an ad hoc basis, ICTs are standing bodies. Tomuschat defines ICTs as 'permanent judicial bodies made up of independent judges, which are entrusted with adju-dicating international disputes on the basis of international law, according to a pre-determined set of rules of procedure and rendering decisions, which are binding on the parties'.[37] The difference with international arbitration is that 'the composition does not reflect the configuration of the parties'.[38]

ICTs render binding decisions, issue preliminary rulings or advisory opin-ions, and grant interim measures.[39] Their jurisdiction is based on the principle of sovereign equality and is conditional to State consent.[40] For example, Article 33 of the UN Charter, leaves the choice of an appropriate forum explicitly to the will of the parties.[41]

Another characteristic of ICTs is their restricted access. Traditionally speak-ing, only States have standing in front of ICTs. This is expressed in Article 34(1) of the Statute of the International Court of Justice (ICJ).[42] However, fol-lowing the proliferation of Human Rights Courts, individuals and legal persons have gained access to ICTs over the past decades.[43]

The composition of ICTs follows, in general, two different models.[44] Either every State party to the statute is granted one seat on the ICT for one of their nationals, the best example being the CJEU, or a special selection formula applies for the selection of judges.[45] That formula operates according to a general principal of just representation, as contained in Article 9 of the ICJ Statute and Article 2 of the Statute of the International Tribunal for the Law of the Sea (ITLOS). The disadvantage of the first model is that ICTs with a lot of State parties to the statute would easily grow to the size of a parliament and would henceforth become unworkable. The disadvantage of the second model is that unrepresented States might question the authority of the court,

---

[36]   Charles H Brower II, 'Arbitration' *The Max Planck Encyclopedia of Public International Law* (2007), para 4.

[37]   Christian Tomuschat, 'International Courts and Tribunals' *The Max Planck Encyclopedia of Public International Law* (2011), para 1.

[38]   Ibid.

[39]   Ibid., 35 et seq.

[40]   Ibid., 48.

[41]   Ibid.

[42]   Ibid., 54.

[43]   Ibid., 58.

[44]   Ibid., 59.

[45]   Ibid.

and a general feeling of being patronised by the court and the foreign judges can arise.

Exigencies of space preclude a detailed analysis of all available statues of ICTs. This chapter uses the ICJ statute as a comparator. This is because the ICJ is the most prominent forum used for the resolution of State–State disputes.

2.2.1   Appointment and term – a standing body

Article 25 of the ICJ Statute stipulates that 'the full Court shall sit', except when it is expressly provided otherwise in the statute. Therefore, the parties to the dispute do not have any influence on the composition of the Court. The Court may form chambers composed of three or more judges to deal with particular cases, which shall be determined by the Court itself.[46]

The Statute of the Court provides for a detailed method of appointment. Pursuant to Article 4 of the ICJ Statute, the judges will be elected by the General Assembly of the United Nations and the Security Council, from a list presented by the national groups of the Permanent Court of Arbitration. They need to obtain an absolute majority of votes in both chambers in order to get elected.[47] In the body as a whole the representation of the main forms of civilization and of the principal legal systems of the world should be assured.[48]

The ICJ judges hold office for nine years and, similar to ICSID arbitration, may be re-elected.[49] However, if they are about to get replaced, they are supposed to finish any cases they have begun.[50]

2.2.2   Qualifications – the ICJ's focus on competence

The ICJ is the principal judicial organ of the United Nations and gives high importance to the qualifications of its judges. Article 2 of the ICJ Statute provides for the requirements of becoming an ICJ judge.[51] The qualifications include independence and the possession of the qualifications for appointment to the highest judicial office in their respective countries, or the quality of being a jurisconsult of recognised competence in international law.[52] Similar to the ICSID Convention, the text requires the judges to be of 'high moral character'.[53] The term had already been employed by the 1899 and 1907 Hague Conventions and can be defined as follows: 'Only persons of a truly high moral

---

[46]   Art 26-1.2 ICJ Statute.
[47]   Art 10 ICJ Statute.
[48]   Art 9 ICJ Statute.
[49]   Art 13-1 ICJ Statute.
[50]   Art 13-3 ICJ Statute.
[51]   Art 1 ICJ Statute.
[52]   Art 2 ICJ Statute.
[53]   Art 14(1) ICSID Convention.

character can oppose any kind of strong pressure, linking his or her personal ethics with their tenure as judges.'[54] Article 20 of the Statute unsurprisingly expects the judges to be impartial. All of the above-mentioned requirements apply to ad hoc judges as well.[55]

2.2.3 Law governing the proceedings

Just like ICSID, Chapter III of the ICJ Statute contains rules of procedure on language,[56] representation,[57] and conduct.[58] Furthermore, the detailed 'Rules of the Court' are applied. The reason for the detailed Rules is that the drafters 'had to devise a procedure capable of satisfying the sense of justice of the greatest possible number of potential litigants and of placing them on a footing of strict equality'.[59]

2.2.4 Appeal

As already mentioned, ICTs tend not to have an appellate mechanism. Where the ICSID Convention states five grounds for annulment, the ICJ Statute clearly excludes any appeal.[60] Every judgment is final and without appeal,[61] with the only exception being Article 61 of the ICJ Statute, which contains a safeguard mechanism. It opens the doors for an application for revision of a judgment in the event of the discovery of new facts that would have had a decisive impact on the outcome of the judgment.

Yet, in the world of international trade and investment adjudication, another well-known institution exists that does have an appeal mechanism and hence constitutes an exception: the World Trade Organisation. It is one of the rare standing trade bodies and provides for a compulsory, binding and enforceable dispute settlement that has become one of the most important and widely used international tribunals.[62] If a party to a dispute would like to have a decision of an ad hoc panel reviewed, it has the right to have recourse to the appellate body. The latter is a standing body composed of seven persons of recognised authority, with demonstrated expertise in law, international trade and the

---

[54] Andreas Zimmermann et al (eds), *The Statute of the International Court of Justice: A Commentary* (3rd edn, OUP 2019) Art 2, 289, paras 16–17.

[55] Art 31-6 ICJ Statute.

[56] Art 39 ICJ Statute.

[57] Art 42 ICJ Statute.

[58] Art 43 ICJ Statute.

[59] *Handbook of the International Court of Justice*, 48 https://www.icj-cij.org/files/publications/handbook-of-the-court-en.pdf, accessed 2 July 2021.

[60] Art 60 ICJ Statute.

[61] Ibid.

[62] Arwel Davies, Simon Lester and Bryan Mercurio, *World Trade Law: Text, Materials and Commentary* (3rd edn, Hart Publishing 2018) 149.

subject matter of the covered agreements.[63] Appeals are limited to issues of law covered in the panel report and interpretations developed by the panel.[64]

2.2.5 Enforcement – not foreseen in the ICJ Statute

In contrast to the ICSID Convention, the ICJ Statute does not provide for an enforcement mechanism. In general, the enforcement of ICJ decisions is a delicate topic as it touches upon both public international law and the law of the UN.[65] Still, there is a provision that refers to the principles of *pacta sunt servanda* and good faith (*bona fides*).[66] By virtue of Article 94(1) of the UN Charter, each member of the UN confirms that it will comply with the decision of the ICJ in any case to which it is a disputing party. However, this does not constitute an enforcement mechanism. The only possibility to seek enforcement of an ICJ decision is to have recourse to the United Nations Security Council, which, on the basis of Article 94(2) of the UN Charter, has the power to make recommendations or to decide upon measures to be taken to give effect to the judgment. The formulation of this provision is very broad and can be interpreted in many ways. Nonetheless, it does not provide exclusive authority for the Security Council to be the 'ultimate and sole enforcer'.[67]

2.3 The Investment Court System

This chapter now turns to the provisions on the ICS, to find out where the ICS finds its place among international courts and investment tribunals, also commenting on the impact of the hybrid nature on the dispute resolution system as a whole. It leaves out 'enforcement' and addresses it in a separate section, as the serious impact of the hybrid nature will be felt when it comes to enforcing ICS decisions.

The first obvious difference between ISDS, international courts and the new ICS in terms of set-up and composition, lays in the terminology employed. Against the 'judges' sitting on international courts and the 'arbitrators' deciding investment arbitration cases, disputes before the ICS are to be heard by 'divisions' of three 'members of the tribunal'. These divisions are composed of

---

[63] Art 17(3) Dispute Settlement Understanding.

[64] Art 17(6) Dispute Settlement Understanding.

[65] Attila Tanzi, 'Problems of Enforcement of Decisions of the International Court of Justice and the Law of the United Nations' (1995) 6(4) *European Journal of International Law* 539.

[66] Mutlaq Majed Al-Qahtani, 'Enforcement of International Judicial Decisions of the International Court of Justice in Public International Law' (PhD Thesis, University of Glasgow 2003) 12.

[67] Ibid., iii.

one EU-citizen, one Canadian/Vietnamese and a national of a third State, with the latter being the chair.[68]

Similar to investment arbitration, individuals are granted standing in front of the ICS. As mentioned above, this is not the case in front of the ICJ. This is an important aspect, which shows how similar the ICS is to investment arbitration.

Interestingly, one particular provision increases the access to the ICS. Articles 8.27-9 CETA and 12.9 Chapter 8, Section 3, EUVFTA, open the door for the parties to the dispute to agree on a sole-member Tribunal, who is required to be a national of a third State. The choice to allow one-member Tribunals resides in reasons of cost: one-member tribunals are foreseen in relation to cases where either the claimant is a small- or medium-sized enterprise, or the compensation and damages claimed are relatively low.[69]

The lower cost of the proceedings in cases where one-member tribunals are provided, are likely to facilitate access to dispute settlement mechanism for smaller businesses investing in Canada/Vietnam or in the EU. It is expected that this will also make proceedings considerably shorter, and therefore more efficient, considering that decisions by one person are likely to be swifter compared to those taken by several people who must deliberate and draft a decision together. As the members can disagree on the decision, the whole process is more time-consuming.

2.3.1   Appointment of ICS members
Whereas the ICS constitutes a standing body similar to an ICT, its appointment mechanism follows the ICSID model. However, unlike the ICSID mechanism, in which the panel of arbitrators is much more of a recommendation of who to appoint, the ICS is arranged in a mandatory two-step system composed of rigorous and detailed provisions.

The first step is the appointment by a committee comprised of State representatives. As a reminder, the ICS Tribunal (the Tribunal) consists of five/three nationals of a member State of the EU, five/three nationals of Canada or Vietnam and five/three nationals of third countries. These members are appointed by the CETA Joint Committee and the Trade Committee respec-

---

[68]   Art 8.27-6 of the Comprehensive Economic and Trade Agreement (CETA) between Canada, of the one part, and the European Union and its Member States, of the other part [2017] OJ L11/23 (CETA); Art 12.6, Ch 8, Section 3 of the EU-Vietnam Free Trade Agreement (EUVFTA).

[69]   Simon Weber, 'Open Doors for Small or Medium Sized Enterprises to Investor State Dispute Resolution?' (*Regulating for Globalization*, 24 January 2019) http://regulatingforglobalization.com/2019/01/24/open-doors-for-small-or-medium-sized-enterprises-to-investor-state-dispute-resolution/, accessed 24 February 2019.

tively.[70] The committees comprise representatives of the EU and the other contracting party of the FTA.[71] Their decisions are taken by mutual consent and are of a political nature.[72] The texts do not include a clear solution for a stalemate if Canada/Vietnam and the EU cannot agree on a proposed member of the Tribunal. This includes the members the other party proposed. It is impossible to say at this point if the appointment of the members will pose a problem or not. However, it cannot be excluded.

As for the duration of the term of the ICS members, Article 8.27-5 CETA states that they are appointed for five years with the chance of one reappointment. As a result, the maximum term is ten years.[73] Similar to the ICJ Statute, CETA stipulates that, if the members of the Tribunal are sitting on a division of the Tribunal, they remain in office until the final award is issued.[74]

The second step is the appointment to a division. Within 90 days after the submission of the claim, the President of the Tribunal appoints the members on a 'rotation basis' to sit on a division.[75] This happens for two reasons.

The first reason is to ensure that the composition of the division is random and unpredictable.[76] Neither party to the dispute will be able to appoint an individual that might be more open to certain arguments the party wishes to put forward. Henceforth, the parties' influence on the composition of the arbitral tribunal is gone. The composition of the division does not reflect the configuration of the parties anymore. On the other hand, one must not forget that it is the States through the Joint Committee that decide on the members of the Tribunal. Ultimately, the influence of the States on the composition of the ICS is considerably higher than the influence of investors bringing a claim. Furthermore, in contrast to ordinary arbitration, it seems as if the ICS appointment mechanism is more likely to ensure the member of the Tribunal's independence and impartiality. This again illustrates the high importance Canada

---

[70]   Art 8.27-2 CETA; Art 12.2 Ch 8 Section 3 EUVFTA.
[71]   The CETA Joint Committee comprises representatives of the EU, representatives of Canada and is co-chaired by the Minister for International Trade of Canada and the member of the European Commission responsible for Trade (Art 26.1 CETA). The Trade Committee comprises representatives of the EU and representatives of Vietnam.
[72]   Art 26.3-3 CETA; Ch 17, Ch XX Art X.5.3 EUVFTA.
[73]   Only in the beginning seven members of the Tribunal will serve for six years in order to avoid a situation where the whole tribunal would be replaced every five years.
[74]   Art 12.5. Ch 8 Section 3 EUVFTA resembles CETA apart from one detail: 'The members of the Tribunal [...] shall be appointed for a four-year term [...].' The term of the EUVFTA ICS members is therefore one year shorter than of the CETA ICS members.
[75]   Art 8.27.7 CETA; Art 12.7 Ch 8 Section 3 EUVFTA
[76]   Art 8.27.7 CETA; Art 12.7 Ch 8 Section 3 EUVFTA.

and the EU seem to attach to impartiality and transparency.[77] During the negotiations of EUVFTA the same provisions were incorporated in the text, as the contracting parties wish to guarantee full transparency of the proceedings.[78]

The second reason is that all members of the Tribunal will serve and sit on a division. Interestingly, some ICSID panellists have never heard a case.[79] However, as the composition of the arbitral tribunal under the ICSID Convention reflects the configurations of the parties who have the right to appoint the arbitrator on their own, it is no surprise that some arbitrators have never been appointed. There is no mechanism that assures that a panellist will ever hear a case. In contrast, the ICS ensures a regular case rotation among the members of the Tribunal.[80]

It is likely that this contributes to coherence in the decisions and for a harmonised interpretation of the different treaty standards. Given that ICS divisions will only apply and interpret the very FTAs, it seems like an opportunity for the outcome of the proceedings to become more predictable and coherent. As a result, the appointment mechanism is nowhere near the appointment mechanism in investment arbitration, as it takes away the disputing parties' autonomy to decide on their own decision makers. Whereas the internal mechanism for the ICT members shows some similarities to the ICSID two-step system, it cannot be equated with ICSID at all. The ICS appointment mechanism is a feature that was taken from international adjudication.

2.3.2   Qualifications – ICS's level of detail

Canada, Vietnam, and the EU seem to give high importance to the qualifications of the members of the Tribunal. Both in CETA and in the EUVTA, various provisions list detailed qualification requirements.[81]

First, similar to the ICJ Statute, the ICS requires the members of the Tribunal to possess the qualifications required in their respective countries for appointment to judicial office or to be jurists of recognised competence.[82] They shall have demonstrated expertise in public international law and desirably possess expertise in international investment law, international trade law, dispute reso-

---

[77] Commission, 'Investment Provisions in the EU-Canada Free Trade Agreement (CETA)' http://trade.ec.europa.eu/doclib/docs/2013/november/tradoc_151918.pdf, accessed 3 July 2021.

[78] Commission, 'Guide to the EU-Vietnam Free Trade Agreement', 55 http://trade.ec.europa.eu/doclib/docs/2016/june/tradoc_154622.pdf, accessed 13 March 2018.

[79] E.g., Vladimir Balas (named arbitrator by Czech Republic on 13.12.2007), Ian Barker (named arbitrator by New Zealand on 14.07.2012) and many more.

[80] Art 8.27.7 CETA; Art 12.7 Ch 8 Section 3 EUVFTA.

[81] Art 8.27-4 and 8.30 CETA; Art 12.4 Ch 8 Section 3, Art 14 Ch 8 Section 3 and Ch 13 b Annex II Code of Conduct EUVFTA.

[82] Art 8.27-4 CETA; Art 12.4 Ch 8 Section 3 EUVFTA.

lution arising under international investment agreements or international trade agreements.[83] These requirements are fairly similar to both the requirements of the ICSID Convention and the ICJ Statute. Additionally, the ICS incorporates a provision entitled 'Ethics' including further requirements.[84]

These very articles add to the requirement of independence.[85] CETA clarifies that the member shall not be affiliated with any government or organisation, shall comply with the IBA Guidelines on Conflicts of Interests in International Arbitration and other rules pursuant to Article 8.44.2 CETA. These additional rules include a code of conduct with regards to topics including disclosure obligations, independence and impartiality of the members of the Tribunal and confidentiality.[86] EUVFTA clarifies that the members' impartiality is of utmost importance and that they 'shall not participate in the consideration of any disputes that would create a direct or indirect conflict of interest'.[87]

Furthermore, the members of the Tribunal are not allowed to act as counsel, party-appointed expert, or witness in any pending or new investment dispute under CETA or any other international agreement.[88] This rule will prohibit their appointment as arbitrator in arbitral proceedings under other agreements such as bilateral or multilateral investment treaties. Consequently, it solves the issue of double-hatting with regards to the members of the ICS. However, if the reform process currently discussed in UNCITRAL working group III does not lead to a multilateral investment court or another reform of the entire ISDR system, which will prohibit double-hatting, the ICS will only constitute a drop in the ocean.

It is noteworthy that a potential challenge of a member of the Tribunal under CETA on the ground of a conflict of interest shall be decided by the President of the ICJ.[89] Similar to the possible stalemate regarding the appointment of arbitrators by a neutral official under ICSID, this includes the risk that the appointing authority is not willing to, or simply does not exercise, the right expressly conferred.[90]

The solution in EUVFTA is different to CETA and avoids a stalemate. A potential challenge to a member of the Tribunal is decided by the President

---

[83]   Ibid.
[84]   Art 8.30 CETA; Art 14 Ch 8 Section 3 EUVFTA.
[85]   Art 8.27-4 and Art 12.4 Ch 8 Section 3 EUVFTA adding to 8.30-1 CETA and Art 14 Chapter 8 Section 3 EUVFTA.
[86]   Art 8.44-2 CETA.
[87]   Art 14.1 Ch 8 Section 3 EUVFTA Resolution of Investment Disputes.
[88]   Art 8.30-1 CETA.
[89]   Arts 8.30-2 and 8.30-3 CETA.
[90]   Schreuer (n 8), 481.

of the Tribunal or to the President of the Appeal Tribunal, respectively.[91] Hence the authority in charge is part of the EUVFTA dispute resolution mechanism, which avoids the risk of the competent authority not exercising its rights.[92]

In conclusion, the new FTAs provide for more requirements that will ensure the competence of the members of the ICSs and help to avoid situations in which conflicts of interest will arise. As the members of the Tribunal will be professional decision makers, they will not be able to represent investors or States in other proceedings in front of the ICS.[93] This is an attempt to make the system bulletproof but, of course, cannot prevent conflicts of interests in other, ordinary investment arbitrations, not involving ICTs members. Similar to the ICJ Statute, competence and a high moral character are important for ICS members. However, investment dispute resolution clauses also give great importance to the qualification of the arbitrators. As a result, the provisions on qualification are similar to both dispute resolution mechanisms.

2.3.3   Applicable procedural rules

In removing the freedom to appoint their own arbitrators from the parties, and instead allowing the States to decide on the members of the Tribunal, CETA and EUVFTA do not seem to accord great importance to strict equality between the disputing parties. However, this cannot be proven by analysing the Rules of Procedure as, interestingly, they are not clearly determined. Article 8.23-2 CETA provides for four ways on how a claim may be submitted to the Tribunal. Either the claim will be submitted under the ICSID Convention and Rules of Procedure for Arbitration Proceedings, under the ICSID Additional Facility Rules if the conditions for proceedings under paragraph (a) do not apply,[94] under the UNCITRAL Arbitration Rules, or 'any other rules on agreement of the disputing parties'.[95] Article 7, Chapter 8, Section 3 EUVFTA, contains the same provision.

'Other rules' that can be used are the PCA Arbitration Rules, the LCIA Arbitration Rules, the ICC Arbitration Rules, any of the arbitration rules by an arbitral institution, or the procedural rules incorporated in national law.[96] Even if unlikely, the parties could agree on their very own set of rules, drafted

---

[91]   Art 14.2 Ch 8 Section 3 EUVFTA Resolution of Investment Disputes.

[92]   Schreuer (n 8), 481.

[93]   The use of the terms 'arbitrator' or 'judge' is disputable due to the hybrid nature of the tribunal.

[94]   This means that the conditions for proceedings under the ICSID Convention are not satisfied. One good example hereof is that the State party to the dispute is not a contracting State of the ICSID Convention.

[95]   Art 8.23-2 (d) CETA.

[96]   ICC Rules of Arbitration.

ad hoc, only for the purposes of the very dispute at stake. By incorporating these sets of rules of procedure, the nature of the proceedings will be similar to arbitration.

The current investment arbitration system is often criticised for its lack of efficiency, high costs and the duration of the proceedings. The ICS, as contained in CETA and EUVFTA, does not address and solve these concerns. It might be true that the procedure for small- and medium-sized enterprises will be faster than ordinary proceedings. However, by incorporating the procedural rules of the ICSID system, the UNCITRAL Arbitration Rules or 'any other rules on agreement of the disputing parties',[97] the ICS does not find a solution for the lack of efficiency concern. The procedural rules will not change and will therefore not have an impact on the efficiency of the system. Yet, this will potentially make the adoption of the new system by practitioners, easier and could provide for a smooth transition to the acceptance of a standing court by the arbitration community.

Finally, it is obvious that this feature has been inspired by international investment arbitration. The procedural rules can usually be chosen by the disputing parties and are not predetermined.

2.3.4   The ICS's big innovation: the appellate body

The ICS introduces an innovation to ISDR: a standing appellate body. The appellate body has the right to uphold, modify, or reverse a Tribunal's award, based on errors in the application or interpretation of applicable law, manifest errors in the appreciation of the facts, and the abovementioned grounds of Article 52(1) of the ICSID Convention.[98] Just as the Tribunal, the appellate body consists of a list of members of the Appellate Body, which will be appointed by a decision of the CETA Joint Committee.[99]

CETA only provides for very few provisions on the Appellate Body. It specifies that the members have to meet the same requirements as the members of the Tribunal[100] and that a division shall consist of three randomly appointed members of the Tribunal.[101] Notably, it is unclear who will have the competence to appoint the divisions. One could be forgiven for assuming that Canada and the EU were not able to either agree on a complete set-up or wanted to wait until a final decision has been made. They leave it open to the CETA Joint Committee to adopt a decision regarding the functioning of the Appellate Tribunal including administrative support, procedures for the initiation and

---

[97]   Art 8.23-2 (d) CETA; Art 7 Ch 8 Section 3 EUVFTA.
[98]   Art 8.28.2 CETA.
[99]   Art 8.28.3 CETA.
[100]   Art 8.27.4 / 8.30 CETA.
[101]   Art 8.28.5 CETA.

conduct of appeals, procedures for filling vacancies of the Appellate Tribunal, remuneration of the members of the Appellate Tribunal, provisions related to the costs of appeals, the number of members of the Appellate Tribunal and any other elements it determines to be necessary for the effective functioning of the Appellate Tribunal.[102]

The European Commission and Vietnam also include an appeal mechanism in the text of their FTA. Article 13, Chapter 8, Section 3 EUVFTA, establishes a permanent appeal tribunal composed of six members that are appointed by the Trade Committee on a four-year term. They shall have demonstrated expertise in public international law and possess the qualifications required in their respective countries for appointment to the highest judicial offices, or be jurists of recognised competence.[103] Article 28, Chapter 8, Section 3 EUVFTA, adds rules on the appeal procedure to the text, stating the grounds for appeal:

(a)   that the Tribunal has erred in the interpretation or application of the applicable law;
(b)   that the Tribunal has manifestly erred in the appreciation of the facts, including the appreciation of relevant domestic law; or
(c)   those provided for in Article 52 of the ICSID Convention, in so far as they are not covered by (a) and (b).

Even though the Appellate Tribunal lacks structure and clarity in its organisation, the contracting parties broke with traditional customs by setting-up an appeal system. Such a body has never existed before in international investment arbitration and constitutes a fundamental change, making it impossible to call the ICS an investment tribunal. Accepting the WTO as a comparator only in this regard, an appellate body is therefore inspired by international adjudicative dispute resolution systems.

Further, this has major implications for the system. A review of decisions is now possible, which contributes to rule of law considerations, to coherence, uniformity and interpretative harmonisation. It is arguable that the legal correctness of the decisions will increase. Even though the structure and clarity of the set-up may well be criticised, the Appellate Body opens new doors to review decisions. This contributes to rule of law considerations, to coherence, uniformity and harmonisation of the decisions. The same effect stems from the fact that the members of the Tribunal will be professional decision makers that derive their legitimacy from the fact that they have been appointed by the States that decided to subject their sovereignty to the judgement of the appointed members of the Tribunal.

---

[102]   Art 8.28.7 CETA.
[103]   Art 13.7 Ch 8 Section 3 EUVFTA Resolution of Investment Disputes.

3.   THE IMPACT OF THE HYBRID NATURE ON ENFORCEMENT

The above discussion demonstrated that the ICS combines features of both investment (arbitration) tribunals and ICTs. This is because two institutional aspects are copied from classic ICTs. First, the ICS is a standing body, composed of tenured decision makers that are appointed by the contracting parties to the FTA. Second, it allows for an appeal, similar to the WTO – a feature entirely unknown to investment arbitration. However, two aspects are taken from investment arbitration. First, the ICS, despite being composed of up to 15 members, only sits as a three-member division or sole-member division, chosen on an ad hoc basis. Second, the procedure is not predetermined and can be chosen by the parties to the dispute.

Yet, the most striking impact of the hybrid nature can be seen in the enforcement mechanism, which is imported from arbitration. Similar to the ICSID Convention, both CETA and EUVFTA contain a provision dedicated to the enforcement of awards.[104] All awards rendered by a division of the ICS are recognised as binding between the disputing parties, which recognise that '(a) final award issued pursuant to this Section is an arbitral award that is deemed to relate to claims arising out of a commercial relationship or transaction for the purposes of Article I of the New York Convention'.

As a result, the ICS is attempting to import the enforcement mechanism from investment arbitration. Yet, this constitutes a major deficiency of the system as the awards will only be enforceable in the EU and in the territory of its trading partners. Third States have not consented to the enforcement of ICS decisions. In the following this chapter lays out why an enforcement mechanism based on the New York Convention is a dead end. It furthermore uses the Iran-US Claims Tribunal (IUSCT) as an example of why decisions rendered by a standing body having similarities to arbitration will cause issues at the enforcement stage.

3.1   The New York Convention is Inapplicable

There are serious doubts as to whether ICS awards satisfy the conditions set forth in the New York Convention.[105] Article I 2. of the New York Convention (NYC) expressly states that '[t]he term "arbitral awards" shall include not only awards made by arbitrators appointed for each case but also those made

---

[104] Art 8.41 CETA and Arts 29.1, 31.1, 31.2 and 31.7 Ch 8 Section 3 EUVFTA provide for a mechanism similar to Arts 53 and 54 ICSID Convention.
[105] Kaufmann-Kohler and Potesta (n 9), para 138.

by permanent arbitral bodies to which the parties have submitted'. The ICS is a permanent body. However, the ICS does not constitute a permanent 'arbitral' body, since the nature of the dispute resolution mechanism is, as this chapter argues, 'hybrid'. Some have argued that the drafters of the NYC envisaged the preservation of the voluntary nature of arbitration as paramount and opposed to party autonomy encompassing the freedom to appoint the arbitrators.[106]

The very same issue arises under the requirements of Article II 1. of the New York Convention, which states that '[e]ach Contracting State shall recognize an agreement in writing under which the parties undertake to submit to arbitration all or any differences which have arisen [...]'. In this regard, the dispute resolution clause, as contained in CETA and EUVFTA, can be considered to constitute an arbitration agreement. The State hereby manifests its offer and agreement to arbitrate. If an investor brings a claim in front of the ICS it does agree to submit the dispute to the jurisdiction of the tribunal. However, they do not submit their dispute 'to arbitration'. This is, again, because the nature of the ICS is not purely 'arbitration' but hybrid.

A third issue arises as to the territorial requirements of the NYC. Would an ICS award qualify as a 'foreign' award under the Convention? Article I 1. NYC spells out that the Convention applies to 'awards made in the territory of a State other than the State where the recognition and enforcement of such awards are sought' and 'non-domestic awards' that are 'awards not considered as domestic awards in the State where their recognition and enforcement are sought'. The proceedings of the ICS are not subject to any domestic *lex arbitri* and are hence not deemed to be made under the laws of the Tribunal's seat. It does therefore not meet the territorial requirements. However, in this regard, the ICS's awards are similar to awards rendered by delocalised ICSID tribunals. Even though this issue has been raised and discussed in the past, it is now widely accepted that awards rendered by said tribunals fall under the scope of the New York Convention.[107]

In conclusion, the hybrid nature of the ICS, including the lack of party autonomy as well as the built-in appeal mechanism, make the NYC likely not applicable to its awards. The overall process cannot be regarded as arbitration. Therefore, decisions rendered by the ICS are not enforceable under the NYC.[108] The European Commission seems to be aware of the issue, as can be inferred by the way it treats the issue of enforcement of decisions rendered by a hypothetical multilateral investment court. The Commission opines, in the 'Submission of the European Union and its Member States to UNCITRAL

---

[106] Ibid.
[107] Ibid., 157.
[108] See to the contrary ibid., 164.

Working Group III', dated 18 January 2019, that, of course, the 'effective enforcement of awards of a standing mechanism is vital'.[109] Furthermore, the Commission states that, in addition to its own enforcement regime, the decisions of a hypothetical Multilateral Investment Court (MIC) can be enforced under the NYC.[110] As the above demonstrates, this assumption is wrong.

3.2   The Iran-US Claims Tribunal – Another Hybrid Tribunal?

One might argue that the Iran-US Claims Tribunal (IUSCT) constitutes a permanent arbitral body, similar to the ICS, rendering enforceable 'arbitral awards'.[111] However, this is not entirely true. Two mechanisms attempt to ensure the recognition and enforcement of the decisions.

First, there is a specific procedure for US nationals. In the Algiers Declaration, Iran agreed in General Declaration paragraph 7 to establish a Security Account of US$1 billion 'to be used for the sole purpose of securing payment of, and paying, claims against Iran in accordance with the Claims Settlement Declaration'. This account is held at the Netherlands Bank for Settlement, in the name of the Central Bank of Algeria, that would make sure that an American claimant would receive his money in due course.[112] The Contracting Parties thereby made sure that the decisions rendered in favour of US nationals are being enforced and the sum of money due is being paid. Yet, the enforcement mechanism is not the mechanism used by the NYC.

Second, Iranian nationals do not benefit from a specific procedure and will have to rely upon the US judiciary. In this regard, the Claims Settlement Declaration contains a safeguard mechanism in Article IV 3. that renders '(a)ny award which the Tribunal may render against either government [...] enforceable against such government in the courts of any nation in accordance with its laws'.[113] Iranian nationals must have recourse to US courts to enforce decisions in their favour or attempt to enforce the award in another country.[114]

---

[109]   UNCITRAL, 'Submission of the European Union and Its member States to UNCITRAL Working Group III' (18 January 2019), para 30.

[110]   Ibid., paras 31–32.

[111]   Hans Bagner, 'Article I', Herbert Kronke, Patricia Nacimiento et al (eds), *Recognition and Enforcement of Foreign Arbitral Awards: A Global Commentary on the New York Convention* (Kluwer Law International 2010) 29.

[112]   Christopher Pinto and Bridie McAsey, 'Iran-United States Claims Tribunal' *The Max Planck Encyclopedia of Public International Law* (2013), para 51.

[113]   Declaration Of The Government Of The Democratic And Popular Republic Of Algeria Concerning The Settlement Of Claims By The Government Of The United States Of America And The Government Of The Islamic Republic Of Iran 1981.

[114]   Jamal Seifi, 'State Responsibility for Failure to Enforce Iran-United States Claims Tribunal Awards by the Respective National Courts – International Character

As the Algiers Declaration is not binding upon any other State it cannot guarantee the enforcement of the decisions under other legal systems. The Declaration correctly points out that the decisions to enforce the award must be taken in accordance with the laws of the State in which enforcement is sought:

> [i]n other words, the obligation for the United States to enforce Tribunal awards derives from the Algiers Declarations. The fact that the United States has chosen the New York Convention mechanism to enforce Tribunal's awards cannot obscure the real source of its enforcement obligation, with the result that no exception to enforcement is permitted.[115]

The result of this analysis is an obligation for US courts to enforce the decisions, but not for the courts of third States. Yet, depending on the 'varying interpretations given to the scope of application of the New York Convention in different States' the decisions will be enforced or not.[116] In two cases the US courts decided to enforce the award of the Tribunal.[117] However, in *Dallal v Bank Mellat*, Judge Hobhouse disagreed, and stated that 'it would have been convenient and advantageous if the awards of The Hague tribunal had satisfied the requirements for recognition under the New York Convention'.[118] The IUSCT itself noted in Case A27 that some of the Algiers Convention's exceptions to enforcement 'are problematic in the context of Tribunal awards, particularly when viewed in the light of the States Parties' obligations under the Algiers Declarations'.[119] This refers to 'certain uniform criteria applicable to the making of the award' under the NYC, as argued above.[120]

In the context of the ICS, the threat this poses to the winning party is that of a third State refusing to recognise or enforce an ICS award for not complying with the requirements of the NYC, for the same reasons IUSCT decisions are not enforced.

---

and Non-Reviewability of the Awards Reconfirmed' (1999) 16 *Journal of International Arbitration* 7.

[115] Ibid., 21.

[116] Ibid., 22.

[117] *Ministry of Defense of the Islamic Republic of Iran v Gould Inc and others*, US District Court (Central District of California) [1989] ICCA Yearbook Commercial Arbitration 763 et seq; *Gould Inc, Gould Marketing v Hoffman Export Corporation, Gould International, Inc v Ministry of Defense of the Islamic Republic of Iran* (US Court of Appeals, 9th Circ) 887 F.2d 1357.

[118] *Dallal v Bank Mellat* [1986] 1 All ER 239.

[119] Iran-US Claims Tribunal Award No. 27 (585-A27-27), June 5 1998, (1999) XXIV YB Com Arb, 513, para 63.

[120] Pinto and McAsey (n 112), para 55.

4.   CONCLUSIONS

This chapter has shown that the ICS combines features of both investment
arbitration tribunals and ICTs. It appears to be a hybrid creature, halfway
between an investment tribunal and an international court.[121] The ICS is the
first step to accustom the world of international investment dispute resolution
to a standing body, not only administering investment disputes like ICSID, but
by providing a standing bench of decision makers.

Two institutional aspects are copied from classic ICTs. First, the ICS is
a standing body, with tenured decision makers appointed by the contracting
parties to the FTA. Second, it allows for an appeal, similar to the WTO –
a feature entirely unknown to investment arbitration. However, two aspects
are taken from investment arbitration, with a third one inspired by arbitration.
First, the ICS, despite being composed of up to 15 members, only sits as
three-member division or sole-member division selected on an ad hoc basis.
Second, the procedure is not predetermined, and can be chosen by the parties
to the dispute. Third, the enforcement mechanism is based on the (inapplicable) New York Convention on the Recognition and Enforcement of Foreign
Arbitral Awards – as the name already says, a mechanism used for 'arbitral'
awards.

As noted, the drafters included useful changes to the ISDR mechanism,
which will improve the access to ISDR, the legitimacy and credibility of
the decision makers, and will most likely contribute to coherent and correct
decisions. However, the combination of ICT and investment arbitration features renders the ICS a hybrid tribunal, which has severe consequences on the
enforcement of its decisions.

Said enforcement mechanism constitutes a major deficiency of the ICS. The
current provisions state that the decisions of the ICS do satisfy the requirements of the NYC. Yet, the decision is by no means an arbitral award. The
ICS is a permanent body. However, the ICS cannot be said to be a permanent
'arbitral' body under Article I 2. of the NYC, since the nature of the dispute
resolution mechanism is, as this chapter argues, 'hybrid'. Second, the very
same issue arises under the requirements of Article II 1. of the NYC, which
states that '[e]ach Contracting State shall recognize an agreement in writing
under which the parties undertake to submit to arbitration all or any differences
which have arisen [...]'. If an investor brings a claim in front of the ICS it does
agree to submit the dispute to the jurisdiction of the tribunal. However, they do
not submit 'to arbitration' – again, because the nature of the ICS is not purely
'arbitration' but hybrid.

---

[121]   Kaufmann-Kohler and Potesta (n 9), para 83.

It is to be seen how the EU and its partners solve these issues. The ICS is a step in the right direction, addressing some of the concerns expressed by the public and by people working in the field. For the identified issues, practical solutions will need to be found.

12. Human rights scrutiny under the EU Generalised Scheme of Preferences: The Uzbek cotton industry as a case study

Rosana Garciandia[1]

1. INTRODUCTION

Uzbekistan is one of the countries benefiting from the EU Generalised Scheme of Preferences (GSP), a development initiative that provides preferential tariffs for various sectors of the Uzbek economy as incentives for development and for the enhancement of human rights. These include the state-managed cotton industry, which has long been accused of deploying forced and child labour. The GSP framework establishes the requirements for Uzbekistan to be eligible as beneficiary of a GSP+ arrangement, and the mechanisms through which the EU monitors compliance with those requirements. In applying this framework, the EU must comply with international law and human rights. Hence, the ongoing negotiations between the EU and Uzbekistan for a more beneficial arrangement for Uzbekistan (GSP+)[2] require an enhanced scrutiny of the EU framework for adoption and monitoring of GSP+ benefits.

The normative framework of the EU GSP scheme consists of Regulation 978/2012, applying a scheme of generalised tariff preferences,[3] and of certain

---

[1]   The author would like to thank Prof Philippa Webb, the Global Legal Action Network, and Joanna Eward-James for their comments on earlier drafts.
[2]   GSP+ is a special incentive arrangement under the GSP scheme, designed for encouraging sustainable development and good governance. Certain countries considered to be vulnerable due to a lack of diversification and insufficient integration within the international trading system are eligible, if they fulfil other conditions, for special tariff preferences.
[3]   Regulation 978/2012 of the European Parliament and of the Council of 25 October 2012 applying a scheme of generalised tariff preferences and repealing Council Regulation (EC) No 732/2008 [2012] OJ L 303.

'constitutional' provisions of the EU Treaties.[4] The EU GSP scheme consists of three preferential trading regimes for developing countries: the GSP arrangement, the GSP+ regime, and the 'Everything but Arms' programme. The three regimes offer developing countries such as Uzbekistan tariff concessions on certain goods under the condition that they uphold certain human rights commitments. If the beneficiary country does not respect those human rights commitments, the EU can trigger a temporary withdrawal of some or all the preferences that the country benefits from.[5]

This chapter explores the EU framework establishing the requirements for Uzbekistan to be awarded GSP+ benefits, and the functioning of the mechanisms to monitor compliance with those requirements. It also reflects on the interaction of the EU system with the World Trade Organisation (WTO) and the International Labour Organisation (ILO) in the functioning of that framework. It concludes that the EU should incorporate human rights impact assessment in its examination of the Uzbek request and that reports from civil society should play a more important role in monitoring Uzbek compliance with GSP+ requirements.

The chapter is structured in three parts. Part 1 presents an overview of the existing EU-Uzbek cooperation and background information on the forced labour allegations on the cotton industry. Part 2 looks at the functioning of the EU framework assessing if the Uzbek request meets the GSP+ requirements. Part 3 explores how that same framework would monitor Uzbek compliance with those requirements if GSP+ benefits are granted.

2. THE EU-UZBEK COOPERATION AND THE COTTON SECTOR

This section presents an overview of the EU-Uzbek cooperation under the GSP scheme and background information on the forced labour allegations on the cotton industry. Under the current Partnership and Cooperation Agreement (PCA) with the EU,[6] Uzbekistan benefits from tariff preferences under the GSP, conditioned to upholding certain human rights standards. For many years, allegations of forced and child labour in the state-controlled cotton

---

[4]   The EU constitutional framework will be analysed in more details in Parts 2 and 3. See Arts 3.5 and 21 Consolidated Version of the Treaty on European Union [2012] OJ C/326/01 (TEU); Arts 207 and 208 Consolidated version of the Treaty on the Functioning of the European Union [2012] OJ C/326/01 (TFEU).

[5]   See section 3.

[6]   Partnership and Cooperation Agreement between the EU and the Republic of Uzbekistan (signed on 21 June 1996 and in force since 1 July 1999).

industry led the EU not to include textiles in its preferential arrangement with Uzbekistan.

Indeed, the Uzbek government was accused of deploying forced labour and child labour to achieve its self-imposed annual production quotas.[7] According to the ILO, it threatened farmers and forced national ministry employees (medical professionals, teachers), as well as students, to participate in cotton picking under menace of penalty. Working conditions in the cotton industry were reported as harsh, the pay poor and sometimes withheld, and punishments deployed if cotton quotas were not met.[8] The UN Human Rights Committee, the Committee on Economic, Social and Cultural Rights, the Committee on the Elimination of Discrimination Against Women (CEDAW Committee) and the Committee on the Rights of the Child also expressed concerns about reported child labour and its effects on children's education, and made recommendations on how to guarantee the rights of the child.[9] In June 2011, at the 100th session of the International Labour Conference in Geneva, the EU itself also reiterated its serious concern in this regard, and urged the Uzbek government to grant an ILO tripartite monitoring mission unrestricted access to the 2011 cotton harvest.[10]

Nevertheless, the European Commission remained favourable throughout to maintaining trade relations with the country and open communication with the national authorities in order to gradually eliminate child labour in Uzbekistan.[11] This soft approach, followed by the EU also for other beneficiary countries such as Bangladesh after the Rana Plaza factory collapse, could be justified to avoid the negative consequences that a more punitive approach could eventually trigger for the country or its population.[12]

---

[7]   Bakhodyr Muradov and Alisher Ilkhamov, 'Uzbekistan's Cotton Sector: Financial Flows and Distribution of Resources' (October 2014) OSF Working Paper.

[8]   ILO, 'Child Labour in Cotton' (2016), 12; ILO, 'Third-party monitoring of measures against child labour and forced labour during the 2015 cotton harvest in Uzbekistan' (2018), 13, para 41.

[9]   Concluding observations of the Human Rights Committee on the International Covenant on Civil and Political Rights on Uzbekistan (2005; 2010); Report of the Human Rights Council Working Group on the Universal Periodic Review on Uzbekistan (2008); Concluding observations of the Committee on Economic, Social and Cultural Rights on Uzbekistan (2006); Concluding observations of the Committee on Elimination of Discrimination against Women on Uzbekistan (2010); Concluding observations of the Committee on the Rights of the Child on Uzbekistan (2006).

[10]   International Labour Conference, 100th session, EU intervention (June 2011).

[11]   Commission, 'Response to letter from Anti-Slavery International' (26 July 2011) TRADE D1/DE/bmc/D(2011)895170.

[12]   Samantha Velluti, 'Human Rights Conditionality in the EU GSP scheme. A focus on those in Need or a Need to Refocus?', in Nuno Ferreira and Dora Kostakopoulou

2.1   Blockage of the Cotton Sector at the European Parliament

From 1993 to 2005, trade in textiles between the EU and Uzbekistan was regulated by a bilateral agreement separate from the PCA.[13] After that date, the situation was uncertain for EU and Uzbek traders. Although as a member of the WTO the EU had to guarantee the most-favoured nation treatment to all countries, that is, apply to all countries the conditions it applied to the country receiving the most beneficial trading conditions, Uzbekistan, which is not part of the WTO, could unilaterally increase import tariffs.[14] To reduce uncertainty, the European Commission thus proposed to include textiles in the existing PCA through a protocol, known as the 'Textile Protocol' (Protocol).[15] In 2011 the Commission's proposal was however blocked by the European Parliament. A campaign by Anti-Slavery International and the Cotton Campaign Coalition had called for it following the worrying reports produced by UN human rights committees and the ILO, as well as the difficulties to grant ILO observers access to the Uzbek cotton harvesting campaigns.[16] The European Parliament concluded that it would only consider consenting to the conclusion of the Protocol if Uzbek authorities granted access to ILO observers for monitoring purposes and if reforms of the working conditions in the cotton industry resulted in an effective reduction of forced labour and child labour.[17] The European Parliament recommended the Commission to call on the government of Uzbekistan to accept a high-level tripartite observer mission to assess the implementation of the ILO Convention.[18]

Yet, despite the concerning reports that followed,[19] the EU did not initiate the temporary withdrawal mechanism from the GSP scheme of Uzbekistan. While the Commission did not exclude initiating investigations if there were signs of

---

(eds), *The Human Face of the European Union: Are EU Law and Policy Humane Enough?* (2016) 343.

[13]   Agreement between the European Economic Community and Uzbekistan on trade in textile products (17 May 1994).

[14]   European Parliament resolution of 15 December 2011 on the draft Council decision on the conclusion of a Protocol to the PCA, to extend the provisions of the Agreement to bilateral trade in textiles.

[15]   Proposal for a Council Decision on the conclusion of a Protocol to the Partnership and Cooperation Agreement between the European Communities and their Member States, of the one part, and the Republic of Uzbekistan, of the other part, extending the provisions of the Partnership and Cooperation Agreement to bilateral trade in textiles COM/2010/0664 final.

[16]   EP Resolution of 15 December 2011 (n 14).

[17]   Ibid., para 2.

[18]   Ibid., para 1(ii).

[19]   Concluding observations on the fourth periodic report of Uzbekistan on the Convention against Torture, (10 December 2013) UN Doc. CAT/C/UZB/CO/4;

serious and systematic violations of human rights in Uzbekistan, it regarded a sanction-based approach as a last-resort mechanism.[20] The rationale being that, for the Commission, the GSP scheme was created as an incentive-based tool to support development rather than a sanctions-based instrument. Thus, in its approach to Uzbekistan, it regarded instead cooperation, transparency and dialogue as more efficient tools to achieve the EU's objectives.[21]

2.2   Towards the Elimination of Forced Labour?

After 2011, the situation in the Uzbek cotton industry has undergone some changes, with the ILO reporting that forced labour in the cotton harvest has been significantly reduced and that child labour is no longer a concern.[22] Yet, this conclusion is not undisputed: a 2018 cotton campaign by civil society organisations stressed that forced labour remains a problem,[23] and the Uzbek-German Forum has been particularly critical with the ILO positive reports and continues monitoring the situation with worrying outcomes.[24]

These developments also affected the EU-Uzbek trade relations. Following reports that Uzbekistan had taken effective measures against child labour during the cotton harvest, in December 2016[25] the European Parliament lifted

---

Concluding observations on the fourth periodic report of Uzbekistan for the ICCPR, (17 August 2015) UN Doc. CCPR/C/UZB/CO/4, para 19.

[20]   European Parliament, Committee on Petitions, 'Response to Petition 0347/2012 by the association Anti-Slavery International (British), on the exploitation of minors in cotton production in Uzbekistan' CM/914353EN.doc. In its response to a petition by Anti-Slavery International, the Commission disregarded the basis of the claim, which was not only child labour but also forced labour of adults.

[21]   EP Resolution of 15 December 2011 (n 14).

[22]   ILO, 'Major progress on forced labour and child labour in Uzbekistan cotton fields' (22 November 2018).

[23]   See reports by Uzbek German Forum for Human Rights http://uzbekgermanforum .org/, Cotton campaign http://www.cottoncampaign.org/ or Solidarity Centre https:// www.solidaritycenter.org/, all accessed 3 July 2021.

[24]   Uzbek-German Forum, 'Forced Labor in Uzbekistan's Cotton Harvest 2018. Key Findings of Uzbek-German Forum' (February 2019).

[25]   European Parliament legislative resolution of 14 December 2016 on the draft Council decision on the conclusion of a Protocol to the Partnership and Cooperation Agreement establishing a partnership between the European Communities and their Member States, of the one part, and the Republic of Uzbekistan, of the other part, amending the Agreement in order to extend the provisions of the Agreement to bilateral trade in textiles, taking account of the expiry of the bilateral textiles Agreement [2018] OJ C/238.

its suspension of the 'Textile Protocol' to the PCA, which entered into force in 2017.[26]

Despite the conflicting reports, in November 2018 the EU High Representative for Foreign Affairs and Security Policy and the European Commission also initiated negotiations with Uzbekistan for an Enhanced Partnership and Cooperation Agreement (EPCA),[27] under which the country could become beneficiary of the GSP+, thus facilitating even more the flow of trade with Uzbekistan through special tariff preferences.

The European Parliament remains mindful of the situation in Uzbekistan. On 26 March 2019, it adopted a recommendation on the new comprehensive agreement between the EU and Uzbekistan, identifying state-sponsored forced labour in the cotton and silk industries as a problem.[28]

3.   ELIGIBILITY REQUIREMENTS OF GSP+ FOR UZBEKISTAN: THE EU FRAMEWORK

The GSP purports preferential trade incentives to promote human rights and core labour standards, and to contribute to poverty reduction in Uzbekistan. This section looks at eligibility requirements of the GSP+ scheme and reflects on the mechanisms that the EU relies on to assess if those requirements are met. It argues that human rights impact assessment of the GSP+ agreement between the EU and Uzbekistan should be a component of the EU examination of the Uzbek request. It also explores the compatibility of the GSP+ requirements with another supranational framework by which the EU abides: the WTO framework. It argues that the WTO has influenced the way in which the Uzbek request will be assessed against those requirements.

3.1   Incorporating Human Rights Impact Assessment to the EC Examination of the Uzbek Request for a GSP+ Agreement

The normative framework of the GSP is provided by Regulation 978/2012, which contains detailed rules on the requirements for third countries to qualify

---

[26]   Protocol to the Partnership and Cooperation Agreement between the EU and Uzbekistan, amending the Agreement to extend the provisions of the Agreement to bilateral trade in textiles [2017] OJ C/238.

[27]   'The European Union and the Republic of Uzbekistan launch negotiations for a new agreement, 23 November' (EU Press Release, Brussels, 23 November 2018).

[28]   European Parliament recommendation of 26 March 2019 to the Council, the Commission and the Vice-President of the Commission / High Representative of the Union for Foreign Affairs and Security Policy on the new comprehensive agreement between the EU and Uzbekistan [2019] 2018/2236(INI).

as beneficiaries of preferential access to the EU market. Under Article 9 of Regulation 978/2012,[29] Uzbek eligibility for the GSP+ is conditioned, among other requirements, to the ratification of core international conventions, which include the two ILO Conventions on forced labour. According to the EU Regulation, Uzbekistan also cannot formulate reservations that are prohibited by those conventions, and monitoring bodies must not identify any serious failure to effectively implement them.[30]

Article 9.1 of this Regulation also requires that the candidate to benefit from a GSP+ arrangement gives a binding undertaking to ensure the effective implementation of the relevant conventions, to accept regular monitoring of its implementation record and to cooperate with monitoring procedures.[31] The Uzbek request to be granted GSP+ benefits should contain comprehensive information on those undertakings.[32] The examination of this request should be the basis for the European Commission to decide on the application and grant Uzbekistan GSP+ benefits.[33]

This chapter argues in favour of including a human rights impact assessment as part of the EU examination of Uzbekistan's request. Although it is not explicitly required by Regulation 978/2012, the increasing commitment of the European Commission with human rights impact assessment of EU external action[34] could be extended to GSP+ agreements as the one for Uzbekistan, in line with the EU constitutional structure under which this Regulation is framed

---

[29]   Regulation 978/2012 (n 3).
[30]   UNCTAD, 'Generalised System of Preferences. Handbook on the Scheme of the European Union' (2015), 15.
[31]   Art 9.1 d, e and f.
[32]   Art 10.1 and 2.
[33]   Art 10.4.
[34]   The European Commission has progressively included human rights in EU impact assessment 'for legislative and non-legislative proposals, implementing measures and trade agreements that have significant economic, social and environmental impacts, or define future policies': Council (EU), Council Conclusions of 25 June 2012 on Human Rights and Democracy, the EU Strategic Framework on Human Rights and Democracy and an EU Action Plan on Human Rights and Democracy, No 11855/12, Annex III, I.1, at 11. The EU Strategic Framework on Human Rights and Democracy (2012) and the Better Regulation Agenda (2015) (Commission, 'Better regulation for better results - An EU agenda' (Communication) (19 May 2015) COM (2015) 215 final), boosted efforts to include human rights more systematically in impact assessment of EU action, and in 2015 the Commission produced its Guidelines on the analysis of human rights impacts in impact assessments for trade-related policy initiatives: European Commission, Guidelines on the analysis of human rights impacts in impact assessments for trade-related policy initiatives (2015). See also the Operational guidance on taking account of Fundamental Rights in Commission Impact Assessment.

and with guidance from the European Ombudsman and Advocate General Wathelet in the *Frente Polisario* case.[35]

The GSP scheme is framed in the EU constitutional structure laid down in the EU Treaties. Under Article 3.5 TEU, the EU shall contribute to the protection of human rights and to the strict observance and development of international law, which includes the prohibition of forced labour and the promotion of human rights. Under Article 21 TEU, the EU shall define and pursue common policies and actions and work for a high degree of cooperation in all fields of international relations, in order to consolidate and support democracy, the rule of law, human rights and the principles of international law. In addition, under Article 208.2 TFEU, the EU and its Member States 'shall comply with the commitments and take account of the objectives they have approved in the context of the United Nations and other competent international organisations'.

This explicit reference to compliance with international law, reinforced with the Treaty of Lisbon, was also emphasised by the CJEU in 2011, in Case C-366/10 on whether Directive 2008/101/EC[36] amending Directive 2003/87/EC so as to include aviation activities in the scheme for greenhouse gas emission allowance trading within the Community was in violation of a number of international treaties and principles of customary international law. In its judgment, which considered the Directive in accordance with international law, the Court emphasised that under Article 2.5 TEU the EU must contribute to the strict observance and the development of international law and that, as a consequence, its acts are bound to observe 'international law in its entirety'.[37]

Incorporating a human rights impact assessment to the EU examination of the Uzbek request for a GSP+ arrangement would contribute to ensuring that its decision is guided by strict observance of international law, as it would provide the EU with valuable information on how its eventual decision would affect human rights. The European Ombudsman and Advocate General Wathelet in

---

[35] European Ombudsman, Decision on *Case 1409/2014/MHZ on the European Commission's failure to carry out a prior human rights impact assessment of the free trade agreement between the European Union and the Socialist Republic of Vietnam* (26 February 2016).

[36] Directive 2008/101/EC of the European Parliament and of the Council of 19 November 2008 amending Directive 2003/87/EC so as to include aviation activities in the scheme for greenhouse gas emission allowance trading within the Community [2009]OJ L 8/3.

[37] Case C-366/10 *Air Transport Association of America and Others v Secretary of State for Energy and Climate* [2011] ECLI:EU:C:2011:864, para 101.

the *Frente Polisario* case provided guidance that would be consistent with this proposed approach.[38]

A human rights impact assessment is 'an instrument for examining policies, legislation, programs and projects to identify and measure their effects on human rights'.[39] This type of assessment collects information to prevent negative effects and maximise positive effects of any policy, legislation or decision on human rights, with the ultimate goal of making human rights considerations operational in a variety of legal and policy contexts.[40] Inspired in other well-established mechanisms, such as environmental impact assessment or social impact assessment, human rights impact assessment would be advantageous for this specific case, as a mechanism systematising in a well-structured and transparent process the analysis of the effects of the GSP+ agreement for human rights in Uzbekistan.

This assessment would also be a sign of good and diligent administration by the EU and a way to ensure that the EU acts in conformity with EU treaties. In its decision on the European Commission's failure to carry out a prior human rights impact assessment of the free trade agreement between the EU and Vietnam,[41] the European Ombudsman emphasised that it would be in conformity with the spirit of Article 21 TEU to carry out a human rights impact assessment.[42] In his Opinion in Case C-104/16 (*Frente Polisario*)[43] referring to the abovementioned position of the European Ombudsman,[44] Advocate General Wathelet maintained that not providing valid reasons not to perform an impact assessment may constitute maladministration on the part of the European

---

[38] It is true that the *Frente Polisario* case and the decision of the European Ombudsman on an impact assessment of the free trade agreement between the EU and Vietnam look at the human rights impact assessment of trade agreements, and not specifically GSP arrangements, with third countries. However, although the GSP scheme qualifies as a development initiative that uses trade benefits as incentives for development and for the enhancement of human rights, the legal basis for the arguments of the Advocate General and the European Ombudsman apply also to ongoing EU-Uzbek negotiations. Both decisions were motivated on the basis of Arts 21.1 and 21.2 TEU, which, referring to EU's 'action on the international scene' also apply to the EU-Uzbek GSP negotiations.

[39] World Bank, Nordic Trust Fund, 'Study on Human Rights Impact Assessments A Review of the Literature, Differences with other Forms of Assessments and Relevance for Development' (2013), Foreword.

[40] Ibid.

[41] European Ombudsman, Decision on *Case 1409/2014/MHZ* (n 35).

[42] Ibid., para 11.

[43] Case C-104/16 P *Council of the European Union v Front Populaire pour la libération de la saguia-el-hamra et du rio de oro (Front Polisario)* [2016] ECLI:EU:C: 2016:677, para 264.

[44] European Ombudsman, Decision on *Case 1409/2014/MHZ* (n 35).

institutions, and that, for it to not lose its significance, such impact assessment should normally be carried out *before* the international agreement at issue is concluded.[45] In his opinion, Advocate General Wathelet emphasised that the EU can 'best promote its values and objectives, including respect for and protection of human rights' during the period of negotiation of agreements.[46]

The opinion of Advocate General Wathelet was adopted in the context of the appeal to the CJEU of a previous decision of the General Court (T-512/12),[47] which declared annulled Council Decision 2012/497/EU of 8 March 2012 on the conclusion of an Agreement between the European Union and the Kingdom of Morocco concerning reciprocal liberalisation measures on certain products, in so far as it approved the application of that agreement to Western Sahara. While the core issue of the judgment was whether a national liberalisation movement could challenge an EU trade agreement and the CJEU decided on appeal to quash the General Court's decision denying legal standing for the Front Polisario,[48] the judgment of the General Court included interesting references to human rights impact assessment that were then followed by Advocate General Wathelet and not ruled out by the CJEU.

The General Court found that the Council had 'made manifest errors of assessment' as it did not examine the relevant facts before adopting a decision on a trade agreement that could affect the human rights of Western Saharans.[49] Concerning agreements to facilitate the export to the EU of products originating in a third country, it acknowledged that 'the Council must examine, carefully and impartially, all the relevant facts [...] to ensure' that the production of those products does not entail infringement of the rights contained in the EU Charter for Fundamental Rights (EU Charter), including the rights to human dignity, to life and to the integrity of the person (Arts 1–3 EU Charter), the prohibition of slavery and forced labour (Art 5 EU Charter), the right to fair and just working conditions and the prohibition of child labour and protection of young people at work (Arts 31 and 32 EU Charter).[50] The General Court also emphasised that, although the EU cannot be liable for actions committed

---

[45] Case C-104/16 P *Council of the European Union v Front Populaire pour la libération de la saguia-el-hamra et du rio de oro (Front Polisario)* [2016] ECLI:EU:C:2016:677, Opinion of AG Wathelet, para 266.
[46] Ibid.
[47] Case T-512/12 *Front populaire pour la libération de la saguia-el-hamra et du rio de oro (Front Polisario) v Council of the European Union* [2015] ECLI:EU:T:2015:953.
[48] Case C-104/16 P *Front Polisario* (n 43).
[49] Case T-512/12 *Front Polisario* (n 47), para 224.
[50] Ibid., para 228.

by that country, 'if the European Union allows' that to happen, it may be considered to 'indirectly encourage such infringements or profit from them'.[51]

The opinion of Advocate General Whathelet calls for EU human rights impact assessment, aligned with the broader claim made by the General Court.[52] The judgment of the CJEU did not consider these aspects, as it quashed the General Court's decision on other grounds, but it left the door open for a role of EU fundamental rights 'as a benchmark for EU trade policies'.[53]

Information provided by the EU to civil society organisations does not give clear indications of a systematic human rights impact assessment currently being carried out in relation to negotiations with Uzbekistan, and no information on any human rights impact assessment check is publicly available. According to the European External Action Service (EEAS), a frank assessment of the human rights situation in Uzbekistan has been carried out, including for the cotton sector, and human rights considerations play an important role in exchanges with the relevant stakeholders. At the same time, the EEAS has however argued that those considerations are being exchanged informally and the documents containing such assessment are not publicly accessible as it could be 'detrimental to the diplomatic efforts and standing of the European Union'.[54] Be the levels of transparency as they may, including a human rights impact assessment in the examination of the Uzbek request for GSP+ benefits would allow the EU to better assess, in full observance of international law, whether the request fulfils the requirements of Regulation 978/2012.

3.2   The WTO Influence on the Current GSP+ Framework

Another area of international law that the EU must observe when applying the GSP+ scheme is the WTO framework. As mentioned above, the GSP scheme is not defined as a trade agreement but trade incentives are one of its core elements. This section illustrates how the WTO has influenced the way in which the EU shapes its GSP arrangements and argues that it will play a role in ongoing negotiations with Uzbekistan.

---

[51]   Ibid., paras 230–231.
[52]   Opinion of AG Wathelet (n 45), paras 259, 276.
[53]   Vivian Kube, 'The Polisario case: Do EU fundamental rights matter for EU trade policies?' (*EJIL:Talk! Blog of the European Journal of International Law*, 3 February 2017) https://www.ejiltalk.org/the-polisario-case-do-eu-fundamental-rights-matter-for -eu-trade-polices/, accessed 3 July 2021.
[54]   The EEAS referred, particularly, to the EU Heads of Missions on the Human Rights and Democracy Country Strategy for Uzbekistan as the document containing such frank assessment.

Such influence has occurred mainly through a decision of the WTO Appellate Body (Appellate Body) dealing with the controversial question on the legality of the GSP scheme under the WTO framework, in particular on how it was compatible with the WTO most favoured nation principle. In its report on the case brought by India against the *European Communities on Conditions for the Granting of Tariff Preferences to Developing Countries*, the Appellate Body confirmed that the GSP scheme falls under the WTO enabling clause. This clause allows its contracting parties to accord 'differential and more favourable treatment to developing countries, without according such treatment to other contracting parties'.[55]

In that case against the *European Communities on Conditions for the Granting of Tariff Preferences to Developing Countries*, the Appellate Body considered India's challenge to the EU's 'drugs arrangement', a GSP programme which allowed developing countries to benefit from additional trade preferences conditioned to certain controls in the production and trafficking of narcotics. The scheme was originally offered to 11 Latin American countries and Pakistan. The inclusion of this latter country as a beneficiary of the GSP programme prompted India's complaint.[56] The Appellate Body confirmed the GSP's legality under the enabling clause, only if the special preference granted was in accordance with the WTO principle of non-discrimination. For that to happen, preferences must be offered on similar terms to similarly situated states and be based on objective criteria.[57] The Appellate Body considered that granting a special preference to certain developing countries with similar characteristics would be in accordance with the notion of non-discrimination.[58] It also found that 'a sufficient nexus should exist' between the special preference granted and the alleviation of the specific need of the beneficiary country.[59] For the preference to be in accordance with the WTO notion of non-discrimination, it should be a preference arguably able to alleviate a specific need of the beneficiary country.

---

[55]   GATT Document L/4903, 28 November 1979, BISD 26S/203, para 3(c)1.

[56]   James Yap, 'Beyond "Don't Be Evil": The European Union GSP+ Trade Preference Scheme and the Incentivisation of the Sri Lankan Garment Industry to Foster Human Rights' (2013) 19 *European Law Journal* 283, 286.

[57]   WTO Appellate Body, 'European Communities – Conditions for the Granting of Tariff Preferences to Developing Countries' (Report) (20 April 2004) WT/DS246/AB/R. See also Lorand Bartels, 'The WTO Legality of the EU's GSP+ Arrangement' (2007) 10 *Journal of International Economic Law* 869, 870; James Harrison, 'Incentives for Development: the EC's Generalized System of Preferences, India's WTO Challenge and Reform' (2005) 42 *Common Market Law Review* 1663.

[58]   WTO Appellate Body, ibid.

[59]   Ibid., para 164.

The position of the Appellate Body on the legality of the GSP scheme under the WTO framework has been criticised by some scholars who consider it difficult to see a clear connection between the human rights commitments of the GSP scheme and the needs of developing countries, as it is often difficult to justify a 'sufficient nexus' between the two. On that basis, they argue that GSP arrangements do not qualify as an exception to the most favoured nation requirement of Article I:1 of the General Agreement on Tariffs and Trade.[60]

While this critique is justified for certain cases, focusing on forced labour cases there is a clear connection between the protection from forced labour and the alleviation of the difficult circumstances in the country's population. As the UN Special Rapporteur on Contemporary Forms of Slavery recently emphasised, slavery and forced labour are 'economically clearly unprofitable' as they lead to broader public health costs, productivity losses, negative environmental externalities and lost income.[61] Therefore, the special treatment underlying the GSP agreement with Uzbekistan would fit within the Appellate Body's description of a preference compatible with the WTO framework.

The decision of the Appellate Body in *European Communities on Conditions for the Granting of Tariff Preferences to Developing Countries* conditioned the design and implementation of the currently existing GSP framework. It was in response to this ruling that the EU implemented the GSP+ programme, as a renewed GSP scheme available to all similarly situated countries pursuant to an objective standard.[62]

The WTO framework will influence the negotiation and shaping of the specific terms of the GSP+ scheme with Uzbekistan. This influence is twofold: on the one hand, Regulation 978/2012 is a consequence of the Appellate Body's decision in the *European Communities on Conditions for the Granting of Tariff Preferences to Developing Countries* case; on the other hand, the EU is aware that a GSP+ arrangement not meeting the Appellate Body's test for legality of this scheme under the WTO framework is susceptible of being considered incompatible with it in a future decision of this body.

---

[60]   Ibid.
[61]   OHCHR, '10,000 People a Day Must be Freed to End Slavery by 2030' (19 September 2019) https://www.ohchr.org/EN/NewsEvents/Pages/Endingtodaysslavery.aspx, accessed 3 July 2021. See also Sasha Reed, Stephen Roe, James Grimshaw and Rhys Oliver, 'The economic and social costs of modern slavery. Research Report 100' (UK Home Office, July 2018).
[62]   Brice Wardhaugh, 'GSP+ and Human Rights: Is the EU's Approach the Right One?' (2013) 16 *Journal of International Economic Law* 827, 829.

4. MONITORING UZBEK COMPLIANCE WITH HUMAN RIGHTS REQUIREMENTS

Uzbekistan is subject to a number of obligations under international human rights treaties such as the International Covenant on Civil and Political Rights (ICCPR, ratified in 1995),[63] and ILO conventions, in particular the ILO Convention on Forced Labour (1929),[64] ratified in 1992, and the ILO Convention on Abolition of Forced Labour (1957),[65] ratified in 1997. These include the obligation to prevent, protect and punish any actor (public or private) deploying forced labour, as well as the obligation not to deploy forced labour.[66]

Yet, in the face of numerous reports on Uzbekstan's poor compliance with its human rights obligations, the only significant measure that appears to have been taken by the EU was the blockage of the Textile Protocol by the European Parliament.[67] As Uzbekistan could soon benefit from a GSP+ arrangement, this section explores the mechanisms that the GSP scheme provides for monitoring Uzbek compliance with the imposed human rights requirements, and the role that civil society organisations could play in that exercise.

4.1 The Use of the Temporary Withdrawal Mechanism

Under Regulation 978/2012 the EU may decide to withdraw temporarily the preferential treatment granted to a country in respect of all or of certain products listed in the GSP+ agreement,[68] if the most recent conclusions of the 'relevant monitoring bodies' (the ILO and UN human rights treaty bodies monitoring the core conventions referred to in Art 9) identify any 'serious and systematic violations' of its human rights commitments.

The Union's approach to the poor handling of human rights protection in Uzbekistan is a signal of the broader issue that the temporary withdrawal from

---

[63]   International Covenant on Civil and Political Rights (1966, 173 States Parties).

[64]   ILO Convention concerning Forced or Compulsory Labour, N. 29 (1929, 178 States Parties).

[65]   ILO Convention concerning the Abolition of Forced Labour, N. 105 (175 States Parties).

[66]   The obligation to prevent and punish implies the prohibition of the commission of forced labour by the State, following the reasoning of the ICJ on the prohibition of genocide (Application of the Genocide Convention, ICJ Rep 2007, paras 166–179). See Philippa Webb and Rosana Garciandia, 'State Responsibility for Modern Slavery: Uncovering and Bridging the Gap' (2019) 68 *International and Comparative Law Quarterly* 552.

[67]   See section 1.1.

[68]   See Art 21 of Regulation 978/2012, (n 3).

GSP agreements is, in practice, barely used. The withdrawal procedure has been activated only in a few occasions, never for Uzbekistan: for Myanmar (1997) on the grounds of deployment of forced labour; for Belarus (2006) for serious and systematic violations of ILO Conventions 87 and 98; and for Sri Lanka (2010) given shortcomings in respect of its implementation of the International Covenant on Civil and Political Rights, the Convention against Torture and the Convention on the Rights of the Child.[69] In addition, a common critique to the GSP framework has been the 'selective conditionality practices' carried out by the EU, applying different standards to different countries.[70]

The scarce number of cases of withdrawal may admittedly be, inter alia, a consequence of the fact that the system presented a number of challenges that the enhanced procedure of Regulation 1083/2013[71] has tried to overcome, such as lack of clarity in some of its provisions. The new regulation provides more transparent rules and clearer processes for the inclusion or exclusion of beneficiaries.[72] This is a positive development that could contribute to a stronger monitoring of the GSP scheme in line with the spirit of the EU constitutional framework regarding human rights. In February 2019, the EU triggered the procedure to suspend temporarily trade preferences for Cambodia over concerns related to serious human and labour rights violations.[73] It will be interesting to see if the trend that consolidates in the near future is aligned with a more effective[74] and less selective[75] use of temporary withdrawal.

4.2   ILO Reports: What Role for Reports of Civil Society?

As mentioned above, eligibility for the GSP+ under Article 9 of Regulation 978/2012[76] is conditioned, among other requirements, to the unconditional

---

[69]   Regulation (EU) No 143/2010 of the Council temporarily withdrawing the special incentive arrangement for sustainable development and good governance with respect to Sri Lanka [2010] OJ/L 45/1.

[70]   J Orbie and L Tortell, 'The New GSP+ Beneficiaries: Ticking the Box or Truly Consistent with ILO Findings?' (2009) 14 *European Foreign Affairs Review* 663.

[71]   Commission Delegated Regulation (EU) No. 1083/2013 of 28 August 2013 establishing rules related to the procedure for temporary withdrawal of tariff preferences and adoption of general safeguard measures under Regulation (EU) No 978/2012 [2013] OJ L 293/16.

[72]   It also addresses some of the concerns that the WTO Appellate Body noted in relation to it: see Part 3 and Wardhaugh, (n 62), 832.

[73]   Commission, 'EU triggers procedure to temporarily suspend trade preferences for Cambodia' (Fact Sheet) (Brussels, 11 February 2019).

[74]   This is what the European Commission has recently called for: see Commission, 'Mid-Term Evaluation of the EU's GSP' (2018), 247.

[75]   Orbie and Tortell (n 70).

[76]   Regulation 978/2012 (n 3).

ratification of core international conventions, including the ILO Convention on Forced Labour (1929),[77] which Uzbekistan ratified in 1992, and the ILO Convention on Abolition of Forced Labour (1957),[78] also ratified by Uzbekistan in 1997, and to the positive reporting about their effective implementation by monitoring bodies.[79]

Under Article 13.21 of Regulation 978/2012, the European Commission must keep under review the status of ratification of the relevant conventions and shall monitor their effective implementation and the beneficiary country's cooperation with the relevant monitoring bodies, by examining the conclusions and recommendations of those monitoring bodies. The GSP+ thus imposes a dialogue between the EU and the ILO: to check eligibility and continuity of GSP+ benefits, the EU turns to observations of the Committee of Experts on the Application of Conventions and Recommendations (CEACR) under the ILO regular supervision system, as well as to additional ILO reports.[80] Conversely, the ILO relies on the EU institutions, on employment and social affairs related issues under the EU-ILO strategic partnership, although this aspect of the dialogue is not directly and exclusively related to the GSP scheme.[81]

Article 14.3 of the Regulation incorporates an important point to the monitoring exercise that the European Commission must undertake. When referring to the biannual report that the European Commission must present to the European Parliament and to the Council on the status of ratification of the relevant conventions, the compliance of the GSP+ beneficiary countries with any reporting obligations under those conventions and the status of their effective implementation, this provision allows the European Commission to consider, beyond reports of the relevant monitoring bodies, information submitted by third parties, including civil society, social partners, the European Parliament or the Council. This chapter argues for a stronger application of this option by

---

[77]   ILO Convention concerning Forced or Compulsory Labour, N. 29 (1929, 178 States Parties).

[78]   ILO Convention concerning the Abolition of Forced Labour, N. 105 (175 States Parties).

[79]   UNCTAD (n 30).

[80]   In addition to periodic reports under the ILO regular supervision system, other ILO mechanisms, which have not been used for Uzbekistan to date, could be relevant in the future, namely representation under Art 24 of the ILO Constitution (by national and international employers' and workers' associations), and the ILO complaint procedure under Arts 26–34 of the ILO Constitution (by another Member State which ratified the same convention, a delegate to the International Labour Conference or the Governing Body in its own capacity. A Commission of Inquiry could follow accusations of persistent and serious violations of ILO Conventions).

[81]   ILO, 'The European Union ILO Cooperation' (May 2019).

the European Commission in the Uzbek case, given the divergence between ILO and other reports.

The most recent observations of the CEACR on forced labour in Uzbekistan were adopted in 2016. The Committee welcomed certain measures adopted for ensuring the voluntary recruitment of cotton pickers, but emphasised that they were not 'robust enough' to bring a decisive change to recruitment practices.[82] It encouraged the government to strengthen the protection system for cotton pickers, to raise awareness about the risks of forced labour, and to continue cooperating with the ILO and other social partners to ensure the 'complete elimination of the use of compulsory labour'.[83] In February 2018, an inquiry was launched on third-party monitoring of measures against child labour and forced labour during the 2017 cotton harvest in Uzbekistan. The resulting report – elaborated by the International Labour Office pursuant to an agreement between the ILO and the World Bank to carry out third-party monitoring of the World Bank-financed projects in agriculture, water and education sectors in Uzbekistan – found no systematic use of child labour in the cotton harvest in the country and acknowledged the implementation of measures to end forced labour. However, it found that, although in the 2017 campaign, most of the cotton pickers (estimated 2.6 million people between September and November) were recruited voluntarily.[84]

The content of these reports was a valuable basis for the EU to assess compliance of Uzbekistan with its commitments under the GSP scheme. However, these reports seem to be contradicted by reports of other organisations working in the field, as illustrated in previous sections. One of the organisations more critical with ILO reports has been the Uzbek-German Forum, which reported in April 2019 that systemic forced labour persisted in Uzbekistan's 2018 cotton harvest,[85] and continues documenting evidence of such allegations. Other organisations gathering evidence of forced labour in the Uzbek cotton harvesting industry and reporting about it are the Cotton campaign[86] or Solidarity Centre.[87]

Given the divergent reports on the Uzbek situation from different sources and the concerns raised about the methodology used in ILO Third Party

---

[82] Observations published in the 106th ILC session (2017).
[83] Ibid.
[84] ILO, World Bank, 'Third-party monitoring of measures against child labour and forced labour during the 2017 cotton harvest in Uzbekistan' (February 2018).
[85] Uzbek-German Forum, 'They said we wouldn't have to pick and now they send us to the fields' *Forced Labor in Uzbekistan's Cotton Harvest 2018,* 24 April 2019.
[86] http://www.cottoncampaign.org/, accessed 3 July 2021.
[87] https://www.solidaritycenter.org/, accessed 3 July 2021.

Monitoring in Uzbekistan,[88] as the dialogue with the ILO continues, the European Commission should, making use of the provision under Article 14.3 of the Regulation that allows it to engage with civil society organisations, pay attention also to reports from other relevant stakeholders in the region. This will ensure that the EU assesses Uzbek compliance with GSP+ human rights requirements more accurately, incorporating as much evidence as possible.

5. CONCLUSIONS

As negotiations are underway for a GSP+ arrangement between the EU and Uzbekistan, this chapter explores the EU framework for the protection and monitoring of human rights under such arrangement and how the dialogue that the EU maintains with other relevant organizations therein contributes to its implementation.

After framing the GSP within the EU constitutional framework, this work highlights certain aspects of its functioning in the Uzbek cotton industry, in light of the overarching aims of human rights protection of the EU set out under Article 3.5 TEU. In terms of eligibility for the GSP+ regime, it was noted that the process by which the EU examines the Uzbek request would benefit of the inclusion of human rights impact assessment. Such assessment would allow the EU to assess, in full observance of international law, whether the Uzbek request fulfils the requirements of Regulation 978/2012, incorporating in its analysis a systematic study of the impact of a GSP+ arrangement on human rights. It also emphasised the influence that the WTO framework will have in the conclusion of the GSP+ decision, mainly under the influence of a past decision of the WTO Appellate Body on the WTO legality of the GSP scheme.

In terms of the functioning of the monitoring system of the GSP+ scheme, it noted that the use of the temporary withdrawal mechanism has been used in a selective and not very effective way, and identified the procedure to suspend temporarily trade preferences for Cambodia, currently under consideration, as an opportunity to identify new trends in the use of the temporary withdrawal mechanism. This work further advances the claim that, given the conflicting

---

[88]   Observation of the ILO Third Party monitoring in Uzbekistan led Lasslett and Gstrein to identify the following shortcomings as concerns: failure to obtain informed consent from vulnerable participants, a risk that participants did not participate voluntarily in interviews, confidentiality and anonymity issues, exposure of interviewees to risks of retaliation, methodological concerns, weaknesses in quality control and concerns over independence (Kristian Lasslett, Vanessa Gstrein, 'Measuring Forced Labour in an Authoritarian Context. An Evaluation of ILO Third Party Monitoring in Uzbekistan', (2018) The Corruption and Human Rights Initiative).

reports published by international organisations and civil society organisations on forced labour in Uzbekistan, incorporating other actors to the dialogue between EU and international organisations operating in the human rights field would benefit the protection of human rights in EU-Uzbek relations.

13. New tendencies in Free Trade Agreement drafting: International financial standards in the EU Free Trade Agreements

Elisa Longoni[1]

1.   INTRODUCTION

Free Trade Agreements (FTAs), namely treaties promoting international trade, have progressively expanded their scope to the point that they frequently overreach trade obligations set by the World Trade Organization (WTO). In doing so, FTAs sometimes incorporate voluntary regulatory sources, such as international standards. This is the case for the financial sector, where a tendency to incorporate international financial standards into FTAs has emerged, at least in the most recent EU FTAs. This scenario raises two questions. First, whether the nature of international financial standards changes from voluntary to compulsory by their incorporation into FTAs. Second, whether FTA provisions related to financial standards are used by the WTO adjudicative bodies in dispute settlement for interpretative reasons, or in the assessment of a trade restrictive measures in the financial sector.

The main goal of this chapter is to investigate whether the widely recognized voluntary nature of international financial standards has been illegitimately upgraded to legally binding through FTAs, or the use of them in dispute settlement. In answering this question, the chapter will explain first, the increasing use of FTAs and the evolution of their scope. It will then assess how frequently international financial standards are included in FTAs and if their voluntary nature changes to compulsory. Finally, the focus will be on the use of international financial standards in the WTO dispute settlement. The results will show

[1]   The views and opinions expressed in the text are those of the author and do not necessarily reflect the official policy or position of the author's employer or any other agency, or organization.

that EU FTAs simply refer to international financial standards in a hortatory and declaratory way, which does not produce legally binding effects. The unchanged nature of international financial standards is also confirmed by the relevant WTO case law, where recourse to these voluntary instruments is very limited, both for interpretative and substantive purposes.

2.   THE PROGRESSIVE USE OF FTAs IN INTERNATIONAL TRADE LAW AND THE EVOLUTION OF THEIR SCOPE

The term 'Free Trade Agreements' refers to treaties concluded by a subset of states that accord to trade parties preferential treatment in derogation from the WTO non-discrimination principle. As defined in Article 24 of the General Agreement on Tariffs and Trade (GATT) and Article 5 of the General Agreement on Trade in Services (GATS), FTAs are used to attain wider and deeper trade liberalization.[2] Originally conceived as an exception, FTAs are nowadays one of the most recurrent legal tools in international trade.[3] Indeed, the use of FTAs has grown remarkably over the past decades, leading to practically every country signing at least one FTA, regardless of their economic model or level of development.[4]

The exceptionality of the phenomenon does not simply concern the massive number of FTAs concluded globally, or the number of countries that utilise them, but also their scope. From purely trade-driven goals, such as tariffs and quotas, FTAs have extended their coverage to societal values, including environmental sustainability, human rights, financial stability, investment protection and so forth. The enlargement of their scope has drawn scholars'

---

[2]   Peter Van den Bossche and Werner Zdouc, *The Law and Policy of the World Trade Organization: Text, Cases and Materials* (3rd edn, CUP 2013) 648; Michael J Trebilcock, Robert Howse and Antonia Eliason, *The Regulation of International Trade* (4th edn, Routledge 2013) 83; Mitsuo Matsushita Thomas J Schoenbaum, Petros C Mavroidis, and Michael J Hahn (eds), *The World Trade Organization: Law, Practice, and Policy* (OUP 2015) 105.

[3]   Richard E Baldwin and Patrick Low, *Multilateralizing Regionalism* (CUP 2009); Joseph Weiler, *The EU, the WTO, and the NAFTA: Towards a Common Law of International Trade?* (OUP 2013); Thomas Cottier and Panagiotis Delimatsis, *The Prospects of International Trade Regulation: from Fragmentation to Coherence* (CUP 2011); Simon Lester and Mercurio Bryan, *Bilateral and Regional Trade Agreements: Commentary and Analysis* (CUP 2007); Jean-Christophe Maur, 'Regionalism and Trade Facilitation: A Primer' (2008) 42 *Journal of World Trade* 979.

[4]   Lorand Bartels and Federico Ortino, *Regional Trade Agreements and the WTO Legal System* (OUP 2010) 3. The total number of FTAs is estimated at around 600, with almost 300 notified to the WTO: Andreas Dür and Manfred Elsig, *Trade Cooperation: The Purpose, Design and Effects of Preferential Trade Agreements* (CUP 2011).

attention to assessing obligations in FTAs against the commitments under-taken in the WTO legal framework and the developing notions of WTO plus (WTO+) and WTO extra (WTO-X) provisions.[5] Specifically, the term WTO+ embraces FTA obligations in disciplinary areas already regulated by the WTO regime, but deepens the commitment already undertaken at the multilateral level. Examples of WTO+ provisions for financial services can vary largely from a detailed definition of the term 'prudential' to a specification of condi-tions under which a branch of a bank can be established in a foreign territory. The so-called WTO-X provisions introduce commitments in areas that have not been covered by the WTO regime in a substantive manner. In financial services, for example, a WTO-X provision can dictate specific requirements for issuing bond or capital requirements for banks in order to preserve financial stability.[6]

In regulating the financial sector, WTO-X and WTO+ provisions in FTAs can be based on other voluntary tools, such as international financial standards set by, for example, the Basel Committee on Banking Supervision (Basel Committee) and the International Organization of Securities Commissions (IOSCO).[7] This implies that FTA provisions can produce new obligations upon contracting parties based on standards that originally belong to soft law.[8] Consequently, it is important to ascertain the legal value of financial standards after their incorporation into FTAs. A first step is to verify whether, and if so

---

[5]   Rohini Acharya, *Regional Trade Agreements and the Multilateral Trading System* (CUP 2016) 5–14; Jo-Ann Crawford and Roberto V Fiorentino, 'The Changing Landscape of Regional Trade Agreements' (WTO publications 2005).

[6]   For further examples of WTO+ and WTO-X provisions in various sectors, see: Henrik Horn, Petros Mavroidis and André Sapir, 'Beyond the WTO? An Anatomy of EU and US Preferential Trade Agreements' (2009) 7 Bruegel blueprint series 1; Joost Pauwelyn and Alschner Wolfgang, 'Forget About the WTO: The Network of Relations between Preferential Trade Agreements (PTAs); and "Double PTAs"' in Andreas Dür and Manfred Elsig (eds), *Trade Cooperation: The Purpose, Design and Effects of Preferential Trade Agreements* (CUP 2011) 497–532.

[7]   Enrico Milano and Niccolò Zugliani, 'Capturing Commitment in Informal, Soft Law Instruments: A Case Study on the Basel Committee' (2019) 22 Journal of International Economic Law 163.

[8]   Among a vast literature on the voluntary soft nature of international standards, see: Chris Brummer, *Soft Law and the Global Financial System: Rulemaking in the 21st Century* (CUP 2012); Sabino Cassese, *Research Handbook on Global Administrative Law* (Edward Elgar 2016); Anne-Marie Slaughter, *A New World Order* (PUP 2004); David Zaring, 'Informal Procedure, Hard and Soft, in International Administration' 5(2) *Chicago Journal of International Law* 547; Armin Von Bogdandy, Matthias Goldmann and Ingo Venzke, 'From Public International to International Public Law: Translating World Public Opinion into International Public Authority' (2016) MPIL Research Papers 1–37; and Joost Pauwelyn, Ramses A Wessel and Jan Wouters, *Informal International Lawmaking* (OUP 2012).

how frequently, these standards are included in FTAs. The second step is to examine how they are incorporated, considering whether financial standards produce new obligations upon states, in which case they become legally binding.

Previous studies investigated the progressively wider scope of FTAs, and from the findings of these earlier studies, the key assumptions for the analysis of modern EU FTAs have been adopted in this chapter. The first assumption is that FTAs have a wider scope compared to WTO agreements, as Marchetti and Roy demonstrated in their cross-country and cross-sectoral quantitative research.[9] The two authors selected 28 FTAs notified at the WTO and analysed both the number of sectors covered by the FTAs (coverage) and the level of commitment accorded (depth). They then compared the level of commitment accorded in the examined FTAs with the best offer proposed by the same countries in the Doha Round of the GATS. By using the level of commitment undertaken in the GATS as a benchmark, they concluded that the coverage and the depth of FTAs are far-reaching.[10]

The second assumption is that EU FTAs enjoy a broader scope than the US FTAs. Trachtman provided a robust cross-country analysis, comparing WTO obligations with provisions in both US FTAs and EU FTAs. He concluded that the European approach is more ambitious than the American one due to the harmonization imperative underpinning the project of the EU's integrated market.[11] Similarly, Horn, Mavroidis and Sapir investigated the scope and depth of FTA obligations. The latter was considered to mean the legal enforceability of FTA provisions, essentially the likelihood of successfully bringing a claim before an international adjudicative body in the case of non-compliance by one of the parties.[12] The authors concluded that while the EU FTAs included many WTO+ and WTO-X provisions, their value remained frequently hortatory. This mismatch between scope and depth in EU FTAs showed a significant legal expansion between the number of areas covered and the commitment undertaken.[13]

---

[9]   Juan Marchetti and Martin Roy (eds), 'Services Liberalization in the WTO and in FTAs' in *Opening Markets for Trade in Services: Countries and Sectors in Bilateral and WTO Negotiations* (CUP 2008).

[10]   Ibid., 31–35.

[11]   Trachtman referred to *Cassis-de-Dijon* to exemplify the EU's 'institutional machinery' that drives harmonization: Joel P Trachtman, 'Trade in Financial Services under GATS, NAFTA and the EC: A Regulatory Jurisdiction Analysis' (1995) 341 *Columbia Journal of Transnational Law* 37, 120.

[12]   Horn, Mavroidis, Sapir (n 6).

[13]   The authors considered 28 FTAs in this study (14 EU FTAs and 14 US FTAs) and identified 52 areas belonging to either WTO+ or WTO-X, particularly in the EU FTAs: ibid., 7.

The third assumption is that the EU-Chile FTA constitutes the baseline for the present analysis of FTAs. The work of Bourgeois, Dawar and Evenett identified the EU-Chile FTA as the most far-reaching FTA, among those concluded by the EU since 2002, and in comparison with WTO obligations. It contains the highest level of concessions in absolute terms compared to both the EU's best GATS offer in the Doha round and the EU FTAs signed before 2002.[14]

The fourth assumption is that different FTA templates influence the level of concessions agreed by the parties. Moreover, according to the template used, the obligations for the financial sector are covered under different disciplines. Latrille, Adulung and Mamdouh, identified two main templates for FTAs: the GATS model and the North American Free Trade Agreement (NAFTA) template. The latter contains a far-reaching approach, because all market access and national treatment obligations generally apply unless specific sectors are exempted in the annexed schedule of concessions.[15] In addition, the NAFTA-based FTAs cover commitments in the financial sector in both the dedicated stand-alone chapter (for modes of supply 1, 2, and 4) and the investment protection chapter (for modes of supply 3 also known as 'commercial presence').[16] In contrast, the GATS-based FTAs do not have a separate chapter for financial services, so obligations for the financial sector are instead included under the general chapter of trade in services. The analysis offered therefore considers the general chapter on trade in services (for

---

[14] Jaques Bourgeois, Kamala Dawar and Simon J Evenett, 'A Comparative Analysis of Selected Provisions in Free Trade Agreements' (Technical Report, European Commission 2007).

[15] NAFTA-based FTAs have the so-called 'negative listing', which opposes the 'positive listing' of the GATS model where only the sectors to which the obligations apply are listed. Rudolf Adlung and Hamid Mamdouh, 'How to Design Trade Agreements in Services: Top down or Bottom-Up?' [2014] *Journal of World Trade* 191; Pierre Latrille, 'Services Rules in Regional Trade Agreements: How Diverse and Creative Are They Compared to the Multilateral Rules' in Rohini Acharya (ed), *Regional Trade Agreements and the Multilateral Trading System* (CUP 2016).

[16] The definition of trade in services in Art 1(2) GATS distinguishes between four different modalities or modes of supply. Mode 1, also called cross-border supply, is a service provided abroad; Mode 2, or 'consumption abroad', consists of a service that is enjoyed by a foreigner within the domestic border of the state of the supplier; Mode 3, or 'commercial presence', is a service supplied through the presence of any type of business or professional establishment in the territory of another state. Finally, Mode 4, refers to a service that is delivered within the territory of the Member through the presence of a natural person. Bart De Meester, 'Liberalization of Financial Flows and Trade in Financial Services under the GATS' (2012) 46 *Journal of World* Trade 733, 759–761; Pierre Sauvé and Robert Mitchell Stern, *GATS 2000 New Directions in Services Trade Liberalization* (Brookings Institution Press 2000).

the GATS-based FTAs), the financial services chapter, and the investment protection chapter, along with the respective schedule of concessions (for the NAFTA-based FTAs).[17]

The final assumption is that geographical proximity, and the level of economic development of the EU's trade partners, are explanatory factors for the level of commitment accorded. Borlini and Dordi showed that the EU's trade policy is influenced by whether the commercial partner is a potential candidate for the EU enlargement, a regional neighbour, or a strategic global player.[18] Also, the level of economic development implies a different level of assistance and value export.[19] This explains why agreements with potentially new EU members present deeper commitments than those agreed with international trade partners and why a stringent standard alignment is usually required to neighbouring economies in transition.[20] These two explanatory factors will help determine whether the European trend to incorporate financial standards occurs only with certain type of trade partners, or of it is widespread.

3.   METHODOLOGICAL PREMISE AND THE STUDY OF MODERN EU FTAs

The analysis provided in this chapter examines modern EU FTAs. This means FTAs negotiated by the EU (given the established far-reaching scope of its FTAs), signed from 2002 onwards and regulating the financial sector. The aim is twofold. First, to understand whether there is a recurrent trend to incorporate international financial standards into EU FTAs, and second, to establish whether the voluntary nature of these standards turn into legally binding obligations.

As a preliminary step, a selection of the most recent EU FTAs has been conducted. Consequently, only FTAs with a finalized text have been shortlisted. The FTAs in early stages of negotiations or lacking a largely agreed text (such as the TTIP),[21] have been excluded from the analysis because they are incapa-

---

[17]   Adlung and Mamdouh (n 15), Latrille (n 15).

[18]   Leonardo Borlini and Claudio Dordi, 'Deepening International Systems of Subsidy Control: The (Different) Legal Regimes of Subsidies in the EU Bilateral Preferential Trade Agreements' (2017) 23 *Columbia Journal of European Law* 551.

[19]   For a further analysis on how PTAs, and more generally bilateral agreements, are used as a means to export specific policy or standards, see Jean-Christophe Maur, 'Exporting Europe's Trade Policy' (2005) 28 *World Economy* 1565.

[20]   Country classification according to the UN Department of Economic and Social Affairs (UN DESA) https://www.un.org/en/development/desa/policy/wesp/wesp _current/2014wesp_country_classification.pdf, accessed 4 July 2021.

[21]   Acronym for Transatlantic Trade and Investment Partnership between the EU and the US.

ble of providing reliable data and capturing a stable trend. With the exception of the Trade in Services Agreement (TiSA), only FTAs with a signed-off text, or in force (even provisionally), have been considered. The main reason for the inclusion of TiSA relates to the relevance of this treaty for the financial services sector, since it consists of a multilateral agreement involving 23 WTO members, accounting for approximately 70 per cent of world trade in services. Moreover, the TiSA's text on financial services was reported as being almost stabilized, with the exclusion of a few provisions.[22]

The EU FTAs have been ordered chronologically, and those lacking financial services, or signed by non-WTO members, have been discarded.[23] The presence of financial services is essential to assessing the inclusion of voluntary financial standards into FTAs and their potentially 'hardened' nature into compulsory treaty provisions. Similarly, in order to explore the use of these standards by WTO adjudicative bodies in dispute settlement, the FTA parties need to be WTO members.

With the aim of capturing any modern tendency in FTA drafting, the first 16 EU FTAs have been chosen for analysis.[24] In addition to those, TiSA has been added as well as the EU-Chile FTA, which has served as a baseline.[25] Therefore, the 18 FTAs analysed are shown in Table 13.1.

From a methodological point of view, a mapping exercise has been conducted to verify if financial standards have been incorporated into the FTAs, and where, namely the chapter and the section. The latter refers to sections headed 'domestic regulation', 'transparency' or 'prudential measures'. This is to understand when international financial standards become relevant, if at all, meaning that they generally relate to trade policy design or, more specifically, prudential measures.[26]

An examination of the wording of the FTA provisions follows. This is to ascertain the parties' intention to create legally binding commitments,

---

[22]   Commission, 'Report of the 21st TiSA Negotiation - Round 2' (10 November 2016). The relevance of TiSA also lies in the EU's ultimate goal to 'multilateralise' it in a second phase, EU Parliament resolution of 3 February 2016 Containing the European Parliament's Recommendations to the Commission on the negotiations for the Trade in Services Agreement (TiSA) [2016] No P8_TA(2016)0041.

[23]   The year taken as a reference is the year the text was signed. It allowed for chronological ordering of the EU FTAs, according to the expression of consent, regardless of the length of each country's ratification procedure.

[24]   Some relevant FTAs are currently under review, such as the 1999 EU-Azerbaijan Partnership and Cooperation Agreement, so their preliminary texts have not been analysed.

[25]   Based on the studies of Bourgeois, Dawar and Evenett (n 13).

[26]   The analysis of the features refers to the work of Adlung and Mamdouh (n 15), as well as Latrille's (n 15).

Table 13.1   List of FTAs considered

FTA	Sign-off	In force
EU-Japan Economic and Partnership Agreement	2018	2019
EU-Armenia Comprehensive and Enhanced Partnership Agreement	2017	2018*
New EU-Mexico Trade Agreement[a]	2018	Not yet
EU-Canada Comprehensive Economic Trade Agreement (CETA)[b]	2016	Not yet
EU-Vietnam FTA[c]	2016	2017*
Economic Partnership with SADC EPA	2016	2018
Enhanced Partnership and Cooperation Agreement between the EU and Kazakhstan[d]	2015	2020
EU-Ghana Economic Partnership	2015	2016*
Association Agreement with Georgia	2014	2016
Association Agreement with Moldova	2014	2016
EU-Singapore FTA	2014	2019
EU-Ukraine Deep and Comprehensive FTA	2014	2016
Association Agreement with Central America[e]	2012	Not yet
Trade Agreement with Colombia and Peru	2012	2016
EU-South Korea FTA	2010	2015
Stabilization and Association Agreement with Montenegro	2007	2010
Trade in Services Agreement (TiSA)	n/a	n/a
Association Agreement with Chile[f]	2002	2003

Notes: *   provisionally applied
[a]   The new EU-Mexico agreement was published on the EU Commission's official website in April 2018. The text of the chapter on financial services has been finalized and considered in the present study. This revised agreement in not yet into force but it will replace the 2000 EU-Mexico FTA.
[b]   Provisional application as from 21 September 2017 (Art 30.7)
[c]   The text considered in the present analysis is the 2016 EU-Vietnam FTA. At the moment of writing, a new EU-Vietnam FTA has been signed off, which is not entered into force yet.
[d]   Although the text of the 2015 EU-Kazakhstan FTA has been examined, a revision is planned by 2019 as part of the EU's strategy for Central Asia: European Parliament, 'Briefing on the New Central Asia Strategy' No EPRS BRI(2019)633162.
[e]   Part IV of the Agreement has been provisionally applied since 2013.
[f]   The text considered is the 2002 EU-Chile FTA, which is currently under review.

meaning the 'legal enforceability' of the provisions. Therefore, provisions containing 'shall' have been distinguished from those containing 'should', to discern between a genuine commitment as against aspirational goals.[27] This

---

[27]   The concept of legal enforceability applied in this study is the same concept conceived in the comparative study of Horn, Mavroidis and Sapir (n 6). This means the likelihood that a provision is 'successfully invoked by a complainant in a dispute settle-

exercise will establish the legal value of financial standard-related provisions and ascertain whether they create new commitments for states.

4. THE UNCHANGED VOLUNTARY NATURE OF INTERNATIONAL FINANCIAL STANDARDS INCORPORATED INTO EU FTAs

The analysis has shown that 13 FTAs out of 18 have included an express reference to international financial standards.[28] Most of the 13 FTAs have incorporated international financial standards into the financial services chapter, be it in a section under the general chapter on trade in services, or a stand-alone chapter. In most cases, the financial standard-related provisions have been inserted under the heading 'regulatory framework' within the discipline 'domestic regulation', as in the FTAs with Moldova, Georgia, Ukraine, South Korea, Columbia, Central America and Chile, for example.

By comparison, in the TiSA and the EU-Armenia FTA, a reference to international financial standards has been included under the subject 'transparency', this is within the financial services chapter in the TiSA, and within the general chapter on services in the EU-Armenia FTA. The EU-Vietnam FTA and the EU-Singapore FTA constitute peculiar examples, as a reference to international financial standards has been included under the subject of 'prudential measures'.

The wording of the financial standard-related provisions is very similar across the various FTAs. Despite minor differences, the provisions overall read as follows, 'Each Party shall make its best endeavor to ensure that internationally agreed standards for regulation and supervision in the financial services sector are implemented and applied in its territory.'[29] This wording, also known as the 'best-endeavour' clause, has a rather declaratory value. Some FTAs, along with the reference to international financial standards, also contain a very high-level cooperation principle, pursuant to ensuring standard compliance and provide a non-exhaustive list of international financial standards to be considered. For example, in a subset of FTAs with trade partners that can be classified as transition economies, the wording often includes an express reference to international standard-setters, such as the Basel Committee,

---

ment proceeding' and it does not automatically refer to the legally binding nature of the obligation itself derived from its inclusion into a hard law instrument, such as a treaty.

[28]   The FTAs that include financial standard-related provisions are TiSA and the FTAs negotiated with Armenia, Mexico, Vietnam, Kazakhstan, Georgia, Moldova, Singapore, Ukraine, Central American Countries, Peru, South Korea, and Chile.

[29]   TiSA, 2016 leaked text, Annex on Financial Services, X.15 'Transparency', para 6. Similar wording in the EU-Central America FTA and in the EU-Chile FTA.

IOSCO, the International Organization of Insurance Supervisors (IAIS), the Organization for Economic co-operation and Development (OECD), G20 and the Financial Action Task Force on Money Laundering (FATF).[30]

Overall, despite the presence of the word 'shall', the best-endeavour clause has a weak prescriptive power. The requirement upon the states is to apply and implement international financial standards through their best endeavour, which is susceptible to interpretation by those states as limiting the burden upon them to the minimum extent possible. In other words, these provisions simply encourage contracting parties to take into account international standards when regulating the financial sector, but without constituting a prescriptive imperative. It therefore appears that such provisions have a rather hortatory and aspirational value and they cannot limit a states' right to regulate the financial sector. Even in the EU-Vietnam FTA and in the EU-Singapore FTA, where a reference to international financial standards has been included under the prudential subject title, an effective obligation to build prudential measures on these standards remains questionable. Consequently, the legal enforceability of the FTA provisions, namely the likelihood of successfully bringing and winning a claim, is extremely weak. The original voluntary nature of international financial standards can arguably be 'hardened' by their mere inclusion in international treaties, given the lack of compulsory value attached to the relevant FTA provisions. This is relevant because international standards have frequently been accused of legitimacy and transparency deficits. Particularly in the financial sector, the standard-setting process of the Basel Committee, among other international bodies, has been heavily criticized for its limited participation, open to mostly advanced economies and just formally to developing countries, which do not get to influence decisional processes.[31] In this context, the production of voluntary financial standards is not contentious since it allows states to freely decide whether to follow them or not. A very different situation would occur if international financial standards, allegedly designed mainly by advanced economies, become compulsory by their incorporation into FTAs. In this regard, the present analysis shows that despite the incorporation of international financial standards into treaties, their voluntary nature remains unchanged.

As a note of clarification, the five FTAs that include no reference to international financial standards have not been further analysed. This is because

---

[30] A list of international standard-setters was included in the FTAs that the EU signed with Georgia, South-Korea, Columbia and Peru.
[31] Maziar Peihani, *Basel Committee on Banking Supervision. Part II: An Assessment of Governance and Legitimacy* (Brill 2016); Micheal S Barr and Geoffrey P Miller, 'Global Administrative Law: The View from Basel' (2006) 17 *European Journal of International Law* 15.

the FTAs that did not incorporate international financial standards comprised less than 30 per cent of the total cases, and could not therefore be deemed representative of the EU's recursive strategy in FTA drafting. Furthermore, the lack of reference to international financial standards in FTAs did not question the voluntary nature of these standards, which constitutes the question at issue.

However, CETA and the EU-Japan FTAs need to be singled out among the subset of FTAs that does not contain reference to international financial standards.[32] Given that Canada and Japan are the most similar trade partners to the EU, among the sample of countries analysed, both in terms of economic model and level of development, the lack of inclusion of international standards into their FTAs requires further reflection. While one could possibly argue that two instances are insufficient on which to base a theory, some speculations can be formulated. First, similar economic development allows for equivalent standards to be applied cross-country, with no need for a specific reference in FTAs. Second, geographical distance prevents these countries from being suitable candidates to the EU enlargement in pursuant of which the EU has shown more stringent standard alignment with its trading partners. This hypothesis is supported by the far-reaching harmonization objectives included in the FTAs with countries close to the EU borders, such as Armenia, where commitments to adjust to the EU framework are expressed as follows:

> The parties recognize the importance of the adequate regulation of financial services to ensure financial stability [...]. For such regulation of financial services the international best-practice standards provide the overall benchmark, in particular in the way they are implemented in the European Union. In that context, the Republic of Armenia shall approximate its regulation of financial services, as appropriate, to the legislation of the European Union.[33]

Therefore, geographical proximity, the EU's enlargement policy, and the level of economic development of trade partners, seem to play a role in the EU's FTA drafting. Whilst interesting, the influence that these factors have on the EU's policy design falls outside the scope of the present study, so it has not been investigated further.

---

[32]   The treaties are CETA and the FTAs with Japan, SADC, Montenegro and Ghana. The later three do not contain a proper section on financial services but rather an exhortation of a cooperative effort. This could be justified by assuming that the financial sector is not a key driver in their economies.

[33]   Art 189 of the EU-Armenia PTA.

5.   THE (NON) USE OF INTERNATIONAL FINANCIAL STANDARDS IN DISPUTE SETTLEMENT

Apart from the examination of the legal nature of international financial standards which have been incorporated into FTAs, the question as to whether these standards are used in dispute settlement, for interpretative reasons, or to assess the reasonableness of a measure, is equally relevant. Financial standard-related provisions in FTAs can come in handy to clarify treaty terms, such as 'prudential measures'. Similarly, international financial standards can be used as a benchmark to assess the 'reasonableness' of a trade restrictive measure. For example, they could help gauge whether specific requirements, such as capital requirements for banks, are reasonable or excessively high, compared to the level set by international financial standards.

Consequently, the use of international financial standards in dispute settlement becomes crucial to truly understand the role that these standards play in international economic law. The unchanged voluntary nature of the international financial standards incorporated into FTAs implies that these standards do not produce new obligations upon treaty parties, but it does not explain their international relevance. If WTO adjudicative bodies rely upon international financial standards in dispute settlement, their relevance would change from international guidelines to interpretative and assessment tools for the WTO regime.

As a practical example, we can consider the EU-Singapore FTA, which contains a financial standard-related provision under the prudential subject heading.[34] This provision would allow Singapore to introduce liquidity requirements for all banks operating in its market, based on international financial standards, in order to preserve domestic financial stability. Assuming that the liquidity requirements are consistent with both the EU-Singapore FTA and international financial standards, although potentially trade restrictive being contrary to WTO obligations, it is important to examine whether the WTO panel can, and should, consider the FTA and international financial standards in its analysis.

Theoretically, international financial standards could be useful to WTO adjudicative bodies in three circumstances. First, for interpretative reasons. Second, in cases where a presumption of consistency between international financial standards and the WTO regime exists, this would guarantee that a national measure based on financial standards is conformed with the WTO system. Third, when assessing the reasonableness of a measure, so using

---

[34]   Art 8.50 of the EU-Singapore FTA.

financial standards as a technical benchmark to establish whether the measure is justifiable or excessively burdensome.

In relation to the purpose of interpretation, as declared in Article 31(3)(c) of the Vienna Convention on the Law of Treaties (VCLT), any relevant rules of international law applicable to relations between the parties can be taken into account, together with the context, to clarify treaty terms. This means that the WTO Panel can refer to FTAs and financial standards as interpretative ancillary tools to clarify the meaning of WTO obligations.[35] While the use of external sources to WTO treaties for interpretative purposes is envisaged in Article 31(3)(c) VCLT, in reality, the number of cases where this exercise has been conducted is very low.[36] In order to use an external source to WTO treaties, the legal source has to be simultaneously a relevant rule of international law, applicable to the parties in a dispute and related to the same subject matter at issue.[37] The WTO case law shows that the use of legal sources which differ from the WTO treaties has been extremely rare.[38] As clearly emerged in the *EC-Banana* case, the recourse to sources other than the WTO agreements (in that case it was the Lomé Convention) are limited '[to] the extent necessary to interpret and apply WTO provisions'.[39] This approach acknowledges that not all disputes deal with ambiguities in treaty provisions, and that frequent clarifications can be found directly in the treaty without the need to consider external sources.

---

[35] Art 31 VCLT. As noted by the UN International Law Commission, different approaches to treaty interpretation can be adopted, such as the subjective, the textual and the teleological interpretation: ILC, 'Draft Articles on the Law of Treaties with Commentaries' (1966) 2 *Yearbook of the International Law Commission* 218.

[36] For a comprehensive analysis, see Isabelle Van Damme, 'What Role Is There for Regional International Law in the Interpretation of the WTO Agreements?' in Lorand Bartels and Federico Ortino (eds), *Regional Trade Agreements and the WTO Legal System* (OUP 2007); and Isabelle Van Damme, *Treaty Interpretation by the WTO Appellate Body* (OUP 2009).

[37] The WTO adjudicative bodies confirmed in the EC-Poultry case that the use of non-WTO law is generally excluded unless the treaty provisions are unclear and the subject matter of the external source is coincident with the subject matter in the dispute: WTO, *European Communities – Measures Affecting Importation of Certain Poultry Products – Report of the Appellate Body* (13 July 1998) WT/DS69/AB/R.

[38] Van Damme, 'What Role Is There for Regional International Law in the Interpretation of the WTO Agreements?' (n 36), 360–368. The Biotech Products case is one of the few exeptions where reliance upon external resources was shown: WTO, *European Communities – Measures Affecting the Approval and Marketing of Biotech Products – Report of the Panel* (29 September 2006) WT/DS291/R, WT/DS292/R, WT/DS293/R [7.67]–[7.70].

[39] WTO, *European Communities – Regime for the Importation, Sale and Distribution of Bananas – Report of the Appellate Body* (9 September 1997) WTO/DS27/AB/R [162]– [170]; *Report of the Panel* (22 May 1997) WTO/DS27/R [7.98].

The second use of international financial standards in dispute settlement relates to a general presumption of conformity of international standards to the WTO regime. The WTO adjudicative bodies could refer to international financial standards if a national measure that is based on these standards is automatically acknowledged as conforming to the WTO system. A presumption of conformity in the food sector has been stated in both Article 2 of the Agreement on Technical Barriers to Trade (TBT) and Article 3 of the Agreement on the Application of Sanitary and Phytosanitary Measures (SPS) and confirmed by the WTO jurisprudence.[40] Article 3(2) SPS reads, 'Sanitary or phytosanitary measures which conform to international standards, guidelines or recommendations shall be deemed to be necessary to protect human, animal or plant life or health, and presumed to be consistent with the relevant provisions of this Agreement and of GATT 1994.'[41] A similar presumption of conformity is expressed in the TBT agreement, which also allows WTO adjudicative bodies to use international standards when assessing the consistency of a national measure with the WTO regime.

By comparison, a similar presumption of conformity cannot be drawn from the GATS and the GATS Annex on financial services (the Annex). Not only does the WTO content on financial services lack any mention of international financial standards, but it also does not express any requirement to base national policies on them. In addition, while the SPS agreement lists the relevant international bodies that adopt food standards, the GATS and its Annex do not.[42] The difference between the food sector, on one hand, and the financial sector, on the other, challenges the assertion that a presumption of conformity of international financial standards to the WTO regime exists. Therefore, the WTO panel should not use international financial standards in dispute settlements to verify conformity to WTO agreements.

Finally, international financial standards can help in testing the adequacy of a measure, by providing numerical and economic data that can serve to gauge

---

[40]   A presumption of conformity in the food sector has been established in the WTO case law. Among others, see WTO, *European Communities – Measures Concerning Meat and Meat Products (Hormones) – Report of the Panel* (18 August 1997) WTO/DS26/R; *Report of the Appellate Body* (16 January 1998) WTO/DS26/AB/R. For TBT-related WTO cases see WTO, *European Communities – Trade Description of Sardines – Report of the Panel* (29 May 2002) WTO/DS231/R.

[41]   Art 3 of the Sanitary and Phytosanitary Agreement.

[42]   The list of the relevant international bodies is provided in para 3(a) and(c) of the SPS Annex A. For an overview of food safety regulation from a transnational perspective, see Hüller Thorsten and Maier M Leonhard, 'Fixing the Codex?: Global Food-Safety Governance under Review' in Christian Joerges and Ernst-Ulrich Petersmann (eds), *Constitutionalism, Multilevel Trade Governance and International Economic Law* (Hart Publishing 2011).

how reasonable and justifiable a measure is. For example, Basel III, adopted by Basel Committee, sets new minimum risk-based capital requirements for financial institutions, which should have as their total common equity 7 per cent of risked weighted assets, to demonstrate the soundness of their banking system.[43] If a state prescribes to Basel III requirements, the measures could be challenged before the WTO Dispute Settlement Body (DSB), if another state feels that they impair its rights or limit market access. If these capital requirements are incorporated into FTAs, the introduction of FTA-consistent measures by a state party can create trade restrictive effects and be challenged before the WTO DSB. The question is whether the WTO adjudicative bodies can assess the reasonableness of a measure against international financial standards or FTA obligations.

So far, recourse to international financial standards in WTO dispute settlement has never occurred. The WTO content on financial services has barely been challenged, with only the Argentina-Financial Services case being brought before the WTO DSB.[44] The dispute concerned eight financial and taxation measures imposed by Argentina on services and service suppliers from countries defined as 'non-cooperative jurisdictions', according to the international standards drafted by the FATF.[45] Argentina invoked the general exception, Article 16 of the GATS, and the prudential carve-out, paragraph 2(a) of the Annex,[46] to justify the claims raised by Panama. The adjudicative bodies partially addressed the application of the prudential carve-out. The panel clarified that a three-step test for prudential measures is required. First, verifying that a contested measure falls within the scope of paragraph 2(a) of the Annex. Second, ascertaining the causal link between the measure and the

---

[43] Basel III capital requirements are set to cover unexpected losses: Juan Ramirez, *Handbook of Basel III Capital: Enhancing Bank Capital in Practice* (John Wiley & Sons 2017).

[44] WTO, *Argentina – Measures Relating to Trade in Goods and Services – Report of the Panel* (30 September 2015) WTO/DS453/R; *Report of the Appellate Body* (14 April 2016) WTO/DS453/AB/R.

[45] The FATF has adopted several good practice guidelines to fight money laundering and terrorism. Argentina was a FATF member, whereas Panama was not. The latter was classified as a high-risk jurisdiction when the case arose http://www.fatfgafi.org/publications/fatfrecommendations, accessed August 2019.

[46] Para 2(a) of the Annex reads:
Notwithstanding any other provisions of the Agreement, a Member shall not be prevented from taking measures for prudential reasons, including for the protection of investors, depositors, policy holders or persons to whom a fiduciary duty is owed by a financial service supplier, or to ensure the integrity and stability of the financial system. Where such measures do not conform with the provisions of the Agreement, they shall not be used as a means of avoiding the Member's commitments or obligations under the Agreement.

prudential rationale behind it. Third, excluding the possibility that the measure was introduced to escape other WTO commitments.[47] However, neither the panel nor the appellate body mentioned FATF standards, or used them as a benchmark in the adequacy test of Argentina's taxation measures.

From a wider analysis of the WTO case law, recourse to sources which differ from WTO agreements overall remains limited. In the Brazil-tyres case, for example, the WTO Appellate body affirmed that the adequacy of a measure has to be assessed within WTO content, and should not be based on external legal sources or international tribunal rulings.[48] The Brazilian government banned imported retreated tyres in order to reduce the number of non-collected tyres, which was a major cause of mosquito-borne diseases. The EU challenged the measure at different stages, including before WTO DSB.[49] The appellate body found the measures inconsistent with the WTO agreements and clarified that the 'arbitrariness' and 'unjustifiability' of a measure should be assessed according to the object and the purpose of the measure itself, and not in consideration of a presumed compatibility with an international tribunal's ruling. Therefore, the causal effect between the rationale and the measure is not conditional upon an external legal source, but rather based on the adequacy test vis-à-vis the WTO regime.[50]

Finally, in the Peru-agricultural products case, the appellate body went even further by 'locking down' the WTO system from FTAs. It reaffirmed that the compatibility of a national measure with the WTO regime – and any potential justification – needs to be assessed within the WTO legal framework and not be based on external regulatory sources.[51] In this case, Peru introduced

---

[47]   WTO, *Argentina – Measures Relating to Trade in Goods and Services – Report of the Panel* (n 44) [7.931].

[48]   WTO, *Brazil – Measures Affecting Imports of Retreaded Tyres – Report of the Panel* (12 June 2007) WTO/DS332/R; *Report of the Appellate Body* (3 December 2007) WTO/DS332/AB/R.

[49]   First, the measure was challenged in the context of the MERCOSUR tribunal and the Brazilian government adopted some measures to comply with the tribunal's ruling. MERCOSUR ad hoc Arbitral Tribunal, *Import Prohibition of Remoulded Tyres from Uruguay (Uruguay v. Brazil)*, Award (Jan. 9, 2002).

[50]   WTO, *Brazil – Measures Affecting Imports of Retreated Tyres – Report of the Appellate Body* (n 48) [227]–[228].

[51]   More broadly, the case delved into the general compatibility of FTAs and the WTO regime. The present analysis focuses exclusively on the lack of recourse to FTAs in the adequacy test of a potentially trade restrictive measure. WTO, *Peru – Additional Duty on Imports of Certain Agricultural Products – Report of the Panel* (27 November 2014) WTO/DS457/R and *Report of the Appellate Body* (20 July 2015) WTO/DS457/AB/R.

a system that imposed additional duties on certain food products.[52] In response to Guatemala's claims, Peru justified the measure under the Peru-Guatemala FTA,[53] affirming that this subsequent agreement would modify WTO obligations between the treaty parties.[54] While the FTA was not considered because it was not in force, the appellate bodies clarified that, in all cases, the compatibility of an FTA should be ascertained under the WTO legal framework, rather than under principles of international law (Art 41 VCLT). This implies that relevant FTA provisions first need to be assessed against the WTO legal basis for FTAs (Arts 24 of the GATT and 5 of the GATS) and, if compatible, they may be used in the adequacy test for a challenged measure.[55] Given such a strict approach towards FTA provisions that contain substantive obligations, the reliance upon financial standard-related provisions in dispute settlement with a hortatory value, appears even more doubtful.

6.   CONCLUSION

FTAs have progressively widened their scope and overreached commitments undertaken within the WTO framework. At times, FTA provisions have been based on voluntary regulatory sources, such as international financial standards. The latter are highly technical instruments adopted by international standard-setters. They are characterized by a limited representation, which does not sufficiently involve transition and developing economies, and an opaque decision-making process, frequently referred to as a closed-door process.[56] The voluntary nature of international financial standards, recognized by a vast literature, does not raise concerns, as it allows states to utilise their

---

[52]   *Peru – Additional Duty on Imports of Certain Agricultural Products – Report of the Appellate Body,* ibid., [5.26]–[5.28].

[53]   Para 9 of Annex 2.3 of Tratado de Libre Comercio Guatemala-Peru signed on 6 December 2011, stated that 'Peru may maintain its PRS'. The FTA was not in force during the dispute settlement since both parties signed the FTA in December 2011 but only Guatemala ratified it in February 2014.

[54]   Subsequent treaty as defined in Art 41 of the VCLT.

[55]   *Peru – Additional Duty on Imports of Certain Agricultural Products – Report of the Appellate Body* (n 52) [5.94], [5.112]–[5.113]. For a rebuttal view on how different sources of international law should interact see: Lorand Bartels, 'Applicable Law in WTO Dispute Settlement Proceedings' (2001) 353 *Journal of World Trade* 499; Joost Pauwelyn, 'The Role of Public International Law in the WTO: How Far Can We Go?' (2001) 95 *American Journal of International Law* 535; and 'How to Win a World Trade Organization Dispute Based on Non-World Trade Organization Law?' (2003) 37 *Journal of World Trade* 997.

[56]   Jean Cohen and Charles F Sabel, 'Global Democracy' (2005) 37 *NYU Journal of International Law and Policy* 763; Roman Grynberg and Sacha Silva, 'Harmonization without Representation: Small States, the Basel Committee, and the WTO', (2006) 34

discretion to decide whether to follow these regulatory tools. Conversely, if the original nature of these standards became compulsory through their incorporation of into FTAs, questions on legitimacy and legality will quickly emerge. Therefore, the first part of this chapter examined whether the nature of financial standards 'hardened' by their incorporation into treaties. The analysis of the most recent EU FTAs has shown a recurrent trend to incorporate financial standards into EU's FTAs. However, the financial standards-related provisions have a rather hortatory value. Indeed, the so called 'best-endeavour' clause introduces an aspirational goal by encouraging states to take financial standards into account when regulating the financial sector, but without imposing any prescriptive obligations upon them. Even if the FTAs concluded with potential EU members and neighbouring trade partners aim at a more stringent alignment of standards, the wording used to incorporate financial standards into the thirteen FTAs considered can doubtfully create new obligations upon states. For this reason, they are unlikely to produce legally binding effects, which demonstrates the unchanged voluntary nature of financial standards.

However, the examination of their legal value does not sufficiently clarify the role that financial standards play in international trade law. Indeed, the hortatory value of the financial standard-related provisions does not prevent WTO adjudicative bodies from considering them in dispute settlement. Financial standards and FTA provisions can come in handy for interpretative purposes and in the adequacy test of a trade measure, which includes the assessment of its reasonableness and justifiability. The second part of the chapter has been devoted to WTO case law. Overall, the WTO jurisprudence has revealed a limited reliance upon external sources to WTO treaties. For interpretative reasons, recourse to Article 31(3)(c), which allows the use of 'any relevant rules of international law', has been extremely rare. Ambiguities in treaty terms have been solved by looking at WTO treaties, rather than elsewhere. Likewise, a presumption of conformity of national measures based on international financial standards to the WTO regime, has been rejected. While the SPS agreement and the TBT agreement contain an open presumption of conformity of international food standards with the WTO treaties, GATS and the Annex on financial services, do not. No use of international financial standards or FTA provisions in the assessment of an allegedly trade restrictive measure has emerged from the WTO case law. In the Argentina-financial services case, FATF standards were not considered by the appellate body, even if the challenged measure was based on these standards. Similarly, in the Brazil-tyres case and the Peru-agricultural products case, the appellate body affirmed that

World Development 1223; Lazaros E Panourgias, *Banking Regulation and World Trade Law* (Hart Publishing 2006).

the adequacy test of a measure – and any justification – need to be based on the WTO legal framework and not on external regulatory sources.

To conclude, the mere inclusion of voluntary financial standards in treaties does not automatically 'harden' their nature. The wording of the relevant provisions reveal that the parties' aim in the case of financial standards is aspirational. The unchanged voluntary nature of financial standards has been confirmed by the WTO adjudicative bodies, which have not relied upon financial standards and standard-related FTA provisions in dispute settlement. This counters the assertion that international financial standards, mainly negotiated by developed countries, have illegitimately turned into compulsory FTA requirements. Therefore, from the analysis of both EU FTAs and WTO jurisprudence, states' right to regulate the financial sector remains preserved.

PART III

International courts and tribunals upholding the rule of law

14. Some remarks on the contribution of UN courts and tribunals to the rule of law and the unity of international law

Fausto Pocar

1. Any discussion regarding the contribution offered by international courts and tribunals in building the international rule of law is by no means straight-forward. The main difficulty lies in defining the rule of law while taking into account the multifaceted features of international society as opposed to the more structured nature of a community organised as a state, as well as in the role of the sources of international law as compared with the sources of state law. Thus, the debate inevitably starts with a preliminary but fundamental question: is there an international rule of law?

In light of the Charter of the United Nations – the guiding document of the world's pre-eminent intergovernmental organisation – this question may seem an easy one, with the answer being found in the Charter itself, as well as in the numerous declarations subsequently adopted for its implementation. The preamble of this globally accepted treaty appears to contain elements that suitably characterise a rule of law applicable in an international context, most evident in one of the organisation's aims 'to establish conditions under which justice and respect for the obligations arising from treaties and other sources of international law can be maintained'.[1]

Without mentioning the numerous UN documents referring – directly or indirectly – to the rule of law, it is worth noting that a meeting was convened in 2012 by the General Assembly, with a view of defining this concept and strengthening the states' commitment to observe it. Following the meeting a declaration was adopted on the rule of law at both the national and interna-tional levels,[2] which underlines the fundamental importance of the rule of law for the development of the three main pillars upon which the UN is built: inter-

---

[1]   Preamble of the Charter of the United Nations (24 October 1945) 1 UNTS XVI, 3rd recital.
[2]   UNGA, Declaration of the High-level Meeting of the General Assembly on the Rule of Law at the National and International Levels (24 September 2012) A/Res/67/1.

national peace and security, human rights and development. The Declaration further recognises that the rule of law 'applies to all States equally, and to international organisations, including the UN and its principal organs, and that respect for and promotion of the rule of law should guide all of their activities and accord predictability and legitimacy to their actions'.[3] With respect to UN institutions, including the International Court of Justice (ICJ) and other international courts and tribunals, it recognises their positive contribution in advancing the rule of law at both the national and international levels.[4]

Despite this clear institutional approach, the existence of an international rule of law has been challenged in legal literature. It has been pointed out on one hand, that in understanding public international law, an approach solely based on legal positivism neglects to consider the variety of actors that partic-ipate in the international politico-legal sphere besides states, especially inter-national organisations whose practice produces an informal 'soft' law, which should also be regarded as law.[5] In that respect, a mere reference to the sources of international law – codified in Article 38 of the Statute of the International Court of Justice – does not capture the variety of the sources of the rules that are applicable to international life. On the other hand, the myriad of existing international organisations make the assessment of an international rule of law rather problematic as is appears that there are no clear rules which make such organisations, including the UN, accountable for human rights violations, with the general rule on jurisdictional immunity tending to prevail in any case.[6]

In this context, and in refraining to dwell further on the possibility of defining a comprehensive and well-established notion of the rule of law which would govern international life, this chapter will only refer to elements commonly perceived as essential to any description of the rule of law and will attempt to discuss how UN international courts and tribunals may and have already con-tributed to ensuring respect for such fundamental elements. In doing so, this chapter will take as a postulate that any description of the rule of law would accept the principle that the law should be applied by a court in a coherent and consistent manner, with a view to ensuring legal predictability. Consequently,

---

[3]   Ibid., para 2.
[4]   Ibid., paras 31–32. The Declaration deals separately (para 23) with the role of the International Criminal Court, as the ICC is not a UN institution.
[5]   See particularly Jose E Alvarez, *The Impact of International Organizations on International Law* (Leiden 2017) 1 et seq.
[6]   See e.g., Supreme Court of The Netherlands, *Mothers of Srebrenica et al v The Netherlands and the United Nations,* Judgement of 13 April 2012, Asser Institute www .internationalcrimesdatabase.org, accessed 4 July 2021, concluding that the UN enjoys absolute immunity from jurisdiction, regardless of the extreme seriousness of the accu-sations brought by the claimants (victims of the crime of genocide) in that case.

this chapter will briefly discuss whether UN courts and tribunals are structured in such a way that favours the consistency of international law, and whether they can avoid fragmentation of the law and ensure legal predictability.

2. The judicial system of the UN is developed only to a limited extent, as compared with the judicial system of other international organisations, e.g., the European Union, and is essentially based on the International Court of Justice (ICJ). While Article 92 of the UN Charter declares that 'the International Court of Justice is the principal judicial organ of the United Nations', no other judicial body is instituted, or has its creation envisaged within the Charter itself. Rather, Article 95 seems to exclude the establishment of other tribunals by stating that 'nothing in the present Charter shall prevent Members of the United Nations from entrusting the solution of their differences to other tribunals by virtue of agreements already in existence or which may be concluded in the future'. Moreover, this provision is in line with the nature of the ICJ's jurisdiction, which is not compulsory and must be accepted by the state parties in order for a dispute to be be submitted to the Court. As recalled by the ICJ itself, 'its jurisdiction is based on the consent of the parties and is confined to the extent accepted by them'.[7]

Under these circumstances, any issues of inconsistency and fragmentation of the applicable law were hardly foreseeable before one single court, and the characterisation of the ICJ as the 'principal' judicial organ of the UN was regarded as an expression of homage to the Court as opposed to an operative provision. The Court's relationship with the United Nations Administrative Tribunal (UNAT) did not require such characterisation with the latter's jurisdiction being limited to decide upon alleged violations of employment contracts or terms of staff members of the organisation's Secretariat.[8] Moreover, in terms of the applicable law by UNAT, which is limited to internal pertinent regulations and rules in force at the time of their alleged non observance, any inconsistency with the law applicable by the ICJ would have been difficult to envisage, save perhaps for fundamental principles of human rights law, even if a specific reference to them was not made in the UNAT statute.[9]

---

[7]   *Immunities and Criminal Proceedings (Equatorial Guinea v France)*, Preliminary Objections, Judgment [2018] ICJ Rep (I) 307, para 42.

[8]   Art 2(1) of the UNAT Statute (24 November 1949) A/RES/351 A (IV).

[9]   The situation has not changed with the replacement of the UNAT by the UN Appeals Tribunal. See August Reinisch and Christina Knahr, 'From the United Nations Administrative Tribunal to the United Nations Appeals Tribunal – Reform of the Administration of Justice System within the United Nations' (2008)12 *Max Planck UNYB* 474-475.

3. Notwithstanding this institutional framework, it is well known that subsequently two ad hoc tribunals – the International Criminal Tribunal for the former Yugoslavia (ICTY) in 1993[10] and the International Criminal Tribunal for Rwanda (ICTR) in 1994[11] – were established by the Security Council under Chapter VII of the Charter to face the threat to peace and security presented by the serious and widespread violations of international humanitarian law during the conflict in the former Yugoslavia and by the Rwandan genocide respectively. Although these two tribunals were not permanent courts and could be regarded as subsidiary organs of the Security Council, they were judicial organs of the UN. They were requested to report on their activity not only to the Security Council but also to the General Assembly, with their judges being elected by the General Assembly from a list submitted by the Security Council as well as being given the same status as their ICJ counterparts. Moreover, these tribunals were given criminal jurisdiction for the prosecution of individuals responsible for the violations of international humanitarian law and for genocide, but they had no jurisdiction over possible state responsibility for such violations, if committed by state agents. Consequently, their jurisdiction did not overlap with the jurisdiction of the ICJ, as only states may be parties in cases before the court.[12]

However, the law that these new judicial organs of the UN were called to apply was customary international law[13] and, to some extent, treaty law.[14] Moreover, by its nature, the application of international criminal law implied, besides the identification of the elements of the crimes under international law, a wide and frequent reference to principles recognised as law to be drawn from domestic legal systems, particularly with respect to the criteria governing individual criminal responsibility.[15] In sum, the same sources of law applied that the ICJ is mandated to refer to when deciding interstate disputes in accordance with international law.[16] Consequently, the possibility of different assessments and interpretations of the law could arise, and could lead to a divergent or

---

[10]   S/RES/827 (1993) of 25 May 1993.
[11]   S/RES/955 (1994) of 8 November 1994.
[12]   Art 34 ICJ Statute.
[13]   See Report of the Secretary-General pursuant to Paragraph 2 of SC Resolution 808 (1993) (3 May 1993) S/25704, para 34.
[14]   See *Prosecutor v Dusko Tadic*, Case No. IT-94-1-AR 72, Decision on the Defence motion for Interlocutory Appeal on Jurisdiction (2 October 1995), para 74.
[15]   Except for some principles that were specifically elaborated on criminal responsibility for crimes under international law after the Nuremberg experience (command and superior responsibility, liability for implementing illegal orders, no immunity for heads of states and members of governments).
[16]   Art 38 ICJ Statute.

fragmented application of international law, with a possible negative impact on its predictability.

This was a known issue to the drafters of the statutes of the ICTY and of the ICTR. However, since there was no overlap of jurisdiction between the ICJ and these new tribunals, they only took care to prevent inconsistencies in the case law of these two courts, by adopting a provision whereby the members of the Appeals Chamber of the ICTY were also mandated to serve as the members of the Appeals Chamber of the ICTR.[17] The same composition of the chamber at the appeal stage helped to prevent inconsistencies not only in the application of the substantive law, but also in the procedural approaches to the treatment of the cases brought to the attention of each of these tribunals.[18] With regard to that it should also be noted that the ICTY Appeals Chamber decided that 'in the interest of certainty and predictability' it would follow its own precedent, except for being free to depart from it 'for cogent reasons in the interests of justice', but that such an exception was not available to the lower chambers, as 'a proper construction of the Statute requires that the *ratio decidendi* of its decisions is binding on Trials Chambers'.[19] Although this decision formally sets an obligation for the trial chambers of the ICTY, in light of the composition of the Appeals Chamber of the ICTR it also applied to the latter's trial chambers.

4. By contrast, the risk that there might be inconsistencies in the interpretation and application of international law by the newly created international criminal tribunals and the ICJ did materialise with the famous dispute about the degree of control required to attribute the acts of a military or paramilitary group to a state, for the purposes of characterising a prima facie domestic conflict as international. The ICJ had concluded that 'effective control' was necessary,[20] while the ICTY criticised that conclusion as being unpersuasive and at variance with judicial and state practice and maintained that 'overall control' was sufficient.[21]

---

[17]   Art 12 ICTR Statute. This provision was subsequently supplemented by an amendment whereby the number of the appeals judges was increased by two judges to be appointed by the president of the ICTR from within its members.

[18]   It should be recalled that the rules of procedure and evidence of the two ad hoc tribunals were almost identical, as the ICTR adopted those adopted one year earlier by the ICTY only with minor amendments.

[19]   *Prosecutor v Zlatko Aleksovski*, Case No. IT-95-14/1-A, Judgment (24 March 2000), paras 197, 113.

[20]   *Military and Paramilitary Activities in and against Nicaragua (Nicaragua v United States of America)*, Judgment (Merits) [1986] ICJ Rep 14, para 115.

[21]   *Prosecutor v Dusko Tadic*, Case No. IT-94-1-A, Judgment (15 July 1999), para 131.

Without going into the details of this well-known debate, it is worth recalling that this prompted a further debate on whether the consideration that the ICJ is the principal judicial organ of the UN should lead it to formally establish a hierarchy between the ICJ and other judicial organs.

Taking into account this view, it has been suggested that the ICJ should have the authority to determine the applicable standards and substance of international law via an appellate or review jurisdiction over decisions of the other judicial organs, or perhaps relying on the establishment of a procedure whereby other judicial organs may seek advisory opinions from the ICJ concerning important, unresolved points of general international law raised by the cases before them.[22] Additionally, this procedure could be extended to international courts that are not UN bodies,[23] thus contributing more generally to avoiding fragmentation and ensuring the certainty and predictability of international law.

This position has been challenged as being unworkable with its shortcomings outweighing possible advantages. A different view has been maintained, advocating interaction between international courts as a preferable approach to ensure coherence in both the interpretation and application of international law and reduce the risk of a fragmentation that may affect certainty and predictability.[24] Through this approach, it should be for judges to keep information on each other's judgments, to have respect for each other's judicial work, and try to preserve unity among decisions unless context prevents this.[25]

This second approach is not just largely preferable but it is also the only viable solution in a context where no clear hierarchy between UN courts is discernible, and the ICJ jurisdiction is based on the consent of the parties to submit a dispute to its consideration.

Following this approach, a forthright dialogue between the interested judicial organs of the UN resolved the main legal divergence that occurred between them, i.e., the legal dispute on the degree of control over the military or paramilitary required to make a domestic armed conflict into an international one. It is true that, when it reverted to this issue in the *Genocide* case,[26] the ICJ

---

[22]　See particularly Gilbert Guillaume, 'Advantages and Risks of Proliferation. A Blueprint for Action', (2004) 2 *Journal of International Criminal Justice* 300, 302.

[23]　Ibid., 303.

[24]　See particularly for this approach Rosalyn Higgins, 'A Babel of Judicial Voices? Ruminations from the Bench', in Rosalyn Higgins, *Themes and Theories. Selected Essays, Speeches, and Writings in International Law, vol 2*, (2009)1256, 1263.

[25]　Ibid.

[26]　*Application of the Convention on the Prevention and Punishment of the Crime of Genocide (Bosnia and Herzegovina v Serbia and Montenegro)*, Judgment [2007] ICJ Reports 43, paras 396–406.

responded to the arguments raised by the ICTY in the *Tadic* judgment[27] and reaffirmed the position it had taken in the *Nicaragua* case.[28] But it also stated that the position referred only to assessing state responsibility, an issue that was to be regarded as distinguished from individual criminal responsibility, and limited itself to finding that the 'overall control' test immensely broadened the scope of state responsibility well beyond the fundamental principle governing the law of international responsibility. Thus, it left open the possibility that such a test may be applicable and suitable with respect to individual criminal responsibility. It is a credit to the ICJ to have gone for a such a composition of the dispute, rather than for extending it with additional arguments, although the solution taken may not be final, as it had been considered and rejected in the *Tadic* judgment.[29] However, no further response came from the ICTY.

5. Furthermore, an approach based on a dialogue between courts is preferable and should be encouraged as it may contribute to achieving unity of interpretation and solutions. This dialogue-based approach would not only be preferable with respect to the judicial bodies of the UN, but also in addressing the divergent approaches between such bodies and the quasi-judicial bodies of the UN. These quasi-judicial bodies include the monitoring bodies established on the basis of UN human rights conventions, particularly when they deal with individual communications. Also between them and judicial tribunals and courts with UN participation such as the International Tribunal for the Law of the Sea, the International Criminal Court, several hybrid criminal courts established by country-specific agreements concluded by the UN and even between international judicial bodies entirely external to the UN, as it the case of many regional courts.

First, the examples of cases where decisions taken in an international court have been influential upon decisions taken in another international or regional court are numerous and cannot be discussed here. In the absence of any hierarchy between them, there is no obligation of any such court to follow the case law of another court as a precedent, barring exceptional cases. However, it is understandable for any international court to be inclined to take into account the views expressed by another international court in reaching its decision, especially on a point of law.[30] This is largely due to the specialised subject

---

27   *Prosecutor v Dusko Tadic*, Judgment (n 21).
28   *Military and Paramilitary Activities in and against Nicaragua* (n 20).
29   *Prosecutor v Dusko Tadic*, Judgment (n 21), paras 102–114.
30   Less frequently it may also occur with respect to the assessment of facts, especially when a court is not equipped for hearing a large number of witnesses, as it was the case of the ICJ in the *Genocide* case (n 26), where the conclusion that genocide occurred in Srebrenica was largely grounded on the assessment of facts made by the ICTY in the *Krstic* case.

matter jurisdiction which many international courts and tribunals have. This invites other courts that may have to deal with an incidental issue concerning that subject matter to take into account the conclusions adopted by the specialised court. This is particularly the case with respect to human rights courts. Human rights incidental issues may arise in any kind of jurisdiction, and courts not specifically devoted to adjudicating these issues frequently rely on the jurisprudence of specialised courts or specialised quasi-judicial bodies to address them.[31]

6. Additionally, a dialogue between courts may not only contribute to the maintenance of the unity of international law by showing regard for the precedent established by another court, or by resolving a conflict between diverging positions arising in different courts, but also by clarifying a legal issue when contradictory views have been expressed by different chambers of one court.

An example is useful in this respect. Reference can be made to the debate within the ICTY regarding the definition of the mode of criminal responsibility being of 'aiding and abetting'. The ICTY jurisprudence had found, after an exhaustive analysis of international practice that, under customary international law, liability for aiding and abetting required providing substantial contribution to the commission of a crime, accompanied by the awareness that the assistance provided represented a substantial contribution.[32] This was the consistent case law for many years, and was repeatedly confirmed by the Appeal Chamber,[33] until an appeal judgment, in the *Perisic* case, deviated from the consolidated case law by adding a requirement to the definition of this mode of liability – in a case in which the accused was remote from the crime scene – represented by the 'specific direction' of the assistance (in the specific case, provision of weapons) to the commission of the crime.[34] This judgment was highly criticised both inside and outside the ICTY, and was later discussed in the Special Court for Sierra Leone (SCSL), which had to decide, in the *Taylor*

---

[31]   See, e.g., on the concept of torture the reference made by the ICTY to the Human Rights Committee under the ICCPR, in *Prosecutor v Dragoljub Kunarac et al*, Case No. IT-96-23-T, Judgment (22 February 2001), paras 480–481.

[32]   *Prosecutor v Anto Furundija*, Case No. IT-95-17/1-T, Judgment (10 December 1998), para 249.

[33]   See *Prosecutor v Tihomir Blaskic*, Case No. IT-95-14-A, Judgment (29 July 2004), para 46; *Prosecutor v Mile Mrskic and Veselin Sljivancanin*, Case No. IT-95-13/1-A, Judgment (5 May 2009), para 159; *Prosecutor v Milan Lukic and Sredoje Lukic*, Case No. IT-98-32/1-A, Judgment (4 December 2012), para 424.

[34]   *Prosecutor v Momcilo Perisic*, Case No. IT-04-81-A, Judgment (28 February 2013), para 36. It must be noted that the conclusion in this case was reached on the ground of a cursory interpretation of the previous case law, rather than on a concrete assessment of customary international law.

case,[35] on whether the accused aided and abetted the crimes perpetrated by rebel forces in Sierra Leone. The SCSL Appeals Chamber conducted detailed research into international practice and concluded that the *Perisic* decision was incorrect and inconsistent with customary international law.[36] A few months later, the ICTY Appeals Chamber reconsidered the question, in the light of new research also including the decision reached by the SCSL, and concluded in the *Sainovic* case,[37] that the *Perisic* approach was in direct and material conflict with the prevailing jurisprudence on the *actus reus* of aiding and abetting and with customary international law, thereby returning to the previous case law of the tribunal on the matter. A subsequent appeal judgment of the ICTY, in the *Stanisic and Simatovic* case, further concluded the debate by quashing a trial judgment which had applied the notion of aiding and abetting characterised by the specific direction requirement, and ordering a retrial based on the notion as affirmed by the case law without such a requirement.[38]

Here it is notable that a consensus was reached regarding a legal issue through both the role of case law of an international court and the contribution of another court. The example given also shows how the dialogue between different courts and tribunals may concur to clarifications, which has potential to have a significant impact on general questions of international law, an example being the individual criminal responsibility for providing weapons that may be used to commit crimes under international law.

7. In the light of the above, one could conclude that the UN courts and tribunals' substantial contribution to an international rule of law has so far succeeded in preventing fragmentation of international law, notwithstanding the proliferation of these judicial bodies and the absence of any mechanism for structured coordination between them. Divergent positions were expressed, and will no doubt be expressed in the future, but this is inherent in any legal debate, and does not mean that it leads to fragmentation of the law. Rather, if it is carried out seriously and with reasoned arguments, it enriches the law and contributes to its development. Any field of law is not static; it is a process which develops within the society from which it applies and according to the development of that said society, influencing or reflecting such development. This is especially the case for international law, which applies in a 'society'

---

[35] *Prosecutor v Charles Ghankay Taylor*, Case No. SCSL-03-01-A, Judgment (26 September 2013), paras 466–486.

[36] Ibid., para 481.

[37] *Prosecutor v Nikola Sainovic et al*, Case No. IT-05-87-A, Judgment (23 January 2014), para 1650.

[38] *Prosecutor v. Jovica Stanisic and Franko Simatovic*, Case No. IT-03-69-A, Judgment (9 December 2015), paras 108 and 131.

that lacks strong structures such as the international community and is characterised by sources with a strong customary component. Therefore, a debate between judicial actors about such a normative process is not surprising and is worth encouraging rather than restricting.

The dialogue in which international courts and tribunals have been engaged has been generally productive, particularly when it has focused on issues concerning the interpretation and application of customary international law. The situation may be different when the application of international conventions, whether general or particular, has been the object of a dispute. This is unavoidable to a certain extent because, in deciding a dispute on the grounds of a treaty, a court must rely on the rules specifically recognized by the parties to the treaty, who are – in principle – entitled to derogate from general law in favour of a special regulation of their relationship, which they deem more suitable to protect their interests. But no duty to prevent or avoid fragmentation may reasonably be ascribed to a court when fragmentation lies in the law it is called to apply.

A special consideration may have to be observed regarding general international conventions aimed at codifying customary international law, while at the same time developing it and filling in gaps, with a view to making its interpretation easier and its application more predictable. These conventions significantly contribute to unity and predictability of international law, but only if they are ratified by most of the states or if they are regarded as merely reflecting customary international law, entirely or in part, at the time in which they are applied, which may of course be different from the time of their conclusion. If this is not the case they may, paradoxically, contribute to the fragmentation of international law, especially when they do not codify customary law entirely, but only to a limited extent.

How could international courts and tribunals, established on the basis of such general conventions or mandated to apply them, contribute to the unity of international law in those situations? It is proposed that a tool they should make use of is to consider interpreting these conventions in the light of customary international law, thereby achieving unitary solutions. A couple of examples may clarify when such an approach would be justified to prevent fragmentation of international law.

Article III of the Convention on the Prevention and Punishment of the Crime of Genocide,[39] which unanimously reflects customary international law, lists the acts that shall be punishable with respect to genocide, comprising among them 'conspiracy to commit genocide' (lett. *c*). Unlike the statutes of the ICTY and of the ICTR, when dealing with genocide, the Rome Statute of the

---

[39]   Adopted by the UNGA on 9 December 1948, 78 UNTS 277 (1951).

ICC does not reproduce textually Article III of the Convention, but uses its provisions within the framework of a general rule on the modes of individual criminal liability (Article 25). In doing so, it omits to mention conspiracy, with the consequence that conspiracy would not be punishable as a crime per se, irrespective of the actual occurrence of genocide, but only if genocide is perpetrated. Should a case of mere conspiracy be brought before the ICC, an acquittal of the accused would run against the convictions that have been pronounced by the ICTY and ICTR under customary international law, as reflected in the 1948 Convention.[40] Should, in such a case, the ICC resort to customary international law to maintain the unity of international law thus preventing a fragmentation due to an incomplete codification of the international law on genocide? In my view it should to the extent that its statute allows it to apply, where appropriate, the principles and rules of international law.[41]

A similar approach would be further justified when the restriction of the law applicable under the Rome Statute as compared with customary international law may impact on human rights protection, as is the case of the crime of persecution, which is punishable under the ICC Statute only when it is committed in connection with another crime within the jurisdiction of the Court,[42] while this connection is not required under customary international law. Furthermore, as the application and interpretation of the law made by the Court must be consistent with internationally recognised human rights.[43]

In conclusion, an appropriate reference to customary international law by international courts and tribunal may play a significant role in contributing to keep the unity of international law also when fragmentation is due to conventional legislation.[44] The international judiciary has here an important role to play.

---

[40]   See, e.g., as to the ICTY and the ICTR respectively: *Prosecutor v Vujadin Popovic et al*, Case No. IT-05-88-A, Judgment (30 January 2015), para 538; and *Prosecutor v Jean-Baptiste Gatete*, Case No. ICTR-00-61-A, Judgment (9 October 2012), para 260.

[41]   Art 21(1)(b) ICC Statute.

[42]   Art 7(1)(h) ICC Statute.

[43]   Art 21(3) ICC Statute.

[44]   See also Fausto Pocar, 'Transformation of Customary Law through ICC Practice' (2018)112 *American Journal of International Law Unbound* 182.

15. Old stage, new actors: The PCA as a platform for an evolving rule of law

Hugo H. Siblesz

1.   INTRODUCTION

This chapter will look at the role of international dispute settlement mechanisms in upholding the rule of law. It will do this from the perspective of the Permanent Court of Arbitration (PCA), the very first intergovernmental organisation specifically created in 1899 to deal with State-related international disputes through arbitration, mediation, conciliation and fact-finding.

Over time, the docket of cases that the PCA handles has broadened beyond inter-State disputes to also include 'mixed disputes', i.e., disputes involving a public element, anything from contractual disputes involving State-owned or State-related entities, to disputes involving international organisations and, last but not least, investor-State arbitrations under treaties for the protection of investment and investment laws.

So much so for the PCA's pedigree.

Around 400 years ago the Globe theatre held a performance of Shakespeare's 'Richard II'. The setting for the opening scene, as you may know, is an arbitration. King Richard has been called upon to resolve a dispute between two noblemen that concerns the fall-out from an act of violence and allegations of misuse of State funds. At the time of the III LAwTTIP Conference, March 2019, that same play was being performed at the Globe. Like the theatre itself, the production was updated since the 1600s. The new cast was made up entirely of women of colour and the production was described as a 'post-Empire reflection on what it means to be British in the light of the Windrush anniversary and as we leave the European Union'.[1] The performance has been acclaimed as a pioneering retelling, 'buzz[ing] with Brexit topicality'.[2]

---

[1]   'Richard II' (*Shakespeare Globe: What's on*, March 2019) https://www.shakespearesglobe.com/whats-on-2018/richard-ii, accessed 21 November 2020.
[2]   Michael Billington, 'Richard II Review – Women of Colour's Blazing Show Reflects our Current Chaos' https://www.theguardian.com/stage/2019/mar/07/richard

Old Theatre. New Actors. New Context

This illustrates the theme of this chapter, which is how the PCA has adapted to accommodate new actors, in the context of new challenges. To that purpose, this chapter will share examples from the PCA's 120-year history in which tribunals supported by the PCA have upheld the rule of law for an evolving cast of actors – traditionally States, but also today international or 'supranational' organisations such as the EU, NGOs, companies, trade unions, and individuals. This evolution has led the PCA to become involved in a wide range of instruments relating to modern-day concerns – not only the Brexit Withdrawal Agreement[3] – but also in the context of feuds over frontiers, free trade, fisheries, and fast fashion.

The chapter is organised as follows: it first provides an overview of the original rationale for the creation of international arbitration as a tool to resolve cross-border differences peacefully and of the role of the PCA (2). It then moves to analyse some of the key areas of current work of the PCA (3) (4). Section 5 looks at how its neutrality and flexibility allow arbitration to live up to new challenges in upholding the rule of law internationally, giving the example of business and human rights arbitration. The chapter concludes with some thoughts on what's next.

2.   ARBITRATION AS AN ALTERNATIVE TO VIOLENCE

King Richard II, in Shakespeare's account, may not have been the ideal arbitrator from a modern perspective. For one, his independence was dubious – as the cousin of one party, the nephew of the murder victim, and indeed a suspect in the underlying crime. Second, he did not deploy the most sensible measures as arbitrator: when it all got too difficult, he chose to rely on divine intervention and a duel by swords to resolve the dispute, only to change his mind again and banish both parties from the kingdom.[4]

-ii-review-lynette-linton-adjoa-andoh-sam-wanamaker-playhouse,   accessed   21 November 2020.

[3]   UK Government, Agreement on the withdrawal of the United Kingdom of Great Britain and Northern Ireland from the European Union and the European Atomic Energy Community (Withdrawal Agreement) https://www.gov.uk/government/publications/new-withdrawal-agreement-and-political-declaration, accessed 21 November 2020.

[4]   William Shakespeare, *Richard II*, Sam Johnson, Geo Stevens (eds) (Bell 1786) Act I, Scene 1, 15: 'There shall your swords and lances arbitrate; The swelling difference of your settled hate.'

In the Netherlands, not long after Richard II was performed for the first time at the Globe, the scholar Hugo Grotius set out:

> three Ways whereby Misunderstandings among Princes may be accommodated without a War:
>
>> The first is by a Conference (i.e., *negotiation*) [...]
>>
>> The second way to prevent War between those, who, not belonging to the same Jurisdiction, have no common Judge to appeal to, is to put the Matter to Arbitration [...]
>>
>> The third Way to prevent War is to determine Differences by casting lots.[5]

The key features of arbitration were memorialised in the PCA's founding document – the 1899 Hague Convention for the Pacific Settlement of International Disputes (1899 Hague Conference). The treaty was the product of the first Hague Peace Conference held at the initiative of Tsar Nicholas II of Russia.[6] The PCA's founding fathers envisaged a world governed by the rule of law, rather than force. The contrast with the way Europe 'sleepwalked' into the Great War only 15 years later could not be greater.

The 1899 Hague Conference recognised arbitration as the 'most equitable and efficient means of resolving disputes where diplomacy has failed', whereby consent to refer their dispute to decision-makers of their choosing, on the basis of respect for law, applying flexible procedures to be agreed to suit the circumstances of the case. The treaty also established the PCA as a permanent framework to be 'accessible at all times' with the 'object of facilitating an immediate recourse to arbitration for international differences'.[7]

The role of arbitration as a means to settle disputes between states continues to be recognised in international agreements (cf, the UN Charter and the UN

---

[5] Hugo Grotius, *Of the Rights of War and Peace: In Three Volumes: in which are Explained the Laws and Claims of Nature and Nations, and the Principal Points that Relate Either to Public Government, Or the Conduct of Private Life: Together with the Author's Own Notes: Done Into English by Several Hands: with the Addition of the Author's Life by the Translators: Dedicated to His Royal Highness the Prince of Wales*, Vol 2 (Printed for D Brown, T Ward, W Meares 1715), 595–600.

[6] See generally, Brooks W Daly, 'Permanent Court of Arbitration' in Chiara Giorgetti (ed) *The Rules, Practice, and Jurisprudence of International Courts and Tribunals* (Brill 2012) 37; Hans Jonkman, 'The Role of the Permanent Court of Arbitration in International Dispute Resolution' [1999] 12 *Recueil des Cours*, 279.

[7] Convention for the Pacific Settlement of International Disputes (29 July 1899) [1901] UKTS No. 9.

Convention on the Law of the Sea (UNCLOS))[8] and maintains its rightful place as an important tool to deal with conflict in international relations.

A global institution from the beginning, the PCA nowadays comprises 122 contracting parties – Mongolia being the newest member as of May 2019. The PCA's caseload consists of over 160 pending registry cases, involving public entities from over 50 different States. The cases, each with different tribunals appointed specifically to deal with particular disputes, are administered by an International Bureau, made up of over 70 lawyers and administrative staff under my direction as Secretary-General.

3.   ARBITRATION AND PEACE

In the types of dispute envisaged by the PCA's founders, the main actors were States, and a prime reason for their recourse to the PCA was to avoid armed conflict. It is worthy of note that in quite a number of the early PCA-administered cases States initiated arbitration against another in order to defend the interests of one or more of its nationals.

It is not an exaggeration to say that, even recently, tribunals at the PCA have dealt directly with matters of war and peace. In 2018 a decision rendered by a PCA Boundary Commission from 2002 was recognised and implemented by Ethiopia, completing an essential step in the ultimate resolution of its war with Eritrea and the following September a border crossing reopened between the two States for the first time in 20 years.[9]

The international community has not only resorted to the PCA for inter-State conflicts but also intra-State disputes. A new type of actor entered the PCA stage in 2009 in the *Abyei Arbitration* between the Government of Sudan and the Sudanese People's Liberation Movement/Army – the latter challenging the central government in Khartoum with political and military means. The

---

[8]   Arts 33 and 36–37 of the Charter of the United Nations (24 October 1945) 1 UNTS XVI; Arts 187, 188, and Annexes VII and VIII, UNGA, Convention on the Law of the Sea (10 December 1982) ('UNCLOS'). See also video-message from UN Secretary-General Guterres https://files.pca-cpa.org/pcadocs/MSG%20SG %20COURT%20OF%20ARBITRATION%20NEW%20YORK%2001%20NOV %2018.mp4, accessed 21 November 2020.

[9]   Joint Declaration of Peace and Friendship between Eritrea and Ethiopia (9 July 2018) https://www.peaceagreements.org/viewmasterdocument/2097. The documents relating to this case are available on the PCA website, *Eritrea-Ethiopia Boundary Commission (The State of Eritrea and The Federal Democratic Republic of Ethiopia)*, PCA Case No. 2001-01 https://pca-cpa.org/en/cases/99/. Hadra Ahmed, 'Ethiopia-Eritrea Border Opens for First Time in 20 Years' *New York Times* (11 September 2018) https://www.nytimes.com/2018/09/11/world/africa/ethiopia-eritrea -border-opens.html, all accessed 21 November 2020.

PCA helped constitute and administered the tribunal that had to decide on the boundary between what is today Sudan and South Sudan, enabling the referendum over South Sudan's independence to go forward.

The *Abyei Arbitration* proceedings illustrate the flexibility of arbitration, and how it may be creatively designed by the parties to suit the particular needs of the case.[10] Parties for example agreed on a special appointment procedure, with each side nominating two arbitrators and a fifth to be agreed or chosen by the PCA Secretary-General from a bespoke list of past and present PCA arbitrators or PCA members of the court. On costs, the parties agreed to apply to the PCA's Financial Assistance Fund. The arbitration was fully transparent: all documents were published, hearings were open, and were the first of their kind to be webcast from the Great Hall of Justice in the Peace Palace to the world. Parties agreed on tight timeframe – 90 days to issue the award after the hearing, for nine months in total – due to an impending referendum.

More recently, the Revitalized Agreement for the Resolution of the Conflict in the Republic of South Sudan, agreed last September, draws on the *Abyei Arbitration* experience, and provides for PCA arbitration of disputes within that State arising from a boundary commission's conclusions.[11] It is a further example of non-State actors finding their place on the stage of the PCA.

Disputes among States in maritime matters continue to form a key part of the PCA's work, including three pending cases under UNCLOS.[12] The ways in which tribunals have operated in 13 arbitrations under UNCLOS at the PCA illustrate further the flexible procedures available to parties in arbitrations:[13] Hearings, for example, can be arranged anywhere, less than half of PCA

---

[10]   The documents relating to this case are available on the PCA website *The Government of Sudan/The Sudan People's Liberation Movement/Army (Abyei Arbitration)* PCA Case No. 2008-07 https://pca-cpa.org/en/cases/92/, accessed 21 November 2020. See also Brooks W Daly, 'The *Abyei Arbitration*: Procedural Aspects of an Intra-state Border Arbitration' (2010) 23(4) *Leiden Journal of International Law* 801.

[11]   Art 1.14.18.7 of the Revitalized Agreement for the Resolution of the Conflict in the Republic of South Sudan (12 September 2018) https://www.peaceagreements.org/wview/2112/Revitalised%20Agreement%20on%20the%20Resolution%20of%20the%20Conflict%20in%20the%20Republic%20of%20South%20Sudan%20(R-ARCSS), accessed 22 November 2020.

[12]   *Dispute Concerning Coastal State Rights in the Black Sea, Sea of Azov, and Kerch Strait (Ukraine v the Russian Federation)*, PCA Case No. 2017-06 https://pca-cpa.org/en/cases/149/; *The 'Enrica Lexie' Incident (Italy v India)*, PCA Case No. 2014-28 https://pca-cpa.org/en/cases/117/; *The Duzgit Integrity Arbitration (Malta v São Tomé and Príncipe)* PCA Case No. 2014-07 https://pca-cpa.org/en/cases/53/, all accessed 22 November 2020.

[13]   See generally, Judith Levine and Garth Schofield, 'Navigating Uncharted Procedural Waters in a Rising Sea of Cases at the Permanent Court of Arbitration' in

hearings are held at our headquarters in the Peace Palace. In *Arctic Sunrise*, which involved the Netherlands as a party, hearings were held in Vienna; and in *Mauritius v United Kingdom* the tribunal met with the parties in Dubai and Istanbul. It is open to parties to agree on different levels of transparency. Some proceedings in the *Enrica Lexie* Incident between Italy and India have been open to the public. In the case of *Faroe Islands v The European Union*, the hearings were also to proceed in public.[14] That dispute, which concerned shared stock of Atlanto-Scandian herring, was the first international proceeding in which the EU participated in its own right. European and intergovernmental organisations have become an important category of 'new actors' on the PCA stage – having administered 33 cases with inter-governmental organisations as parties.[15]

Arbitration at the PCA has also led to innovating procedures. In *Guyana v Suriname*, the PCA assisted the tribunal in appointing a hydrographic expert and PCA staff accompanied him on a site visit to take coordinates of a colonial era boundary marker whose location was crucial to the case. The expert reported back to the tribunal on a discrete issue, which the tribunal adopted as part of its award. The same tribunal also retained and adopted the findings of a legal expert to review Dutch colonial archives.[16] The process of referring discrete tasks to independent technical experts was also used in the *South China Sea* and *Arctic Sunrise* arbitrations.[17]

We have thus seen that the flexibility of arbitration allows parties to play a role in creating a process suitable to their dispute, and that this might entail devising special appointment procedures, setting strict timeframes, using an established institution for administrative assistance, or the tribunal referring discrete issues to a separate entity.

These were all aspects of the dispute settlement provisions agreed by the UK and the EU in the Withdrawal Agreement in October 2019.[18] Article 171 of the Withdrawal Agreement provides for establishment of a list of qualified jurists willing and able to serve as arbitrators and a system for their selection to

---

Stephan Minas, H Jordan Diamond and Holly Doremus (eds), *Stress Testing the Law of the Sea* (Brill 2018).

[14] *The Atlanto-Scandian Herring Arbitration (The Kingdom of Denmark in respect of the Faroe Islands v The European Union)*, PCA Case No. 2013-30, Rules of Procedure (15 March 2014) https://pcacases.com/web/sendAttach/305, accessed 22 November 2020.

[15] For public listings, see https://pca-cpa.org/en/cases/25/, accessed 22 November 2020, two of which are contract cases involving the EU.

[16] *Guyana v Suriname*, PCA Case No. 2004-04, Award (17 September 2007) https://pcacases.com/web/sendAttach/902, accessed 22 November 2020.

[17] See discussion in Levine and Schofield (n 13).

[18] Withdrawal Agreement (n 3).

a five-member panel, to be finalised with assistance of the PCA if necessary. Article 170 and Annex IX rely on the PCA as a channel of communications and secretariat. Article 173 sets tight timeframes for the panel to make a ruling. Article 174, perhaps most interesting for themes of this volume, provides that where a dispute raises a question of interpretation of a concept of EU law, the arbitral panel shall not decide such question but shall request the Court of Justice of the European Union to give a ruling on the question, which the arbitral panel must then follow.

Similar mechanisms are included in the November 2018 draft Framework Agreement between the EU and Switzerland.[19] Regardless of its fate, both this latter agreement and the Withdrawal Agreement remain instructive examples of how parties can design dispute resolution mechanisms to suit their needs.

Parties are also increasingly resorting to the PCA to facilitate alternative forms of dispute resolution amongst States in the context of treaty arrangements for management of fish stocks,[20] such as regional treaty review panels; and conciliation, such as the ground-breaking conciliation between Timor Leste and Australia that led to a new maritime boundary treaty in 2018.[21] One interesting aspect of the *Timor Sea Conciliation* is that the two States also engaged with the Operation Sunrise Joint Venture that had been granted concession rights to exploit natural gas in the disputed area.

It is the involvement of such private actors, and foreign investors in particular, to which this chapter now briefly turns.

4.   TRADE AND INVESTMENT DISPUTES

In the last 20 years the PCA has administered nearly 200 investor-State arbitrations. Some well-known examples include *Philip Morris v Australia*; *Chevron v Ecuador*; *Achmea v Slovak Republic*; *Yukos v Russian Federation*; several NAFTA cases, and a recent slew of renewable energy related disputes involving European States.

---

[19]   Art 10 and Protocol 3, Accord Facilitant les Relations Bilatérales entre l'Union Européenne et la Confédération Suisse dans les Parties du Marché Intérieur Auxquelles la Suisse Participe (only available in French) (23 November 2018) https://www.fdfa.admin.ch/dam/dea/fr/documents/abkommen/Acccord-inst-Projet-de-texte_fr.pdf, accessed 22 November 2020.

[20]   See the two review panel decisions initiated by the Russian Federation (PCA Case No. 2013-14) and Ecuador (PCA Case No. 2018-13), both finalised within six-week timeframes per the treaty terms https://pca-cpa.org/en/cases/, accessed 22 November 2020.

[21]   *Timor Sea Conciliation (Timor-Leste v Australia)*, Report and Recommendations of the Compulsory Conciliation Commission (9 May 2018) https://pcacases.com/web/sendAttach/2327, accessed 22 November 2020.

The PCA's involvement with these so-called 'mixed arbitrations', where one of the parties is a private entity or person, represents a response to the growing demands of its users in the past couple of decades. Some of the PCA's early State-to-State disputes concerned in fact interests of private individuals or entities. Their States of nationality defended those interests as if their own. Examples are the *Japanese House Tax* case of 1902, concerning a government's alleged failure to live up to promises in respect of taxation of investments,[22] and the *Orinoco Steamship Case* of 1907 about the claims of American investors against Venezuela.[23]

Such cases can in fact be considered as the precursors to modern investment arbitration. Authorised by its contracting parties, the PCA administered for the first time an arbitration directly opposing a private entity and a State, in *Radio Corporation of America v China*,[24] which involved a claim to exclusive broadcasting rights. The case set a precedent for the handling of disputes between private parties and States, founded on contracts and later investment treaties.[25]

Nowadays the majority of all known UNCITRAL investor-State proceedings are administered by the PCA, of which there are over 100 pending. As

---

[22]   *Japanese House Tax (Germany, France, and Great Britain/Japan)*, PCA Case No. 1902-02 https://pca-cpa.org/en/cases/69/, accessed 22 November 2020. The case concerned perpetual leases entered into by Japan with foreigners. The leases were aimed at giving the foreigners access to real property for the establishment of foreign settlements. Such settlements were to remain outside the Japanese municipal system, and their occupants were not obliged to pay taxes. Such tax benefits were granted by virtue of treaties between Japan, Great Britain, Germany, and France. A dispute arose when Japan asserted that only the land itself, but not the building on it, enjoyed the tax exemption.

[23]   *The Orinico Steamship Company (United States of America v Venezuela)*, PCA Case No. 1909-02 https://pca-cpa.org/en/cases/78/, accessed 22 November 2020. As a result of an economic dispute involving a steamship company owned by American nationals, the two States had severed diplomatic relations. A mixed commission was established to decide on the claims of the US citizens against Venezuela. The verdict of that Commission, however, was unacceptable to the United States for various reasons, including perceived fundamental errors. The two Governments overcame the diplomatic deadlock by signing an arbitration agreement referring to the PCA. The ensuing arbitration provided not only for a resolution of the legal disputes but also led to the reestablishment of political relations.

[24]   *Radio Corporation of America v China*, PCA Case No. 1934-01 https://pca-cpa .org/en/cases/16/, accessed 22 November 2020.

[25]   A more recent example of a contract-based dispute between private parties and states is *The Eurotunnel Arbitration*, PCA Case No. 2003-06, https://pca-cpa.org/en/ cases/70/, accessed 22 November 2020. The PCA has also administered one of the few inter-State proceedings under an investment treaty in *Republic of Ecuador v United States of America*, PCA Case No. 2012-05 https://pca-cpa.org/en/cases/83/, accessed 22 November 2020.

with the inter-State disputes, these mixed arbitrations enjoy a large degree of procedural flexibility and have accommodated a new range of actors. These first include non-parties, including the European Commission and NGOs, who have provided submissions to tribunals in NAFTA, Energy Charter Treaty and bilateral investment treaty cases.[26] The PCA is also notably administering the first ever investor-State case against the EU, *Nord Stream 2 AG v The European Union*, arisen in the framework of the Energy Charter Treaty.[27] Investment tribunals have also retained independent experts on matters of environmental damage, forensic analysis and calculation of damages.[28]

Hearings in these cases have been held the world over to suit the needs of the parties and participants, including in States where the PCA has concluded Host Country Agreements. Our most recent such agreement was signed with the Republic of Ireland to provide the same privileges and immunities as participants have under our headquarters agreement with the Netherlands, and free hearing facilities in Dublin.

In three cases, the parties to the arbitrations have chosen to apply the UNCITRAL 2013 Transparency Rules, even though they might not automatically have applied.[29] In a few instances, parties have themselves expressly agreed to seek diversity in arbitral appointments.

Plenty has been discussed – at the III LAwTTIP conference and outside – on investor-State dispute settlement arbitration reform. The PCA takes no view as to the desirability of particular reforms in this system. In our view, it is the prerogative of governments to select the dispute settlement mechanism that they regard most appropriate, taking into account their policy preferences and interests. That said, given the depth of experience in administering investor-State disputes, the PCA is assisting the UNCITRAL Working Group

---

[26] *Achmea BV (formerly known as 'Eureko BV') v The Slovak Republic*, PCA Case No. 2008-13 https://pca-cpa.org/en/cases/28/; *Voltaic Network GmbH v Czech Republic*, PCA Case No. 2014-20, https://www.italaw.com/cases/2515; *Resolute Forest Products Inc. v The Government of Canada*, PCA Case No. 2016-13 https://pca -cpa.org/en/cases/142/, all accessed 22 November 2020. For intervention of non-parties in inter-State disputes, see discussion in Levine and Schofield (n 13).

[27] *Nord Stream 2 AG v The European Union*, PCA Case No. 2020-07 https://pca -cpa.org/en/cases/239/, accessed 22 November 2020.

[28] *Saluka Investments BV v Czech Republic*, PCA Case No. 2001-04 https://pca -cpa.org/en/cases/101/; *NJSC Naftogaz of Ukraine et al (its 6 subsidiaries) v Russia*, PCA Case No. 2017-16 https://pca-cpa.org/en/cases/151/, all accessed 22 November 2020. Site visits have been undertaken in at least two investor-State arbitrations at the PCA. See Judith Levine and Nicola Peart, 'Procedural Issues and Innovations in Environment-Related Investor-State Disputes' in Kate Miles (ed), *Research Handbook on Investment Law and the Environment* (Edward Elgar 2019).

[29] See PCA website search at https://pca-cpa.org/en/cases/151/, last accessed 22 November 2020.

III process at the technical level, in an effort to assist States in ensuring that any new approaches lead to efficient and fair dispute resolution mechanisms.[30]

What remains perhaps under-explored is the possibility of mediating investment disputes. The PCA has supported the work of a number of projects to develop rules and guides on investment mediations,[31] and has also recently administered three conciliations including one between private parties under the PCA's conciliation rules for environmental disputes.[32]

This leads to a final observation about new frontiers for the PCA.

5.   NEW FRONTIERS

Due to the neutrality and flexibility of arbitration, and the enforceability of awards, some have suggested arbitration as a prospective forum for so-called business and human rights disputes, so long as there is consent by all relevant parties.[33]

In 2016 two arbitrations were commenced under the Bangladesh Accord on Fire and Building Safety by two labour unions against two global fashion brands. The Accord is a unique instrument negotiated in the aftermath of the 2013 Rana Plaza Factory collapse that killed over 1100 workers in the Ready-Made Garment industry.[34] It aims to enable a working environment in which no worker needs to fear fires, building collapses or other accidents, and establishes a safety inspection regime and obligations on signatory brands to ensure supplier factories comply. It also features a binding arbitration clause.

---

[30] See submissions from Intergovernmental Organizations on the website of UNCITRAL Working Group III https://uncitral.un.org/en/working_groups/3/investor -state, accessed 22 November 2020.

[31] International Bar Association Council, International Bar Association Mediation Committee, State Mediation Subcommittee, 'IBA Rules for Investor-State Mediation' (4 October 2012) https://www.ibanet.org/Document/Default.aspx?DocumentUid= 8120ED11-F3C8-4A66-BE81-77CB3FDB9E9F; Energy Charter Conference, '2016 Guide on Investment Mediation' https://www.energycharter.org/web/Metadata/Temp/ 1600688265__614_CCDEC201612.pdf, both accessed 21 November 2020.

[32] Levine and Peart (n 28), referencing PCA conciliations in a construction dispute between a company and State-owned entity in Costa Rica; an NGO and the International Criminal Court; and two parties involved in a clean development mechanism project under the Kyoto Protocol, which used the PCA's Conciliation Rules for environmental disputes.

[33] Judith Levine and Ashwita Ambast, 'The Bangladesh Accord Arbitrations: Arbitrating Business and Human Rights Disputes' [2020] 1 *Transnational Commercial Law Review* 116.

[34] Accord on Fire and Building Safety in Bangladesh, 13 May 2013 http://www .industriall-union.org/sites/default/files/uploads/documents/2013-05-13_-_accord_on _fire_and_building_safety_in_bangladesh.pdf, accessed 22 November 2020.

In the two cases mentioned, the PCA was asked to appoint the chair and act as registry. The tribunal acknowledged the genuine public interests at stake in the proceedings when ruling on a transparency and confidentiality regime.[35] The cases settled last year before going to hearing. The outcomes were welcomed as 'proof that legally binding mechanisms can hold multinational companies to account' and as showing the 'validity of the arbitral process and a turning point for business and human rights'.[36]

The new 2018 Bangladesh Accord incorporates the UNCITRAL Rules, provides for The Hague as the seat of arbitration and specifies the PCA as the administering institution.[37]

More recently the PCA was chosen as the default administering institution for business and human rights arbitrations in the Hague Rules on Business and Human Rights arbitration.[38] These arbitration rules, launched on 12 December 2019 at a ceremony held at the Peace Palace,[39] provide the possibility of a remedy for those affected by the human rights impacts of business activities, as set forth in Pillar III and principle 31 of the UN Guiding Principles on Business and Human Rights (UNGPs).[40] They also provide businesses with

[35] See *Bangladesh Accord Arbitrations*, PCA Cases Nos. 2016-36 and 2016-37 https://pca-cpa.org/en/cases/152/, Procedural Order No. 2 (4 September 2017) https://pcacases.com/web/sendAttach/2234, both accessed 22 November 2020.

[36] 'Clean Clothes' (Tweet, 23 January 2018) https://twitter.com/cleanclothes/status/955853902108332033; Christy Hoffman, UNI Global Union's deputy general secretary, cited in: Dominic Rushe, 'Unions reach $2.3m settlement on Bangladesh textile factory safety' *The Guardian* (22 January 2018) https://www.theguardian.com/business/2018/jan/22/bandgladesh-textile-factory-safety-unions-settlement, both accessed 22 November 2020.

[37] Art 3 of the Accord on Fire and Building Safety in Bangladesh (May 2018) https://bangladesh.wpengine.com/wp-content/uploads/2020/11/2018-Accord.pdf, accessed 22 November 2020.

[38] Art 1(5) of The Hague Rules on Business and Human Rights (December 2019) https://www.cilc.nl/cms/wp-content/uploads/2019/12/The-Hague-Rules-on-Business-and-Human-Rights-Arbitration_CILC-digital-version.pdf. For an overview of the Project, see https://www.cilc.nl/project/the-hague-rules-on-business-and-human-rights-arbitration/.

[39] Report of the Launch symposium of The Hague Rules on Business and Human Rights Arbitration, held on 12 December 2019, at the Peace Palace, The Hague, The Netherlands https://www.cilc.nl/cms/wp-content/uploads/2020/02/The-Hague-Rules-on-Business-and-Human-Rights-Arbitration_Launch-Report-.pdf, accessed 22 November 2020.

[40] Guiding Principles on Business and Human Rights: Implementing the United Nations 'protect, Respect and Remedy' Framework (2011) https://www.ohchr.org/documents/publications/guidingprinciplesbusinesshr_en.pdf, accessed 22 November 2020.

a mechanism for addressing adverse human rights impacts with which they are involved, as set forth in Pillar II and Principles 11 and 13 of the UNGPs.

While the categories of disputes that arbitration is used to resolve are continually broadening and, at times, have expanded to include human rights, the Hague Rules on Business and Human Rights arbitration have been specifically tailored to meet the effectiveness criteria for dispute resolution procedures between businesses and those affected by potential human rights violations of the former as set out in the UNGPs – including legitimacy, accessibility, predictability and rights-compatibility of the outcomes, as well as equitableness and transparency of the procedures.

6.   CONCLUSIONS

This chapter has demonstrated that, as old theatres can provide a new stage to new actors in the context of new challenges, so can old international institutions, such as the PCA.

The continuing confidence of the international community in the PCA has evolved with the creative approach also by parties – including the EU in the context of trade – so that peaceful dispute resolution structures may continue to flourish for the benefit of peaceful relations under the rule of law.

16. WTO dispute settlement: A curse or a bliss in international trade relations?

Federico Ortino

1.   FROM SUCCESS TO PARALYSIS

Until recently, anyone casting an eye on the dispute settlement system of the World Trade Organisation (WTO) would have seen an (almost) idyllic picture (a 'bliss'). Former WTO Director General, Pascal Lamy, famously described the WTO dispute settlement system as the 'jewel in the crown of the WTO'. When considering the number of disputes that have been brought before the WTO, the number of decisions rendered by panels and the impressive record of WTO Members complying with decisions, the dispute settlement system of the WTO must be seen as a success story.

Much of the credit for this success rests with an institution that was created during the Uruguay Round and sits at the centre and apex of the WTO dispute settlement system: the Appellate Body. Despite its unpretentious name, the Appellate Body is considered by many to be the de facto World Trade Court. The Appellate Body is a standing body and hears possible appeals on issues of law against WTO panel decisions (formally called 'reports'). It is composed of seven individuals ('members') and appointed (based on a balanced geographic distribution) by the WTO membership on a four-year term, which is renewable once. Proceedings before the Appellate Body are generally not to exceed 60 days, although the absolute maximum limit is 90 days. The Appellate Body has elaborated its own 'working procedures', provided for by the Dispute Settlement Understanding (DSU). Particularly in its early years, the Appellate Body appears to have focused its interpretative approach on 'text' and 'context', and has since then elaborated a relatively coherent body of jurisprudence and practice. Overall, the Appellate Body has achieved a level of independence, credibility and legitimacy that any adjudicative body aspires to. In this sense, many have recognised the Appellate Body, through its existence and operations, as having made a significant contribution to the development of a full-fledged international 'rule of law'.[1]

Is it all bliss then? Well, if one visits Geneva today, not all is bliss, unfortunately. In fact, it is the opposite. The WTO dispute settlement system, 'the jewel in the crown of the WTO', is on the brink of paralysis. While some rumblings were apparent over ten years ago, this near paralysis is mainly down to the current US administration's decision to block the appointment of any new Appellate Body members since 2017. Accordingly, since October 2018, there have been only three Appellate Body members in place: Bhatia (a national of India), Graham (United States) and Zhao (China). As the Appellate Body operates in divisions of three, it is currently still operational, although proceedings are taking much longer as all the work is being carried out by three rather than seven members. However, and crucially, at the end of 2019 the terms of two of the remaining three members expired, meaning that no new appeals have been able to be examined and thus the entire dispute settlement system (and possibly the WTO system overall) has been be jeopardised (a 'curse').

The repercussions of this paralysis extend beyond the world trading system. For example, the current efforts to reform Investor-State dispute settlement include the introduction of a standing appeal mechanism and even a standing multilateral tribunal, which take inspiration directly from the WTO dispute settlement system.[2]

2.   WHAT ARE THE CLAIMS ADVANCED BY THE UNITED STATES FOR SUCH IMPENDING PARALYSIS?

In their 2018 Trade Policy Agenda, the United States Trade Representative (USTR) stated that the 'United States has grown increasingly concerned with the activist approach of the Appellate Body on procedural issues, interpretative approach, and substantive interpretations.'[3] Over the course of the last 18 months, the US has further elaborated some of these concerns.

---

[1]   Jennifer Hillman, 'An Emerging International Rule of Law? – The WTO Dispute Settlement System's Role in its Evolution' (2010–2011) 42 *Ottawa Law Review* 269.

[2]   See the work carried out by the UNCITRAL Working Group III on Investor-State Dispute Settlement Reform https://uncitral.un.org/en/working_groups/3/investor-state, accessed 5 July 2021.

[3]   Office of the United States Trade Representative (USTR), '2018 Trade Policy Agenda and 2017 Annual Report' (March 2018), 28 https://ustr.gov/sites/default/files/files/Press/Reports/2018/AR/2018%20Annual%20Report%20FINAL.PDF, accessed 5 July 2021.

2.1   Procedural Issues: 90-Day Rule and Rule 15

With regard to procedural rules, the US first of all complained about the failure of the Appellate Body to adhere to the 90-day deadline for the issuance of its reports. While Article 17.5 of the DSU states that 'as a general rule', the proceedings before the Appellate Body shall not exceed 60 days from the date a party formally notifies its intention to appeal a panel report, that same provision also provides that '[i]n no case shall the proceedings [...] exceeds 90 days'.[4] The US has recently argued that since 2011 the Appellate Body has ignored the 90-day requirement, while often failing to consult and obtain the parties' consent when deciding it could not meet the 90-day requirement.[5] The US has also noted that since the 2011 change of approach, the average length of appeals has increased: Before 2011 the average was approximately 90 days, however since then the average is approximately 149 days (excluding the EU and US large civil aircraft disputes). And since May 2014, no single appeal has been completed within the 90-day deadline, with the average being 163 days.[6] The US argues that there is a risk that the length of appeals may continue to grow and thus the dispute settlement system may move further away from the principle of prompt settlement as reflected in Article 3 of the DSU.[7]

Second, the US has complained of the Appellate Body's failure to comply with the rules in the DSU when it has allowed members to serve on the AB beyond the expiration of their terms according to Rule 15 of the Appellate Body Working Procedures, in order for them to complete the disposition of cases assigned prior to the expiry of their term of office.[8] The US argues that 'the Appellate Body simply does not have the authority to deem someone who is not an Appellate Body member to be a member'.[9] While Rule 15 of the Appellate Body Working Procedures provides for such an extension, the US argues that, under the WTO Agreement, it is the Dispute Settlement Body, not the Appellate Body, that has the authority and responsibility to decide whether a person whose term of appointment has expired should continue serving. The US emphasises that, while before 2017 Rule 15 was invoked sparingly and was used to cover relatively short extensions, since then the Appellate Body has invoked Rule 15 in a number of disputes, for indefinite and extended periods

---

[4]   2018 Trade Policy Agenda, ibid., 24–25.
[5]   Statements by the United States at the Meeting of the WTO Dispute Settlement Body (Geneva, 22 June 2018), 13.
[6]   Ibid., 17.
[7]   Ibid., 21.
[8]   Minutes of the DSB meeting of 31 August 2017 (WT/DSB/M/400), para 5.4 et seq.
[9]   2018 Trade Policy Agenda (n 3), 25.

of time, even on appeals where work had not begun before the member's term expired. The US has noted that this is 'an important issue of principle whether WTO Members are going to respect their own rules and take appropriate action'.[10]

2.2 Interpretative Approach: Issues of Fact, Advisory Opinions, Precedent

The United States has also raised three concerns that more directly relate to the way the Appellate Body has exercised its adjudicative functions.

Issues of fact. First, the US has complained that the Appellate Body has violated Article 17.6 of the DSU, which limits appeals to 'issues of law covered in the panel report and legal interpretations developed by the panel'. The US has argued that the Appellate Body has (1) 'invented' its authority to review panel fact-finding and (2) has incorrectly asserted that it can review panel findings concerning the meaning of a Member's municipal law, which is often the key fact to be demonstrated in any dispute.[11]

With regard to the first argument, the US has argued that the Appellate Body has incorrectly relied on Article 11 DSU, which states that 'a panel should make an objective assessment [...] of the facts of the case', to expand its authority over issues of fact. In particular, the US points to the word 'should' in Article 11 and argues that, while the Appellate Body never engaged in a textual analysis of that word, it did find that Article 11 established an applicable standard of review for a panel's factual findings, thus recognising that the Appellate Body has the authority to review whether a panel has indeed made an 'objective assessment' of factual issues.

The US has noted that the decision to review panel fact finding has had a number of adverse effects on the dispute settlement system, including: (a) an increased workload for the Appellate Body (due to the complexity of appeals, length of submissions and the need to devote time and resources to a panel's factual findings);[12] (b) undermining the value of interim reviews of panel reports (as the availability of an Appellate Body review of the facts may refrain a party from providing corrections or clarifications of the factual section of a panel's interim report);[13] and (c) the inability of the Appellate Body to determine a consistent approach to the applicable 'standard of review' (it initially set a very high threshold that focused on a panel's 'egregious errors', however

---

[10] Ibid., 26.
[11] Statements by the United States at the Meeting of the WTO Dispute Settlement Body (Geneva, 27 August 2018), 10.
[12] Ibid., 13.
[13] Ibid., 14.

more recently it shifted to a more intrusive approach that focuses on whether the panel has provided a 'reasoned and adequate' explanation for its findings and coherent reasoning).[14]

With regard to the second argument, the US has claimed that the Appellate Body has not treated panel findings concerning the meaning of municipal law as a factual issue. Instead, in the United States' view, the Appellate Body has treated the meaning of municipal law as a matter of WTO law, to be decided by the Appellate Body *de novo* in an appeal under Article 17.6 of the DSU.[15] The US has argued that the Appellate Body has given 'no interpretation of the text of the DSU for its statement that the meaning of domestic law is an issue of law in the WTO dispute settlement system'.[16] Furthermore, the US has specified that in at least 15 instances, other WTO Members have expressed disagreement with the Appellate Body's assertion that it has the authority to review a panel's factual findings on the meaning of a WTO Member's domestic law. The Appellate Body has nevertheless not reconsidered its view.[17]

Advisory opinions. The second criticism raised by the US with regard to the Appellate Body's interpretative approach deals with the claim that the Appellate Body's (and often the panel's) reports include findings that are either superfluous or are on issues not presented in the dispute.[18] The US has argued as follows: the purpose of the dispute settlement system is not to produce reports or to 'make law', but rather to help Members resolve trade disputes among them. WTO Members have not given panels or the Appellate Body the power to give 'advisory opinions'.[19]

In particular, the US has highlighted several instances where the Appellate Body addressed issues raised by the parties that were not necessary to solve the dispute. For example, in *Argentina – Financial Services* (DS453), having reversed the panel's findings on 'likeness' for purposes of Article II and Article XVII GATS, the Appellate Body was no longer required to address the panel's findings on 'less favourable treatment' and on the prudential carve-out in the GATS Annex on Financial Services. However, the Appellate Body decided nonetheless to address those issues, with two-thirds of their overall analysis (46 pages) being *obiter dicta*.[20] In the US' view, the Appellate Body

---

[14]   Ibid.

[15]   Ibid., 22.

[16]   Ibid., 23.

[17]   Ibid., 22.

[18]   Statements by the United States at the Meeting of the WTO Dispute Settlement Body (Geneva, 29 October 2018), 10–26.

[19]   2018 Trade Policy Agenda (n 3), 26.

[20]   Statements by the United States at the Meeting of the WTO Dispute Settlement Body (Geneva, 29 October 2018), 23.

does not have the authority to provide 'interpretation in the abstract', as that authority is expressly attributed to the membership in Article IX:2 of the WTO Agreement (which grants WTO Members the power to adopt 'authoritative interpretations').

As with the previous complaint, the US has pointed out that several other WTO Members have also spoken out on this issue. It has cited, for example, *Canada – Continued Suspension* and *United States – Continued Suspension*, whereby ten WTO Members spoke in the DSB to question the Appellate Body's authority to 'recommend' that the DSB requests that certain Members initiate further dispute settlement proceedings.[21] The US has argued that the issuance of advisory opinions by WTO adjudicators (and increasingly by the Appellate Body), represents 'a failure by the Appellate Body to follow the rules agreed by Members in the WTO agreements.'[22]

In terms of systemic consequences, in the view of the US, advisory opinions add time and complexity to a proceeding and risk not taking into account all the facets of an issue (if the parties have not engaged fully with issues that are not before the WTO adjudicator or if the relevant facts have not been fully developed by the parties).[23]

Precedent. Third, the US has complained that the Appellate Body, without an express basis in the DSU, claims that its reports are entitled to be treated as precedent by subsequent panels absent 'cogent reasons'. In the view of the US, the Appellate Body's approach with regard to 'precedent' seeks to usurp the authority expressly reserved for WTO Members. The US has argued that there is 'no provision in the DSU that establishes a system of "case-law" or "precedent", or otherwise requires that a panel applies the provisions of the covered agreements consistently with the adopted findings of previous panels or the Appellate Body'.[24] In the US' view, to say that an Appellate Body's interpretation in one dispute forms a precedent for later disputes would effectively convert that interpretation into an authoritative interpretation of the covered agreements, which would directly contradict Article IX:2 of the WTO Agreement which grants 'the exclusive authority to adopt interpretations' of the covered agreements to the Ministerial Conference and the General Council.[25] According to the US, a prior panel or Appellate Body interpretation only has a 'persuasive' value.[26]

---

[21] Ibid., 20–21.
[22] Ibid., 25.
[23] Ibid.
[24] Statements by the United States at the Meeting of the WTO Dispute Settlement Body (Geneva, 18 December 2018), 13–14.
[25] Ibid., 14.
[26] Ibid., 15.

The US has pointed out that, while early decisions by the Appellate Body had recognised that prior reports could only have persuasive value, the Appellate Body report in *United States – Stainless Steel (Mexico)* (DS 344) contains the Appellate Body's first effort to introduce the concept of 'cogent reasons'. In the view of the US, the Appellate Body's statement concerning 'cogent reasons' in *United States – Stainless Steel (Mexico)* is 'profoundly flawed' in several respects, including: (1) a failure to properly appreciate the functions of panels and the Appellate Body within the WTO dispute settlement system; (2) an erroneous interpretation of Article 3.2 DSU; (3) a misunderstanding of why parties cite prior reports; (4) inappropriate and incomplete analogies to other international adjudicative for a; and (5) incorrect assumptions concerning the existence of a hierarchical structure that does not reflect the limited task assigned to the Appellate Body in the DSU.[27]

Moreover, the US pointed out that, together with the US, other WTO Members (such as Chile, Argentina, Colombia and Mexico) criticised the Appellate Body's statement on precedent when the reports in *United States – Stainless Steel (Mexico)* were considered by the DSB.[28]

2.3 Substantive Interpretations

The third set of criticisms that have been put forward by the US focus on the interpretation given by the Appellate Body of certain substantive provisions. The US has complained that the Appellate Body has interpreted some of the WTO covered agreements in a way that adds to or diminishes the US' rights or obligations, something which is expressly prohibited by the DSU (Art 3.2). In particular, the US has focused on the way the Appellate Body has interpreted the Agreement on Subsidies and Countervailing Measures (SCM), the Agreement on Anti-dumping, the Agreement on Safeguards and the Agreement on Technical Barriers to Trade (TBT). In the President's 2018 Trade Policy Report, the US has provided the following examples:[29]

(1)   The US has expressed significant concern with several the Appellate Body's interpretations that would significantly restrict the ability of WTO Members to counteract trade-distorting subsidies provided through State-Owned Enterprises (SOEs). In particular, the US has criticised the Appellate Body's findings on 'public body' (whether an SOE can be deemed to confer a subsidy) and on the simultaneous application

---

[27]   Ibid., 21–22.
[28]   Ibid, 31–32.
[29]   2018 Trade Policy Agenda (n 3), 23–24.

of countervailing duties and antidumping duties under a non-market economy methodology.

(2)   In several disputes, the US has expressed concerns with the Appellate Body's interpretation of the non-discrimination obligation under the TBT Agreement, which calls for a review of factors that are not related to any difference in treatment due to national origin. The US has pointed out that this approach may find that the identical treatment of domestic and imported products could nonetheless be found to discriminate against imported products due to differences in market impact. There is nothing in the text or negotiating history of the TBT Agreement to suggest that Members had ever negotiated or agreed to such an approach.[30]

(3)   The US disagreed with panel and Appellate Body reports in the *US – FSC* dispute, which offered an interpretation of WTO rules that do not treat different (worldwide vs. territorial) tax systems fairly. This dispute disregarded the broader perspective that, in the GATT, Members had agreed to an understanding that a country did not need to tax foreign income, and there was no evidence that the US FSC distorted trade or was more distortive than the territorial tax system used by most other WTO Members.

(4)   In a number of disputes, the United States has expressed concerns that the Appellate Body's non-text-based interpretation of Article XIX of the GATT 1994 and the Safeguards Agreement has seriously undermined the ability of Members to use safeguards measures. The Appellate Body has disregarded the agreed WTO text and read text into the Agreement, applying standards of its own devising.[31]

(5)   Another area of concern is that the Appellate Body in effect created a new category of prohibited subsidies that was neither negotiated nor agreed by WTO Members (*US – CDSOA*) (DS217) The US Congress had made a policy decision to assist industries harmed by illegal dumping and subsidization, and no provision in the WTO Agreement limits how a WTO Member might choose to make use of the funds collected through antidumping and countervailing duties.

---

[30]   See e.g., Minutes of the 13 June 2012 DSB meeting (WT/DSB/M/317), para 13 et seq; and 23 July 2012 DSB meeting (WT/DSB/M/320), para 94 et seq.

[31]   See e.g., Minutes of the 16 May 2001 DSB meeting (WT/DSB/M/105), para 41 et seq; and 8 March 2002 (WT/DSB/M/121), para 35 et seq.

3.   WHAT ARE THE REAL REASONS UNDERLYING THE IMPENDING PARALYSIS?

In my view, there are three possible readings of the US' recent stance vis-à-vis the WTO Appellate Body.

The first reading of the US' position is that the US (and its current administration in particular) is critical of an international dispute settlement system that behaves very much like a domestic judicial branch with strong 'rule of law' features (i.e., a 'rule-oriented' system). Taken individually, none of the procedural and interpretative concerns raised by the US seem to justify such a drastic approach vis-à-vis the Appellate Body. For example, is the fact that Appellate Body proceedings last five months instead of three the real issue? Similarly, does *obiter dicta* not help 'to clarify the existing provisions' of the covered agreements and thus provide 'security and predictability to the multilateral trading system' pursuant to Article 3.2 DSU? If one takes these various issues together, however, one gets the sense that the US may indeed be happier going back to the old-GATT panel practice of dispute settlement (with no precedential effect, no consistency, no coherent jurisprudence), which Professor Weiler has famously called 'diplomacy through other means'.[32] That would appear to be a system that at least in principle is more easily controllable, particularly by those WTO Members enjoying greater political clout, like the US. And this is what may indeed happen, at least in practice, when in December 2019, there will only be one Appellate Body member still standing and thus the Appellate Body will no longer be able to deal with new appeals.

A second possible reading of the US' position is that their main bone of contention is with the way the Appellate Body has interpreted certain key provisions of WTO substantive law, in particular with regard to trade remedies. In other words, this is about issues such as the controversial 'standard of review' under Article 17.6(ii) of the Anti-Dumping Agreement (ADA),[33] or whether 'zeroing' as a technique to calculate dumping margin is prohibited by the ADA.[34] One can even see the links between these specific issues (where the Appellate Body has allegedly provided an incorrect interpretation of the underlying substantive agreements) and some of the more systemic/interpretative

---

[32]   Joseph Weiler, 'The Rule of Lawyers and the Ethos of Diplomats: Reflections on the Internal and External Legitimacy of WTO Dispute Settlement' (2001) 35 *Journal of World Trade* 191.

[33]   See John H Jackson and Steven P Croley, 'WTO Dispute Settlement Procedures, Standard of Review and Deference to National Governments', (1996) 90 *American Journal of International Law* 193.

[34]   See Edwin Vermulst and Daniel Ikenson, 'Zeroing Under the WTO Anti-Dumping Agreement: Where Do We Stand?' (2007) *Global Trade and Customs Journal* 231.

concerns raised by the US. For example, there is a clear link between the issue of the special 'standard of review' under the ADA and the US' criticism of the Appellate Body's position that municipal law is an issue of law rather than an issue of fact. Similarly, there is a clear link between the issue of zeroing and the US' criticism of the Appellate Body's position with regard to the precedential value of its reports (the (in)famous Appellate Body report in *United States – Stainless Steel (Mexico)*, analysed above, was indeed about zeroing). Interestingly, one of the solutions to these various issues is a change in the interpretation of the key provisions of the WTO dispute settlement system, ideally by the Appellate Body.

A third possible reading of the US' position is that their real concern goes beyond any of the specific issues that they have formally raised (whether procedural, interpretative or substantive) and is about the realisation that many of the WTO rules of the game (whether as written or interpreted) are inadequate or unfair, in the sense that they no longer properly regulate today's global trade. This reading is clearly linked with the rise and impact of China in the global economy. As USTR Robert Lighthizer stated to the US Congress in February 2019:

> We are here to talk about China. I agree with those who see our large and growing trade deficit and their unfair trade practices – including technology transfer issues, failure to protect intellectual property, large subsidies, cyber theft of commercial secrets and other problems – as major threats to our economy. We can compete with anyone in the world but we must have rules – enforced rules – that make sure market outcomes, not state-capitalism and technology theft, determine winners.[35]

In this sense, the US' concerns with the Appellate Body's interpretations in the area of trade remedies are only a piece of the broader puzzle. Accordingly, these various broader concerns may not be dealt fully by different interpretations of the existing agreements but they will instead require new provisions or even new agreements. And this is where a further realisation kicks in: that of the extreme difficulty in changing any rules within an institution of 164 Members (with different economies and priorities) that still operates, at least de facto, on the basis of consensus. If this third reading is indeed correct, then the US' stance vis-à-vis the Appellate Body (as well as in its unilateral trade measures) can be seen as an attempt to merely create leverage within the WTO Membership in order to bring about these changes.

---

[35] Opening Statement of USTR Robert Lighthizer to the House Ways and Means Committee (Washington DC, 27 February 2019) https://ustr.gov/about-us/policy-offices/press-office/press-releases/2019/february/opening-statement-ustr-robert, accessed 5 July 2021.

It is difficult to determine which (if any) of the above readings is the correct one and thus it is difficult to identify possible solutions to the current impasse. In any event, the saga of the WTO dispute settlement system is far from over and future months will hopefully bring about more clarity regarding the true reasons underlying the US' stance. In the short term, the WTO dispute settlement system, described as 'an extraordinary achievement that comes close to a miracle',[36] is the one that risks the most, even if it may not be the main culprit.

---

[36]   Claus-Dieter Ehlermann, 'Six Year on the Bench of the "World Trade Court": Some Personal Experiences as Member of the Appellate Body of the World Trade Organization' (2002) 36 Journal of World Trade 605, 639.

17. Judicial protection in the EEA

Frank J. Büchel and Carsten Zatschler

1. MORE THAN A MERE FREE TRADE AGREEMENT

The European Economic Area Agreement has since 1994 extended the European Union's internal market to European Free Trade Area States.[1] Even after 25 years, it remains the EU's most advanced and most comprehensive free trade agreement. The Norwegian Prime Minister recently described it as 'the world's best trade agreement',[2] and she is certainly right that it is an agreement that not only delivers effectively frictionless trade, but also delivers much more than meets the eye.

The EEA Agreement may in some respects be the embodiment of a less far-reaching vision of European integration. It does not envisage an 'ever closer Union' of the people of Europe and eschews any attempt at creating a single European polity. The EEA is about economic integration on the same terms as the EU, but without political integration.

Yet – and this is important also in the context of the ongoing quest to define the level of interaction between the UK and the internal market – the deep economic integration and cooperation between advanced economies exemplified by the EEA must necessarily be based on common values and a high degree of mutual trust, including trust in each others' judicial systems and a shared commitment to equal treatment and a level playing field.

The EU's internal market, which the EEA Agreement extends to the three EEA EFTA States – Iceland, Liechtenstein and Norway – is 'an area without

---

[1]   Pursuant to Art 128 EEA, the Swiss Confederation or any European State becoming a member of EFTA may apply to become a party to the EEA Agreement. The Swiss Confederation has so far refrained from exercising this right.

[2]   Solberg, 'EØS-avtalen er verdens beste handelsavtale' (Speech to NHO Norwegian business association, 9 January 2019) https://www.abcnyheter.no/penger/makrookonomi/2019/01/09/195490323/solberg-eos-avtalen-er-verdens-beste-handelsavtale   https://navva.org/norway/norway/solberg-the-eea-agreement-is-the-worlds-best-trade-agreement/, accessed 6 July 2021.

internal frontiers in which the free movement of goods, persons, services and capital is ensured'.[3] To bring this about, of course tariffs must be tackled and regulations aligned, but also the multitude of smaller obstacles which mean that it still makes a difference in which European country one is – everything from roaming charges to the recognition of diplomas, or the need to set up a new bank account and get different payment cards. Incidentally, these obstacles increasingly originate beyond national regulations, in the form of barriers erected along national borders by private companies, for example, in the pursuit of profit maximisation through price discrimination,[4] so that prices of products differ in better- and worse-off markets.[5] As legislative barriers are rolled back, our vigilance needs to shift so that they should not be replaced by equally restrictive measures taken by private companies.

One simply cannot build an ambitious project like the internal market on self-interest alone, or even build it on mutual economic interest alone. Just because, for example, Liechtenstein's GDP per capita is the highest in the world[6] and is with close to 40 per cent of its economy underpinned by industrial production the most highly industrialised country in Europe, comprising notably world leading manufacturers of dental products[7] and power tools,[8] that would not on its own have enabled Liechtenstein to negotiate the complete market access it has today to the internal market.

---

[3]   Art 26(2) TFEU: 'The internal market shall comprise an area without internal frontiers in which the free movement of goods, persons, services and capital is ensured in accordance with the provisions of the Treaties.'

[4]   In the economic sense as a pricing strategy where the same goods are sold at different prices in different markets: see Paul R Krugman and Maurice Obstfeld, *International Economics: Theory and Policy* (Boston, 2003), 142.

[5]   Regulation (EU) 2018/302 has been applicable in all EU Member States since 3 December 2018 and addresses unjustified online sales discrimination based on customers' nationality, place of residence or place of establishment within the internal market. Joint Committee Decision No 311/2019 incorporating the Regulation into the EEA Agreement was adopted on 13 December 2019 but only entered into force on 1 August 2020 as 'constitutional requirements' had been indicated pursuant to Art 103 EEA.

[6]   US\$ 166,022, just ahead of Monaco (US\$ 165,421) and Luxembourg (US\$ 106,806). Bermuda and Macao are then followed by the other three EFTA States on spots 6, 7 and 8 of the list: Switzerland (US\$ 80,101), Norway (US\$ 75,295) and Iceland (US\$ 73,060): United Nations Statistics Division, National Accounts Main Aggregates Database 2017, accessed 16 March 2019.

[7]   Ivoclar Vivadent AG, headquartered in Schaan, Liechtenstein, generates an annual turnover of some CHF 800 million with a range of products and systems for dentists and dental technicians. It has subsidiaries and marketing offices in 29 countries and employs approximately 3,500 people.

[8]   Hilti AG, headquartered in Schaan, Liechtenstein, employs 29,000 people worldwide.

From a purely economic point of view, in order to unleash the full potential of market integration between advanced economies, one has to go beyond merely improving the terms of trade. To enable the complex value chains and cross-border services collaboration, not only goods, but also people need to move freely across national borders. Economic studies have consistently shown that the internal market is by way of consequence one of the biggest drivers of prosperity in Europe. Although some regions gain more than others, everyone wins.[9] Interestingly, the EEA EFTA States appear to be among the biggest winners in terms of per capita welfare gains from the internal market. This is at the same time consistent with the advanced nature of the economies in question, with a strong representation of high value-added production, and testimony to the fact that their integration into the internal market functions well even without EU membership. More importantly, economic integration alone would not be capable of commanding popular support in the longer term without a strong social component and ensuring that not only businesses but also people benefit. In any event, by reason of the manifold close cultural ties among European countries, their common heritage and shared values make it relatively easy to find a common denominator also as regards the approach to be taken to social and consumer protection issues. There are by way of consequence considerable substantive rights which flow from the EEA Agreement for people, be that in their capacity as consumers, workers, students, pensioners or simply cross-border travellers. Importantly, many of these rights benefit people who do not even leave their home country: EEA law makes our food safer, choice in supermarkets wider, and prices lower, to name just a few advantages.

A more than merely symbolic component of the EEA are the EEA Grants which the EEA EFTA States make available to contribute to a more equal Europe by reducing social and economic disparities.[10]

The EEA Agreement therefore really is much more than a free trade agreement. Firstly, it is not only, and arguably not even primarily, about businesses and traders, but about people. The much-vaunted free movement of people

---

[9]   Aart De Geus, chairman and CEO of the Bertelsmann Stiftung, summarising the findings of a 2019 Bertelsmann Stiftung study 'Estimating economic benefits of the Single Market for European countries and regions' by Giordano Mion and Dominic Ponattu.

[10]   The EEA Grants are funded jointly by all three donor countries – Iceland, Liechtenstein and Norway. The donor countries contribute according to their size and GDP – Norway provides approximately 95.8 per cent, Iceland 3 per cent and Liechtenstein 1.2 per cent. During the 2014–2021 funding period, the EEA Grants amount to €1.5 billion:see eeagrants.org, accessed 6 July 2021. In addition, the Norway Grants are funded by Norway alone and consist of an additional €1.3 billion during the 2014–2021 funding period.

serves as a representative illustration here. Secondly, it creates a *sui generis* legal order which bestows legal rights on individuals and simultaneously entrenches the shared fundamental values on which the EEA as a whole is founded. These two aspects will be explored further below, before delving into the two main mechanisms by which EEA law is enforced and concluding in setting out the fundamental roles which the judicial enforcement mechanisms play for the viability of the EEA legal order as a whole.

1.1   Free Movement of People

Approached purely from the point of view of their wording, the fundamental freedoms as laid down in the EU Treaties are concerned with economic operators rather than people. It is true that Title IV of Part Three of the TFEU is entitled 'Free movement of *persons*, services and capital', which together with the free movement of goods dealt with in Title II constitute the famous 'four freedoms'. As reading the substantive provisions however immediately reveals, 'persons' is shorthand in this context for workers, covered in Chapter 1, and establishment of self-employed persons and undertakings[11] in Chapter 2. One can thus understand that readers of only these provisions may be misled into thinking that individuals can benefit from the freedoms only for the purposes of pursuing an economic activity. That sort of blinkered approach would however ignore the consistent case law of the EFTA Court and the CJEU, as well as the fundamental common values of the contracting parties, which form the wider context in which the EEA Agreement must be seen.

The four freedoms, as fundamental objectives of the EU and the EEA, are given a wide interpretation. Thus, the freedom to provide services for example includes the freedom for the recipients of services to go to another State in order to receive a service there, without being obstructed by restrictions, and notably tourists must be regarded as recipients of services.[12]

The EEA Agreement has moreover ever since its entry into force contained measures of EU secondary legislation operationalising the freedom of movement of persons as workers and as economically inactive EEA nationals, in both cases including their family members.[13] It is useful to recall in this regard

---

[11]   While a wider concept that merely covering companies or firms with legal personality (see Case E-3/13 and E-20/13 *Fred. Olsen*, confirmed in C-646/15 *Trustees of the P Panayi Accumulation & Maintenance Settlements*, EU:C:2017:682), it is notable that Art 54(2) TFEU excludes non-profit-making entities from the concept.

[12]   Case 186/87 *Cowan* EU:C:1989:47, para 15 and the case law cited therein; Case C-897/19 PPU *Ruska Federacija v IN*, paras 52–53.

[13]   Directives 90/364/EEC, 90/365/EEC and 93/96/EEC were referred to in Annex VIII to the EEA Agreement on freedom of establishment.

that the EEA Agreement is dynamic in nature and does not operate subject to the strict hierarchy of norms as the EU Treaties. By way of consequence, the acts of EU secondary legislation incorporated into the EEA Agreement have in principle equal ranking alongside the main provisions of the Agreement. As a matter of EEA law, there is no marked distinction between a right being conferred by an act contained in an annex, or a principal article.

As the main provisions of the EEA Agreement have never been amended, there is no equivalent to be found in them to the concept of Union citizenship introduced by the Maastricht Treaty.[14] This consolidates intervening developments and clarifies that free movement rights are independent of economic activity. According to Article 21(1) TFEU, a Union citizen shall have a right to move and reside freely within the territory of the EU States, subject to the limitations and conditions laid down in EU law. However, the absence of such a clear statement in the main provisions of the EEA Agreement is legally immaterial in any event since the incorporation of the Citizens' Rights Directive[15] into the EEA Agreement.

The Citizens' Rights Directive regulates the freedom of EEA nationals to move and reside freely within the territory of the EEA States, and Articles 6 and 7 confer the right of residence for both economic and non-economic purposes. Those provisions make operational not only the free movement of workers and the freedom of establishment, but also the free movement of EEA nationals generally. Nationals of EEA EFTA States are for these purposes placed on the same footing as EU citizens and derive the same free movement rights from the Directive.

It is useful to emphasise that the Citizens' Rights Directive in many respects only clarifies rights which find their roots in the acquis that was taken into the EEA Agreement on its adoption, be that the then existing secondary legislation or the case law of the CJEU such as *Cowan*,[16] as well as the shared fundamental values of EEA States. The obvious link with the right to family life, protected by the ECHR, was made by the EFTA Court in *Jabbi*, holding that 'all the EEA States are parties to the European Convention on Human Rights,

---

[14]   This concept is now expressed in Part II of the TFEU. Every person holding the nationality of an EU State is a Union citizen. Union citizenship is additional to national citizenship of an EU State and entails certain rights under EU law.

[15]   As there is no concept of 'EEA Citizenship', this is referred to as the 'Residence Directive' in the non-EU EEA States. This semantic point aside, the Directive was incorporated into the EEA Agreement without substantive adaptations or modifications, albeit with a Joint Declaration that 'The concept of Union Citizenship as introduced by the Treaty of Maastricht (now Arts 17 et seq EC Treaty) has no equivalent in the EEA Agreement.'

[16]   *Cowan* (n 12).

which enshrines in Article 8(1) the right to respect for private and family life. According to established case law, provisions of the EEA Agreement are to be interpreted in the light of fundamental rights'.[17]

The EFTA Court has consistently, in its *Gunnarsson*,[18] *Jabbi*[19] and *Campbell*[20] judgments upheld an interpretation of the provisions of the EEA Agreement whereby nationals of EEA EFTA States enjoy the same free movement rights as EU citizens, independently of any economic activity. The Court has thereby at the same time safeguarded the principle of homogeneity.[21]

Similar considerations have now led the CJEU to go arguably even further and conclude that nationals of EEA EFTA States can be considered to be in a situation that is objectively comparable with that of an EU citizen to whom, in accordance with Article 3(2) TEU, the EU offers an area of freedom, security and justice without internal frontiers, in which the free movement of persons is ensured.[22] Evidently, this also does not have the effect of importing the TFEU's citizenship provisions into the EEA: notably the political rights find no reflection in EEA law,[23] and the equivalence is merely achieved as regards the free movement of people.

In summary, the most tangible and important achievement of the EEA Agreement is that, through free movement of people, it allows the nationals of its contracting parties to treat the whole EEA as their 'home'.

As a final point in this regard, it must be noted that in certain quarters a rearguard action still seems to be fought trying to limit the reach of the EEA Agreement and the benefits which nationals of EEA EFTA States can derive from it. Sometimes, this can come from surprising corners, such as notably the Norwegian Government's position before the European courts. It is striking that any State should be arguing against the obvious interests of its own citizens, but the stance becomes even more puzzling when seen against the Norwegian Government's formal line, which has consistently been to bolster the EEA Agreement and its role for citizens' rights. In the current official strat-

---

[17]   Case E-28/15 *Yankuba Jabbi v The Norwegian Government*, [2016] EFTA Ct Rep 575, para 81.
[18]   Case E-26/13 *The Icelandic State v Gunnarsson* [2014] EFTA Ct Rep 254.
[19]   *Yankuba Jabbi* (n 17).
[20]   Case E-4/19 *Campbell v The Norwegian Government*.
[21]   *Yankuba Jabbi* (n 17), para 68.
[22]   *Ruska Federacija v IN* (n 12), para 75.
[23]   Provisions of Part II of the TFEU entitle Union citizens to political rights including certain electoral rights and a right of petition to the European Parliament including access to the European Ombudsman.

egy for cooperation with the EU, the Norwegian Minister of Foreign Affairs states:

> Under the EEA Agreement, Norwegian citizens have opportunities they could not have dreamed of in the past, when Norway only had a classic trade agreement with the EU. Many Norwegians make use of their rights under the Agreement to cross borders, live, work, invest, and study in other EEA countries. Younger generations take these opportunities for granted. The Government sees it as one of its main tasks to increase awareness of the importance of the EEA Agreement for safeguarding fundamental Norwegian interests.[24]

The Government's submissions in European Courts have not been consistent with this approach and have at times veered to the comically anachronistic. Having twice already had the EFTA Court confirm its position regarding the applicability of the Citizens' Rights Directive in *Gunnarsson*[25] and *Jabbi*,[26] it seems that the Norwegian Government nevertheless asked the Norwegian Supreme Court for a – wholly unnecessary – reference on the same issue in *Campbell*,[27] predictably yielding the same answer. It can then only be qualified as astonishing, that Norway yet again appears to be rearguing the same ground hardly six months later in the *NAV* cases.[28]

In the same vein, it was a courageous line indeed to argue, in a 2020 Grand Chamber CJEU case, that there were doubts as to the applicability of the fundamental freedoms to the situation of an EEA national who had been arrested in another EEA State, as it was in essence not clear whether he had purchased a bus ticket (and thus become a recipient of services) and seeing that criminal matters fell outside the EEA Agreement.[29] While those arguments might have been considered serious in the 1970s, they were seriously out of place 50 years later. It also does not appear clear what objective might conceivably be pursued by such submissions, which – had they been successful – could have

---

[24] Ine Eriksen Søreide, Minister of Foreign Affairs, 'Norway in Europe – The Norwegian Government's strategy for cooperation with the EU 2018–2021', Foreword https://www.regjeringen.no/globalassets/departementene/ud/dokumenter/eu/eu_strategy.pdf, accessed November 2020.

[25] *Gunnarsson* (n 18).

[26] *Yankuba Jabbi* (n 17).

[27] *Campbell v The Norwegian Government* (n 20).

[28] Cases E-8/20, E-13/20 and E-15/20, pending at the time of writing.

[29] *Ruska Federacija v IN* (n 12). Being a PPU case, where only the parties to the original proceedings and the Commission have an opportunity of submitting written observations, the submissions were made orally at the hearing, where ESA was represented by one of the authors. The submissions are recorded in summary by Advocate General Tanchev in his opinion: EU:C:2020:128, paras 55–59.

deprived an EEA national of the full protections that EEA law offers, and would moreover have undermined the standing of the whole EFTA pillar.

Indeed, also the position taken by Norway in the same case that the Surrender Procedure Agreement between Iceland and Norway was to be seen as a regular international treaty that forms no part of EEA law[30] appears to ignore the obvious reliance of that treaty on the same common values which are being consistently strengthened and operationalised through the EEA Agreement, and be short-sighted in the extreme when it comes to defending the interests of Norwegian citizens. Equal treatment of EEA EFTA nationals and EU citizens could never have been achieved in as sensitive an area as the sphere of the European Arrest Warrant and concomitant Surrender Procedure without the fertile ground of common values, mutual trust and effective enforcement mechanisms, which have been continuously strengthened within the EEA Agreement. The fact that EEA EFTA States may opt to keep certain aspects of multilateral cooperation with the EU formally outside the EEA Agreement and adopt acts alongside it, does not detract from the fact that, without the EEA Agreement as a basis, much of this would not be possible.

1.2   A *Sui Generis* Legal Order, Conferring Rights on Individuals

The emphasis on people at the core of the EEA Agreement is a feature shared with the EU's legal order. Other ones are the fact that the EEA Agreement should be concerned with non-economic obstacles and that there is no *de minimis* threshold below which rights would be unenforceable. Contrary to ordinary free trade agreements, enforceable rights are conferred on individuals and the starting point is that there should be no obstacles, so that any restriction needs to be explained – it must be 'justified and proportionate' in the language of the settled case law of the European courts.

In its *van Gend en Loos* judgment, the CJEU famously held that the Community constitutes a new legal order of international law for the benefit of which the States have limited their sovereign rights, albeit within limited fields, and the subjects of which comprise not only Member States but also their nationals.[31] The EEA Agreement does not comprise all of the hallmarks of EU law, notably direct effect and primacy, but nevertheless also does give rise to a *sui generis* legal order, which aims at achieving notably homogeneity[32] and reciprocity[33] through different means, and compensates

---

[30]   Summarised by Advocate General Tanchev in his opinion: ibid., para 57.
[31]   Case 26/62 *Van Gend en Loos* EU:C:1963:1.
[32]   Philipp Speitler, 'Judicial Homogeneity as a Fundamental Principle of the EEA' in Carl Baudenbacher (ed), *The Fundamental Principles of EEA Law* (Springer 2017).
[33]   Carl Baudenbacher, 'Reciprocity' in Baudenbacher, ibid.

through other mechanisms such as the rule of precedence in Protocol 35 to the EEA Agreement and the principle of State liability for breaches of EEA law. Absolutely fundamental in this respect is the duty to interpret national law in conformity with EEA law. As the EFTA Court recalled in *Irish Bank*,[34] the objective of establishing a dynamic and homogeneous EEA can only be achieved if EFTA and EU citizens and economic operators enjoy, relying upon EEA law, the same rights in both EU and EFTA countries. National courts are bound to interpret domestic law, so far as possible, in the light of the wording and the purpose of EEA law in order to achieve the result sought by it and consequently comply with Articles 3 and 7 EEA and Protocol 35 to the EEA Agreement.

It is only where the principle of conform interpretation cannot yield the result required by EEA law that State liability will come into play. It was in the *Sveinbjörnsdóttir* case[35] that the EFTA Court found State liability to be part of EEA law. The Court based itself on three reasons: homogeneity; protection of individuals and economic operators; and the duty of loyalty.[36] On this basis, the Court held 'that the EEA Agreement is an international treaty *sui generis* which contains a distinct legal order of its own'.

A crucial part of the EEA legal order is the proper application of little-known Protocol 35 to the EEA Agreement, which the EFTA Court notably referred to in *Irish Bank* as forming part of the basis of the principle of conform interpretation of national law in line with EEA law. From the perspective of an EU lawyer, this protocol merely states what is obvious, namely that implemented EEA law enjoys primacy over national law. Its sole article reads:

> For cases of possible conflicts between implemented EEA rules and other statutory provisions, the EFTA States undertake to introduce, if necessary, a statutory provision to the effect that EEA rules prevail in these cases.

The first observations of the EFTA Court on Protocol 35 EEA arose in the Court's first case, *Restamark*,[37] where the Court held it to be inherent in the nature of Protocol 35 EEA that, in cases of conflict, individuals and economic operators must be entitled to invoke and claim, at the national level, any rights that can be derived from the provisions of the EEA Agreement that have been

---

[34] Case E-18/11 *Irish Bank*, paras 121–124. See also Case E-1/07 *Criminal Proceedings against A* [2007] EFTA Ct Rep 246, para 39.

[35] Case E-9/97 *Erla María Sveinbjörnsdóttir v Iceland* [1998] EFTA Ct Rep 95, paras 62 et seq; and see Case E-4/01 *Karlsson* [2002] EFTA Ct Rep 240, paras 25 and 37–48.

[36] Art 3 EEA.

[37] Case E-1/94 *Restamark* [1994–1995] EFTA Ct Rep 15, para 77.

made part of the national legal order, if they are unconditional and sufficiently precise.

The EFTA Court has repeatedly held that it follows from Protocol 35 EEA that EEA rules that have been implemented into national law must prevail over other conflicting national provisions, provided that the former are unconditional and sufficiently precise.[38] This is thus capable of giving rise to a form of direct effect, albeit in full respect of legislative sovereignty of the EFTA States (as there actually has to have been an implementation of the EEA rules in question into national law for the principle to become operational).

In view of the high threshold for State liability actions (in addition to the rather heavy-handed nature of resorting to State liability), it is of utmost practical importance that the courts properly apply the principle of conform interpretation, and that Protocol 35 EEA is implemented to the extent necessary. In Iceland, there unfortunately continue to be problems in this respect, with the consequence that even the fundamental provisions of the EEA Agreement on the fundamental freedoms cannot be relied upon in cases of a (possible) conflict with other national provisions, despite the fact that the four freedoms are implemented into Icelandic law and comply with the requirement of being unconditional and sufficiently precise. This deprives these main provisions of the EEA Agreement of their core purpose, that is to prevent unjustified restrictions on free movement, and entails that individuals and economic operators are unable to rely on their rights derived from the EEA Agreement. ESA has accordingly addressed a Reasoned Opinion to Iceland on the matter.[39] What is unfortunate in this context is the circumstance that the Icelandic Supreme Court has been involved in a string of cases where provisions implementing EEA law were being invoked in the face of other, conflicting, national legislation, but the court has not felt able to comply with the obligations incumbent on all organs of the State by virtue of Protocol 35.

As will be explored in more detail below against the background of some recent jurisprudence in the field of public procurement, in addition to complicating the practical application of EEA law, it is essential that national judges contribute to upholding the mutual trust and cooperation characterised by the closeness of shared fundamental values of the EU and EFTA States.

As already touched upon, the internal market, as a concept at the core of EU law, has never been narrow in outlook. It is as much about people as about

---

[38]   Case E-1/01 *Einarsson* [2002] EFTA Ct Rep 1, para 50; Case E-2/12 *HOB-vín ehf* [2012] EFTA Ct Rep 1092, para 122; Case E-11/12 *Koch* [2013] EFTA Ct Rep 272, para 119; Case E-6/12 *ESA v Norway* [2013] EFTA Ct Rep 618, para 66; Case E-15/12 *Wahl* [2013] EFTA Ct Rep 534, para 54 and Case E-12/13 *ESA v Iceland* [2014], EFTA Ct Rep 58, para 73.

[39]   Decision 002/20/COL of 30 September 2020.

business. It is not just about making the big deals possible, but also about removing the small, everyday obstacles to free movement. This means also tackling national restrictions that may not have a direct quantifiable financial impact, but that nevertheless hamper free movement of people or have a chilling effect on them exercising their rights. Given this context, there is a particular burden on the judiciary to ensure that the concrete rights in the service of aspirational ideals do not end up being seen as empty messages.

2.   TWO COMPLEMENTARY ENFORCEMENT MECHANISMS

The fact that the internal market aims at more ambitious market integration than traditional free trade agreements, and requires overcoming also smaller-scale obstacles, and even ones that might be seen as *de minimis*, is reflected in the institutional and procedural framework.

There are two potent enforcement mechanisms in the EEA EFTA model which, while based on equivalent ones in the EU, are not commonly found in ordinary free trade agreements: public enforcement by an independent surveillance authority and private enforcement through the national courts.[40]

2.1   Independent Surveillance and Enforcement by the EFTA Surveillance Authority and the European Commission

First, there is an independent surveillance mechanism. The EEA EFTA pillar is 'self-policing': in EU Member States, the European Commission fulfils the function of 'guardian of the treaties'. In the EFTA States parties to the EEA – Norway, Liechtenstein and Iceland – the EFTA Surveillance Authority (commonly known as 'ESA') fulfils that task. The EFTA Surveillance Authority broadly enjoys the same powers as the Commission does in carrying out investigations and in bringing infringement actions. Indeed, ESA cooperates with the Commission very directly, for example, in joint competition dawn raids or veterinary inspections.

Enforcement by an organisation charged with compliance is particularly important where there are restrictions that are small enough that individuals would not go to the length of launching an expensive enforcement action themselves. An independent surveillance mechanism can also be important where fundamental values of society, such as environmental standards or general health protection are in issue – or indeed the rule of law.

---

[40]   Actions for annulment will be left to one side for present purposes.

A particular point of concern where intervention by ESA is required are national legislative practices in breach of the principle of legal certainty. This principle requires that rules of EEA law be clear and precise so that interested parties can ascertain their position in situations and legal relationships governed by EEA law. This is enunciated in settled case law of the EFTA Court[41] as well as the CJEU.[42] Moreover, '[e]ven if, in practice, the authorities of a Member State do not apply a national provision which is at variance with [EEA] law, the principle of legal certainty nevertheless requires that that provision be amended'.

ESA has not always endeared itself to the national administrations when it investigates seemingly minor restrictions to free movement. It can at times also be quite challenging to explain to interested journalists and citizens why ESA is spending resources on matters such as type-approval certificates for second-hand lawnmowers, or why we pester national authorities over the recognition of professional qualifications which are maybe held by only a single practitioner on their territory.[43] The answer tends to be broadly the same: the benefits of the internal market require reducing all obstacles to free movement; restrictions are rarely isolated and even if they apply only to a narrow field are liable to have a wider deterrent chilling effect on people deciding to exercise free movement rights. And finally, and crucially, if we as the authority specifically entrusted with this task do not take up a matter, then who will?

2.2   Enforcement Through the National Courts

Secondly, enforceable rights are given directly to people. Rights are given to students, to workers, to people travelling or buying goods or services in another EEA State. EEA law transposed into the national legal orders can be relied upon by anyone in front of national courts to enforce rights. Where EEA law is incorrectly implemented, a damages remedy is available against that State.[44] Again, it is the national courts where such actions can be brought. The

---

[41]   See Joined Cases E-4/10, E-6/10 and E-7/10 *Liechtenstein v ESA* [2011] EFTA Ct Rep 16, para 156; also E-17/10 and E-6/11 *Liechtenstein and VTM Fundmanagement v ESA* [2012] EFTA Ct Rep 114, para 142; E-9/11 *ESA v. Norway* [2012] EFTA Ct Rep 442, para 100.

[42]   Case T-115/94 *Opel Austria* EU:T:1997:3, para 124 and case law cited therein. See also e.g., Case C-29/84 *Commission v Germany* ECLI:EU:C:1985:229, para 23 and Case C-119/92 *Commission v Italy* ECLI:EU:C:1994:46, para 17.

[43]   See e.g., Case E-17/14 *EFTA Surveillance Authority v Liechtenstein*, concerning restrictions on pursuit of the profession of 'Dentist' in Liechtenstein.

[44]   *Erla María Sveinbjörnsdóttir* (n 35), para 63.

national courts are thus the cornerstone of the system rather than the CJEU or the EFTA Court.

Conferring rights on individuals accelerates the development of a legal order in a way that no institutional or diplomatic mechanism could. The eighth recital of the EEA Agreement has been premonitory in recording the conviction of the contracting parties 'of the important role that individuals will play in the European Economic Area through the exercise of the rights conferred on them by this Agreement and through the judicial defence of these rights'.

Rights – and procedural rights of suit – in the hands of individuals make every single natural and legal person potentially an agent of the development of the law. Where private enforcement works well, the whole machinery of justice is put to work to flesh out the provisions of the EEA Agreement both in terms of providing clarity as regards what those rights mean in practice, and in terms of developing and extending those rights to the extent that that is necessary to fulfil the underlying ambition of equal treatment for all and the respect for the fundamental principles of the *sui generis* legal order created by the Agreement.

Private enforcement simultaneously provides an important disciplining factor regarding the action of public authorities and ensures that it is not only the national legislator and the central government authorities that are concerned with proper implementation of EEA law. Every local authority, specialist agency and devolved administration is provided with a tangible incentive to comply with EEA law on pain of seeing its decisions scrutinised by the courts at the suit of an individual.

The possibility of developing EEA law through private enforcement moreover ensures that the body of those rules develops in ways that are relevant to individuals: the time and financial costs of litigation will be born freely only by those who have something tangible to gain from a clarification of a particular aspect of the law. In the same way that Adam Smith's 'invisible hand' ensures the efficiency of the market, the constant interplay of individual pressures brought to bear on the development of the law contribute to the coherence and practical relevance of the resulting edifice.

An ancillary point in this regard is that private enforcement can also provide a useful backstop to public enforcement, even as regards cases that have been taken up by the relevant surveillance body (ESA or the Commission), but which may not be progressed as rapidly as desired by the private persons concerned. While private parties usually cannot force ESA to take up a particular case,[45] if their interests are affected in a tangible way, private parties

---

[45] ESA in particular has a practically unfettered discretion as to whether to initiate or progress the infringement procedure against States for infringement of EEA law

can enforce those rights through the national courts irrespective of what stance ESA has taken.

A good example is the field of public procurement, where there has been a lag in bringing procurement practices into line with the relevant EEA legislation, and where there continue to be occasional problems in particular at local level.[46] Until 2011, ESA's policy in the field had been limited to establishing a breach of EEA law and, subsequently, requesting recognition of the infringement by the State concerned. ESA changed its policy in the light of the CJEU's judgments in the 'Brunswick cases'[47] as well as the consequent change in policy on the part of the Commission to pursue infringement cases as long as the contract continues to produce effects and the State has taken no measures to remedy the effects of the breach. Under its current policy, ESA no longer closes infringement cases when the State merely acknowledges its breach of the public procurement rules and, instead, seeking rescission of the contract has in principle become the standard.[48]

In Case E-4/17 *ESA v Norway*, ESA for the first time pursued to judgment an infringement procedure in the public procurement field. The case concerned multiple infringements of Directive 2004/18/EC[49] in relation to the construction and operation of an underground car park in Kristiansand/Norway. As the economic centre of gravity of the contract, consisting in the construction works, had already been performed, ESA nevertheless closed the follow-up case notwithstanding the fact that the measures taken reduced, but did not eliminate, the ongoing negative effects of the breaches of EEA public procurement law. The construction of the car park itself had itself already been concluded by the time the procedure had come to fruition and the unlawfully awarded contract continued to produce effects only as regards the continued operation of the car park (its maintenance in return for the collection of parking fees). While this was due to continue for an exceptionally long period of poten-

---

under Art 31 SCA. See Case E-13/10 *Aleris Ungplan* [2011] EFTA Ct Rep 5, paras 26 and 27 and Case E-2/13 *Bentzen Transport* [2013] EFTA Ct Rep 803, para 40.

[46]   Though, as Case E-8/19 *Scanteam AS v Norway* demonstrates, slipups can happen even when it comes to central Government procurement, *in casu* through the Norwegian Ministry of Foreign affairs acting through its Embassy in Luanda/Angola.

[47]   Joined Cases C-20/01 and C-28/01 *Commission v Germany* EU:C:2003:220, para 36.

[48]   Decision 236/11/COL of 18 July 2011 to adopt a new policy on pursuing infringement cases in the field of public procurement.

[49]   Directive 2004/18/EC of the European Parliament and of the Council of 31 March 2004 on the coordination of procedures for the award of public works contracts, public supply contracts and public service contracts, act previously referred to at point 2 of Annex XVI to the EEA Agreement (replaced by Joint Committee Decision No 97/2016) [2004] OJ L 134/114.

tially up to 60 years, ESA expressly concluded that it was in the exercise of its discretion pursuant to Article 31 SCA, that it did not consider it opportune to pursue this case further.[50]

This rather lenient stance is best seen against the background that – while more than 15 years after the CJEU's Brunswick judgments, it was the first case to be taken 'all the way' in the EFTA pillar of the EEA Agreement. The case already has an obvious pedagogical value for public authorities engaging in public procurement and from a public enforcement point of view, little would have been gained from taking the matter to the EFTA Court anew in order to achieve complete compliance with the judgment in Case E-4/17. While such an action would, in the light of the clear case law of the CJEU, almost certainly have been successful, from ESA's point of view, that was not necessary at this stage in the development of EEA law to ensure that useful conclusions would be drawn from the case.

Importantly for present purposes, ESA's forbearance in insisting on rescission of the contract concerning the operation of the contract, of course has no effect on the ability of private parties to bring the matter before national courts. It would seem that – in particular in the light of the EFTA Court's judgment in Case E-4/17 – the contract in question is voidable. It is merely important to draw a distinction in this respect between the types of actions available to private parties. There is a fundamental difference as regard the conditions attached in this regard between an action sounding in damages for State liability (which has to conform to relatively high standards, notably as regards the seriousness of the breach to be established) and an action based on the deficient procurement procedure (whether that sounds in contract, tort or an intermediate cause of action such as *culpa in contrahendo*). While an action for State liability is, pursuant to the settled case law subject to stringent criteria,[51] public authorities are under a primary duty to remedy all breaches of EEA law, which is the consequence of, and an adjunct to, the rights conferred on individuals by the relevant EEA law.[52]

---

[50] Decision 127/20/COL of 11 November 2020 closing an own initiative case concerning compliance by Norway with the judgment of the EFTA Court in Case E-4/17 in relation to the construction and operation of an underground car park.

[51] According to the principle of State liability, an EEA State may be held responsible for breaches of its obligations under EEA law when three conditions are met: first, the rule of law infringed must be intended to confer rights on individuals and economic operators; secondly, the breach must be sufficiently serious; and, thirdly, there must be a direct causal link between the breach of the obligation resting on the State and the damage sustained by the injured party. See Case E-7/18 *Fosen-Linjen II* [2019], para 117.

[52] The point is an obvious one, but see e.g., Case C-199/82 *San Giorgio*, EU:C: 1983:318, para 12.

State liability, which the EFTA Court established in the EFTA pillar legal order in the landmark *Sveinbjörnsdóttir* case,[53] is in many ways the ultimate, and usually inadequate, backstop to a failure to comply with EEA law. Damages are usually inadequate – in particular where lives of individuals have been upset, but also when it comes to assessing the true measure of losses of commercial undertakings, particularly when this encompasses lost future profit (*lucrum cessans*) in addition to loss suffered (*damnum emergens*).[54] That is why specific performance is usually to be preferred to an award of damages when it comes to doing justice.

The important consequence for the purposes of EEA law is that there is an additional resulting burden placed on the need to interpret national law – including national procedural law – to the extent possible so as to ensure the full effectiveness of EEA law.[55] The first reflex of any judge thus has to be to achieve justice in the individual case with the tools at their disposal. Any breach of the law is in principle sufficient to trigger liability sounding in damages to compensate the person harmed for the damage incurred, in the same way as in any other commercial relationship.[56] In application of the principle of national procedural autonomy,[57] it is then for the national courts to ensure that the whole body of national law is interpreted in such a way as to give effect to EEA law.[58] It is only where that this is not possible, i.e., usually where EEA law has not been incorporated into the national legal order, or where it has been insufficiently or incorrectly incorporated, so that the national judge cannot provide a remedy for a breach – that State liability with its traditionally higher 'sufficiently serious breach' liability bar comes into play.[59]

The important point for present purposes is that private enforcement is, to function effectively, dependent on national judges impartially giving full effect to the rules of EEA law, even if that requires them to resort to novel methods of interpretation or a different approach than what they would normally have considered orthodox. Especially because litigation concerning points of EEA law will usually pit 'outsiders' – people from another EEA State – against

---

[53]   *Erla María Sveinbjörnsdóttir* (n 35), paras 62 et seq.; and see *Karlsson* (n 35), paras 25 and 37–48.

[54]   Cf Art 7.4.2, 2004 UNIDROIT Principles: 'The aggrieved party is entitled to full compensation for harm [that] includes both any loss which it suffered and any gain of which it was deprived [...].'

[55]   The obligation to perform consistent interpretations extends to 'national law as a whole' (e.g., Case C-397-403/01 *Pfeiffer* ECLI:EU:C:2004:584).

[56]   See Case E-16/16 *Fosen-Linjen I* [2017] EFTA Ct Rep 617, paras 64, 80 and 82.

[57]   *Fosen-Linjen II* (n 51), para 113; *Fosen-Linjen I*, ibid., para 70.

[58]   *Irish Bank* (n 34), paras 123–124. See also Case C-282/10 *Dominguez* EU:C:2012:33, para 27 and the case law cited therein.

[59]   *Fosen-Linjen II* (n 51), paras 117–120. See also *Irish Bank* (n 34), para 125.

locals, that it is all the more important that the judiciary called upon to adjudicate on those disputes be seen to be scrupulously impartial and diligent in its application of the law. Any public impression that EEA law rights are difficult or uncertain in their application or outcome is liable to have a chilling effect on individuals contemplating engaging in cross-border free movement.

3. ACCESS TO JUSTICE AND JUDICIAL INDEPENDENCE

When it comes to protecting the rule of law, enforcement through the Commission and the EFTA Surveillance Authority are at least equally potent to private enforcement, maybe even more so. The Article 7 TEU mechanism on the EU side is a special example. But the mere fact that there is some monitoring by an independent authority clearly has a salutary effect on rule of law compliance as well.

We would of course all like to think that our own States are immune from rule of law deviations. But as recently as 2019, the European Court of Human Rights found that Iceland had infringed Article 6(1) of the ECHR in selecting the judges for its newly-established Court of Appeal.[60] The Court found that the process had amounted to a 'flagrant' breach of the applicable rules at the material time. It had been 'to the detriment of the confidence that the judiciary in a democratic society must inspire in the public and had contravened the very essence of the principle that a tribunal must be established by law'.

In another recent judgment, the ECtHR had the occasion to examine the judicial protection mechanisms in the EFTA pillar of the EEA Agreement in the context of a case against Norway. Here, the EFTA Court's standing requirements were challenged as regards the right of access to a tribunal under Article 6 of the ECHR.[61] ESA intervened in this matter, making submissions to the Strasbourg Court on how access to justice is ensured in the EEA court system. The EEA legal system is strengthened by being subject to judicial scrutiny on human rights. In the event, the application was dismissed as inadmissible, but the ECtHR's judgment contains a number of clarifications concerning the compliance of the EFTA pillar judicial mechanism with the ECHR, in particular as regards the applicability of the so-called Bosphorus presumption.[62]

---

[60] *Guðmundur Andri Ástráðsson v Iceland* App no 26374/18 (ECtHR, 12 March 2019).

[61] *Konkurrenten.no AS v Norway* App no 47341/15 (ECtHR, 5 November 2019).

[62] Named after *Bosphorus Hava Yolları Turizm ve Ticaret Anonim Şirketi v. Ireland* ECHR 2005-VI, paras 152–153. According to the Bosphorus presumption, when a State implements its obligations arising from the membership in an interna-

The ECtHR started by holding that the basis for the Bosphorus presumption was in principle lacking when it comes to the implementation of EEA law at domestic level within the framework of the EEA Agreement. In coming to this conclusion, the ECtHR highlighted two features of distinction as between the EU and EFTA pillars of the EEA Agreement. First, within the framework of the EEA Agreement itself there is no direct effect and no supremacy of EEA law over national law.[63] Secondly, and although the EFTA Court has expressed the view that the provisions of the EEA Agreement 'are to be interpreted in the light of fundamental rights' in order to enhance coherency between EEA law and EU law,[64] the EEA Agreement does not include the EU Charter of Fundamental Rights, or any reference whatsoever to other legal instruments having the same effect, such as the Convention.

The ECtHR nevertheless went on to establish a 'Bosphorus light' presumption in favour of the EFTA pillar judicial control mechanism.[65] It observed that the issue was whether Norway was responsible for an alleged denial of access to a court by the EFTA Court when it dismissed the applicant's case. This responsibility will in any event only come into play if, and to the extent that, the alleged violation can be attributed to a structural shortcoming in the procedural guarantees afforded under the organisational and procedural regime of the EFTA Court, the test being whether the procedural regime is manifestly deficient when compared with the Convention requirements. The ECtHR then took into account the fact that the EFTA Court was set up to operate as a judicial body similar to the CJEU, and that the essential procedural principles governing the operation of the EFTA Court were inspired by those of the CJEU. The only starting point could then be that there are no such manifest deficiencies. The ECtHR further held that this was confirmed by specific provisions in the EEA and ESA/Court Agreements, the EFTA Court's Rules of Procedure and its case law as the parties and ESA had presented it. In this connection, the ECtHR noted in particular that the EFTA Court is a body of independent and impartial judges who deliver reasoned decisions based on proceedings that are public and adversarial.

As a final point in this regard, history has taught us that while judges potentially wield the strongest powers within any State subject to the rule of law, they are also potentially the most vulnerable in the face of any concerted effort to undermine the rule of law. Judges are supposed to be scrupulously

---

tional organisation, the State is presumed acting in compliance with the Convention, provided that protection of human rights in that international organisation is equivalent to that provided by the Convention.

[63]   Contrast *Bosphorus*, ibid., para 164.
[64]   *Yankuba Jabbi* (n 17), para 81.
[65]   *Konkurrenten.no AS v Norway* (n 61), paras 44–45.

impartial, which is why it is delicate for them to take sides and advocate for causes – even if it so happens that the side is their own and the cause the rule of law. The judicial power is largely dependent on the other branches of the State for support and protection. ESA monitors rule of law issues particularly closely when they relate to the judicial enforcement of the EEA Agreement, be it within the EFTA or the EU States. This means the Authority ensures that appointments to the EFTA Court are made in accordance with the rules, and of course more generally must uphold the independence of both the EFTA Court and itself as an institution.

3.1   Judicial Protection of the Rule of Law

All national courts within the EU/EEA system operate in a European capacity when applying the law derived from the respective treaties. It is essential that they are able to fulfil their function having regard to the law only, and free from any direct or indirect external influence.

As eloquently put in an Order of the President of the EFTA Court:

> the Court assumes an essential role in the EEA legal order and the proper composition of the Court is key to the observance of the rights and obligations flowing from the EEA Agreement. Without an independent court, the purpose of the Agreement would be rendered nugatory and the EFTA States would fail to safeguard the protection of the rights of individuals and economic operators. To maintain the independence of the judiciary is not a privilege for judges, but a guarantee for the respect of these rights and a bulwark of the democratic order.[66]

In the EU, the infringement action brought by the Commission against Poland to protect the independence of the Polish Supreme Court[67] is a good example. Formal infringement action was also accompanied by a number of preliminary references from all levels of the Polish judiciary to the Court of Justice of the EU. Again, ESA participated in a number of these cases and submitted observations as regards why it considered the reforms of the Polish judiciary to be problematic.

ESA will always be vigilant when it comes to upholding the rule of law. It is not just about access to justice in concrete individual cases. Problems in access to justice in an EEA State would profoundly affect the position of individuals and economic operators from other EEA States seeking to assert their internal market rights. Such an individual may lose some money or rights if no fair

---

[66]   Case E-21/16 *Pascal Nobile and DAS Rechtsschutz-Versicherungs AG,* Order of the President of the EFTA Court (20 February 2017), para 25.

[67]   Case C-619/18 *Commission v Poland* EU:C:2019:531.

and independent hearing is possible. Such an individual may also return home disappointed, and less inclined to go into foreign ventures again. That is as such bad for the individual, and it is also bad for the internal market because of its deterrent chilling effect.

As already mentioned, the fact that EEA law confers enforceable rights on individuals is one of the key aspects which sets the internal market apart from less ambitious trade deals. It is what gives confidence to individuals and economic operators to treat the whole of the EEA as their 'home'. If the rule of law is compromised, their trust to exercise or enforce their rights is undermined.

Observance of the rule of law, by way of the independence of the judiciary and access to justice, is at the very core of democracy and essential to upholding the highest human rights standards. We see this reflected in the political debate in the EU these days. Safeguarding the rule of law is not only a precondition for a well-functioning EU, it is a precondition for close economic integration in the entire EEA as well, and by necessity a shared core value.

Although the legal order established by the EEA Agreement differs in many respects from the EU legal order and pursues a less far-reaching level of integration,[68] these differences do not, at any rate, extend to the very foundations and values on which both legal orders are based. More specifically, both legal orders are based equally and fundamentally on the respect for the rule of law in all its emanations. As is affirmed in the Preamble to the EEA Agreement, the relationship between the EU, its Member States and the EEA EFTA States[69] is based on *'long standing common values and European identity'*.[70]

The EEA Agreement may not contain any express equivalent to Articles 2 and 7 of the TEU, but the values enshrined and protected by those provisions are no less part of the EEA legal order and underpin our operation and existence. It is clear that respect for the values enunciated expressly in the TEU equally are preconditions for participation in the EEA.

3.2   Judicial Dialogue

The fact that these same fundamental values are shared across the EEA is the principal reason why the 'self-policing' aspect of the EEA Agreement works, without the need for any cross-pillar checks and balances. There is no EFTA judge on the CJEU and no EU judge on the EFTA Court, even when these courts adjudicate, say, on the rights of a Liechtensteiner receiving healthcare

---

[68]   *Erla María Sveinbjörnsdóttir and The Government of Iceland* (n 35), para 59.
[69]   EEA EFTA States are the EFTA States that are Contracting Parties to the EEA Agreement (namely Iceland, Liechtenstein and Norway).
[70]   See the written observations of the EFTA Surveillance Authority of 20 November 2018 in Case C-522/18, *DS v Zakład Ubezpieczeń Społecznych,* paras 1 and 4.

in Spain,[71] an Icelandic citizen being arrested in Croatia pursuant to a Russian arrest warrant,[72] or a Norwegian indicted for spending time in Italy.[73]

It is rather instructive to contrast this 'self-policing' approach based on deep mutual trust under the EEA Agreement with the approach being currently put forward by the EU in other contexts. Both the Withdrawal Agreement with the UK and the draft Institutional Agreement with Switzerland provide for less freedom and require closer alignment notably with the case law of the CJEU.

Article 4(2) of the draft EU-Switzerland agreement provides, under the heading 'Principle of uniform interpretation' that all provisions of the agreement 'shall be interpreted and applied in accordance with the case law of the CJEU' both 'before or after the signature of the agreement'.[74] The UK Withdrawal Agreement (which is of course not intended to represent the permanent settlement) goes even further and provides for direct jurisdiction of the CJEU.

This approach is in contrast with the formal position under the EEA Agreement, in a number of respects. First, it is only the CJEU case law prior to signature of the agreement which is actually binding.[75] Second, as regards later case law, it is only the EFTA States who have unilaterally asked the EFTA Court to 'pay due account to' CJEU rulings,[76] and third, it is only with the consent of the parties that the CJEU may be asked to give a ruling on the interpretation of rules of EEA law which are identical in substance to Union law.[77]

There are thus no circumstances where the EEA Agreement attributes anything like the jurisdiction to the CJEU as the one it enjoys under the agreements with the UK and Switzerland. The arbitration mechanism under Protocol 33 to the EEA Agreement likewise docs not foresee the possibility of the arbitral tribunal there established making references to the CJEU.[78] Any divergence of views between the courts is ultimately resolved through judicial

---

[71]   Case E-2/18 *C v Concordia Schweizerische Kranken- und Unfallversicherung AG.*

[72]   *Ruska Federacija v IN* (n 12).

[73]   Case E-8/20 *Criminal Proceedings against N.*

[74]   In so far as their application involves concepts of European Union law, the provisions of this Agreement and the agreements concerned and the European Union legal acts referred to therein shall be interpreted and applied in accordance with the case law of the Court of Justice of the European Union, before or after the signature of the agreement concerned. (Unofficial translation.)

[75]   Art 6 EEA.

[76]   Art 3(2) of the Agreement between the EFTA States on the Establishment of a Surveillance Authority and a Court of Justice (Surveillance and Court Agreement).

[77]   Art 111(3) EEA.

[78]   The arbitration at the same time cannot concern a point of interpretation of EEA Law identical to Union law: Art 111(4) EEA.

dialogue. Both the EFTA Surveillance Authority and the EFTA Court are instrumental in ensuring the cohesion and homogeneity of the internal market as such. This is essential for the credibility of the EFTA pillar and of the EEA Agreement as such.

By way of conclusion, it can be said that the features of the institutional and judicial protection framework in the EEA exemplify the deeply shared common values and the high degree of mutual trust between EU and EFTA States. None of this would be possible without a deeply-rooted respect for the rule of law, but once that respect is there, everything else falls into place, making a lot of the safeguards lawyers may think of practically unnecessary. This starts with the rights of the citizen, and the ability to exercise those rights directly. And this is the ultimate illustration of the principle recognised by the European Parliament that 'developed economies with properly functioning judiciaries render the need for investor-state dispute settlement mechanisms less important'.[79]

The rule of law is both a precondition for the will to confer far-reaching substantive rights and the guarantee that those rights will actually be enforceable.

---

[79]   European Parliament non-legislative resolution of 13 February 2019 on the draft Council decision on the conclusion on behalf of the European Union of the Investment Protection Agreement between the European Union and its Member States, of the one part, and the Republic of Singapore, of the other part (07979/2018 – C8-0447/2018 – 2018/0095M(NLE)), Recital K.

Index